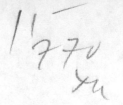

STUBBORN

WEEDS

STUBBORN WEEDS

Popular and Controversial

Chinese Literature after

the Cultural Revolution

Edited by Perry Link

INDIANA UNIVERSITY PRESS

Bloomington

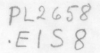
Copyright © 1983 by Indiana University Press

Manufactured in the United States of America

Library of Congress Cataloging in Publication Data
Main entry under title:

Stubborn weeds.

(Chinese literature in translation)
1. Chinese literature—20th century—Translations into English.   2. English literature—Translations from Chinese.   I. Link, E. Perry (Eugene Perry), 1944–
II. Series.
PL2658.E1S78   1983   895.1′08′005   82-48268
ISBN 0-253-35512-5
1   2   3   4   5   87   86   85   84   83

In Fond Memory of Kai-yu Hsu (1922–1982)

Contents

DRAMA

POPULAR PERFORMING ARTS

Comedians' Dialogues

Fast Clappertales

Shandong Fast Tales

STUBBORN

WEEDS

Introduction

Most people who think and talk about the literature of the People's Republic of China want to understand the question of literary control. This is generally as true inside China as outside. Chinese readers and writers, especially during the years represented in this book, have paid much attention to the "scope" allowed to writers and to the forces that have made this scope expand or contract. The Western reader, although prevented from seeing very much of the immensely complex dynamics of Chinese literary politics, nevertheless remains curious about the question of control and tends to ask about it first. A few Chinese writers were pleading in 1980 that people stop focusing on the control question and pay more attention to literary quality. From foreigners, these writers wished dearly to know how their works would be classified and rated by international standards. To these writers I sincerely apologize for focusing this introduction on the more popular topic of control; my purpose is not to slight the question of artistry but to place it in its societal context—explaining how certain ideological pressures are applied, resisted, modulated, reapplied, etc.—and thereby perhaps to help the Western reader to contemplate the artistic question with more insight.

THE SYSTEM OF LITERARY CONTROL

Mao Zedong, in his "Talks at the Yan'an Conference on Literature and Art" in 1942, laid down some basic rules for the control of literature in China's Communist areas. Although the vicissitudes of literary politics have been many since 1942, the fundamental importance of Mao's rules has not changed. Literature should serve political aims; individual literary works are to be judged by both political and artistic criteria, with the political criteria taking precedence. These and others of Mao's theoretical pronouncements on literary control have been well analyzed elsewhere;[1] here, rather than summarize that work, I will offer an analysis of the actual practice of literary control as I was able to observe it in China during the course of research there in 1979–80. But first a warning: in speaking of a "system" of literary control and in analyzing its workings, I do not mean to give the impression of a fixed set of standards that writers, editors, and readers can

1

confidently rely upon. Sometimes, as when the liberal Hundred Flowers period of 1956[2] suddenly turned into the Anti-Rightist Campaign of 1957, the entire system has been known to lurch from one direction to another in a manner that is quite unpredictable to most of the people involved.

The primary rule of literary control is that literature must support the current political leadership or, to the extent that literature can be apolitical, at least not oppose the leadership. Five significant groups are involved: readers, writers, editors and publishers, critics, and the top leadership. By top leadership I mean literally the highest levels— Party chairmen and vice-chairmen monitor contemporary literature and worry about its implications; writers cultivate friendships with the children of high officials in order to learn what the Party Secretariat is saying about them. By critics I mean officials whose job is to analyze literary works and, if necessary, to criticize authors according to the political criteria the top leadership has chosen for the present day. This role differs in obvious ways from that of a literary critic in the West. Some critics in China, especially in academia, do entertain questions of literary technique, but these critics usually have very little access to the public media. By readers I mean primarily urban readers. This is not to slight the peasant masses in China but simply to note the plain fact that they are not yet part of the literature-reading public.[3]

These five groups interact in extremely complex ways but always, of necessity, under a strong influence from the demands of the literary control system. To understand this influence, we "bourgeois" Westerners must first set aside our notions about the primacy of the writer. From the standpoint of the control system, the primary relationship on the literary scene is that between readers and top leadership. The whole point of literature, so viewed, is to cause readers to think what the top leadership feels it is best that they think. Correct thoughts in turn serve Party policy as well as the interests of society as a whole. Party theorists, borrowing a term from Stalin, explain that literature is a tool for "engineering the souls" of readers.[4] Thus the prescribed roles (but not always the actual roles—more on this later) of writers, editors, publishers, and critics are to ensure in their various ways that the primary relationship is properly built and protected. Critics are supposed to mediate the thought of the top leadership for writers, editors, and publishers; these groups, in turn, mediate correct thought for the masses of readers. The relations of these various roles on the literary scene are, moreover, hierarchical in a way that resembles the traditional Chinese family system. This is not just because the top leadership is elderly, while most readers are young and most writers and editors are in between; it is because Chinese political culture still rests, as it has for centuries, on the family analogy. Top leaders in many ways function as parternalistic authority figures for citizens of all ages. This theoretically benevolent authoritarianism, as it applies to literature, is frequently expressed in a medical metaphor. A good literary work is "healthful" to its readers; a bad work is "unhealthful" or even "poisonous." The implication is that a wise prescriber of medicine (the top leader) knows what is best for patients (readers) better than the patients themselves can know. Whether the medicine tastes good is a separate point.

A separate point, but hardly an ignored one. The leadership can be embarrassed if it becomes too obvious that readers do not enjoy the literature that is prescribed for them. Hence the fiction is maintained that readers do like it. A prescribed medicine also becomes a prescribed preference of the palate. Such preferences must be distinguished, of course, from genuine palatability; in fact, it will be useful in many contexts to use the following almost as technical terms: *actual reader preferences* are what readers enjoy; *prescribed reader preferences* are what the top leadership feels readers ought to enjoy.[5]

One could, with care, draw a kind of graph of the years since the Yan'an Conference in 1942, showing when and to what extent actual reader preferences and prescribed reader preferences have converged or diverged. (Separate graphs might have to be drawn for certain works or certain kinds of works.) There was indubitably a high degree of convergence for resist-Japan war stories in the liberated areas through 1945 (especially when the anti-Japanese message was delivered through oral or performing media that circumvented the problem of illiteracy). On the other hand, pronouncements that the proletarian masses loved the subtle art of the great modern writer Lu Xun, at that time and ever since, are a good example of extreme divergence between actual and prescribed preferences. Another area of relative convergence would be the optimistic years of the 1950s, at least until the Great Leap Forward in 1958. Many readers genuinely liked 1950s' stories of the revolutionary struggle and early socialist transformation—works such as Yang Mo's *Song of Youth* or Zhou Erfu's *Morning in Shanghai*. In the 1950s, the horrendous problems of the 1930s and 1940s were still vivid in readers' minds, and the self-sacrificing idealism projected in these works was considered fresh, hopeful, and attractive. Several years were required before the impracticality of this idealism began to emerge and to lead to alienation and wide divergence between actual and prescribed reader preferences.

An interesting thing happened, in the terms we are using here, during the Cultural Revolution (1966–76). We would have to invent a new graph to chart it. Literature became so politically bowdlerized that actual reader preferences were frightened almost entirely out of sight. Yet there was a sense in which enthusiastic Red Guards did enjoy such literature. The key to understanding this paradox is to see that they were not really enjoying the literature *as readers*. Chairman Mao's "little generals," in emulation of the Great Leader, conceived themselves as dispensers, not consumers, of truth. They asked themselves less whether they liked a story than whether it was good medicine for society—meaning, essentially, for other people. It was primarily this *role* in the use of Cultural Revolution literature that was so enjoyable.

With the fall of the Maoist "Gang of Four" in October 1976, the way was cleared for a great popular outpouring against "ultraleftism," "socialist fascism," "remnants of feudalism," etc. The main avenues for this great outpouring became the mushrooming literary magazines of the late 1970s, which changed the face of contemporary Chinese literature dramatically. But it is important to recognize that these changes did not happen outside the same basic system of literary control that had begun in 1942. The crucial change was in the top leadership, who, partly from a wish to legitimize their departures from the *ancien regime*, could to some degree approve of the vitriol directed against that regime and life under it. As a result, prescribed reader preferences and actual reader preferences coincided for a time as never before, and little "engineering" was necessary to foster literary works that satisfied everyone. With little need for engineering, all elements in the system could relax somewhat.

This relaxation had some side effects. For one, writers and editors could, to an unprecedented degree in the Peoples Republic, take their own initiatives with nothing to fear except what might happen when conditions changed again. Critics could also be less rigid in their work because the new degree of harmony among leadership, writers, and readers meant that the critics' job of keeping writers in line was for the time being unimportant. (To be sure, there was some anxiety among critics over the very fact of their sudden marginal role, and there must have been a secret hankering in some of them for a return to the status quo.) The most noticeable and refreshing effect was that literary works became much more lively and much more reflective of actual society and popular thought. In early 1979 it appeared that a fundamental change may have happened in the political control of literature. But within a year it was clear that the relaxation had resulted from the temporary internal configuration of the system, not from its demise or its radical change. In 1980 prescribed reader preferences and actual reader preferences began to diverge again (although not nearly as much as before), and the system became accordingly more rigid.

The 1980 retrenchment happened for two related reasons. First, the leadership felt that its goal of discrediting its predecessors had been adequately achieved. To continue excoriating the recent past encouraged spillover into discontent with the present and could undermine current leadership, despite their efforts to assign blame for most problems to "remnants" and "residues" of the Gang of Four. Second, with the increased elbow room that writers enjoyed in the late 1970s, they had begun departing from their assigned role of transmitting received wisdom and were now expressing their own views on social morality and the fate of the nation. Among the more conscience-ridden and outspoken writers, there was a general drift during 1979 away from explicit attacks on the Gang of Four and toward works that examined basic problems not easily attributable to only four people. In some cases, the drift included works that clearly referred to major questions in the present. The play "What If I Really Were?" ("Jiaru wo shi zhende"), which is included here, is an important example. Written in summer 1979, it explicitly identifies its time of action as after the Gang of Four. Its satire of official corruption was received with great enthusiasm by the public, especially urban youth, and eventually the leadership singled it out as an example of a tendency that had to be curbed.

THE WRITER'S DILEMMA: CONSCIENCE VERSUS RISK

The trend in the late 1970s which saw writers begin "expressing their own views on social morality and the fate of the nation," as we have just described it, was a trend less toward "bourgeois" interests than toward an ancient concept of the writer's role in China. To understand this role we must remind ourselves of the traditional Chinese idea of the near synonymy of literature, morality, and politics. The Chinese classics were not only literature but also, for centuries, the crucible of the morality that uniquely qualified one for political office. Historical writing was also literature, one of its main purposes being to establish the legitimacy of the current dynasty by "correctly" describing the wrongs of the previous one. Dissenters, too, shared assumptions about the moral-political duty of writers: the famous poet Qu Yuan (ca. 340–278 B.C.) took his life in protest of a weak and corrupt state; the equally famous Du Fu (A.D. 712–770) spoke for the cold and the hungry. In the popular tradition, heterodox sects and peasant rebellions nearly always had a "heavenly document" which they considered fundamental. Even when literature that was primarily for entertainment did emerge, roughly a thousand years ago, its departure from serious moral-political purposes caused it to be denigrated—together with visiting teahouses and brothels or watching itinerant jugglers—as something that diverted people from their proper Confucian roles. Although these attitudes have softened in recent centuries, especially the early twentieth century, the synonymy of literature-morality-politics is still a prevalent notion. Mao

Zedong himself, in laying down the rules for the "scientific" control of literature at Yan'an in 1942, was not only borrowing concepts from Marxism-Leninism but also appropriating some deep-seated Chinese assumptions about the written word and the patriotic responsibilities of a writer. In the late 1970s, these same deep-seated assumptions ironically were working in opposition to much of Mao's own post-Liberation legacy.

What kind of problems did writers point to? Perhaps most fundamental in the whole protest of the late 1970s was the question of telling the plain truth. China's vexing and sometimes massive problems had never been adequately illuminated by the ersatz light of "revolutionary romanticism," and in many writers the nagging sense of a duty to tell the plain truth would not go away. In recent history there had been much to mention: broken families, suicides, floods (it is said a million died in a flood in Henan in 1975, and who knows?), acute hunger, horrible prisons, and many other things that had not been truthfully, or even half-truthfully, reported. To be sure, much was already known through the informal word-of-mouth network that in many ways is the functional equivalent in China of a low-quality newspaper in the West. But, given the moral and political prestige of the written word in Chinese tradition, it was still exciting, and very important, for readers to see the truth in print. And the weightier and more official the medium, the better. We in the West (I include Hong Kong and Taiwan as part of the "West" for present purposes) often overemphasize the significance of "underground" literature in China. It is quite true that the greater the distance between literary creation and extraneous political pressure, the better the chance for high-quality creation. But this fact is greatly overpowered by another—that readers and writers at all levels in China feel it is better to be above ground than under and, while above ground, better to be in official publications than in unofficial or semi-official ones. One's writing counts for more in an official journal—not primarily because the circulation is bigger but because of the prestige.

Telling the truth naturally led in the late 1970s to criticism of those who had not been telling the truth. Hence much of the outpouring of conscience became an unofficial campaign against hypocrisy. The stalwarts of this trend, being democratic in spirit, were largely uninterested in hypocrisy among the lowly, but focused attention on glaring hypocrisy in officialdom. Mao Zedong had warned of "the emergence of a new ruling class" when he launched the Cultural Revolution. Although writers seldom invoked Mao in 1979 and never used his phrase, it still comes as close as any to describing their concerns.[6] The most obvious offenses of the new class, especially in the view of young writers, were its special comforts—better food, finer clothers, larger homes, and access to automobiles, to the "soft" class on the railroad, to private hospital rooms, to vacation resorts, to stores where others could not shop, to theaters where others could not enter, etc.—all governed by an immensely complex system of formal and informal privileges, some of which could be bartered. It is not an exaggeration to describe the whole system as a kind of "economy," related and in some ways parallel to the money economy, where privilege and political power could and often had to substitute for cash in the distribution of goods and services.

These special privileges were eye-catching in the late 1970s, especially to youth. But some of the more mature, mostly middle-aged, writers could see a deeper issue. They were opposed to the system of special privileges less for its unequal distribution of material comforts than for its cruel betrayal of the ideals of the revolution and its shameless establishment of a gap between verbiage and practice. In the 1930s and 1940s, a person risked life itself to join the Communists, and many did so from high idealism. But now manipulation, cynicism, and hypocrisy had taken over. Officials who benefited could easily see the injustices but feared to tamper with a system whose ropes they had mastered only after the investment of much effort and whose protection of their own narrow margin of safety and comfort required steady vigilance. There was no return, perhaps, after one-time socialists learned that pursuit of an item of private interest had to be made even when the loss to the collective weal far outweighed the private gain itself.

Some of the literary works that revealed these problems stated or implied that they were common problems, in fact endemic ones. This implication drew fire from the political critics, because it made it harder to separate problems and to attribute them to either aberration or the Gang of Four. But on the other hand, works that might appear to lampoon specific people, such as, in this collection, "A Bundle of Letters" by Bai Hua or "Foundation" by Jiang Zilong, could cause problems if it were not perfectly clear who the person lampooned was supposed to be. Certain people were not to be attacked. Sometimes an author would create a villain from his own imagination, based on general observations, only to have his editor receive dozens of letters from real-life individuals protesting that the alleged villany was not so—or (more interestingly, since it implied a degree of guilt) not *quite* so. This circumstance was widespread enough to acquire the nickname of "self-assigned seating." Amusing though it seems, authors could face serious trouble for it.

Honest reflection of actual social problems was inevitably controversial. The issue created a kind of protracted tug-of-war between advocates for and against a greater scope for such honesty. The expansion of the scope in 1979 bears definite resemblances to a similar "thaw" in the Soviet Union in 1956: both came three years after the death of a Great Leader; both exposed social and psychological sores that had been festering under the proud facade the Great Leader had enforced; in both cases some of the bolder pieces, like "What If I Really Were?" in China, could be openly published only outside the country; and in both cases the thaw ended in the following year, 1957 and 1980 respectively. The gradual refreezing that then occurred had a similar rationale in each case.

Yet the analogy to the Soviet thaw can be misleading if pressed too far. The bold writers on the Soviet scene reached their audience by slipping some literary bombs into a few key volumes—the journal *New World* and two large anthologies called *Literary Moscow*. Their Chinese counterparts—more mobile, more deft, using smaller weapons, and in general more like guerrilla warriors—published from time to time in several places, availing themselves of sympathetic editors who themselves were involved in precarious balancing acts. The repressive side in China also has differed from that in the Soviet Union. Less mechanical and heavy-handed, China's subtler approach to psychological engineering has also been more effective in its suffocation of dissent. The modern Chinese, to paraphrase Simon Leys's ironic insight, bear an added burden because of the superior sophistication of their civilization.

The mechanics that determine the scope allowed to Chinese writers have been complex, and we can sketch them here only briefly. One must begin by exorcising the illusion, which can also arise by analogy to the Soviet Union, of a joust between Party and non-Party forces. Many, perhaps most, of the courageous and truthful writers and editors in China have been Party members. It might be objected that this is so because a true dissenter from the Party would speak out only at forbidding cost. And this is true, but it is also true that non-Party people, provided they are not *anti*-Party, have generally been given a wider scope for public expression than Party members have. Hence it is a true paradox that many of the bolder writers have been in the Party. Even those writers (mostly youth) who have gone so far as to suggest dismantling the whole system have sometimes been Party members.

Other labels for the advocacy of a larger or smaller scope for writers are similarly problematic. "Liberal" and "conservative" might seem reasonable. The term "conservative" is in fact used, widely but informally, inside China. But the term "liberal" cannot be used because the 1981 campaign against "bourgeois liberalism" has made it politically repugnant, a "heavy hat" no person can afford to wear. "Left" and "right" will not do either, because they are hopelessly entangled in differing usages, both inside China and between China and the West. The most culturally conservative people in China (those who, for example, oppose bell-bottom trousers from an antipathy for things that are "un-Chinese") are sometimes the same as the most politically orthodox people (who, for example, regard the Marxist classics as scripture even though they do not read them very sensitively). It may seem strange to a Westerner, as it does to some intellectuals in China, that these two overlapping groups are sometimes called the "left," or even the "ultra-left". Often associated with the military, they advocate rigid control of many things, including literature. On the other hand, people who have opposed militaristic rigidity and have advocated tolerance in publishing, tolerance of foreign influences, and a more democratic political style have been the objects of campaigns against "rightism." These rightists, ironically, have much less in common with the old "reactionary right" of the KMT in the 1940s than do some of the people on today's "left." The situation is as complex as the labels are unclear.

But, troublesome though it is, we cannot abandon the search for labels for the two opposing poles of thought that are called in Chinese political-literary discourse *shou* (advocating more restriction) and *fang* (advocating more tolerance). There is, of course, a range of opinion between these two poles. There are also many people who conceal their opinions in order to stay somewhere in the middle where they can hedge their bets. But no other two words are as good as *shou* and *fang* to describe the polarity involved, and hence I propose here to adhere rather closely to the Chinese terms and to refer below to "restrictiveness" and "tolerance." The reader should bear in mind, however, that these terms in English do not carry the same weight of political connotation that *shou* and *fang* do.

THE MECHANICS OF EXPANSION OF THE SCOPE FOR WRITERS

How does the pull between the advocates of tolerance and restrictiveness actually cause the scope for writers to expand or contract? It is fair to conceive of an almost constant pressure from the "tolerance" group of writers and editors to expand this scope. But the pressure they exert also varies considerably with what is called in China the "wind." The wind—a metaphor for messages from the top leadership that are usually oral or, if written, oblique—shifts direction in subtle ways, and people are well advised to adjust their weather vanes carefully. In literary politics, people usually refer to wind "temperature," which is either "warm" or "cold," indicating tolerance or restrictiveness. To be sure, the top leadership often intends more complex instructions than merely "warm" or "cold," but by the time the wind blows all the way down from the mountaintop, having been repropelled by functionaries at many intermediate stations, only its temperature is sensible in the valleys. The leadership's reasons for ordering changes in wind temperature are seldom very clear—they

Introduction

are often the subject of speculation through the grapevine inside China as well as in the Hong Kong press. Raising the wind temperature sometimes seems to be aimed at winning the support of intellectuals, as, for instance, when a modernization drive begins; or, as we have seen, it can serve to encourage an outpouring of complaint about former leaders; or, as many say of the Hundred Flowers campaign in 1956, it might be used to lure dissenting opinion into the open. A drop in wind temperature can reflect a renewed burst of faith in "restrictivist" philosophy. Since a cold wind can be a weapon of great strength and flexibility in the hands of local officials, it can also be used to reimpose social control when public behavior has grown lax or unruly. Changes in wind direction further can be a reflection of political accommodation between advocates of tolerance and restriveness at the top.

Happily, however, the question of why wind temperature changes is beyond our scope here; our topic is the effect that a warm or cold wind has on everyone in the political-literary system. In general we can observe that a higher temperature increases the pressure exerted by writers and editors against the "scope" of permissibility that surrounds them, and that a drop in temperature correspondingly reduces that pressure. (The metaphor could not fit more nicely with what Charles' Law in physics has to say about the relation of temperatures and pressures.) When the wind blows warm, the effect is not only to lend moral support to writers who would speak out but, more importantly, to increase the likelihood that a foray outside the currently prescribed scope will go unpunished. Such forays always involve the risk of criticism, and criticism, in the People's Republic, has often led to more serious consequences.

A writer or editor who would make such a foray therefore does whatever is possible to ensure in advance that it will meet with approval rather than criticism. The way to gain such assurance is to find what is called "backstage support" from someone who wields some power. It is not a Catch-22 to say one needs official permission to break an official barrier, because officialdom, including Partydom, includes many shades of both tolerance and restrictiveness. Frequently one writer and his backstage support will face off against corresponding adersaries on an opposing side. This happened, for example, in 1977, when the editors of the literary magazine *Literary Works* in Guangzhou decided to risk a series of articles criticizing Hao Ran, who in the latter part of the Cultural Revolution had been promoted as the only significant contemporary Chinese novelist. In this case, the question became one of whether Hao Ran's backstage support could outweigh that of *Literary Works*. Such a question turns not only on the relative weight of the two backstage supporters but on their distance (meaning political distance, although geographical distance also plays its part) from the site of publication. If someone dares to publish a criticism of Hao Ran in Guangzhou, and if his backstage support resides in Guangzhou, he needs less powerful support than he would need to accomplish the same thing in Beijing. Conversely, the opposition, in order to outweigh a challenge from Guangzhou and silence it, needs more clout in Beijing than might be necessary locally. And one does have to *out*weigh the opposition in order to silence him; a tie in the weight of backstage support, even a very approximate tie, usually means, under the conditions of a warm wind, that both sides get to say what they want. Thus it happens that Chinese writers can benefit from their country's unmanageable size. During a warm wind they can send their manuscripts to various provinces in search of leaderships with varying emphases; those who would oppose such writers can be thwarted purely by the bureaucratic headaches involved in trying to stamp out a bubble under a rug.

Backstage support can also be analyzed for "firmness." The firmest support comes in cases where a writer simply speaks for his backstage support, with prior understanding on both sides of what is happening. For example, the "restrictive" ideas in the essay entitled "Praise and Shame" (*Hebei wenyi*, June 1979) by Li Jian, a previously unknown young man, belonged to his backstage support, who apparently were people close to the famous veteran poet Tian Jian. But usually a writer cannot get specific, before-the-fact approval from his backstage support. A supporter cannot know in advance how something might be phrased, and even if he could, to assume all the responsibility would be an unfair division of the risk. Besides, in the face of criticism, it is much easier for backstage support to defend a few key points in someone else's bold *fait accompli* than to take responsibility for originating the idea. A less firm kind of backstage support provides a vaguer, more general license, without implying approval of any specific piece. This was generally the case in Anhui Province, where First Secretary of the Party Wan Li supported a generally tolerant trend among literary journals in the late 1970s. At its softest, backstage support can be symbolic and nearly impossible to pin down. But even then it is useful; if a supporter is powerful, weight can compensate for lack of firmness. In late 1978, for example, students at Zhongshan University in Guangzhou were having difficulty in launching their literary magazine, *The Red Beans (Hongdou)*. When Zhou Yang, vice-chairman of the All-China Writers' Association, came to town for a meeting, a student sought him out with a question: "What do you think of our plan to start a magazine, respected Comrade Zhou Yang?"

"Very good," Zhou reportedly answered.

"Will you do us the honor of donating your calligraphy?"

Zhou Yang did, and using the calligraphy for their front cover, the students got a subsidy of 1,000 *yuan* (about $650 U.S.) from their university and the magazine was born. It is hard to say whether Zhou Yang's very abstract and temporary patronage had anything to do with *The Red Beans*'s daring to be one of the more outspoken student magazines in China, or its being the last of these magazines to fall in the chilly wind of 1980. This is possible, but its success certainly also had to do with the relatively enlightened policies of the Guangdong provincial leadership. In cases where backstage support is abstract, the involved parties themselves cannot say with precision just what is being done, and being made possible, by their relationship.

In some cases a writer may not know who is supporting his piece. When the wind blows warm, one can send a pathbreaking piece to an editorial board, and with luck an editor will notice it and champion it. This does not happen very often, but warm winds can cause many aspiring young writers to assume that it will happen to them. Editorial boards will receive piles of manuscripts every day— more than they can read and hundreds of times more than they can use. Prominent literary officials will also receive stacks of manuscripts from youth who feel their genius has been snubbed by editorial boards but will certainly be recognized by a wise and fair literary official.

From these stacks of manuscripts it emerges that besides self-expression and truth-telling, another incentive exists for writing boldly. For if one's breakthrough is not criticized, and if official opinion eventually affirms it, one can be credited as a *chuangjiang* or "groundbreaking hero." After Liu Xinwu's famous story "The Homeroom Teacher" (November 1977) and Lu Xinhua's equally famous "Scar" (August 1978),[7] thousands of youngsters wrote stories in imitation and mailed them to literary magazines. But only the first to make the plunge, of course, is the groundbreaking hero. During the Cultural Revolution it had been a rather well known trick to write a false diary detailing one's self-sacrifices and secret loyalty to Chairman Mao and then to "lose" the diary on a sidewalk and wait for one's hidden virtue to be discovered and rewarded. Without detracting for a moment from the honesty and courage of the writers who brave cold winds, it is also true that during warm winds there has been a certain speculative mentality in figuring how to become tagged as a "groundbreaking hero" with "liberated thought." In fact playing the ups and downs of literary politics in China, at least during its livelier periods, can be something like playing the stock market in the West: in both cases one can speculate on future trends; both can bring success or ruin; both do have their logic, but a logic that is easier to see after the fact than before; and about both there circulate inside "tips."

No one other than the top leadership can declare that the wind will blow warm and that the scope for writers will expand markedly. The power of local political leaders is moderate by comparison. Editors, another notch lower, are left mainly to maneuver among the larger forces. But occasionally even editors can influence the temperature of the wind in limited times and places. This usually has to be accomplished through some sort of cleverness, such as finding a bold piece written by an important person's son. Another device, to pick but one example, is the selective publication of letters to the editor— one can publish the sincere diatribe of an opponent of tolerance, knowing full well that to many readers it will read like self-satire.[8] But while editors by themselves can do little to expand the scope for writers, they can easily bring the opposite result by impatiently attempting to expand the scope too quickly. Rash action can anger the leadership and tip the balance at that level to favor the advocates of restrictiveness. The more progressive editors around the country therefore monitor one another and attempt to go forward in concert— not precisely together, since a slightly erratic march can keep the opposition off balance, but also never so far apart that the one in front might be picked off and made a negative example for everyone.

THE MECHANICS OF CONTRACTION OF THE SCOPE FOR WRITERS

A cold wind is always attributed, at least officially, to the masses, because the masses are the theoretical basis for political legitimacy. In early 1980, for example, it was an official view that the masses were getting tired of literature that exposed psychological sores and were demanding more stories about the heroes of the Four Modernizations. In reality, judging from all available evidence,[9] no such shift in popular tastes occurred. In November and December 1979, the editors of *People's Literature* surveyed reader preferences in short stories, and the editors of *Yalu River* in Shenyang surveyed reader preferences in poetry. The results—which showed a continued strong preference for protest and exposure of sores—were classified "for internal circulation only."[10] The gap between actual and prescribed reader preferences could not be publicly admitted.

Like reader preferences, the whole dynamic of a cold wind admits a distinction between the theoretical and the actual. The case of the cold wind of 1981 that blew around the writer Bai Hua will serve as an example. Theoretically, the masses read Bai Hua's film script "Unrequited Love"[11] and discovered that the author hankers after bourgeois liberalism (why the masses had not made this discovery two years earlier, when the piece first appeared, is not part of the theory); the leadership then took action on behalf of the masses but reminded them that *ad hominem* attacks must not be made on Bai Hua, but rather that the *issue* of bourgeois liberalism must be singled out

Introduction

wherever it appears. The theoretical causal chain, in other words, starts with mass opinion and ends with a warning to all writers. The actual causal chain is more nearly this: the top leadership determines that writers must be warned; an example is sought and Bai Hua is found; a literary example within Bai Hua's work is sought and "Unrequited Love" is found; it is then proclaimed that the masses object to "Unrequited Love."[12] (We need to remind ourselves that any statement about the views of the *masses* is moot, because actually they are not involved. The readers of contemporary literature, as noted above, are primarily educated urban youth who constitute less than 10 percent of the population.)

By far the most important force in the contraction of the scope for literary expression, and in inducing writers to stay within it, is a vague but omnipresent fear of criticism and punishment. This fear is the great anchor that exerts a constant, directed pull on all the little sailboats of subtle crisscrosssing suggestion. During the Cultural Revolution one's house could be ransacked, one could be paraded through the streets with excrement on one's head, and one could be shot. In the late 1970s no punishments approaching this severity were being applied, but the vivid memory of such things and the perpetual uncertainly of Chinese politics were enough to make even mild criticism a very effective disincentive. At times the leadership exhorted writers to rid themselves of "residual fear" of the Gang of Four and to overcome the kind of paranoiac conditioned reflexes that had developed during the Cultural Revolution. Yet could something like the Cultural Revolution happen again? No one expected that it would, but few denied that, if the leadership changed, it could. (Actually to *expect* another Cultural Revolution might have been psychologically impossible—and if not that, then politically impossible to express.) Moreover, the leadership, despite its pronouncements to the contrary, quietly exacerbated the problem of residual fear by continuing to use the implied threat of criticism to control writers. Thus in 1979–80 it was still true that, for writers and editors, no disincentive loomed as large as the danger to one's career, family, and self that might result from political criticism. That fear of criticism was the major means of control on literary expression was another circumstance distinguishing China from the Soviet Union, where, in the three decades since Stalin, a more settled system of pre-publication censorship and economic measures such as firing and blacklisting has largely replaced overt political criticism in the control of writers.

The manipulation of fear in literary control in China can be quite subtle and, on the face of it, even gentle. One device, for example, is to begin by isolating the object of criticism. If in 1981 "the masses" suddenly felt revulsion at "bourgeois liberalism," it follows that those tainted by it are "a tiny minority." In a major speech in September

1981—a speech that blew the coldest wind since 1976—Party Chairman Hu Yaobang used the "tiny minority" phrase several times.[13] He fleshed out his point with the simile of lice on the body of a great lion. To an outsider this might appear odd. If the opposition were indeed as minor as lice are to a lion, one might wonder why the Party Chairman would deliver an austere and well publicized speech about "the crucial need to maintain vigilance" against this "grave danger." But to wonder this is to look in the wrong direction. The point of the lice simile and the "tiny minority" phrase is not to estimate the size of any group but to work on the psychology of everyone.

First, to tag the opposition as a tiny minority automatically removes their legitimacy, since legitimacy rests on the wishes of the masses. Second, such a tag says to the majority of writers and editors who are involved in complex compromises and balancing acts that, if they will be docile, they will be safe; after all, it is only the "tiny minority" who are causing trouble. Writers who have been provocative toward the leadership can be forgiven if they change their ways. If they do, their actions have propaganda value for the leadership. An example is Sha Yexin, the main author of "What If I Really Were?," who refused to alter this work even under considerable pressure; but when he followed it by another called "Mayor Chen Yi," a clever and enjoyable play that praised a revolutionary elder, the critics found him quite acceptable and gave the new play much publicity.

A third and most important aspect of the "tiny minority" phrase is its vagueness. What tiny minority? Who? Since everyone knows that *some* traces of bourgeois liberalism, "correctly" interpreted, might be found anywhere, the ambiguity of the "tiny minority" phrase is a fearsome thing. But this ambiguity also has its purpose: with almost no one able to rule himself out, almost everyone has an incentive to play things safer. The same kind of vagueness attends the borderlines of the "scope" for permissible expression. What exactly *is* bourgeois liberalism? How does one square it with the injunction to "liberate" one's mind? (Contradictory warnings are a favorite tool in literary control. The impossibility of compliance tends to bring everything to a halt, and this, for advocates of restrictiveness, as well as for time-serving bureaucrats, is ideal.) True, a writer can be shown Bai Hua's "Unrequited Love" as a concrete negative example. But why would this film script be objectionable when many pieces that go even further are apparently acceptable? If one wishes to be safe, one can only stay well inside the vague boundaries.

Another very important sword in the arsenal of vagueness is ambiguity about the seriousness of a case. When a literary work is criticized for "casting a shadow over our socialist motherland," the author cannot know whether this is a reminder to be a little more optimistic next time or an innuendo that one is anti-socialist, therefore anti-Party. Even if the charge seems clear when it is made, its gravity could change abruptly in the future after a change in wind temperature. But at least shouldn't the *writer* of the criticism know what is meant? Not even this is necessarily true. If he is writing with backstage support, which is the norm in major cases, he is representing partly the intentions of another, and this relationship must also be protected with some vagueness.

The ambiguity that results when top leaders speak through critics instead of directly also has its use in bringing pressure on writers. When the leaders speak publicly, they can confine themselves to general principles, leaving their complaints about specific works to be expounded by critics. As it impinges on writers, this division of labor amounts to that between carrot-holder and stick-holder. A top leader's general principles can welcome writers warmly to side with the masses against the tiny minority of troublemakers. There is, after all, no need to comment on a writer's work if he will be nice enough to curb himself. But if this approach fails and a critical attack does become necessary, the critic can come forth to play the negative role. The separation of roles is important because it leaves the writer, even after an attack, with enough face before the leadership to apologize and to accept, as if on second thought, the leadership's kind invitation to side with the masses.

In formal political-literary discourse, it is not only the author's face that is considered but also—in fact much more—the leadership's. What the leadership often wants to say to writers is, "Don't take potshots at us." (My paraphrasing here is not merely playful; *informal* political-literary discourse within the leadership is apparently often very colloquial.) But the simple fact that potshots are being taken, if admitted formally and in public, can represent a bad loss of face for leadership that is cast in the father-figure mold. Hence political-literary criticism is often oblique. Sometimes a work that is excessively outspoken is criticized for some other reason. For people who are accustomed to interpreting the "wind," there is no great difficulty setting aside the stated reason in order to absorb the true one. As an example, we can refer once again to the play "What If I Really Were?," which was criticized for encouraging youth to sympathize with a deceitful impersonator, "a swindler." It is perfectly obvious that the message of this play is not to glorify deceit. The play's whole point, which could hardly be clearer or more colorfully portrayed, is to denounce deceit, bribery, sycophancy, and string-pulling—not of the impersonator, to be sure, but of the official circles he moves in. (The critics might be credited with considerable originality for pointing out a problem that the audience did not even notice until it was found to be the central problem of the work.) Yet viewed against its own goals, the critics' emphasis on the swindler was brilliant. It drew attention away from the sore point—the play's devastating portrayal of official corruption—and toward an issue where the leadership had not only face but the upper hand. Sympathize with a trickster? Socialist China may have its problems, but what we need are socialist solutions, not bourgeois-individualist solutions.[14] (In fact, the play never presents the protagonist's deceit as a "solution" to the social problem of corruption. Even as a way out for an individual, it is presented as a forbiddingly dangerous stratagem, because at the end—and Chinese audiences always look at the end for the lesson—the young trickster is crushed.) The attack on the play was successful, and as a result one bold challenge to the leadership was squelched—but without any official's having to admit publicly that the squelching was the main point.

In the years since the Cultural Revolution, the leadership has found a need for gentler disincentives than the fear of political criticism. To criticize a writer can be too frightening, and perhaps too far-reaching in its effects. To achieve limited goals in a more precise fashion, a number of other measures, primarily logistical and economic, have been more convenient. One such measure, as the editors of the student journal *Our Generation (Zheiyidai)* discovered in November 1979, was simply to cut off access to printing. This curtailed one's activity without doing gross damage to one's face or career. When Deng Xiaoping sought to crack down on the unofficial press in January 1980, he zeroed in on the question of printing and paper supplies:

> It is absolutely forbidden for a Party member to peddle notions like freedom of speech, freedom of the press, or freedom of assembly if these are extended to counter-revolutionaries. No one may turn his back on the Party by becoming involved with such people. What I mean here is that no one may be sympathetically involved; I am not referring, of course, to our comrades who work as infiltrators. But there are people who genuinely do sympathize. How, for example, did some of those secret publications get printed so prettily? Where did they get their paper? Who did the printing? Don't tell me those people have their own printing presses![15]

Limitation of paper supplies is an even more widespread disincentive than control of printing facilities, and it is also more subtly articulated. All official publications are subject to the scrutiny of the State Publication Administration, a bureaucracy with several functions, but two especially important ones—it checks for material it feels the masses should not read, and it allocates paper. Paper was in chronically short supply for literary magazines in the late 1970s, and although the shortage itself was not the fault of the State Publication

Administration, it could and did make use of the shortage to bring pressure on publishers. Like other pressures, this one too was diffuse. Paper allocations were made not for specific works but for a publisher's entire annual plan, which meant that the whole plan could be in jeopardy because of one or two objectionable items. On the other hand, viewing the trade-off in terms of a publisher who advocated "tolerance," one might be able to slip in a few bold pieces provided they were balanced by more orthodox works.[16]

These considerations were strongly colored by a financial question. Paper allocation was often a question not of more or less volume but of what one would be charged. There were two grades of paper, one fixed at 1,500 *yuan* per ton and the other at 1,350 *yuan* per ton. The difference in quality was not great, and the State Publication Administration enjoyed the financial leverage of determining for each publisher the ratio of the two grades of paper. The resulting difference could be surprisingly important to a publisher's finances in the new economic regime of the late 1970s and early 1980s, when publishers were given progressively greater incentives to operate at a profit. Beginning in 1980, 15 percent of profits could be returned to the staff of a publishing house as a bonus. For the Guangdong People's Publishing House, this meant everyone received 400 *yuan* (about $275) in bonuses for the year. In 1981 bonuses at this publishing house came to 6 *yuan* per person. (The bonus was the same for everyone from chief editor to janitor.) In an economy marked by rising prices, especially for food, bonuses were very important. If it chose to come down hard on a publisher, the State Publication Administration could wipe out bonuses and even force the end of a magazine through financial means. The most radical way of doing this was to wait until a book or magazine was already printed and then forbid its sale, effectively wiping out a publication's entire working capital. This nearly happened in the case of the cartoon version of the story "Maple" until the decision was reversed at the highest levels.

The complexity of literary politics in China often means that when a warm or cold wind blows, it blows with different effects in different places. Guangzhou, Shanghai, Hefei, and Jilin—mostly because of local leadership that favored tolerance—were among the more progressive literary publishing centers during the late 1970s. Since the central leadership was also more tolerant than the provinces, at least before 1980, central journals such as *People's Literature (Renmin wenxue)*, *Poetry (Shikan)*, and *Present Times (Dangdai)*, as well as the journals of the Beijing municipal press, were also livelier than most. But there was also very complex chronological variation. Centers of restrictiveness and tolerance shifted over time, and almost every province did something interesting once in a while. We cannot attempt to trace every development here, but the main fluctuations in the climate as a whole will be briefly reviewed.[17]

A BRIEF CHRONOLOGY OF LITERARY DYNAMICS, 1976–80

It is customary in China to point to April 5, 1976, as the beginning of the major thaw of the late 1970s. That was the date of the famous Tiananmen Incident, when supporters of the relative moderation of Zhou Enlai challenged police in the heart of Beijing. But in fact, no milestone, publicly attributable or not, can compare to September 9, 1976, the day Mao Zedong passed away and supreme power fell within the reach of people with more practical ideas. During the first year after this great watershed, little of note appeared in the literary journals, but there was a paving of the way for future change through the gradual return to prominence of old-guard writers, editors, and critics from the 1930s through the early 1960s.

The first literary work to break significantly into forbidden zones was Liu Xinwu's "The Homeroom Teacher" (*People's Literature*, November 1977). Not only did Liu dare to put China's problem of urban juvenile delinquency into print; he was even more bold, and eventually controversial, in his portrayal of a young woman whose "model leftist" characteristics—energy, unquestioning loyalty, puritanical attitudes, disdain for any view that does not originate in the official press—eventually turn her into an ignorant, insensitive bigot, as flawed in her own way as the juvenile delinquent is in his. Judged by the standards of two years later, "The Homeroom Teacher" seems rather plain; but the excitement it generated in late 1977 coursed through China's literary grapevine as intensely as anything since. In the ensuing months, the cities of Guangzhou and Shanghai successively restored branches of the Chinese Writers' Association and themselves became the scenes of some exciting publishing.

The next work to signal a significant change in the literary weather was Lu Xinhua's "Scar," published in the Shanghai newspaper *Wenhuibao* on August 11, 1978. Basing itself on the fact that the family unit is still supremely important in China, "Scar" tells of a young woman whose relations with her widowed mother (representing her family of birth) and her boyfriend (her would-be family of marriage) are both ruined by mindless and overwhelming political pressures in her environment. For readers, the story provided a vital connection between their own daily lives and the widely trumpeted symbolic evil of the Gang of Four. Although "Scar" is a very simple story, millions read it and thought: This family was ruined! *My* family was ruined! Bravo for this story! But critics asked: Can we allow a story to dwell on the negative, to elicit tears? Where will such a trend stop? Where are the heroic figures and the optimism of "socialist realism"?

While these questions were being debated on the pages of *Wenhuibao* and in conversations across the nation, many other stories like "Scar" appeared, until they came to be known collectively as "Scar literature." Meanwhile the supreme weathermen at the top continued to call for a warming trend. In November 1978, the Tiananmen Incident was officially declared to have been a good, correct, and revolutionary movement. Although this decision might have been anticipated, it was a true surprise when, around the same time, the "rightist" labels were removed from everyone who had carried them since the Anti-Rightist Campaign of 1957. Why would the leadership do something this drastic? Were they really repudiating such a large and significant campaign? Fourteen months later, in January 1980, Deng Xiaoping made it clear that he was not repudiating the Anti-Rightist Campaign but only saying it had been too big.[18] November 1978 had been, however, the planning time for the Third Plenary Session of the Eleventh Party Congress in December. This plenum was to unveil great plans for China's modernization, and without the cooperation of intellectuals, such plans might look like a giant paper tiger. Viewed in this context, the blanket removal of rightist labels was certainly a prudent investment.

The Third Plenum proceeded to call upon intellectuals to liberate their thought, to break into previously forbidden zones, and not to fear a return of repressive policies. Although the purpose behind this appeal was the modernization of China's economy, military, and science—not especially her art or politics—when the wind blows exceeding warm, the whole great land is inevitably heated. In literature and art, the first quarter of 1979 was the warmest season in thirty years.

In April, May, and June, the wind temporarily blew chilly again. Wei Jingsheng, the courageous young editor of the unofficial journal called *Explorations (Tansuo)*, was arrested on March 29. Many editors cautiously donned another layer or two of clothing. In June a young man named Li Jian, representing "restrictive" opinion, published an article called "Praise and Shame" in *Hebei Literature and Art*. He argued that any writer who fails to remember the Great Chairman Mao or to sing the praises of the wonderful socialist motherland is shameful. This piece, although awkwardly written and from an unknown pen, captured national attention as a definitive statement of the so-called "praise faction", i.e., people who supported the Maoist legacy and found "liberation of thought" to be irksome.

But soon the weather changed again. Wang Ruowang, an intrepid veteran literary warrior from Shanghai, attacked Li Jian's "Praise and Shame" in an article called "A Cold Wind in Springtime" that was published on July 20 in *Guangming ribao*, the national newspaper for intellectuals. Overwhelmingly, intellectuals sided with Wang against the praise faction—now dubbed, popularly and less flatteringly, "the whateverists"—meaning that they supported "whatever" Mao said, now and for all time. Li Jian became a pariah; even his girlfriend left him, denouncing his whateverism, and he is said to have attempted suicide. Li Jian found reprieve only when Deng Xiaoping personally summoned him, Wang Ruowang, and editors from *People's Daily* to meet and recognize together that young Li had made some mistakes, to be sure, but that the older people were also wrong simply to attack him. They should guide him instead.

The fine literary weather in autumn 1979 (and extending in the journals to January and February, 1980, because of the publication time lag) was even better than that of the early spring. In speeches at the Fourth Congress of Literary and Art Workers held in Beijing from October 30 to November 15, some long repressed writers brought standing ovations with their challenges to falsity, hypocrisy, and crass political intervention in literature. In addition, Hu Qiaomu, head of the Chinese Academy of Social Sciences, pressed for abandonment of the slogan "Literature in Service of Politics." Hu argued that the record of the past thirty years showed the slogan to have done more harm than good. Members of the praise faction (Huang Zhen, Lin Mohan, Liu Baiyu, and others) were naturally opposed, and key bridge figures such as Zhou Yang remained temporarily uncommitted. But for the interim, while the debate continued, the slogan did disappear from the public media.

In December the chilly wind made its second return of the year. The closing of Democracy Wall in Beijing was much less important in itself than as a signal across the land. And only a month after the unofficial press had been endorsed in the communique of the Congress of Literary and Art Workers, pressure on all unofficial publications increased. The top leadership had apparently decided that it was time to direct the attention of youth away from contemporary social problems. Apparently to soften the blow, they allowed for the time being a certain stress on traditional and foreign literature and art—even such things as an occasional nude statue—so long as these served to reduce youth's preoccupation with criticism of contemporary society.

The wind temperature dropped further with Deng Xiaoping's speech of January 16, 1980. Many youth, Deng said, had been infatuated with bourgeois liberalism and had overlooked the great distinction between socialist democracy and bourgeois democracy. In socialist democracy, literature and art must uphold socialism, Marxism-Leninism-Mao-Zedong-Thought, the dictatorship of the proletariat, and the leadership of the Communist Party. While it may have been be acceptable to set aside the slogan "Literature in Service of Politics," this of course did not mean that "literature can be separate from politics."[19]

A month later, during the middle of February, the line was drawn more clearly for literature at a Conference on Playwriting in Beijing. Hu Yaobang, then Secretary General of the Party's Central Committee, delivered the keynote address, a fact that signaled the importance of the conference. Amid an effusion of verbiage about encouragement of the arts, two film scripts and a play were cited as negative examples. One was "What If I Really Were?," whose problems we have already reviewed. Another, a film script by Wang Jing called "In Society's Archives," tells how a fine young woman is driven to juvenile delinquency after she is raped by a high military official and his son.[20] It was criticized for exaggeration. The third, "Girl Thief" by Li Kewei, although only mildly offensive compared to the other two, was criticized for sympathizing too much with a young gangster who runs circles around bumbling police.[21]

The basic principle that writers were supposed to infer from the Conference on Playwriting was formulated in a slogan that was widely publicized in March—"Writers Should Consider the Social Effects of Their Writing." Leading critics cited examples of the ill effects of irresponsible writing. It was pointed out that somewhere in China children had murdered their siblings after viewing a violent foreign film. But the promulgation of the "social effects" slogan actually led to a mild counterattack from the advocates of tolerance. How, they parried, can a creative artist stand responsible for the immensely complex relations between a work of art and reader or viewer psychology? Or the even more problematic relations between reader psychology and reader behavior? When something goes wrong in society, why assume that it all started with writers? Since when are writers the most powerful influence in the environment?

The leadership had never intended, of course, that writers do research on what readers derive from literature. The behest to consider "social effects" was in fact a face-saving way to press leadership's view of social effects, and one did not need opinion polls in order to grasp this view. The opponents of the policy knew this and followed the rules of the game by pointing out that the only true way to know the social effects of a piece is to let it be published so that the people themselves can decide. Thus, while everyone accepted the slogan superficially, the real issue was argued to a standoff. The wind grew no warmer, but the refreezing tendency also abated for a time. On July 26, the long awaited replacement for the slogan "Literature in Service of Politics" was unveiled. It was itself a carefully wrought compromise: "Literature in Service of the People and in Service of

Socialism." Writers would apparently still have more elbow room than during most of the last twenty years, but works that exposed social problems too baldly would be out of bounds.

By this time, the gifted writer Wang Meng had been experimenting for many months with literary form in ways that were popularly attributed to influences from "stream of consciousness." These experiments, like exposure writing, drew considerable criticism. ("If I can't understand a story, the masses can't; and if the masses can't, it doesn't belong in socialist art.") But in the latter half of 1980, Wang Meng's experiment set a trend among a significant portion of China's serious writers. Basically, it offered these writers a middle way between the Scylla of capitulation and the Charybdis of serious political trouble. But their interest in new techniques continued to bring the opposition not only of restrictivist critics but also of the bold advocates of social exposure, who continued to insist that a writer's first duty is to speak for the people and to tell the truth.

A renewed plea for freedom of art was delivered in early October by the famous film actor Zhao Dan as he lay dying of cancer. "If the Party controls literature and art too closely," he wrote, "literature and art are hopeless—they are finished."[22] Although this piece was published in *People's Daily* and other Party organs, the final verdict on it, delivered from the very top, was negative. Indeed it may have been a factor in bringing about the nationwide movement in 1981 to curb "bourgeois liberalism" through criticism of Bai Hua.

The future of literary politics in China is impossible to predict; the only thing that seems certain is that it will remain a frequent topic of interested speculation. Two underlying forces, major and basically opposed, appear likely to continue causing fluctuation in the Party line, at least for the next few years. First, the top leadership, even if it changes, will not want to relinquish literature and art as tools to "engineer the souls" of readers. Second, as long as modernization remains a primary national goal (which it may not, if there is a change in leadership), the hand of the advocates of tolerance will be relatively strong. Scientists and engineers must be treated reasonably well if modernization is to succeed; although it does not follow that writers must also be treated well, any attack on them that is too severe will, for at least another few years, conjure fears of the across-the-board anti-intellectualism of the Cultural Revolution years. Moreover, China's creative writers will remain a vital bridge between generations. Almost all of the top leadership is over sixty; the majority of the population, including the vast majority of readers of contemporary literature, is under thirty and quite conscious of being a different—and aggrieved—generation. Prominent active writers are a key group because nearly all of them are between thirty and sixty and share some characteristics with the two generations they bridge. The leadership can hardly be unaware of the dangers of silencing them. In sum, the literary weather in China will probably continue, as surely as the stock market, to fluctuate. But the extremes of 1966–72 on the cold side, and 1979 on the warm side, may not be exceeded for some time.

SOME NOTES ON THE PRESENT COLLECTION

This volume is conceived in part as a sequel to Kai-yu Hsu's *Literature of the People's Republic of China* (Bloomington: Indiana University Press, 1980). It attempts the same broad representation of genres but focuses on 1979 and 1980, whereas the Hsu volume spanned all of 1949–79. Our choice of 1979–80 is not accidental, of course; these two years stand out clearly since 1949 in terms of the relaxation of controls on writers and the frankness with which writers were able to reveal some of the profound and complex problems in Chinese society and in recent Chinese history. The year 1956, with its short-lived "hundred flowers" atmosphere, is comparable in these regards but still falls far short of 1979–80.

It is less easy to say that 1979–80 were banner years artistically. Clearly, when the controls were relaxed, the literary quality of published works did improve along with its "outspokenness"; but in general the increase in quality was not as striking as the increase in outspokenness. Why? First we need to remind ourselves that, as pointed out earlier, the distinction between art and outspokenness has for a long time been less clear in China than in the modern West. In China, candor in behalf of one's people and country has long been considered a primary duty of intellectuals and therefore a literary value in itself. Not surprisingly, the traditional sense of a responsibility to speak out has in recent years been magnified by the very fact of controls on expression. It thus can happen, ironically, that when the controls are eased and writers have more leeway to shape their artistic intuitions, they are impelled instead to use their new freedom to complain about controls. Thus when we think of the artistic harm done by the "scope" that writers must stay within, we are mistaken to think only about the fertile areas for inspiration that the scope rules out of bounds. More insidious, and ultimately more damaging, is the simple presence of the "scope" itself, which, even at its broadest, irritates writers enough to draw their attention away from art. Readers in China also become preoccupied with the scope question, and this fact explains why "pathbreaking" works that are highly praised by Chinese readers can seem quite dull to an outsider. Unless one understands how a "forbidden zone" is being opened, and can feel the exhilaration that comes when a long period of enforced silence ends, it is hard to appreciate a story that simply tells about an

Introduction

unfair bureaucrat, or an intellectual separated from his books, or a boy and girl who put love before class background. In the present collection we have tried to include some works with potential staying power for the non-Chinese reader. Liu Zhen's "The Girl Who Seemed to Understand" and Xiao Yi's "The Little Egg Girl" may be particularly successful in this way. But most of the works collected here are basically time-bound and culture-bound. The more one knows and cares about contemporary China, the more meaningful they will be. At a minimum, they are testimonies to human suffering that reached massive proportions in recent years in the world's most populous nation. From this they achieve a certain dignity that transcends cultures, even if their expression is culture-bound.

There were some conspicuous flaws that recurred in the literature of 1979–80 which, for the sake of perspective, deserve a brief review here. The most important problem may have been the tendency to imitate. The theme of the heroic cadre, returning from persecution by the Gang of Four to shoulder the burdens of the Four Modernizations, was repeated nearly *ad nauseam*. Although badly battered, he is always as steady and trustworthy as your favorite uncle. He is self-sacrificing and very humble in spite of the fact that he is never wrong. In sum he embodies morality itself, and this shows in his physical appearance (graying temples if over fifty and bushy eyebrows if under) just as clearly as it does in the heroes of popular Chinese opera and pre-revolutionary popular fiction. Another popular holdover from earlier storytelling was the plot that turns on far-fetched coincidence—long-separated family members reuniting by chance or only because someone recognizes an artifact from childhood, etc. In the category of thrilling device, however, the far-fetched plot had to vie with a modern competitor—the flashback, and flashback-within-flashback, mostly as adapted from Western film. Romantic love, perhaps because it was banned from the printed page for the decade 1966–76, became a hackneyed theme. Even stories whose main interest lay elsewhere often included a touch of melodramatic romance, almost as if a formula required it. Fewer in number, although equally hackneyed, were the accounts of army heroes and their glorious victories over the Vietnamese. But these stories, like the border war itself, were not very popular.

A tremendous volume of literature was published during 1979–80, making the question of a survey quite difficult. The present selection was made after considering suggestions from friends in China and from some of the contributing translators. Considerable emphasis has been put on illustrating the kinds of works that were popular and controversial, and thus there has not been enough space to represent many of the more important authors. Stories like "Maple" and "What Should I Do?" will frustrate the reader who is seeking literary

Introduction

art; they are included here for their popularity in China and for the role they played in the politics of literature during 1979. Similarly, "Cries From Death Row" is meant to give the Western reader a sense of the kind of sensationally accented stories of woe that were commonly told, orally as well as in print, during 1979–80. The comedians' dialogues and clappertales are also included to illustrate popular tastes, and will be most appreciated by readers who are familiar with the performance styles of these genres.

In matters of translation, the editor and translators have emphasized both naturalness in English and fidelity to the Chinese. We feel that in literary translation faithfulness to tone—involving the attempt to write what a native speaker of the target language might write if inspired by the "same" thought (it is hard, of course, to say any thought is precisely the same in different languages)—can be just as important as faithfulness to denotative meaning. Our emphasis has involved trying to match the overall quality of writing in Chinese and English: harsh when it is harsh, subtle when subtle, immature when immature. The effort to give the volume a reasonable uniformity in approach to translation involved a protracted editing process that I know was a burden to some of the translators. My warmest thanks go to all the translators (both those who were oppressively edited and those who were not) for their fine work as well as their remarkable patience and good will over a preparation period that was too long.

For the convenience of the reader, all references to amounts of money have been converted to U.S. dollars at the 1979 exchange rate of approximately 1.5 Chinese *yuan* to $1. Other references to weights and measures in the metric system or in traditional Chinese units have been converted to pounds, feet, acres, etc., except that the metric system has been kept in a few scientific and technical contexts. Except for the introduction to "What If I Really Were?" by Edward M. Gunn, the introductions to individual pieces are by the editor.

This project was conceived and begun in China in 1980 under a fellowship from the Committee on Scholarly Communication with the People's Republic of China. My sincere thanks go to the CSCPRC as well as to my Chinese host organizations, the Chinese Academy of Social Sciences and Zhongshan University. My grateful thanks also go to the Center for Chinese Studies at the University of California at Berkeley for support during this project and to *China Quarterly* for permission to reprint copyrighted lines from the three poems "The New Face of Judas," "Desert Scenes," and "Two Cents," translated by W. J. F. Jenner. Finally, I am delighted to acknowledge my debt to Eugene Eoyang for coming up with the interesting title "Stubborn Weeds"—from his noctural subconscious, I understand.

P.L.

Introduction

NOTES

1. See Bonnie S. McDougall, *Mao Zedong's "Talks at the Yan'an Conference on Literature and Art"* (Ann Arbor: University of Michigan, Center for Chinese Studies, 1980); T.A. Hsia, "Twenty Years After the Yenan Forum," in *The Gate of Darkness* (Seattle: University of Washington Press, 1968); and Merle Goldman, *Literary Dissent in Communist China* (Cambridge: Harvard University Press, 1967).

2. Under the slogan "Let a Hundred Flowers Bloom, Let a Hundred Schools of Thought Contend," intellectuals were urged to speak their minds in the latter half of 1956 and early 1957. See Hualing Nieh, ed., *Literature of The Hundred Flowers* (New York: Columbia University Press, 1981, two volumes).

3. Even among urban readers, we refer primarily to high-school-educated youth. Older readers generally preferred classical literature, the politics of which, at least in 1979-80, were not considered a very important topic. The less educated urban readership preferred detective and spy stories, love stories, and martial arts tales, which in the late 1970s were also regarded as less important items for literary control.

4. Herman Ermolaev, *Soviet Literary Theories, 1917–1934: The Genesis of Socialist Realism* (Berkeley: University of California Press: Publications in Modern Philology, vol. 69, 1963), p. 167.

5. Prescribed reader preferences are easy to infer from the many policy statements and critical articles in the public press in China. Actual reader preferences are more difficult to determine. The statements and assumptions about reader preferences in this essay are based on: (1) interviews with editorial boards of literary magazines, book publishers, and newspaper literature columns in six Chinese cities; these boards in turn base their impressions on readers' letters, their own annual surveys, and a system of *pingshu dian* ("review points"), where an appointed reader in a local work unit is given free literary materials in return for writing reports on how they are received among co-workers; (2) interviews with personnel of the New China bookstore; (3) library borrowing statistics; (4) reader preference surveys that are occasionally published in China; (5) 116 responses to my own questionnaire among readers in Guangzhou and Beijing; and (6) my personal impressions from talks with readers during 1979–80.

6. Some of Mao's original ideas in the Cultural Revolution were aimed at improving conditions that the Cultural Revolution in fact made much worse, but that is another story.

7. Liu Xinwu, "Ban zhuren," *Renmin wenxue*, no. 11, 1977; Lu Xinhua, "Shanghen," *Wenhuibao* (Shanghai) August 11, 1978. Both stories are translated in Geremie Barme and Bennett Lee, eds., *The Wounded* (Hong Kong: Joing Publishing Co., 1979).

8. For example, in May 1979, the very popular magazine *Masses Cinema* printed on its back cover a color photograph of a Chinese actress and actor in the roles of Cinderella and her prince, kissing. In the August issue the editors printed a letter from a Party cadre in Xinjiang Province who was furious: "A foreign poisonous weed is attacking the Party and Chairman Mao!" The letter was so unbridled and outlandish that it drew an immense volume of biting rebuttal, and this pushed the door of tolerance just a bit further open.

9. See note 5.

10. In the survey for short stories, four of the five most popular (I do not know the fifth) were, in order, Jiang Zilong's "Manager Qiao Assumes Office" ("*Qiao changzhang shangren ji*," *Renmin wenxue*, no. 7, 1979); Chen Guokai's "What Should I Do?" ("*Wo yinggai zenmo ban?*," *Zuopin*, no. 2, 1979); Kong Jiesheng's "The Other Side of the Stream" ("*Zai xiaohe neibian*," *Zuopin*, no. 3, 1979); and Dai Qing's "Anticipation" ("*Pan*," *Guangming ribao*, November 25 and December 2, 1979). All were rather hardhitting. Jiang Zilong's story was officially awarded first prize. Chen Guokai's story was listed eighteenth; Kong Jiesheng's and Dai Qing's were denied prizes, although Kong was rewarded by having another of his stories, much more innocuous, listed sixteenth. The survey of reader preferences in poetry was published in *Wenyi qingkuang* (Beijing), February 1980, pp. 1–8.

11. Bai Hua and Peng Ning, "*Kulian*," *Shiyue* (Beijing), no. 3, 1979.

Introduction

12. One might suppose that, in the middle of this causal chain, the reason for singling out Bai Hua was indeed his film script "Unrequited Love." But this would be to misconceive the process fundamentally. The reason for criticizing Bai Hua was that a *societal* tendency had to be curbed. The interesting question that relates to Bai Hua personally is this: Of many possible alternatives, why was Bai Hua the one picked as an example? The answer, alas, is obscure. Many theories have circulated through China's grapevine, and some have appeared in the Hong Kong press. But it would serve little purpose here to review such theories or to explain my own, when the fact remains that no one outside China and only a tiny minority inside can know the truth. This circumstance is the same in more important cases, such as Lin Biao's.

13. Hu Yaobang, "Speech at the Commemorative Convention of the Hundredth Anniversary of the Birth of Lu Xun," in *Guangming ribao* September 26, 1981.

14. Many critics voiced this view in the spring of 1980. Probably the most important statement was from Chen Yong in *People's Daily* March 19, 1980.

15. Deng Xiaoping, "On Our Present Situation and Responsibilities" (Beijing, February 1980), p. 20.

16. Most publishers in China give the size of print runs in the backs of books. But these numbers, which are the ones reported to the State Publication Administration, are not always accurate. The more active publishers often find informal ways to get paper supplies, sometimes more than half of their total supply, outside the State Publication Administration's system. It is prudent for them not to indicate the resultant increased circulation of their preferred books.

17. For a fine introduction to literature in 1979 and the events that made it possible, see W.J.F. Jenner, "1979: A New Start for Literature in China?," *China Quarterly*, no. 86 (June 1981) pp. 274–303.

18. Deng Xiaoping, "On Our Present Situation and Responsibilities," pp. 6–7.

19. Deng Xiaoping, "On Our Present Situation and Responsibilities," p. 23, and paraphrased from pp. 16, 17, and 36.

20. Wang Jing (pseud.), *"Zai shehui de dang'anli,"* was originally published in the unofficial journal *Wotu* (Beijing), no. 1, 1979; it was reprinted in the official journal *Dianying chuangzuo* (Beijing), no. 10, 1979.

21. Li Kewei, *"Nü zei"*, *Dianying chuangzuo*, no. 11, 1979.

22. *People's Daily*, October 8, 1980, p. 5.

SHORT
STORIES

LIU ZHEN   *The Girl Who Seemed to Understand*

One of the items on the truth-telling agenda of Chinese writers during 1979–80 was the condition of the Chinese countryside. Following years of idealization of peasant life in Cultural Revolution propaganda, stories such as "The Girl Who Seemed to Understand" exposed the artificiality of such idealization when measured against enduring problems of poverty, ignorance, and authoritarian social structure. Not since the 1920s and 1930s, with stories by writers like Lu Xun and Wu Zuxiang, have Chinese readers seen such stark portraits of village life. In the present story a young university student, full of theories of the revolution, gradually gains true understanding of an old peasant and thereby a clearer view of herself. Her sojourn in the countryside reminds one of Lu Xun's in "My Home Town": the hopes of an urban intellectual are crushed by the reality of village life, and the crushing is made personally poignant by the stolid submissiveness of a peasant to whom the egalitarian notions of the intellectual are as foreign as they can be. It is a virtue of both stories that the intellectual is moved toward introspection and a skeptical examination of his/her hopes. Liu Zhen's story, though fine realism, lacks Lu Xun's brilliant terseness; but her more overt style was certainly to the liking of Chinese readers in 1979–80, who thirsted to see the truth spelled out.

Liu Zhen (b. 1930) fled her home at age nine to join Communist guerrillas, and at age twelve joined the Party. She never went to school, but learned to read and write from guerrilla elders and after 1949 built a career as a creative writer. In 1959 she was criticized for a "rightist tendency" and sent to work in the countryside. During the Cultural Revolution the attacks on her grew very severe (primarily for trying to "reverse the verdict" on General Peng Dehuai); even after 1976 she was continually turned away from literary jobs for political reasons. In late 1981 she was in poor health and working without official title in the cultural office of a small town in Hebei called Handan.

Originally published in Qingming
(Hefei), No. 2, 1979.

Translated by W. J. F. Jenner.

31

1

Young Qin of the Four Cleanups Work Team and the old bachelor Du sat under the stars eating supper. Looking up at the sky Qin suddenly asked, "Do you know why it is that the moon and the stars stay up in the sky and don't fall down?"

The old man kept his eyes down and continued eating his cornbread and gruel. He had no time for such questions, but as he had to say something he bluntly replied, "I don't care. If they want to fall, let them. If they don't want to, they can stay up there."

At this reaction she cocked her head to one side and asked another question: "Do you know what the moon and stars actually are, and why they shine?"

"It's none of my business," he replied. "They won't keep me from starving or feed me. They won't buy me salt or put clothes on my back."

Qin laughed aloud and pressed on with her questioning: "You've seen them every night for over seventy years. Haven't you ever wondered about them?" Old man Du snorted and turned aside to avoid having to look at her. Her questions meant nothing to him. But she kept at him with the tenacity of a tiresome little ant. She refused to let him go. "Have you ever wondered about anything? In the old days, did you ever dream of building yourself a brick house and having a fine pair of mules or horses to take you on your very own cart to see the bright lights of Tianjin?"

"Only the rich thought about things like that," he answered.

"But what about you?" she asked. "What were your dreams?"

"I dreamed about my belly."

"But you had a belly—why dream about that?"

"Huh! It's a thing to dream about, all right! It's never been full from the day I was born. I'll soon be dead now, and because of that belly all my toil and trouble have got me nowhere."

"Oh," Qin said. She thought for a long time before asking, "Haven't you felt full since Land Reform?"

"In those days," he replied, "I never dared eat my fill. All I got was half an acre. If I'd eaten all the grain I harvested I'd never have been able to get through a drought year. I scrimped and saved, but there was always a hole."

"What do you mean?"

The old man cut the story short to offer a kind of summing-up: "During those three terrible years around 1960 there was one big hole. Everything was thrown into it: oxen, horses, carts, even pots and pans. It well nigh swallowed up everyone in the village."

"What do you think of the Four Cleanups movement?"

"It's all right I guess."

"In what way?"

"Don't ask me. Will all our worries about food and clothing be over when it's finished?"

Stubborn Weeds

32

"Of course they will! There'll be no more corruption or theft. Everyone will work with a will. Production's bound to be good, isn't it?"

"I don't know. I haven't seen it yet."

"Won't you believe anything until you've seen it? Don't you start with any political consciousness?"

"I don't know what 'consciousness' is. I used to believe in it, but then in 1960 I starved, and got starved out of my mind."

It had taken a lot for old man Du to dare to talk to Qin so freely. When the work team first came to the village the pair of them had almost become enemies. That had been in the bitterly cold winter of 1964. Qin, a second-year university student, had come to the country-side for some practical experience and had joined a work team with two older women comrades from the provincial Party committee. One was the leader of the Four Cleanups group in the village. Once a sudden gust of icy wind seemed to have blown their door open in the middle of the night. Frightened, the three women all sat up at once and turned on their flashlights. Three beams of light revealed an old man, wrapped in a tattered sheepskin, kneeling and trembling in the middle of the floor. The two older women pulled on their clothes, told him to get up, and asked what he was doing. Qin, who was on night duty, had just come back from patrol and was sitting on the brick bed-platform, still in her padded clothes.

"Heavens," she said, "you nearly scared me to death! It's you, isn't it?"

The two older women stepped down from the bed-platform and tried to pull him to his feet, but he refused to stand. His mouth, blue with cold, just kept chattering. "I—I—I—" Qin lost her temper.

"What's the matter with you? What do you want? Say something, and quick!"

The group leader pinched Qin in the back as a signal to calm down, then bolted the door and turned back to face the old man.

"We can't have you kneeling there, my good man. You'd better sit on the bed-platform. Look how cold you are. Wrap yourself in this quilt and stop shivering, then you'll be able to talk. How about it?" As she spoke she gave him a hard tug, but he still did not dare to stand up. By then the other woman had lit the kerosene lamp.

The sight of the man kneeling made Qin angrier and angrier. "You feudal old slave! Anyone would think you were looking at the emperor. We won't stand for it! Say whatever it is you have to say, and get up!"

Old Du was a big man, and with those women jabbering all around him he looked like a huge heap as he knelt there. He raised his hands to grab hold of something but lost his nerve. Both hands shook as he spoke: "I—I—I—and Widow Liu—it's wicked!"

When the two older women heard this they burst out laughing.

"A widow and an old bachelor," one of them said. "There's nothing wicked about that. Stand up now. Tomorrow we'll write you an official letter. You and Widow Liu can go to the commune office, register your marriage, and that'll be that."

"Leave it to me," said the group leader. "We'll repaper her cottage with some old newspapers and sweep the place out. You're both getting on—you'll be company for each other, and you ought to look after each other. Nothing wrong with that. Very well then. Up you go." The two of them gave one great heave and dragged Du willy-nilly to his feet. He staggered two paces backward and leaned against the wall, not daring to sit down.

"Do you accept our suggestion?" the group leader asked him. The old man's round, honest face was as expressionless as a log. He kept his eyes on the ground and said nothing. "Go home to bed now," said the leader. "An old worker like you ought to have more backbone. Never kneel to anyone again." Still speechless, the old man turned and shuffled out of the room.

"How weird!" exclaimed Qin. "The Four Cleanups movement isn't supposed to be cleaning up musty old problems like that. He really gave me a scare."

The next day the nimble Qin hurried to Widow Liu's house as early as she could. She wanted to make the old lady happy by giving her the wonderful news. But to her surprise Widow Liu said nothing and showed no emotion. There was an even a bigger surprise to follow. Before then at every mealtime old man Du had been bringing his bowl and a couple of corn buns to eat as he sat on the edge of Widow Liu's bed-platform. Now he stopped coming.

Qin asked another old woman, "Granny, what's all this about? If they've been carrying on in private all these years, why won't they come into the open and get properly married?"

The old woman, who was known in the village as Granny Sharp-tongue, snorted at her. "You don't know half the story. The old man's got no time to think about that sort of thing. When he was guarding the threshing floor in 1960 he knew that officials were stealing grain, but he kept his mouth shut—and the reason he kept his mouth shut was that he was stealing grain himself. If he wasn't stealing, how else do you think he survived when so many other people in the village starved to death? Ever since your group arrived he's been scared out of his wits. A wedding is the last bloody thing on his mind."

Qin's eyes opened wide as she listened. "Oh! Now I understand."

She hurried over to old man Du's mud-brick cottage to see him. He had just come back from hoeing and had not yet had time to wipe the lather of sweat from his forehead. He was sitting in front of the stove, lighting it to cook his midday meal. The stove in his little cottage was built all of a piece with the bed-platform, so that Qin, who was standing beside the bed-platform as he faced the stove, was looking straight at him. She could not hide her fury: "Now I know what you were up to, going on like that and kneeling on our floor in the middle of the night! You only dragged Widow Liu's name in to cover up for your thieving. Who put you up to it? It was a dirty trick, acting stupid like that. It's true, isn't it? If you don't come clean you've had it!" The old man said nothing as he bent before the stove, putting in firewood.

From that day onward the old man would never look Qin in the face, even if they met head on. But neither did he try to avoid her. When they sat on the same big bed-platform during a meeting and he happened to glance at Qin, it was as if she were a thousand miles away. There was no resentment or hostility in his look; it was simply as if she were a complete stranger. No matter how she questioned him, even if she lost her temper, he would always show the same expressionless face. Qin became very upset and reported what had happened to the group leader, adding: "I can't stay in that group any longer. Of all the people in that group, young and old, men and women, he's the key one. He knows what really happened, but he's clammed right up. Nothing will move him. Why don't you switch me over to 'making direct attacks on corrupt cadres'? Anyone would be easier to deal with than him!" The group leader thought this over for a while and said, "I think you'll just have to go and eat with him every day. You're going to get through to him even if it takes you months."

"Heavens!" said Qin, throwing her hands in the air. "That'll be the death of me. Are you going to turn me into a deaf-mute?"

The leader made some suggestions as to how Qin might approach the old man.

"Very well," said Qin after a moment's reflection, "I'll see how it goes; but if it doesn't work you'll have to lend a hand." Then she had second thoughts and went on, "But I can't stoop to waiting on him hand and foot; if I did that, he'd have a lower view of me than ever and be even less willing to talk. I'll have to start out by standing on my dignity with him."

"That's up to you," replied the group leader. "But remember, you're not the county Party secretary, so don't make yourself ridiculous by being too high and mighty."

Qin was not going to give in. "Even a provincial Party secretary would look ridiculous if he were too high and mighty," she replied.

"But he wears the mandarin's winged hat," the group leader replied, "so if he swaggers as he walks down the road the wings of his hat quiver and it's all very impressive. But all you have is bobbed hair and a pair of ears. You could swagger for all you were worth, but there wouldn't be much to quiver, would there? What do you think you'd look like?"

Qin rehearsed all sorts of ways of asserting her dignity before she found what seemed to her the right one. Then she strode into the little mud brick cottage that old man Du had built for himself and sat on the edge of his bed-platform.

"I'm here this evening," she announced, "to inform you that I have been instructed to eat here starting tomorrow."

The old man, crouched beside a kerosene lantern, was squinting intensely in an effort to thread a needle. Try as he might, he just couldn't thread it. When Qin spoke he stopped trying and grunted, "Right." He then went back to his needle but with no more success than before. At the sight of how hard he found it Qin longed to take the needle from him, thread it, and patch his tattered white vest. But then she thought: No, even if she wasn't going to act like a high and mighty provincial Party secretary, she could not cast aside all her dignity.

"Until tomorrow, then," she said.

"Right," he grunted.

She strode out.

2

After eating with him for two days, Qin realized that the old man was not in the least affected by how or whether she stood on her dignity. All he did was cook an extra bowl of rice and some more corn buns, and wash an extra bowl and pair of chopsticks; he noticed nothing else. Qin realized that standing on her dignity was completely useless. He would have paid more attention to a gust of wind that blew some dust into his eye and made him blink. He was like an unshakable mountain crag; nothing moved him. He was like mud; you could dig holes in him without hurting him. He was like an old ox that had toiled hard all its life until it died; no one could say how much land it had plowed or how heavy its burdens had been. How and why could he have become so frightened and cold and gone to kneel before the three women?

Qin just couldn't understand it. But then something else happened. One evening while they were eating the old man started to shiver again. "I—I made another mistake today, a very big one," he said.

Qin stopped eating. "What mistake?" she asked with astonishment. "And what do you mean by 'big'?"

"I was arrested—that big."

"Arrested?"

He confirmed it with a grunt.

"Then why are you sitting here eating your meal? You obviously weren't taken away."

"Coming back today doesn't count. Tomorrow I have to bring them an official letter from the production brigade and a written self-criticism too. I'll only *really* be out if they let me go tomorrow."

"Goodness! What's it all about?"

Slowly he told her the story. Now that Qin had started to eat with him, the branch he was using as a cooking-pot holder was too short for him to cook enough gruel for both of them. He had wanted to cut a longer branch, but whose tree could he cut it from? He couldn't very well take it from someone's privately-owned tree, and to cut it from a publicly-owned one was out of the question. After much thought he had remembered that he had planted some willow saplings around the half-acre which had been assigned to him during Land Reform. Only one had survived, but it was now a big tree beside the new road. Today he had been up in this tree, chopping away, when some men from the Highway Department had suddenly rushed at him shouting, "A saboteur! Get him! Get him! Must be an ex-landlord!" The shouting and the sound of running feet had made the old man shake so badly that he had dropped both the ax and the branch he had just cut, and had almost fallen out of the tree with them. The men who had come charging at him now danced around brandishing his ax. "We've got you this time, you horrible old man," they had cried. "So you're the one who's been doing all the sabotage. Come down here!"

The old man had been too terrified to come down but had just kept shaking his head and trying to defend himself: "No, not me, not me. This is the first time I've come here. I needed a branch very badly."

"Dirty liar. See this rope? If you don't come straight down we'll drag you down."

When they had showed him the rope, going down had been the last thing he wanted to do; instead he had scrambled higher as if the tree had been a ladder to heaven. But in the end a strapping young man had shinnied up and started pulling him by his feet. Old man Du had clung to a branch for dear life and shouted, "Stop, stop! I'll break my neck!"

They had tied him up and hit him as they shoved him into a small hut by the roadside, where an extremely vicious-looking man had demanded to know the reason for his sabotage.

"I never sabotaged anything."

"What's this, then? Who told you to chop it off?"

"It's for my cooking pot, I cut it for myself."

"Why did you chop it off the Highway Department's tree?"

"I planted it."

"*You* planted it, you fucker? When? When the landlord militia came back to the village?"[1]

"No. I planted it just after I got my land during Land Reform. That was before the landlord militia came back."

"Are you a poor peasant?"

"Even poorer than that."

"Then why do you hanker after the days of private farming? Why don't you support socialism?"

"I've never hankered after private farming."

"Never? Then why did you chop a branch off a publicly-owned tree?"

"There was no other tree I could use. I came here because this was the tree I'd planted. The branch I've been using to hold my cooking pot is too short. I couldn't cook enough food."

"I don't believe a word of it. You can go home now, but you'll have to come back with a letter from the head of the Four Cleanups Work Team to say who you are—and bring a written self-criticism, too."

"But please give me that branch for my cooking pot."

"What? You break the law and then expect to take this home for your cooking pot? You must be out of your mind!"

Then he had been untied and given a shove that almost sent him flying. As he started on his way home he heard someone yelling at him, "Old bastard, you got off lightly this time. You bring us that official letter or we'll come for you tomorrow and sort you out!" As the man spoke, old Du had heard his branch being snapped. He had felt thoroughly wretched; that branch had almost cost him his life.

This story made Qin angry and indignant. "What a tough time ordinary people have!" she burst out. "An honest old man like you, and a poor peasant at that, gets beaten up and shoved around just because of a branch." Her last remark reminded her of how she had lost her temper at him, and she realized she had behaved almost like the men from the Highway Department. She blinked several times and then asked if he was still angry with her.

"About what?" he replied.

"About what?" she said, "Have you forgotten what happened the other day?"

He nodded to show that he had forgotten everything.

1. "Landlord militia" were nongovernment forces organized by landowners who sought to recapture their holdings in Communist-run areas during the civil war of 1946–49.

"Have you been bullied so much all of your life that you don't notice one more piece of bullying?" asked Qin.

"That's right," he said, "you just have to take it or you're in *real* trouble."

"But didn't you stand up to struggle against the landlords during Land Reform?"

"I'm no talker, and I'm not a quick thinker either. I just took my share of what the peasants' association was handing out."

"Didn't you take the lead when the mutual-aid teams and the co-ops were formed? Didn't you play cymbals and drums?"

"I joined, sure, and put in the whole half-acre they gave me at Land Reform. But I can't play cymbals and I never touched a drumstick because they all thought I wouldn't hit the drum right."

"So do you feel you've made any contribution to our new China?"

"All I can do is work my guts out. I don't know what all that about 'contribution' means."

By now they had finished their meal. "I'll go and see the Highway people about that business," said Qin. "You can forget all about it."

"Oh no," he said, his eyes staring wide, "that's impossible. They haven't released me yet."

"Then I release you. You've had a hard day. Get some sleep. There's no meeting tonight."

"You may be a big official, but you're not in charge of this case. You're not in the Highway Department."

Qin had already turned on her heel and left.

She wrote two official letters—one explaining who she was and one who old man Du was. Being impetuous, which was hardly surprising for someone only eighteen, she would not wait till morning. She knew where the roadbuilders' cottage was and went there that very evening.

A group of workmen were playing cards; others were standing around watching. She threw her two letters into the middle of the game, startling the players and making them curious to read them. Then the little man who was in charge stood up and invited her to sit. He turned to a wild-looking lad and said to him, "What are you staring at? There's a big pile of branches outside. Trim one into a pot holder for this comrade to take back with her." The youngster went straight to fetch a sickle and started to work by the light of the electric bulb.

Qin sat down on a chair, crossed her legs, and folded her hands on her knee. She looked at each of the men in turn and asked, "Which of you beat him up today?"

Short Stories

The man in charge laughed awkwardly and said, "We didn't beat him up, an old man like that. We just gave him a few gentle shoves."

"If a provincial or even a county Party secretary had been up that tree, cutting down a branch, would you have dared to give him even a few gentle shoves?"

"What an idea!" replied the foreman. "A provincial or county secretary, or even a department head, would be too old to climb a big tree like that."

"Du's old too, isn't he?"

"Come off it. Party secretaries don't go around chopping bits off publicly-owned trees to get branches for their cooking pots. They get all their food from special kitchens. And if they do cook for themselves, they use aluminum pans and don't need branches to hold their pots. Besides, even if they did need a branch, they wouldn't have to go climbing a tree themselves—"

"Precisely," Qin cut in. "It's only an old man of seventy-two, one of our poor, neglected ordinary working people, who has to climb a tree himself and be grabbed by his feet and almost fall and break his neck, then be beaten up, abused and shoved around, and told to come back with a written self-criticism. Just tell me how he's supposed to write it. He's completely illiterate. I'll have to write it for him!"

"Hey, here it is," shouted the young lad, holding out to Qin a pot-holder that had been peeled white and had two pegs on it. "It's a bit long," he explained. "When you get back he can trim it to the size he needs for his pot."

Qin took the pot-holder. "You can't blame him for needing two pegs. One's for himself and one's for me. But when he came he got beaten up, and when I came I got what I wanted. Who needs egalitarianism? If everything were completely even we'd be talking about a plain round rod that would be no use for cooking-pots."

"Let's drop it—it's done with," said the foreman. "It's dark now. We've got a flashlight. We'll see you home. When you get back tell the old fellow he needn't write that self-criticism. He can forget about it."

"But I don't know where he'll get his next pot-holder," she said, standing up. "I can manage, but he can't, and I won't be with him forever."

Only now did she understand why the old man knelt and shivered when anything went wrong. It was appalling. A newborn babe needed the protection and care of a nurse, but who was going to nurse an old man like him?

Thinking these thoughts she left the roadbuilders' hut. When she noticed that some of them were escorting her, she stopped and said, "I grow up as the years go on, but old man Du becomes more and more of a child. There's no need for you to see me home. Just take better care of those poor old children of the future. I don't know why it was, but the famine around 1960 hardened people's hearts with hunger. Old-fashioned morality was starved to death too. If you had pulled him out of the tree and crippled him in the fall, you'd have treated it as a big joke. You're no better than the runners in the country magistrate's office in the old days or the guardian monsters in a temple."

"Well, we hope you'll think better of us later," they said as they left her.

3

When Qin reached the edge of the village she noticed that old Du's hut, located on a slope by the road, was completely dark. Feeling relieved that he must have gone to sleep, she continued on her way. But as she passed Granny Sharptongue's cottage she heard voices and saw that the lamp was still on. She lifted the door-curtain and saw people of all ages crowded on the bed-platform. Old man Du was standing by the wall facing them. It seemed that he had been talking for a long time as he ended with, "Now I've told you everything. That's all there is to it." Everyone was staring at him blankly, disappointment in every pair of eyes.

Granny Sharptongue thumped the side of the bed-platform and said, "I don't believe you, no, I don't. So many people in our production team died. Some people were so starved that their legs were as thin as hemp stalks. They couldn't even walk. How come you always looked so fit and trim through it all?"

"Me?" the old man protested, pointing at his own legs. "Don't tell me that I had legs like tree trunks when everyone else's were like hemp stalks!"

"They may not have been like tree trunks, but at least you could stay upright in a wind."

"Huh," he snorted indignantly. "In the winter of 1960 I had to use a stick and lean on walls when I walked. Didn't you see me?"

"I never saw you," said Granny Sharptongue, "but then I wasn't Widow Liu."

"From then till now," said Widow Liu from the corner, "I've been in my bare bones under this torn padded jacket. I don't even have a vest, and each of my ribs sticks out like a great long eye. I've seen it myself—"

"Keep to the point," interrupted young Bullhead, who had put himself in charge of the meeting. "Let old man Du do the talking. Now, I'm asking you—when you were guarding the harvest for those three months in 1960, did you really take only one jar of corn?"

"I've told you already, haven't I? The officials stole grain five times, and each time they gave me four or five pounds of it. It didn't even last me the autumn."

Bullhead pushed up his sleeves and sprang to his feet: "Do the rest of you believe him or not?"

"No!" shouted everyone except Widow Liu and her son, Liu Nian.

"So what are we going to do?"

"Beat him!"

They all raised their fists, but only to give him a fright, not a real beating. Even so, old man Du was terrified. "You all stole," he blurted out. "The officials stole from the threshing floor, and the rest of you stole the grain as it grew in the fields. Bullhead was in command of the militia squad guarding the fields—he stole more than anyone else. I caught him doing it. If you hadn't stolen, would any of you be alive to shout at me today? You'd all have been under the ground long ago."

A boy scrambled noisily to his feet. "My mother starved to death! We didn't steal! Don't you accuse us!" he cried, grabbing old man Du by the collar. He was about to hit the old man when Qin burst in and shouted at him to stop. The boy was so upset that tears came to his eyes.

Old man Du stepped nearer him and leaned forward. "If you want to hit me, lad," he said, "hit me in the face. Hitting through this old padded jacket won't hurt me."

Qin was so angry that she went straight for Bullhead. "Did you call this meeting?" she demanded.

"Do you think we can't do anything without your stinking help? Does democracy mean nothing to you people?" Bullhead glared at her, his eyes blazing with fury.

Qin bottled up her temper. "There aren't any landlords or rich peasants here to struggle against," she replied. "Are you peasants going to fight among yourselves and beat up your own people?"

"If we don't fight among ourselves, who can we fight with? Your Communist Party? In 1958 the weather was perfect—the crops were the best we'd had in a hundred years. But your lot came in and made such a mess of everything that we starved. Then you said it was just paying a debt. Do you think we're all idiots? Do you think we'd believe that? But we couldn't object, even though we didn't believe it. One peep and we'd have been done for, like Peng Dehuai.[2] Could we face that? If we don't fight among ourselves, can we survive a fight with you?"

2. Peng Dehuai, Minister of Defense, protested the economic policies of Mao Zedong in 1958 and was purged in 1959.

Qin was now in a flaming rage. "You're backward! You haven't got a shred of political awareness!"

Bullhead was not yielding an inch. "If I were head of your Four Cleanups Work Team drawing over $100 a month, I'd be progressive and politically aware too. But I only get a few cents for flogging my guts out all day. I'll just go on being backward and unaware!"

All Qin could find to say was, "Remember the bad old days—"

Bullhead did not wait for her to finish. "That's all you can say, isn't it? I'll tell you the truth—the old people here all say that those three years were worse than the bad old days. In the old days if you had to leave home to go begging you could always find *somewhere* that hadn't been hit by famine. But not that time. The whole country was exactly the same. There was nowhere to hide. You had to starve—it was hopeless. Hunger is more vicious than a savage beast. I don't care what you think!"

Qin bowed her head, thinking that all this was very unfair. She had been only thirteen in 1958—how could she have known?

She endured the onslaught for a while, unable to find a word in reply. Then she realized she had to act more like an official. All she could do was wave her hands and say, "The meeting's over. We can carry on with this conversation another time. At least under socialism we have ways of overcoming our difficulties. One day things will be better."

"Mum, Mum—"

As she left she heard the boy who had lost his mother weeping aloud; he had no other way of showing his anger. Granny Sharp-tongue was saying, "Don't cry, child. I can't bear it when you cry. Qin has told us that things are sure to get better some day. You can't see your mother again. Child—and the rest of you—we'll just have to work as hard as we can."

4

After this encounter Qin plodded slowly back with a heavy heart toward Du's little cottage. It had no yard, walled or otherwise, around it. The old man was sitting in the dark, leaning against the bed-platform. Qin found the matches on top of the stove and lit his little lamp. Its tiny flame was the size of a bean. She had virtually been the target of a struggle meeting alongside the old man, but instead of being indignant she felt only sadness. She handed him the pot-holder.

"Here you are. You don't have to go back tomorrow. I never imagined you'd have so hard a time of it at home too."

He lay the stick beside the stove and stared at it, his head bowed low. "I was done for from the day I was born," he said. "I wish I'd never had a belly. That bottomless pit has made me lose all sense of shame. My life has been one long disaster." Tears rolled down his checks.

Qin turned to look at him for a while before saying, "Uncle, you shouldn't let yourself be put upon. You can tell me what it was you couldn't finish saying just now. According to our policies you don't have to pay back the grain."

The old man raised his head. "If only I could give it back. I'd give my life to see those children stop crying. But there's no way I can do it. I'd hang myself, but what use would that be? But I can't go on living either. I don't know what to do. The others won't let me off the hook, and I don't deserve to be let off."

Qin, now really worried that he might do something rash, tried to console him. "When you've told us everything, that'll be the end of it. We'll believe you. Don't take it so hard." Then after a moment's thought she asked: "That night you came to kneel to us, was it really because of Widow Liu, or was it—?"

Old man Du, who had never in his life interrupted anyone, this time would not let her finish. "It was because of her and because of that pot of corn and because of those four or five pounds of grain. These people, they're no fools! They guessed almost everything. That's why the others never chose me to guard the threshing floor again after 1961. They figured out that I'm a crook. They were starving and they hated me so much they'd have eaten me. I've known this all along. When you group came I was scared. But it was myself I was scared of more than you. When I knelt there I was begging you to turn me back into a good man. I'll soon be dead and buried, and when I'm dead I don't want to be kicked about like a thieving dog. I want to die like a human being, but how can I tear off this filthy hide of mine? I know what sort of man the Communist Party wants me to be, but I haven't reformed. I'm even worse than I was in the old days. Everybody hates me, and with reason too. And you were right to suspect me and tell me off. That night I was too ashamed to tell you everything."

This was too much for Qin. "Why should you be the only one to suffer like this? Didn't you tell me that everyone was stealing?"

"Yes," he said. "But I know that there were some honest people who didn't steal."

"Did the people who starved to death not steal?" asked Qin.

"I wish I'd died with them instead of living like this," said Du. "But I didn't understand until it was too late. I owe a debt now that I couldn't pay back in two lifetimes."

Qin, now indignant, tried to comfort him. "Just open your eyes and look at all those corrupt cadres who have stolen and embezzled and eaten well and grabbed what they want. What you did was

Stubborn Weeds

44

nothing! You shouldn't exaggerate it and make yourself so wretched."

"I'm not going to compare myself with people like that. That would make me even worse than ever."

"Uncle," she said, "you've had a terrible life. Look at this cottage of yours—what kind of home is it? You ought to go ahead and marry Widow Liu. That way you'll have some sort of home for the rest of your life."

His eyes opened wide with horror. "Never. I'm too old; I won't be able to get about much longer. I could never, never make that poor kid Liu Nian look so bad, and give him another idle mouth to feed as well. He wants to get himself a wife, and that'll be hard enough as it is. When I can't move about any more, and get sick too, I'll be able to shut my eyes and die by myself. Then I won't have to worry any more about this belly or put up with disgrace any longer. I'll be ashamed of what I did with Widow Liu long after I've rotted in my grave, and the debt I owe those children I could never pay back in two more lifetimes."

Qin sighed and said, to nobody in particular, "Another debt. One to his old fellow villagers and one to the children. But he's had a really hard life, he's destitute, and he's weighed down with debts that taken together couldn't be repaid in four lifetimes." Then she thought of her own grandfather. Working it out on her fingers, she realized that he was the same age as old man Du. Her grandfather's son and daughter—her own father and aunt—had joined the revolution very early. Grandfather had not wanted to leave his old home. But he had had his youngest son, her uncle, to look after him, and her father and aunt were each sending him $13 a month, making $26 in all, as well as regularly taking him cakes and sweets and sending him high-quality tea and cigarettes. Who, she asked herself, cared at all when someone like Du had trouble? Even if he chanced to find a good-hearted local official, how much relief money would be available? There were simply too many hardship cases. Back when the old revolutionaries like her father and her aunt had first joined the revolution, surely they had not thrown themselves into the struggle just for the sake of their own parents and families. But judging from what actually happened afterward, it seemed that the old revolutionaries had indeed sought to benefit only their own.

Qin suddenly understood Bullhead's angry outburst. She could not blame him. It was as if she had matured several years in that one day. She realized that whenever disaster struck or corruption appeared in officialdom those who were hit first and hardest were the very humblest of the working people. Revolution, revolution, and more revolution had not made much difference from the old society in that respect. She was a history student, and the more she reflected on these things the more depressed she became. She could not recall later how she had left the old man's hut.

That was the end of her attempts to stand on her dignity with old man Du. She realized that such disgraceful posturing not only would be her own ruin but, if adopted by all of her generation, would mean the betrayal of the people and the death of the revolution. She wished that she had taken the needle from the old man that time and patched his tattered vest for him. His eyes were failing, but he would never dream of buying a pair of spectacles; he did not even know what spectacles were for and thought people wore them only to show off how rich they were. He had no yard in which to raise chickens, so he could not even sell eggs to get the money to buy a little salt—spectacles would have been beyond his wildest ambitions. He always called the trucks that sped along the highway "them electrics" and would never have even imagined riding in one himself. And all this poor old man could say, over and over again, was that he owed debts that could not be paid off in several lifetimes.

From the next morning onward, when the old man came back from leveling the fields on the early shift, he found that Qin had always cooked his breakfast for him. His very occasional smile would fill her with painful compassion. She served his rice, handed him his corn buns, and washed his cotton socks, his rough cotton handkerchiefs, and his tattered clothes, mending and patching them when they needed it.

One day Bullhead saw her washing the old man's clothes by the well. "The old so-and-so's got one foot in the grave, and then a nice young girl comes to him from out of the blue. I suppose he won't have to settle his debts now."

But the older people had a reply. "Let it go," they said. "When we see a sight like that we reckon we haven't lived for nothing, and we're happy enough even if the old fellow doesn't pay anything back." As for the old man himself, he never breathed a word of thanks but just continued to live as he always had. When Qin looked at him, his back still ramrod-straight despite a lifetime of hard toil, she reflected that her greatest consolation would be to know he would never again kneel before anyone. On the question of whether he would ever go hungry again, though, she felt less and less certain.

It was the following summer, when this round of the Four Cleanups was still going on, that she kept asking old man Du her silly questions as they ate their supper at the edge of the collectively-owned woods. She would tease him until he plucked up the courage to take issue with her and argue back. Only then did she realize with a bitter kind of satisfaction that in all his life nobody had ever cared about the formation of his character.

When the Cultural Revolution followed upon the Four Cleanups

Stubborn Weeds

movement, Qin behaved rather differently from other young people. When urged to join the Red Guards she asked what difference it would make in solving the peasants' food problem. When others told her that it would be a "great, most timely, and absolutely essential revolution to solve all problems", she replied, "I'll wait and see. If it's right, I'll give it everything; but if it isn't, I'm not going to act like an idiot."

After the overthrow of the Gang of Four, the classmates who had once urged her to join the Cultural Revolution now asked her why she had never been duped. "I suppose I was held back by the misery and hunger of the peasants," she replied.

"You seemed to understand something long ago," said her classmates, who had been arrested several times and had fought bitterly among themselves.

" 'Seemed' is the word for it," she replied. "Many things need to be thoroughly reassessed, including my own attitudes. As time goes on I realize more and more clearly how stupid I used to be. During those ten years a very decent old man I knew died. They had Red Guards where he was, too. But he was dead for two days before his body was discovered in his little cottage. The way you people carried on, a person's death meant no more than an ant's. If the figures were known, the blind folly of that decade probably killed many more people than starvation did during the three hard years. You people destroyed anything successful that you could get your hands on."

At this her former classmates protested with wide-eyed astonishment. "You can't put the blame on us. It's all very well for you to use us as scapegoats, but where can we take our complaints about how *we* were treated?"

"You deserved it all," she retorted, her anger flaring.

"Good heavens!" they said sarcastically. "What a know-it-all! Even if we all hanged ourselves or slit our throats that wouldn't be enough for her."

The mention of hanging made Qin remember old man Du more clearly than ever. Staring through the window at the sky, she whispered to herself, "Uncle Du! You owe nothing to anybody. But what I owe to you could never be repaid in eight lifetimes. You gave your country years of hard work, but until the day of your death nobody took care of you. I should write a frank account of your wretched and miserable life, but I haven't yet. There are too many things that I still don't understand and haven't thought through."

Her classmates, seeing that she was holding a letter that she had just finished reading, snatched it from her and opened it. The signature at the bottom was "Bullhead".

"Hey, this could be one of us," said one of the boys. "We're bullheaded, too!"

Short Stories

"There's no comparison," Qin snapped. "He knows what he's talking about. That's why he wrote apologizing that he didn't look after an old man properly for me." Her thoughts became too much to bear. She put her head on the table and began to sob aloud. She had much to grieve over.

Her former classmates were horrified. Each of them had been like Bullhead in the Cultural Revolution, but Bullhead's fate had been even more wretched than theirs, his sufferings even greater. He was in his thirties now and had been unable to find a wife. He wouldn't end up a poor old bachelor, too, would he? Such were the thoughts Qin wanted to express as she wept.

XU HUI   *Nightmare—Notes from a Mother's Hand*

Public denunciations of the Gang of Four were officially welcomed and extremely common after 1976. But until 1979 most were formulaic, referring to "the interference and destructiveness of the Gang of Four" and telling little that was either detailed or personal. Writers assumed it was their duty to penetrate beyond slogans, but there were difficult problems in doing so. For many, to relive the details of their Cultural Revolution experiences was too painful; there was convenience and a certain comfort in joining the formulaic denunciations and leaving it at that. Besides, to offer one's more intimate experiences in written form for publication meant to re-expose them in the public political arena, where the original hurt had come from and where one still had to temporize in order to fit contemporary standards of expression. For example one could attack the Gang of Four but not the Cultural Revolution itself, which was held somewhat awkwardly distinct from the Gang of Four until late in 1980 when the Chinese media began in concert to write "Cultural Revolution" in quotation marks. Yet even then criticism of Mao Zedong had to be oblique.

"Nightmare," written in early 1979 under several of these burdens, is uncommon in its simple authenticity as a story, but clearly representative of a common tragic experience.

Originally published in Sichuan Wenxue *(Chengdu), No. 4, 1979.*

Translated by William A. Lyell.

Stubborn Weeds

I have had many dreams. After I awake, they usually disappear without leaving so much as a trace. There is one, however, I shall never forget—a nightmare, all too true to life. . . .

I was sitting alone one summer evening, a volume of *Lu Xun's Complete Works*[1] open on the desk before me. The room was like an oven. A whisp of a breeze occasionally fingered its way through the foliage of the parasol tree outside my window, but it brought with it not even the barest hint of coolness. Whenever this kind of weather had prevailed in the past, the benches along the shaded path through the trees were crowded with people taking advantage of the breeze, and if I had already finished correcting my stack of fifth-grade composition books, I would usually go out to catch a breath of air myself. Today the path was totally deserted.

Suddenly from someplace in the distance, there came a sound—a sound that frightened me. Since this ancient city had been liberated without the firing of a single shot, I, like most of the other inhabitants, had never been able to distinguish the sound of firecrackers from that of gunfire.

After a short burst of firing, I was once again surrounded by silence. I sat there staring at my book but had no heart to go on reading. I flipped through a few pages an random and then took a note from my desk drawer, a note so crumpled it looked like the skin of dried bean curd. I had read it dozens of times before.

> Mom:
>   Please don't come looking for me and don't worry about me either. I am taking part in the struggle to protect Chairman Mao and win victory for the Great Proletarian Cultural Revolution. Together with my comrades-in-arms I shall hold and defend our Red Fortress, destroying all enemies who come to besiege it! *FIGHT FOR CHAIRMAN MAO—IF WE WIPE OUT, WE WIPE OUT!* Such is the ironclad oath we Red Guard Warriors have taken!
>
> Your son, July 26, 1967

My gaze lingered on "your son." The two neatly written characters suddenly became a pair of black and flashing eyes; beneath those eyes were a high-bridged nose and a well defined mouth. This was my sixteen-year-old son, Jiping, an only child. He had not come home for three days. He had moved into a tall red brick classroom building without the school compound where he went to high school—the Red Fortress he spoke of in his note. A rival student

---

1. Lu Xun (1881–1936), China's greatest modern writer, was virtually the only prerevolutionary Chinese writer it was safe to read during the Cultural Revolution.

faction had occupied the rice-brown administration building opposite the school's main gate. This was no game of war played by children; both sides had real guns and lethal bullets. What's more, on both sides, the youngsters with those guns and bullets were fired by a fervor bordering on religious faith and filled with intense hatred for their opponents.

Ping! Ping! The guns began again and made me shudder so that the note dropped from my hand and fluttered to the floor. I didn't pick it up. My gaze turned instead to the large photograph of the child's father on top of the book cabinet. I wanted to shout, "If only you were still with us, you'd surely be able to talk him into coming back." The man in the photograph seemed to eye me thoughtfully while a perpetual smile played at the corners of his mouth.

Our son was seven when his father passed away. Cancer of the liver. Close to the end, he lay on a small steel cot in the hospital, his body so wracked with pain that he couldn't speak. But his dry eyes seemed to be searching for something in the room. I realized that he was looking for Jiping. Between sobs, I told him I had left Jiping with our neighbor, Auntie Liu. I hadn't brought him along because I didn't want to cast the slightest dark shadow across our child's heart. Jiping's father seemed to understand, for his gaze ceased to wander and a barely discernible smile crossed his face.

From then on, Jiping became the most important part of my life. If I left work, came home, made supper, and he still wasn't back from school, my imagination would run riot. Could he have taken a spill from the horizontal bar during gym class? What if he had been hit by a car? As the little clock on the desk dully ticked off the minutes, the room would suddenly seem too large, too empty, too quiet. But then, just as suddenly, the door would burst open with a *pow*, and Jiping would come dashing in like a spirited colt. He would take off his book bag, toss it onto the bed, and announce in his crisp, clear voice, "I'm back!" The room would immediately fill with life. It was as though everything in it had started to talk and sing. The tick-tock, tick-tock of the clock was now a happy voice calling, I'm back, I'm back.

After supper I would sit at my desk and correct papers while Jiping sat at a corner of the same desk doing his homework. I would often stop in my work and stare at those jet-black eyes and that mouth tightly pursed in concentration, discovering once again that the face before me was a small replica of his father's. At such times a feeling that would have been hard to put into words welled within me, and I would forget that I still had work to do. Auntie Liu from next door came in one evening when we were sitting like that. With a teasing laugh she said, "Aha! What have we here? Looks just like an imperial tutor attending a little prince at his books!"

If it was still early when Jiping got through with his homework,

Stubborn Weeds

he would pester me to tell him a story. But what stories could I tell? Even though I had been only a struggling scholarship student before Liberation, I was still considered a holdover intellectual from the old society. That meant I had to be on guard not to let the nonproletarian thoughts in my own mind influence my son. So I always made it a point to pick something with a revolutionary theme. Given my professional competence as a language teacher, I could tell the stories in a lively and vivid way, and Jiping was always enthralled. Any time a new character appeared in the narration, Jiping's large and flashing eyes would open wide as he urgently asked, "Is this a good guy or a bad guy?" For the "bad guys," he would angrily clench his teeth as though he wished he could get his hands on them. He showed anxious concern for the fate of the heroes who bravely dedicated their lives to the revolution. He was always thrilled by their successes. At such times, his innocent face would beam with admiration and longing. I was highly amused by these expressions of his boyishness, but at the same time was gladdened that his loves and hates were so clearly distinguished at so early an age.

When Jiping started junior high school, his roundish face began to take on the shape of early manhood and a light line of fuzz appeared on his upper lip. Mornings he went to school with Auntie Liu's son, Xiaoning; evenings he sat by my desk doing homework. At the end of every term he invariably came home with the three brand new notebooks that served as awards for model students in each class. Without really thinking about what I was doing, I would always place them for a while in front of his father's photograph on the book cabinet. Although I was an atheist, somehow I felt it could only make the child's father happy to watch his son maturing.

Shifting my gaze away from the top of the book cabinet, I bent down and picked up Jiping's note again. How had all these unhappy things come about?

The Great Proletarian Cultural Revolution began so quickly that I scarcely had time to give it any thought. My son, in ninth grade at the time, had donned the armband of the Red Guards and set about the task of "Destroying the Four Olds and Establishing the Four News."[2]

Just as I got in the door one day, Jiping handed me a fistful of cash and said, "Mom, I've straightened up the book cabinet and sold all the Four Olds books to a waste station.[3] Here's the money I got."

Flabbergasted, I opened up the book cabinet and looked inside; except for the works of Marx, Lenin, Mao Zedong, and Lu Xun, the shelves were bare! Not to speak of all the other things that were gone, the missing books I had treasured most were an old edition of Romain

2. See "Four Olds" in glossary.
3. Waste stations were set up during the Cultural Revolution to pay people who turned in books containing any of the Four Olds.

Rolland's *Jean Christophe* and a folio of beautifully painted reproductions entitled *A Collection of Rubens's Oils*. This was the first time I ever lost my temper with my son. "Even when 'Destroying the Four Olds,' you ought to talk it over with your mother first. Do you really think those books are all nothing but *waste* paper?"

He had never heard me use such a tone of voice with him, which is probably why he lowered his own voice as he answered. There was, however, not the slightest trace of hesitancy in his words: "Mom, those were bad books. I looked through all of them and they *were* bad books—honest. Take Rubens, for instance, he never painted the heroes of the proletariat—honest." He squinted his eyes just a bit as though expecting that those two "honests" should have been enough to convince me.

For the moment I couldn't think of anything to say. It was true that although one could find Volga boat pullers in Rubens's works, there were also many aristocrats and rich people as well—"honest." And yet those books were also a crystallization of mankind's collective wisdom. Could they simply be dismissed as "bad books"? But how could *I* possibly explain this to my son? Wasn't I the one who had seen to it that he never came into contact with any of those books lest they exert an unwholesome influence on him? It pained me that he had sold my books, but I was even more concerned about his present way of thinking. Were "good" and "bad" to be so easily distinguished?

All the schools had long since taken the advice of the slogan to "stop classes and shake things up with a revolution." And my son? Well, in the afternoons he still came bursting in like a spirited colt; the only difference was that his schoolbag no longer contained books and notebooks but was now packed with handbills. They contained mimeographed slogans, all advising people to *burn* this or *bombard* that.[4]

After everything imaginable had been "burned" or "bombarded," the youngsters who had "set the fires" and "shot the guns" then divided into two factions, each holding religiously to its own "viewpoint." Xiaoning from next door had originally been the best of friends with Jiping, but now, because their "viewpoints" differed, they didn't even greet each other when they met on the street. What's more, this factionalism spread like a contagious disease, and the merest contact was enough to spread the infection.

Auntie Liu had had to leave her job because of it and was now recuperating at home; yet even she had become a faithful disciple of her son's faction and lectured me endlessly with words and phrases that were quite obviously straight from him. People like me were labeled the "disinterested faction."

4. In the early stages of the Cultural Revolution referred to here, high school students used "burn" and "bombard" to mean "attack verbally".

Questions which could not be worked out verbally were settled with fists. And then the time arrived when even fists were insufficient and weapons were brought into play—lethal ones which would quiet one's opponents once and for all.

After the first bullet sliced through the clear blue sky of summer, I called Jiping to me and told him to stay out of armed conflict, no matter what. He agreed. Since Jiping had never been one of those rough children who liked to play with toy guns and clubs, I thought that he really would stay out of it.

After a few days the fighting seemed to escalate. From dawn until dusk there was nothing but gunfire. It was especially bad after sundown. All the shooting and explosions kept the windowpanes rattling in their frames, and once, as I peered into the fathomless depths of night, I actually began to feel that the world was coming to an end. I heard Auntie Liu say that Xiaoning and his faction had already been driven out of the classroom building. Recently Jiping had been leaving earlier and coming back later with every passing day. It looked as though I would have to catch him "on the run" between his conferences.

As I walked into his room that evening, he had just gotten back from school and was noisily washing up in the kitchen. I fluffed the pillow on his bed while I planned what to say. Suddenly my fingers bumped against something hard and ice cold—a gun, a *real* gun! Dumbfounded, I stood staring at that awful thing and wasn't aware of Jiping's approach until he was already standing beside me. I don't know why, but *I* was the one who felt guilty. It was as though he had discovered me in some awful secret.

"Mom, don't be afraid. Our policy is 'Attack with Words and Defend with Weapons.' If anyone starts anything, it will be them!" Cool and collected as you please, it was Jiping who started the conversation.

"You mustn't go, you just mustn't!" I grabbed his sturdy arm, feeling as if he might disappear on the spot. "Jiping, you're the only son your mother has, and bullets don't play favorites. My good, good son, give some thought to your mother!"

For just a moment the lines of my son's face were disturbed by a faint tremor and a gentle light began to appear in his eyes, but then he immediately recovered that cool and collected air of the previous moment and said, "Mom, wasn't it you who used to tell me all those stories about the heroes of the revolution? The mothers in those stories would *never* have said what you're saying now!"

"It's—it's not the same! Back then they were fighting the *enemy!*"

"We're fighting the enemy today!"

"What? Do you mean to tell me that Xiaoning is your enemy?"

My question seemed to have put him at a loss. It was only after a long pause that he answered, with apparent difficulty and in carefully weighed tones, "Xiaoning belongs to the other faction, and that makes him an enemy! Chairman Mao has told us that the Cultural Revolution is the continuation of the long-term struggle between the Communist Party and the Nationalist Party. There used to be people who were duped into serving the Nationalists, but that doesn't matter. Whoever stands on the wrong side is one of the enemy!" He had become so impassioned as he spoke that the last words came between clenched teeth.

After a long silence, Jiping gently pushed my hand from his arm. Eyes radiant with idealism, he looked me full in the face and said, "I'll bet that ten years from now people will write of today's struggle just as they now write of the Huai-Hai Campaign.[5] Think how lucky we are to be able to take part personally in this epic revolution! Mum, there's no need for you to worry!"

I was unable to convince him, and when I awoke the next morning, he had already left. I found a small note under the clock: "I've moved into the school."

My emotions in utter disarray, I headed straight toward the rear gate of the school. Characters as large as bushel baskets were written across the high red brick wall surrounding the school compound: Fight for Chairman Mao—If We Wipe Out, We Wipe Out. On the wall of the administration building, occupied by the opposing faction, the exact same slogan appeared. Had anyone ever seen such a "war"?

An armed "gate guard" blocked my path. Despite the summer heat, this "warrior"—about the same age as my son—was wearing a heavy old army uniform. It was only the pitch of her voice that betrayed her sex, because her hair had been cut very short. When she heard that I wanted to see Jiping, she sternly surveyed me and then pointed self-importantly to a blackboard hanging at one side of the gate. I raised my eyes: Key Military Post—Idlers Keep Out! I was going to say something else, but the hard look in her eyes warned me in no uncertain terms: "You'll be wasting your time no matter what you say."

For a long, long time after reaching home, I sat completely still and depressed. Finally, around suppertime, I opened the door to go out. A note fell from the crack into which it had been wedged—it was that same note I have kept in my drawer and read and reread so many times.

I folded the note until it was as rough as a piece of dried bean curd. Then I unfolded it; and folded it again. The distant sound of gunfire ceased, but the silence which came in its wake was just as frightening. I decided that I would see Jiping the next day, no matter

5. The Huai-Hai Campaign was the second of three decisive campaigns between the Nationalists and the Communists during the civil war (1946–49) that preceded the establishment of the People's Republic of China.

Stubborn Weeds

what! No gate guard was going to intimidate me. Tomorrow I would go to the school. I would beg, plead, scold, and raise such a ruckus that there would be no way for them to get rid of me. If people thought me an uncultivated old bitch, so be it. This time I would bring my prestige as mother into play—something I hadn't resorted to yet. In sum, I would do anything it took to talk my son into coming back home.

All of a sudden I heard a faint, tentative knock at the door. My heart skipped a beat, for my son would never have knocked like that.

"Who is it?" I opened the door and recognized at first glance the gate guard who had chased me off the other day.

"What's happened?" My heart started to beat wildly and uncontrollably.

"It's Jiping—he's wounded!" she said. Now it seemed that those same eyes, which had so intimidated me earlier, no longer dared even to look at me. Even her voice was faint.

An icy chill ran down my spine. Poor innocent child—she hadn't even learned how to lie yet. It would have been so easy to deceive me.

Mechanically following the silent young woman, I made my way through dark street after dark street until we entered the "Red Fortress." The staircase of this former classroom building had been "fortified" by a chaos of desks and chairs which left a path just wide enough to accommodate one person. My mind blank, I made my way up the stairs. Clang! A loud noise startled me. When I collected myself enough to look I saw that my hand had struck the key of a piano which was serving as foundation for a stack of desks and chairs.

I must have been seeing things, for that was certainly my son, my only son, lying on a long table in the large room, a red flag with yellow characters draped across his body. As though I were sleepwalking, I made my way toward him, but the table was so far away, so very far away, that I was afraid I would never reach it—

Why? *Why?* Could anyone tell me why?

My son, my own son on whose heart I had not wanted the slightest shadow to be cast, had now been engulfed by the gigantic shadow of death, completely engulfed. Yet there were no shadows at all on his boyish face. A hank of hair crossed his smooth forehead at a rakish angle; his mouth and eyes were closed in a manner at once natural and serene. It was as though he were fondly dreaming of that distant day when the Cultural Revolution would be victorious—as though he might, at any moment, sit up and ask, "Mom, who are the good guys? Who are the bad guys?"

In my dazed state, I seemed to hear a gentle sobbing voice close to my ear: "Try not to take it so hard. Jiping was very heroic in his sacrifice. We will avenge him, and once the Cultural Revolution is victorious, we will erect a memorial to him."

Peace. Everything was at peace now. All strength drained from my body, I had collapsed on my bed after a few of the young people brought me home. My head ached until I thought it would explode, but that was just as I wanted it, for as long as the pain persisted, I couldn't think.

A sultry night breeze blew in through the window. My headache seemed to have abated somewhat. Woodenly, I looked up at the photograph on top of the book cabinet. And then I heard again the tick-tock, tick-tock of the little clock. So *that* was it! It had only been a dream, a terrible nightmare that had seemed all too true to life! Yes! When the sun came up in the morning, my door would burst open with a *pow*, and Jiping would dash in like a spirited colt. The room would fill with life again; everything in it would start to talk and sing. . . .

Children who were born amid all the gunfire that year are now in fifth-grade classrooms studying their books. Of all the people bustling back and forth between the red brick classroom building and the rice-brown administration building (both have long since been repaired and look as good as new), how many even remember that such a "struggle" once took place on those very school grounds? Besides, most of the inhabitants of this town have never been able to distinguish between firecrackers and gunfire anyway.

This year Xiaoning passed the entrance examinations and went off to the university. He came to see me yesterday accompanied by a girl classmate. As luck would have it, she turned out to be the gate guard of yesteryear. Who would ever have suspected that the awkward child with the stern stare would turn into so lovely a young woman? As I listened to my son's former "comrade-in-arms" and "enemy" prattle on at great length about all the new things they had seen and heard, all the new feelings they had experienced, I thought to myself, "Children, you're the lucky ones." In the course of the long lives before you, those dread days will be no more than a ripple, but for my son they came too quickly and ended too tragically. You are the lucky survivors. You will know happiness!

If history is a fair and impartial judge, then the perpetrators of that catastrophe—Lin Biao and the Gang of Four—will stand as the accused while the plaintiff's place will be empty save for a long, long list of names of people who have departed this world. And behind each and every one of those names, there will lurk a nightmare. . . .

Stubborn Weeds

ZHENG YI *Maple*

Here is a story whose significance lay almost entirely in expanding the scope allowed to literary creation. Although crudely written and psychologically shallow, "Maple" was very important, and nationally famous, for telling the truth in print about armed conflict during the Cultural Revolution. Until the publication of this story, this physical violence had remained a "forbidden zone" for writers.

Zheng Yi (b. 1949?), a student at Shanxi Normal College, must have known that he was challenging this forbidden zone when he submitted his story to several literary magazines in late 1978. None would touch it. But at Fudan University in Shanghai, students began to copy it by hand and pass it around. The student literary society Spring Bamboo recommended it to the editors of Wenhuibao, *who, although they were divided in opinion about the story, did publish it in February 1979. Political critics had mixed reactions, but readers overwhelmingly welcomed it as a breakthrough.*

Still greater controversy surrounded a pictorial version of the story published in Cartoon Strips Lianhuan huabao. Beijing) no. 8, 1979. Chen Yi-*ming, Liu Yulian, and Li Bin, who were young Shanghainese working at the Bureau of Culture in Harbin, painted a color cartoon strip that not only showed violence—machine guns, grenades, and young people lying dead in pools of blood—but also implicated the Great Helmsman Mao Zedong at a time when such implication violated another "forbidden zone." In the cartoon strip, posters of Chairman Mao appear abundantly in the background at Red Guard speeches and parades. Two frames also show dead youngsters at the bases of huge slogan-posters proclaiming "eternal life" for Mao and "loyalty to death" from Red Guards.*

Less than two days after the cartoon strip was released, the Chinese Post Office froze its delivery and asked for instructions from the State Publication Administration. The Administration promptly banned distribution. The editors of Cartoon Strips *then appealed to the Central Propaganda Department of the Communist Party, where the decision of no less a figure than Hu Yaobang was reportedly necessary to reverse it. After a ten-day delay, distribution was resumed.*

But the public controversy had only begun. The stated objection of the State Publication Administration had been farfetched—that the cartoon strip showed both Lin Biao and Jiang Qing with normal, healthy faces. Were these drawings, the Administration asked, covert support for the Gang of Four? Although this issue was debated in political reviews, the real issues, quite clearly, were the penetration of the two forbidden zones: the showing of armed violence and the implied criticism of Chairman Mao. Letters from readers poured in to the editorial offices of Cartoon Strips, *most of them defending the assault on the forbidden zones on the grounds that the young artists were, after all, only telling the truth. Armed with stacks of such letters, the editors of Cartoon Strips hosted two conferences of prominent editors and officials in Beijing in an effort to solidify their support.*

The issue of "Maple" was raised again in late 1980 when the Emei Film Studio in Chengdu produced a movie version. The initial review of the film by the Department of Culture was negative. The main criticisms were three: that the villainous Lin Biao and Jiang Qing were clearly shown in documentary footage from 1967 to be standing next to Mao at Tiananmen Square in Beijing; that when the hero carries the dead heroine into the sunset, a great expanding red sun eventually engulfs them both (the symbolism was too clear); and that the narrator, at the end of the film, explains to his young niece that the protagonists of this story are not heroes, and not martyrs—but simply "history." Since all modern Chinese history is "great and glorious," this attribution would not do.

The film directors managed to accommodate all of these criticisms. The faces of Lin Biao and Jiang Qing in the documentary footage were thrown out of focus; a thick fog was substituted for the big red sun; and the sound track with the narrator's last words was erased. But the picture of his silently moving lips had undeniable effect for those who knew the story of the editing, or those astute enough to infer what he must have been saying.

Originally published in Wenhuibao
(Shanghai), February 11, 1979.

Translated by Douglas Spelman.

1

By October 1967 the struggle between the two factions in our area was at a fever pitch. Representatives were bargaining hard in the "study session" sponsored by the central authorities. On the local level, the two sides were trying to capture strategic positions which had political, military, or economic significance—aiming to achieve *faits accomplis* which would win for them things they could not win at the negotiating table. The three counties which comprised the outer defense ring for the faction called the Rebel Headquarters Regiment (RHR) fell in quick succession as the Jinggang Mountain faction (JM) consolidated the forces of eight counties and brought them to the walls of the city.

At this critical juncture, the Cultural Revolution leaders, meeting in Beijing, expressed their heartfelt concern for the two factions; then, speaking separately to each side, they clarified their position: "Rebellion is justified! You are the true leftists, and we support you!" They also emphasized the principle of Jiang Qing's September 5th speech to "Attack with Words and Defend with Weapons":[1] "We will not be

1. See glossary.

caught barehanded when the class enemies attack," and "We will defend ourselves against any attack, then will counterattack." According to reports from Beijing, both factions had put together excerpts from several of Jiang Qing's speeches on Attack with Words and Defend with Weapons and had distributed these everywhere. Each side thought they were the true leftists, the rebels fighting to defend the revolutionary line of Chairman Mao. Everyone was putting Attack with Words and Defend with Weapons into practice.

The War Department of our RHR decided to strike before the other side completed its deployments for attacking the city. We would seize immediately the Attack with Words and Defend with Weapons broadcasting station in the No. 6 Middle School. This broadcasting station had been like a wedge in the area we controlled. Once the battle for the city got started, JM would need only to launch a thrust from this wedge to put enemy both in our face and at our back, forcing us to wage war on two fronts. If we couldn't hold, and they tore holes in our line, we would have to withdraw from the whole central area and would be squeezed into a remote nook in the northwest. Unthinkable! The task of taking the broadcasting station was given to our Youth Defense Division.

The division's leadership held a lengthy planning meeting that was marked by intense squabbling. Finally Li Honggang, one of the leaders, came to tell me that they had decided to send me to scout out the situation. Their reason was that I, an art teacher, had never taken part in armed combat; all I ever did was run around with my easel, painting watercolors, which had led everyone to suppose that I was a carefree artist. In fact I had already carried out several scouting assignments.

I circled around to the side of the school and carefully climbed over the surrounding wall. Inside, the soft, gentle switches from several rows of tall weeping willows hung to the ground and intertwined with the dense wormwood—it was like a primeval forest untouched by man. I stealthily groped my way through this willow thicket so dense it could shield wind, until I saw a strange scene before me.

The athletic field was all grown over with weeds and crisscrossed with connecting ditches and battle trenches. Several recently constructed machine gun positions stuck up like horns. The main building was pockmarked with battle holes, and a ragged battle flag fluttered in the autumn breeze, now and then revealing the words "Attack with Words and Defend with Weapons." Two rows of red maples encircled the main building, glinting like torches in the noontime autumn sun. Under the trees were big iron stoves packed with gunpowder. I made a quick ink sketch and was hurrying to open my paint box to mix the right colors when the urge to turn and run gripped me, driving away every other thought. So I plastered plain colors onto the paper, first using grass-green to cover the field (I didn't dare actually draw the battle trenches and machine gun positions—I just indicated where they were by little marks in the clumps of grass), then earth-yellow for the main building, lake-blue for the sky, red for the flag, and olive-green for the willows. Finally I mixed a little red with orange-yellow, steadied my hand, and carefully detailed the leaves on each one of the torch-like maple trees. I loved these fire-red maples; I painted them every fall. I also marked among the trees the locations of those fearsome stoves. When the battle came these would be most. . . .

"Don't move! Raise your hands!" A deep, threatening voice came from behind me.

Damn! All at once my heart stopped. The easel in my hand was snatched away before I could react.

"March!" There was nothing to do but shove the branches aside and walk out of the dense willow thicket. Several youths carrying semi-automatic rifles surrounded me.

"What did you come here for?" A boy grabbed my collar. He looked like an eighth-grader at most. Not long ago I probably could have elicited a tearful apology by simply raising my voice at him.

"You RHR bastards!" he cursed venomously. "We haven't finished you off yet?" He thrust his dagger to the base of my neck.

"I didn't paint anything—a picture of the scenery—a pen drawing with a little color—" I was so nervous I could only stammer.

"Still won't cough up the truth, huh? Ya mother! Wanna live or die?" As he was yelling, he prodded me with his gun.

"It's all true!" I ignored the pain as I tried frantically to explain myself. When he started glaring at me again, I just stammered a slogan at him over and over: "The supreme instruction: 'Fight with words, not with weapons!' "

"Hey, you know your *Quotations* pretty well! Let him go, Little Rabbit." A girl walked slowly around from behind me. "Give us another verse! Page 11 of the *Quotations*, hurry up!"

"Revolution is not a dinner party, is not—"

"Is not what? Huh? Cat got your tongue? Hurry up!"

"Is not a dinner party, is not like writing an article, is not like painting or doing embroidery—"

"OK!" She stopped me, took the easel from one of her friends, and waved it in front of me. "It's not like painting or doing embroidery—you can't be gracious, virtuous, respectful, frugal, or deferential! Revolution is violence—understand?"

Then she picked up my painting while several of them gathered around her.

"Look at those maples—pretty!"

"Hah! Really smart! And look at our battle flag, look at that red!"

Stubborn Weeds

60

"You can even see the slogan on our building: 'We will not attack unless attacked; but if attacked, we will certainly counterattack!' "

The group gathered around the painting and began an animated discussion—even the boy pointing the dagger at my chest couldn't keep from twisting his head to look. My heart calmed down a bit; it was a good thing I hadn't left in a rush after all—the color was acting as a camouflage!

The girl in charge raised her eyes and looked me over.

"If you're just sketching, why not draw what's there? Why didn't you paint the battle trenches and the stoves?"

Seeking to blunt her attack as much as possible, I replied calmly. "They ruin the scenery. I couln't put them in the painting."

The hint of a smile flickered in her eyes. She turned her head and said to her classmates: "I'll take him to the main building. You all carry on with your regular duties!"

The remark stopped me cold.

"Let me go, young comrades!" I begged them. "I won't dare come again! This is all a big mistake!"

The girl grabbed her rifle and loaded it.

"Mistake? Even if it's a mistake it's got to be explained! Stop babbling, take your easel, and get going! What are you looking all around for? Don't try to make a break for it—you're a suspect! I'm not going to kill you, but I could snap your leg in two pretty quick!"

That's it! Hopeless! A chill went through me. Once inside the main building, it wouldn't be easy to get out. Even if I didn't crack under interrogation, I'd be right in the middle of the battle that would begin tonight. Should I run? No, that wouldn't do—she looked like she really would fire. Nothing to do but keep marching in terror toward the main building.

We followed a path through weeds that covered our ankles, made a couple of turns, and reached the maples in front of the building. The girl suddenly overtook me with two strides. She raised her gun.

"Teacher Wang," she said softly. "Don't you recognize me?"

A student of mine? A flash of joy and surprise brought me to a halt.

"You're—"

Short hair like a boy's, square face, thin lips, proud arched nose, and under the disheveled bangs a pair of still child-like eyes flashing a haughty light in the shadow of the trees.

"Ours was the first class you taught in 1962, right after you graduated and were sent to our school to teach art!"

She saw that I still couldn't recall her, so she pulled her hair back. "I cut off my braids—Lu Danfeng."

"Danfeng!" I remembered. Now she was an announcer at the JM

broadcasting station, but in her senior year she had been Secretary of the Youth League branch for the C class. I had taught her for a few days in ninth grade.

"Were you really just out for fun, not to spy? You can paint anywhere; why did you have to come here?" she scolded angrily. "And at a time like this!"

All I could do was smile broadly and lie through my teeth.

"I haven't been back to school for almost a year, and I've thought about it a lot—the colors are so rich in fall, the best season for painting scenery—the green of the willows, the poplars already turning yellow. And then the maples—they turn all red as soon as the frost hits them—"

"You're not lying to me? Then—I'll let you go! Follow the base of the wall to the north; when you hear me fire a shot, turn east and you'll come to the willow grove."

Looking into her bright, sincere eyes, I felt the urge to tell her that all hell would break loose tonight—on the good and the evil alike. I wanted to tip her off but couldn't come out with it—the duel to the death between our two factions sealed my lips. I settled for saying, "Danfeng, I've heard they're coming soon to besiege you!"

"Yeah, we knew all along! But struggle demands sacrifice. If you're afraid of dying, you shouldn't make revolution! Besides, we've got *them* surrounded too; they've got nothing on us if they want to fight!" Then, waving the painting in her hand, she said, "You can't take this painting with you, Teacher Wang. If you still want it, I'll have to keep it for you!" She ended by smiling and then declaring stiffly that: "Chairman Mao says, 'After traveling the hard road of battle, the easy road will come.' When our red regime has consolidated its power, when the Great Cultural Revolution is finally victorious, then you can paint however you like!"

All I could do was turn in silence, barely able to restrain my tears.

"Stop! Teacher Wang, you know Li Qian'gang, don't you? I heard he changed his name a while ago. Because the two parts of the character 'Qian' mean 'black' and 'today'—too reactionary—he changed it to Honggang [red steel]. They say he's now a leader of RHR. He used to be in the Student Union."

I nodded.

Danfeng became very pensive, slowly turning her gaze to the maple leaves overhead and saying nothing for a long moment. Suddenly she jumped up lightly and broke off two full red maple leaves. As she brought the leaves up to her face to examine them closely, a faint bashfulness, almost impossible to detect, flickered at the corners of her mouth.

"Take a note to him for me, will you?"

As she spoke, she slung her rifle onto her back, grabbed my

Stubborn Weeds

easel, and with the leaf stems clenched in her mouth, quickly scribbled several lines on a sheet of my sketching paper. Then she deftly folded it and handed it to me.

"Don't let anyone else see it, give it to him yourself—OK?" As she took the leaves out of her mouth, she said, "Give these to him too," and finally smiled unguardedly.

They were two torch-like maple leaves joined at the stem. I took them and put them with the letter in an inside pocket. I remembered that when Li Honggang had applied to join the Youth Defense Division of RHR, some people had objected that he was awfully close to Lu Danfeng, who was a mainstay of JM. Later, after he continued to flatly deny it and because he was so courageous in battle, he was allowed to become a formal member. Now it appeared there really had been something to it. Yet—this evening—I looked at Danfeng with sympathy and foreboding.

Danfeng took her rifle from her shoulder and flipped off the safety. She looked at me with a quiet smile as if to say, OK, go!

I turned and ran.

"Halt! Halt!" Danfeng shouted. I ran even faster. Bam, bam, bam! Her gun sounded and a hail of bullets flew over my head, sending the maple leaves in all directions. Remembering what Danfeng had told me, I turned immediately to the east and plunged into the willow grove. The dense willow branches slapped my face and the irksome weeds pulled at my feet, but I continued running wildly. Suddenly I tumbled into a hole, almost knocking myself out. When I tried to climb out, my legs wouldn't respond. I could already hear the sound of rapid footsteps behind me. At this critical moment I discovered that I had fallen into an uncovered hot air duct. Without another thought I started burrowing into it. No sooner had I crawled in than I heard voices outside.

"Did he crawl into the duct? I didn't see anybody jump over the wall!"

"We'll keep watch here, you go get a flashlight."

Although in great pain, I frantically crawled farther in.

2

When I emerged from the hot air duct I was totally exhausted and looked barely human. My clothes had been ripped to shreds by bolts inside the duct, my body was covered with cuts, and my feet were bare, my shoes having disappeared. If anyone had wanted to paint a "fugitive," they couldn't have found a better model. But even worse, I found that I was inside the main building! I had escaped capture only to deliver myself even more directly into their hands. Yet I was afraid to climb back in, for what if someone came crawling through looking for me? There was nothing to do but replace the cover of the duct, slip into a classroom, and hide.

I had just caught my breath when I heard several rumbling explosions and the crack of rifle fire. They had not waited for me; the battle was on. I leaped to my feet and peered out the window. Several long sections of the wall in front of the school had been blown to rubble. Our troops had already surged in but were pinned down by machine guns from bunkers on the playing field. They were pressed flat on the ground, unable even to raise their heads. Our own machine guns that were providing cover for the attack were howling like the wind but couldn't stop the enemy fire and succeeded only in blowing hundreds of leaves down from the trees.

The battle grew fiercer and fiercer. There was a machine gun right over my head, so my location got lots of special attention. Soon there was no glass left, and even the shutters were shattered. My only resort was to crawl to a classroom on the north side, where I knew there would be no fighting because we had left the north side to them as an escape route. Suddenly a voice came from outside the window.

"Listen, Danfeng, we probably could get out easily to the north. There's a housing area just over the wall. They've surrounded us on three sides and left the north open. It looks like they want to uproot us and drive us out of the city. Get hold of the Front Army Headquarters and get a clear answer from them—are we supposed to hold on here or not? And make sure they know our opinion, which is that we are a dagger pointed straight at RHR's heart, and we will hang on to the finish!"

"We've got to complete our mission! Off we go, Little Rabbit!"

I listened tensely, with bated breath, as the sound of two sets of footsteps faded into the distance. On the north, just as a precaution, we had hidden one machine gun. I hoped my comrades there would obey orders strictly and remain as standbys—not try to lead the attack. A long few minutes passed without any gunfire, and my agitation subsided somewhat.

I lay down under the windowsill, with recollections of Danfeng drifting through my mind—

Danfeng used to be a Youth League cadre and one of the school's most avid readers of Chairman Mao's *Quotations*. When the Cultural Revolution came and Lin Biao published his "Preface to the Second Edition," Danfeng not only committed it all to memory, but—at a schoolwide meeting to exchange experiences in studying Chairman Mao's *Quotations*—actually recited, one by one, every quotation in the little red book and explained how she "repeatedly studied and repeatedly used" them. To illustrate the Chairman's principle of "study first what is urgently needed: erect a pole and immediately see the

Stubborn Weeds

64

shadow" [i.e., get instant results], she abruptly stood up, walked in front of the speaker's table, and, under the glaring spotlight, cast her shadow over the lectern. This had drawn appreciative laughter from the audience. When Danfeng realized how ramrod-straight she was standing on the stage, she couldn't help laughing: "Actually I'm not a pole, you know!" As the entire hall rocked with laughter, Danfeng's ebullient smile and the principle of "erect a pole and see the shadow" were vividly planted together in everyone's mind.

Another time, the students called a meeting to launch a campaign to criticize the school leadership for obstructing the great mass movement to study Chairman Mao's *Quotations.* Someone would read a page number and make the leaders recite a few quotations. It was hilarious. Neither the Party Secretary, the principal, nor the Dean of Students was any good at it, and all made fools of themselves. Principal Zhang grew indignant and complained that nobody could pass by these rules. Danfeng stood up and walked to the stage. She shoved her book of quotations into Principal Zhang's hand and said, "Come on, any section you want!" Principal Zhang was dumbstruck. Then everybody took turns calling out page numbers, about a dozen in all, and discovered that Danfeng could rattle off the obscure quotes as effortlessly as the common ones. Even the chairman of the meeting was dumbstruck. He thumbed through the *Quotations* at some length, then announced his choice—page 271, paragraph two. After everybody flipped through their books, a hush fell over the room. Danfeng thought for a moment before replying.

"The book of quotations has only 270 pages, so there is no page 271, much less a paragraph two." Thunderous applause obliterated the end of her sentence. In the row where all the school authorities sat, one head after another bowed—

The fighting on the south side of the main building seemed to be moving farther away. I lay on the concrete floor completely unmindful of it, inexplicably having allowed myself to become lost in these recollections. Suddenly, a long burst of machine gun fire issued from the north. In fright, I leaped to my feet. It was immediately obvious that it was our precautionary machine gun, hidden on top of the water tower, that was firing.

I saw a rifle-carrying youth—it was Little Rabbit, who had poked me with his gun—fall slowly off the low dirt wall, clutching a case of ammunition. He twitched once and then lay still. Another pair of hands appeared at the top of the wall. The machine gun fired again, and the two hands disappeared. All was silent. Danfeng! Was she finished, just as easily as that? I crumpled to the floor.

I could hear above me a flurry of footsteps, voices, breaking glass. One of the machine guns on the south was apparently being moved—there obviously had been a new development. I stood up

Criticized for showing Lin Biao without distortion.

Broke into forbidden zones by showing violence.

The giant character is "bound" in "May his longevity know no bound."

The "Maple" Cartoon Strip

Criticized for implicating Mao Zedong.

Stubborn Weeds

again. At the base of the dirt wall a hole had appeared—whether made by a bayonet or the barrel of a gun I do not know. Danfeng thrust her hands through it, grabbed one of Little Rabbit's feet, and pulled him in. Presently the hole got bigger, and a moment later someone began pushing their way out. When I squinted I could see that Danfeng had clamped her left arm around Little Rabbit's neck and was using her right hand to pull herself along the ground. She apparently was trying to use the corpse in her embrace to shield herself and thus cross the open stretch of blockaded ground in order to deliver the command from headquarters.

In a flash both sides understood. The RHR machine gun in the water tower began spraying bullets like a rushing torrent. The JM machine gun and rifles over me also started firing wildly in an attempt to give cover to Danfeng. But the RHR in the water tower were not diverted; they kept their aim riveted on Danfeng, surrounding her with dust. She crawled with great difficulty because she was also dragging two ammunition cases and two rifles which were bound to her legs—

Finally! Finally she got to a corner where the machine gun fire could not reach. The people waiting there rushed up to her and picked her up. But she fell kneeling in front of Little Rabbit's corpse and began to wail.

Unable to keep watching, I turned my head away.

3

On the south, the battle raged stubbornly on, back and forth. The JM group had relinquished their front line on the playing field and had withdrawn all their people from the side buildings and back into the main building. They had shortened the battle line and concentrated their forces, but still had made no move to break out of the encirclement. It looked as if the command which Danfeng had struggled so courageously to deliver was to shore up defenses until help could arrive.

The JM forces wouldn't budge an inch. They were waiting until the leaders of the RHR Youth Defense Division realized that they would call on the support of the JM surrounding the city. They would not take the safe route out which RHR had left for them. We had no choice but to steel ourselves, dig in, and intensify the attack.

Several feints by small RHR detachments had succeeded in destroying those awesome "thunderclaps"—the big iron stoves. Our RHR comrades battled their way through a bloodbath and finally managed to surge into the main building, where an intense struggle for control immediately ensued.

On the first floor the sounds of gunfire and grenades had already ceased as the fighting moved toward the second floor. I heard a rush of footsteps in the corridor but was afraid to open the door for fear of walking into a burst of gunfire. Then I heard Li Honggang's deep voice and let out a wild scream, "Li Honggang!" The footsteps stopped. I opened the door and rushed out.

Li Honggang stopped short, then rushed over and grabbed me. A clamoring crowd gathered around. "Aha, when we heard that burst of gunfire at noon we figured you were done for—you're a tough one!" My eyes filled with hot tears from that special emotion which warms the depths of one's being when one unexpectedly meets comrades on a battlefield of life and death. Before I could say anything, two shots rang out from nowhere and one comrade fell to the floor. Everyone else scattered frantically. I grabbed a gun and charged up the stairs with my friends.

The JM troops, in order to conserve ammuntion, began to hurl down on us things which they had stockpiled for the purpose—cement slabs, dismantled radiators, tables, chairs, instruments, and an occasional grenade for good measure. Our casualties were heavy. The urge for revenge goaded each of us to an emotional boiling point. We seemed about to explode. With no thought for our lives we pressed the attack, ever upward floor by floor—

Finally we captured the fifth floor. The remnants of the JM forces had fled to the roof, not stopping even to carry their wounded with them. They were desperately defending the small skylight which gave access to the roof. There was no way to throw grenades up, and guns were of no use. And we were suffering more casualties.

Li Honggang considered the situation, then called for a small bag of gunpowder and put it on a pile of tables which reached to the ceiling. At the same time he ordered those at the skylight to continue their fierce attack. When the powder went off it shattered two ceiling slabs and left a hole half the size of the room. Before the dust had settled, Li Honggang shouted and led a charge to the roof, where he seemed to arrive at a single bound.

"Youth Defense Division comrades! To victory! Charge!" he yelled, spraying bullets in every direction.

Everyone charged up the pile of wrecked tables to the roof. In less than a minute the gunfire stopped and the fighting was over. JM casualties were everywhere. Never again would they use megaphones to shout us down with quotations; never again would they crawl up to slaughter our RHR soldiers with machine guns and grenades.

Sunset came before anyone noticed it. Our bodies went limp as we all sat down to catch our breath. Li Honggang reached over to feel the barrel of my gun, and his parched lips broke into a smile.

"It's a little hot, huh? What do you say, Teacher Wang—you weren't used to it at first? This is the way steel is forged!"

I nodded my head uncertainly, wondering to myself: How could I describe that sensation, novel yet fearsome, when I fired my first shot? These hands of mine, which had always held paintbrushes, had actually picked up a gun and killed people! Is this the way "struggle changes people"?

We suddenly noticed that someone was slowly climbing to her feet in one corner of the roof. Holding two grenades high in her hand, she walked toward us swaying back and forth. And she kept right on coming! We all panicked at this surprising event and flattened ourselves on the roof in spontaneous unison. Li Honggang was first to come to his senses; he jumped up, raised his gun, and shouted, "Put down your weapons! Quick, or I'll fire!"

The attacker stopped and slowly lowered her right arm, which had been holding the grenades aloft. She took off her helmet and threw it to one side. Aha! That short hair even with the ears, that boyish short hair was fluttering softly in the evening breeze—

"Danfeng!" Li Honggang let out a startled whisper and stood stock still, as if he were made of wood and clay.

Danfeng didn't answer. She slipped the grenade ring off her little finger, and as her hand went limp the grenade fell beside her foot. She walked slowly to Li Honggang and reproached him bitterly.

"Why did you have to come? Why did you come? Why? Your hands are smeared with the fresh blood of JM people—executioner! Executioner! Ex—e—cu—tion—er!"

She suddenly grabbed her head with both hands and staggered backwards. Li Honggang sprang forward and caught her around the waist.

"Danfeng! Danfeng! Snap out of it!" Li Honggang was shouting anxiously into her ear.

"Qian'gang, do you still remember me?" Danfeng gradually came to her senses. She seemed exhausted as she ran her hand through her disheveled hair and said with a bitter smile, "Back when it all began, we never would have imagined a final parting like this, would we?"

Tears ran down her cheeks. "How great it would be if I could see the final victory of the Cultural Revolution with my own eyes!" She grabbed the front of Li Honggang's shirt and twisted it tight. "Qian-gang," she implored, "hurry and come to your senses! Come back to the revolutionary line of Chairman Mao! Hurry and point your gun the other way, Qian'gang!"

Fighting tears, Li Honggang turned his face away.

"No! You—*you* surrender!"

Danfeng stiffened with anger and pushed Li Honggang away. She took several steps backward, straightened her old, faded, blood-stained uniform, and flashed a scornful smile.

"I'll be true and faithful even to death! Go ahead and shoot, chicken!"

Li Honggang—the former regimental head of our Youth Defense Division, who never flinched no matter how heavy the fire—now began to tremble all over.

"You've got no guts!" Danfeng yelled at him, then turned and walked to the edge of the building.

"Danfeng! Danfeng! Danfeng!" Li Honggang's shouts were high-pitched, clipped, and filled with terror. The gun in his hand began to shake violently. But Danfeng did not hear, for Li Honggang's cries were drowned out by the slogans she shouted in her strident broad-caster's voice: "Our Jinggang Mountain fighters cannot be an-nihilated! Communism is invincible! Defend to the death Chairman Mao's revolutionary line! Defend to the death Chairman Mao, defend to the death Lin—"

With this last shout, Danfeng took her last step.

Total silence. From below came a dull thud, like a sack of grain hitting the ground.

"Ah—" Li Honggang wailed hysterically and fired a whole clip of bullets into the magnificent glow of evening.

Everyone rushed forward grabbing frantically for his gun, then wrestling him to the rooftop.

I don't know what good soul had straightened her body and arranged her clothes. She was just lying there, quietly lying on the maple leaves which had been shot down during the fighting. The evening breeze wafted by, blowing down a few cinnabar [*dan*] red autumn maple [*feng*] leaves, which swirled down on her full, young breast and landed beside her blood-drained face. It was only then that I remembered the note and the leaves she had asked me to give to Li Honggang, and I now hurriedly pulled them from my pocket. The note was still in one piece, but the leaves had long since been crumpled out of shape. I looked up, thinking to pick two new ones in their place, but even after I pulled several down, I was unable to find any which were joined on a single stem. This surprised me, and only after looking at the tree for a long time did I discover that only the leaves at the very tips of branches are joined on one stem.

I didn't know what I should say to comfort Li Honggang. I stood next to him for a long time before I handed him the note and the joined leaves.

"She asked me to give you these," I said.

"When?"

"Not long ago, at noon, when she released me."

Li Honggang carefully unfolded the letter. Dusk had fallen, so I pulled out a match and struck it. The words could scarcely be made out:

Qian'gang: All's well with you, I trust? I miss you and also hate you—do you still remember the last time we met? I could see then what you would do. I can only long for the day of victory, when, in celebrating victory, all my wishes will come true!

The match went out. Li Honggang's hands trembled as he stared at the leaves dumbly. Noticing his intense gaze, I struck another match for him. Up from the stems, the color of the leaves blended from orange to red until, at those five splendid leaf tips, it was a red as pure, bright, and intense as red agate. Delicate red veins spread over the orange face of the leaves like blood vessels. They were so red it seemed as if life's blood still coursed through them. How beautiful, how moving, these frost-nipped leaves could be!

Li Honggang pulled out his *Quotations*, opened it, and removed two maple leaves from it. These were also a pair joined on one stem, but they had long since withered. Their color was dull and had none of that delicate vitality.

"It was last October, more than a year ago, not long after the movement started, and before RHR and JM had split into two factions—" Li Honggang mumbled his reminiscences as if to himself. "That evening was the last time we opened our hearts to each other. Just before we parted, she plucked two maple leaves and gave them to me. 'Here,' she said, 'for you.' When we parted she said, 'Let's throw ourselves totally into this great revolutionary struggle and together sweep away all forces of evil and fight for the great truth of Communism!' We never even held hands; all we ever did together was talk about life, ideals, struggle—"

The autumn breeze blew gently, rustling the maple leaves. As I imagined myself hearing these wisps of conversation between the two youngsters as their school, I too seemed to meld into that bitter, misty scene.

"Hey—another light?" asked Li Honggang. I struck another match, and Danfeng's beautifully written characters once again appeared on the sketching paper:

But unless you return to the revolutionary line of Chairman Mao, there is no point in speaking of the slightest personal happiness between us! You must turn your weapon the other way, you must see the light!

Otherwise, remember, "revolution is not a dinner party, not like painting or doing embroidery—"You will die by my gun on the field of battle!

Danfeng

Li Honggang's hands fell limp, and the letter and leaves swirled to the ground. He went to one knee at Danfeng's side, one huge tear after another falling to the ground. I lit several matches together, and in that moment of brightness she seemed filled with the same vitality I had seen in her at noon. She still had her short boyish hair, square face, thin lips, and impudent arched nose. But her large childlike eyes had forever lost their proud sparkle.

Li Honggang gently brushed back the hair on her forehead, murmuring: "It turns out I didn't die by your gun—you, you—you died by—oh!"

No longer able to contain himself, he began to sob.

"Danfeng—Danfeng—oh, oh, Danfeng!"

A maple leaf drifted onto Danfeng's mouth, making it seem that she was wistfully kissing goodbye to love, to youth, and to life—kissing everything that she had now left forever.

Everything seemed blurred as tears filled my eyes. The matches went out, and all receded into the indistinct night.

From the distance came the rumble of gunfire; JM had launched its attack on the city. A call to assemble rang across the campus as the newly conquered broadcasting station burst forth with a rousing Mao-quote song: "Develop the style of fighting courageously, never fear sacrifice, never fear exhaustion or continuous warfare." The supremely bitter siege had begun.

Li Honggang forced himself to stand up, wiping the tears from his face with his sleeve. Throwing a final glance at Danfeng, he stumbled toward the assembly bonfire.

4

Two years later, after much seesawing back and forth, our enemies finally gained power. In an effort to consolidate this power, they indicted a group of "war criminals," including two charged with "throwing Lu Danfeng from five stories to her death." One was sentenced to death and one to probation. A few days later, it was charged in a study session that Li Honggang had forced Danfeng to jump at gunpoint. This could not be considered "a life taken in battle," since Danfeng had already put down her weapon. JM spent several days and nights searching everywhere for Li Honggang, who had long since left the RHR and had "drifted" for many months. He was finally found, arrested, and sentenced to immediate execution.

That day, as the police van made its way through the crowd, I couldn't bear to watch. Instead, I took a slow walk, alone with my thoughts, along a quiet out-of-the-way road. The maple trees flanking this road had turned red again, looking like clumps of brightly burning fire. The scarlet tops of the trees looked as if they were covered with blood fresh from a wound—thick, bright, dripping—

CHEN GUOKAI *What Should I Do?*

This immensely popular story circulated in several versions by word of mouth before it was written up by Chen Goukai and published in the Guangzhou literary magazine Literary Works *in February 1979. It quickly established a great new popularity for that magazine throughout China. In the form of officially approved excoriation of the Gang of Four, the story provided an outlet for very intense feelings about personal and family tragedies that had directly affected many people during the Cultural Revolution. After its publication, the editors of* Literary Works *received a record number of letters from readers, overwhelmingly favorable and many stating that they knew of similar cases themselves.*

During the last two months of 1979 People's Literature *conducted a preference poll among readers for short stories of the current year. When the poll was finished a prestigious committee of senior writers, editors, and officials awarded twenty-five prizes using the poll as a "basis." "What Should I Do?" was said to have placed second in the poll but, after consideration, it was listed eighteenth on the prize list. The prize committee probably recognized the story's relative lack of craft and subtlety. But there were other reasons why the story was controversial and could not be rated too highly. For one, the extremely emotional reader response to the contemporary problem of broken families could easily seem detrimental to the official goal of "stability and unity". A second problem was that the story broached the taboo subject of bigamy, and although the suggestion was only barely made, this little irreverent fact accounted for much of the story's fame among readers.*

Chen Guokai (b. 1938) is from a Hakka family in rural Guangdong. A junior high school graduate, he has worked in a chemical fertilizer plant and as an electrician in a repair shop. In October 1979, as a result of the present story, he was invited to become a professional writer with the Guangdong Writers' Association. He has written many stories since then and become quite well known.

Originally published in Zuopin *(Guangzhou), No, 2, 1979.*

Translated by Kenneth Jarrett.

To the girl that I was, life seemed a sunlit road strewn thick with fresh flowers—smooth, pleasant, and beautiful.

Although I lost both my parents when I was young, I had a wonderful aunt—my father's sister—who raised me all by herself. She was an engineer in a research institute of chemical engineering, and a spinster. She had fallen in love as a college student but the affair had ended in heartbreak. This killed her desire for romance and kept her from ever marrying. After my parents passed away, my aunt took meticulous care of me; her love for me exceeded the love most mothers feel for their own daughters.

Probably because of my aunt's melancholy, I was not as fond of singing and dancing as most other girls were. I liked quiet. I liked to be alone, quietly reading a book. My aunt was a stern disciplinarian and paid close attention to my behavior. Once she sighed and said, "Zijun, you're very beautiful. In fact, you're too beautiful—it's a kind of affliction. You'll have to be especially careful in life!" My aunt's advice summed up the lessons of her own life, but these were lost on me. I thought that in our new society, flooded with brilliant sunshine, the Party and Chairman Mao had arranged a happy future for my generation. What affliction could I possibly have?

In a monotonous but pleasant way, our life passed peacefully and quietly, like running mountain streams. My aunt often said wistfully that "if it weren't for the Communist Party and Chairman Mao, I don't know how we two weak women would get by." My aunt's love for the Party and Chairman Mao was deep and sincere. When I became old enough to understand, she often explained to me how without Chairman Mao we would not have a new China or a happy life. Many years earlier, my frugal aunt had used her hard-earned money to buy an expensive statue of Chairman Mao carved in ivory. She had solemnly placed it on a dark wooden table covered with red satin. At the foot of the statue she placed a flower vase with gold ornamental engraving. Every day after work my aunt would stop at a florist to buy some fresh flowers, which she would reverently place in the vase beneath Chairman Mao's statue. Then, each evening, under Chairman Mao's benevolent gaze, we would happily study, work, chat, or listen to fine music. I would often recite passionate poems by Pushkin or He Jingzhi[1] for my aunt. Those days could hardly have been more joyous.

In 1964 I completed an accelerated course at the university. I had excellent grades and was assigned to be a technician in a machine factory. The following year I was sent to a large factory in the provinces for in-service training. The person in charge of my instruction

1. He Jingzhi (1924–), a well-known poet and playwright, and Vice-Minister of Culture during.

Stubborn Weeds

there was a technician named Li Liwen. A brilliant student who had graduated two years earlier from Qinghua University, he had a personality that matched his name—slightly feminine.[2] He was good-looking, but I looked down on him to a certain extent because I felt he lacked masculinity. Whenever I encountered his bashful manner, I would stare at him, challenging him, until he became quite confounded. This gave me great pleasure. But on one occasion I got my just deserts. He was trying to plan a technical improvement, and I was helping him with the sketches. Out of carelessness I drew a machine axle incorrectly. Moreover, I failed to follow the normal procedure, which was to give the plans to him for checking, and instead handed them directly to a craftsman to begin work. Some time later Liwen came looking for me, axle in hand. His face was red with anger as he slammed the axle onto my desktop: "You did this! How idiotic!" Who would have thought a man like him could get so angry? I was dumbstruck. "This is design paper, you know, not a schoolboy's writing pad! Mistakes like this would be hard to make even with your eyes closed! Do you know how much material and work time have been wasted because of your drawing? This is alloyed steel bought with precious foreign currency, not a washing board or a fireplace poker!" With these words he launched a verbal barrage at me. I had never been dressed down by anyone like that before. I was so upset I began to cry, but he just continued to shout. My shame turned to anger, and I finally slapped the table. "I quit!" I covered my face and ran from the room. I was so angry I couldn't eat all day.

At sunset I was still sitting—feeling miserable—in the cool woods of the factory park by the river. As I sat gazing at the meandering stream, he quietly appeared at my side, his head lowered to look at me. He was obviously searching for something appropriate to say, but could not find it even after a long time.

Finally he muttered, "The Party branch secretary criticized me. I—I was wrong. I was rude to a comrade who had come to us from another factory. Will you forgive me?"

I did not answer.

"Please criticize me." After saying this he was quiet again for a long time. Then he placed a bag of something next to me and said, "I bought these fried dumplings at the mess hall. You haven't eaten, have you?"

My heart jumped, but I still didn't look directly at him. He just stood there dumbly. After a long time, he sighed and said, "You probably grew up in a city, so you don't realize how difficult it is to get that kind of imported steel. I was born and raised in a fishing village. During school vacations when I went home I'd go out fishing

2. The first character "li" in the given name Liwen means "beautiful". Although very common in women's names, it is rarely used for men.

Short Stories

with my family. It was really hard work. You can't imagine how much fish and shrimp it takes to earn enough for one piece of alloyed steel. That's why I blew up."

I was deeply stirred by these words. It was as though I had touched a brilliant, glowing heart. My eyes were moist but I still said nothing.

He stood for a while, then quietly left.

Love can come to a young girl in many strange ways. My heart had become inexplicably tied to his by the sudden eruption of this quarrel. I studied hard under his guidance. Sometimes, in order to help me understand some technical problem, he would patiently repeat his explanations again and again. He often stayed busy deep into the night, and I would stay at his side. Under the bright light of lamps, surrounded by the sound of machines in the quiet night, our hearts grew closer and closer. Finally, late one blissful evening, as we were returning from the factory, the smell of machine oil still clinging to our bodies, I timidly offered him my young girl's heart.

I will never forget our parting that evening. We sat in the factory park until late at night. Then for the first time I experienced his awkward embrace; the deep impression of his kiss was left on my lips.

2

For someone in love for the first time, life becomes a source of excitement, anxiety, and restlessness. My sensitive aunt discovered that Cupid's arrow had already pierced my heart. But when she learned that my beloved lived so far away, she became deeply worried. "Do you understand him?" she asked. "Are you sure he truly and sincerely loves you?"

"I understand him as well as I understand myself," I answered.

"Don't be so naive about love," she sighed. "What's going to happen when you have to remain separated for a long time? Remember the old saying about 'too far away for the whip to reach the horse'? You'd be better off finding a good man nearby. It'd save you lots of worry, and let your aunt relax, too."

We could not agree on this point. But she was still very understanding and, except for an occasional sigh, did nothing else to interfere. She just watched anxiously as our love continued to grow.

We communicated our love through letters. I sent one about every three days. Anyone passionately in love hopes to get love letters that are long and detailed, every word revealing a burning, restless heart. But often his letters seemed perfunctory. One time he even requested that we write less frequently because he was busy working on an important technical innovation. I was very angry. But I forgave

Stubborn Weeds

him when I remembered how often he neglected even food and sleep for his work. Not long afterward he sent me a newspaper with his photograph and a description of his achievements. I was indescribably happy and immediately sent him a telegram to congratulate him. The newspaper story also made my aunt feel better about him.

Our romance was at its peak when the Cultural Revolution began. I became drawn in by the tempestuous struggle around me. I watched thousands of young people march through the streets, as though drunk or mad, holding aloft Chairman Mao's little red book. I felt a profound admiration for it all. I believed this great movement to spread Mao Zedong Thought would have tremendous significance in combating and preventing revisionism. But it was quickly obvious that reality was falling far short of my ideals. The movement, begun as a political debate, soon entered its violent stage. I was sickened by the indiscriminate beatings, arrests, public humiliations, and ransacking of people's homes. I felt great sympathy for the cadres, workers, and technicians who were turned overnight into "monsters" of every discription. The high hopes I had begun with were being torn to pieces. I was terrified that some disaster might befall my aunt, who was an intellectual from a merchant background. But luckily the political torrents did not reach our doorstep. My aunt was a cautious person. She had worked many years as a technician, had no quarrel with the world or anyone in it, and hence was spared personal attack at the onset of the Cultural Revolution. She exhorted me repeatedly to be cautious—to give people leeway in whatever I did and to avoid involvement in conflicts.

I felt confused that people's behavior in the movement was so at odds with Chairman Mao's original spirit, and I therefore stood aside from the struggles. I became, in fact, one of the "disinterested faction". But I remained deeply worried about what was happening to my distant lover. I waited for his letters even more anxiously than before. From them I learned that he was still buried in his studies and technical experimentation, but that his spirit was in torment because his work could not proceed as smoothly and effectively as before. He wrote about the vehement criticism of a veteran Party branch secretary who had always helped him carry out technical innovations, about the dissolution of his factory's worker-technician-cadre committee,[3] and about promising innovations turning to pipe dreams. He felt unhappy and hurt, but there was nothing he could do. I could well understand the agitated and despondent feelings of a dedicated technician unable to pursue the work he loved, and I was worried that this despondency would cause him to do something foolish. It

3. This was name for many local administrative bodies before the Culture Revolution; they were later replaced by Revolutionary Committees consisting of soldiers, "revolutionary" cadres, and members of the "revolutionary masses."

Short Stories

seemed to me that only passionate love might relieve his anguish. I decided to move our marriage date earlier so that his agitated spirit could find peace in my warm embrace.

It was in 1967, when the call to "Attack with Words and Defend with Weapons"[4] rang out and "all-out civil war" began, that my lover came to my side. To the accompaniment of gunfire and bomb explosions in the city, we raised our wine glasses and with blushing faces drank a wedding toast in front of my aunt, relatives, and friends.

Around this time, factories were grinding to a halt. Factory Party organizations found themselves with no way to exercise authority amid the bewildering but intense struggle between opposing factions. Our honeymoon months passed in this unusual environment. Marriage caused our feelings for each other to reach new heights, but I discovered that when my husband was quiet, his face would take on a pensive or blank expression. He was thinking about his factory and the technical innovations he had left unfinished. At times, even when he was in my tender embrace, he seemed preoccupied with telling me how his technical innovations would help production leap ahead. That's when I realized that a woman can never command 100 percent of her husband's heart when his love for his work and factory are so deep.

After Chairman Mao issued the call for revolutionary unity, the battles in the factories gradually ceased. When my husband's factory sent him a letter asking him to return, I was already pregnant.

It is always sad when a loving couple has to separate. On the evening before his departure we were awake the whole night; our impassioned conversation was like an endlessly flowing stream, like a thread that couldn't be broken. We talked excitedly about our future home and child, and thought long and hard about a good name for the child. Finally we decided on Li Sijun.[5]

The next day, I faced the freezing wind and saw my husband off at the railroad station. After his train disappeared from sight, I suddenly felt my heart tighten. Tears rolled down my face like pearls off a broken string.

3

I passed several quiet months enjoying the kicking of my unborn child. But less than two months before the baby was due, an ominous shadow suddenly fell over me.

Soon after Liwen returned to his factory, he sent me a letter that contained unusually strong language. His equipment had been to-

4. See glossary.
5. "Jun" is the same character used in Zijun's name; "si" is "thinking of." Hence the child's name suggests "thinking of Zijun."

tally destroyed. Seeing the fruits of several years' work go completely to ruin brought him to tears. His letter expressed intense anger at the outrageous behavior of the "rebels" who were holding the factory. Immediately I began to worry about his own situation.

A month later I received a letter whose language was even stronger. It told how, in the name of purifying the class ranks, the people in charge of the factory had launched an all-out reign of terror against the workers and staff. Some of his good colleagues had been subjected to persecution for no good reason at all. What especially upset him was that the chief mechanical engineer, a founding elder of the factory and a man he respected immensely, had been persecuted to death on groundless charges. His letter expressed his anger: "I cannot keep quiet. I must protest—"

This alarmed me. During those years, to protest injustice was to invite trouble. I hurriedly wrote him a letter asking him to come for a visit, which would place him outside the political maelstrom. After mailing the letter I counted the days on my fingers, but no response came within the expected period of time. Overcome with anxiety, I sent a telegram. But again there was no answer. An ominous feeling came over me. At the same time, a check of the class ranks was begun in my own neighborhood. The frightening atmosphere of arbitrary arrests and beatings increased my feeling of terror. I decided to set out in search of my missing husband.

Two days and nights on the train brought me to my husband's factory. I was received there by the arrogant and domineering head of a special investigation team. He listened to my story and then said, icily, "Your husband is an out-and-out counterrevolutionary. He attacked the rebels, attacked Red political power, and even had the audacity to seek scandalous material against us. He has already met a shameless end. You want to see him? Fine." He went to a room to get something—a bag—that he threw at me. "But you've come a bit too late," he said. "This counterrevolutionary has already committed suicide to escape punishment. He will remain forever an enemy of the people—"

My head throbbed. Losing the last ounce of strength in my body, I fainted. When I regained consciousness I found that I had been dragged into a deserted corridor. No tears would come, for I could not believe that my husband was a counterrevolutionary. I did not believe that a technician who had devoted all his intelligence and strength to socialist construction could be a counterrevolutionary. I just trudged away, holding to my breast the last possessions of my husband. When I reached the railroad station, I peered at those long tracks extending into the dark night. It occurred to me to end my grief by destroying myself. But just as I started walking dumbly toward the rails, the child inside me stirred. This made me realize I had a responsibility toward a little life. I halted, in a daze.

When I got home, completely exhausted, I was dealt another staggering blow. I knocked at my aunt's door and, when the door opened, found to my surprise a strange man standing before me. Inside was a completely different set of furniture and household articles. I was dumbstruck. For a long time I couldn't say a word.

"Your aunt was a suspected enemy agent. She died in the 'cow shed'[6] and has already been cremated. This apartment belongs to our research institute and has been assigned to me." The door slammed shut.

I raced to my aunt's office only to learn that on the third day after I had left home, my aunt had been accused of being a secret enemy agent and put into the "cow shed." This preposterous conclusion had been reached on the basis of her unhappy love affair long ago. While studying in the university, she had fallen in love with a young man of a wealthy family. Although she offered her young girl's love to him, he suddenly abandoned her and married a young woman from another rich family. He ridiculed and insulted my aunt to her face. Afterward, this rich man's son became a member of the CC Clique and a leading figure in the Sino-American Cooperation Institute.[7] At Liberation he fled to Taiwan. Who would have thought that this bitter episode from the past could become "evidence" that my aunt was an enemy agent? Even more absurdly, it was claimed that the reason my aunt had never married was that she wished to remain faithful to this kingpin spy. My aunt had not been in good health. She had been suffering from serious heart trouble and had not been able to stand this mental and physical torture. After a few days in the "cow shed," she had died of a heart attack.

Dragging legs of lead, I left my aunt's institute and headed numbly toward my factory. When I entered my office I saw that my desk had been moved to a corner and was being used as a table for water bottles and miscellaneous items. The head of the design section forced a smile. "Zijun," he said, "the factory investigation office has notified us that because of your relationship to your aunt and husband, you are no longer suitable for work in this section. They also said that you must report to them as soon as you return." The section head looked at my blank expression and added compassionately, "Zijun, you're an honest person. I sympathize deeply. I did ask the investigation office to allow you to remain in the design section while you clear up your problem, but—" He threw up his hands, shrugged his shoulders, and heaved a long sigh. "Cheer up, Zijun. And take care of yourself. Go on living—don't do anything foolish."

6. See glossary.
7. The CC Clique was a powerful faction in the KMT (Nationalist Party) in the 1930s and 1940s. Composed mainly of bankers and businessmen, it was named after its leaders, Chen Lifu and Chen Guofu. The Sino-American Cooperation Organization was a KMT military advisory group based in Chongqing (Chungking).

I went to the investigation office and was given a routine talking-to by one of its members. Then they handed me a small label with the words, "Counterrevolutionary Family Member," which I was to fasten to my blouse as a mark of my status. I was told to join the factory labor brigade to sweep the streets. They also ordered that every evening I write a confession of the crimes I had committed in the past and a report on my thinking that day. Seeing the small, black "Counterrevolutionary Family Member" sign on my chest and feeling the long bamboo broom in my hand, I realized that I had fallen among the dregs of society. My heart was broken—all hope was gone!

Carrying a child about to be born, I quietly swept the streets. I did not cry. I did not even grieve. The blows that had rained upon me had already deadened my emotions. I moved the broom as if I were a robot; it was only the occasional movement of the child that reminded me I was a living thing.

Dusk fell. I was permitted to put down my broom and return home. But where was home? The laws of the state clearly provided that the rights and interests of workers should be protected and that the property and personal freedom of every citizen should be safeguarded. But where was the law now? Where was truth? Where were the people's democratic rights? Who was it that had deprived me—an innocent, ordinary citizen—of my human rights?

I walked aimlessly through the streets. Close to midnight I found myself at the riverbank. Looking at the murmuring, flowing river, I thought that here my body and soul could rest forever.

The cool, salty night breeze gently caressed my hair. The dense evening fog lightly moistened my benumbed skin. I took my last glimpse of the world and with my unborn child threw myself into the river. . . .

4

I don't know how I regained consciousness. I opened my eyes in a daze. When I saw the white curtains, the white bedsheets, and the medical equipment in the room, I realized I was in a hospital for the living and not in the dragon palace at the bottom of the sea.[8]

At my side, watching me wake up, was a kindly woman doctor in a white hospital jacket. She sighed and pointed toward the foot of the bed. "This comrade saved you," she said. "He's watched over you the entire night."

I looked up wearily. Sitting on a long wooden bench—asleep—was a young man about my age. At first the stranger's image was vague, but it gradually became clear to me. It seemed I had seen that

8. In Chinese legend, four dragons—controlling rainfall, storms, lightning, and thunder—reign over the sea.

face somewhere before. Suddenly I remembered. It was my high school classmate Liu Yimin! I was stunned.

Liu was the son of a dock worker. His shoulders were broad, his face dark and square. He had inherited the rough personality of a dockhand; he preferred action to words. In our class he had been known as an arbiter of truth and justice because he liked to stand up to unfairness and was always willing to help his weaker classmates. I had heard that he became a factory worker after graduation, but I had long since forgotten him. Who would have imagined the strange coincidence that would bring us together again in this hospital ward, he in the role of my savior?

From his point of view, perhaps, saving a person from death was a noble act. But from my point of view, there was not the slightest cause for gratitude. In fact I felt bitter: I had already surrendered my sorrow and despair to the endlessly flowing water, and he had only salvaged my suffering and grief and returned them to me. His intentions had been good, but he should have minded his own business!

He awoke and saw that I had regained consciousness. "Comrade Xue Zijun,," he cried happily. "You're awake!"

I closed my eyes wearily and did not answer. My former classmate's voice caused me to recall those student days, so filled with ideals and aspirations. What wonderful times those were! A romantic spirit had filled the air; singing, laughter, and gaiety were everywhere. On quiet evenings we innocent and naive girls would sit outside on the smooth green lawn of the school yard to gaze at the brilliant full moon and count the twinkling stars. Our thoughts seemed to grow wings that carried us across the heavens toward the shining Big Dipper. With vivid imagery we would describe our shining futures in impassioned tones. We all wanted to become like stars, eternally embedded in the vast heavens above our motherland, adding brilliance to our motherland's glorious face. I never imagined that in just a few years' time, the stars of our ideals would turn to scattered dust and that I myself would become an outcast.

I slowly opened my eyes, only to hear my classmate sigh and say, "This is not the way to deal with life."

Life—what was life? The reality before my eyes was like a black fog obscuring my vision; it blocked out the sunshine, cut off the green mountains, smothered my vitality, and cast a heavy, stifling shadow over my heart. I sighed weakly. "You're too meddlesome," I whispered. "You haven't saved me. All you've done is thrown me back into misery." My eyes were brimming with tears.

I heard the sound of footsteps. Two doctors, a man and a woman, appeared at my side. The man spoke. "The two of you must go home," he said. "The patient will be all right." His voice was warm but firm.

Stubborn Weeds

82

"Please let her stay in the hospital a few days. She's weak and—" My former classmate was speaking, but the male doctor interrupted.

"No," he said. "The hospital leadership wants her to leave immediately. They say the hospital is not a place for seeking refuge from class struggle."

Confused though I was, and though my body was as limp as a worn-out sponge, this remark felt like a needle piercing my heart. I strained to get out of bed and began walking toward the door. When I reached the door I almost fell. Liu Yimin supported me as we left the hospital. He called a pedicab and asked, "Where do you live? I'll see you home."

Where was home? "Just take me back where you found me," I answered. "I have no home."

A peculiar expression came over his face. After a moment of silence he said, "Mm   you'd better spend a few days resting at my house!" He helped me into the pedicab.

And so, without ever intending it, I ended up in his home. It was a wooden building on a secluded lane; his apartment was only about a hundred square feet. He told me that both his parents had passed away and that he lived alone. Then I learned that he was a maintenance electrician in one of the city's chemical factories. He said that the previous night, as he was cycling along the riverfront after work, he had suddenly seen someone fall into the river. He had jumped in to save the person. He had no idea the person he was saving was his former classmate until he had brought me to the hospital.

He briefly asked me about a few things, then went to prepare some food. Later he went out again and came back with a kindly-looking old woman. "This is my aunt," he told me. "She's in charge of the neighborhood street association.[9] If you have any problems, just ask her. She lives next door." With this he picked up his simple bedroll and headed for his factory. Only after he left did I notice the money, rice coupons, and other ration tickets that he had left on the table top. With them was a simple note explaining that they were for my use.

What happened that day had been complicated enough for a play. But, completely exhausted both physically and mentally, I was in no condition to ponder its meaning. When Liu and his aunt had left, I closed the door and, still muddle-headed, fell asleep.

I was awakened by an intensely agonizing pain and was taken immediately to an obstetrics hospital. My child was entering the world prematurely. When I looked into the little eyes, as clear as crystal, of this poor child who was fatherless from the moment it

9. Neighborhood street associations mediate disputes, monitor local opinion, and help to enforce public order and security.

Short Stories

joined the world, my maternal instinct returned. For this child I would stay alive no matter what!

5

My relationship with Yimin was rather strange.

He came to visit after the child was born, and I could see that he really liked children. He held the child and began asking about its father. This led me to give him, for the first time, a detailed and tearful account of my misfortunes.

"Your husband really had guts," he said when it was over.

There was a long silence. Then he sighed and said, "These days bad people rule the roost and good people take it on the chin. At first I was all for the Cultural Revolution too. But later the blood and tears of so many old cadres and ordinary citizens helped me to see things more clearly." He was quiet for a while, then continued, "Seems like somebody's manipulating this movement. People wave the banner of the Party and Chairman Mao but in fact are blackening the name of the Party and Chairman Mao."

I had never tried to figure out the complicated background of this round of political struggle. I was only an ordinary person; what concerned me was how my child would survive. I was already at the end of my rope, with nowhere to turn. Suicide counted as "counter-revolutionary behavior" then, and unsuccessful suicide called for return to one's work unit for mass criticism. When the hospital notified my factory that I had jumped into the river, the factory investigation section—probably because they were still capable of a touch of mercy—did not try to trace my whereabouts or drag me back for criticism. All they did was discharge me. Thus I had no work, no relatives, and no home. For the moment, the only person I could depend on was this high school classmate. My fate and that of my child were in his hands. All he had to say was "Please leave," and my child and I would be beggars in the streets. He had saved me out of the goodness of his heart, but he certainly had no obligation to support us.

We sat quietly, without speaking to each other. I felt like a prisoner in the dock, waiting to be sentenced.

Seeming to guess what I was thinking, he decided to speak. His voice was soft but very determined: "Don't worry. You can live here until you find work. Until then, I will cover expenses for you and your child."

Unable to control myself, I began to weep.

"Don't be too sad," he comforted. "The day will come when the black clouds pass and the sun comes out again."

Stubborn Weeds

84

To tell the truth, I felt quite unhappy becoming a heavy burden to a strange man. But what other choice did I have?

Why was this young man, neither well paid nor married, willing to make such a generous sacrifice for an orphan and widow he did not really know? Was it from deep, well considered sympathy or just the emotional impulse of someone acting bravely for the sake of justice? Didn't he know that giving refuge to someone wearing the label "Counterrevolutionary Family Member" could be a heavy burden politically, emotionally, and materially? After a long silence, with tears in my eyes and my voice shaking, I asked, "Why do you want a person like me to stay here?"

"Why?" He was speechless. After thinking a while he finally said, "You ask me why, but I can't really say. Your question reminds me of a story, though." There was another silence before he began.

"When my father was alive, he told me this story many times. Once he was sick. One of the dockyard manager's regulations said that if a permanent dock worker was absent from work because of illness for more than three days, he would be fired. On the fourth day, when the boss was calling the name roster, someone answered my father's name and went off to work. This person even gave the money he earned to my father for medical expenses, until my father was healthy and able to go back to work. It was one of my father's co-workers, a night shift dock worker. In order to help my father stay alive, he did two shifts of coolie labor every day for ten days. This, I think, is our workers' class . . . our class feeling. It was just in this hand-in-hand, shoulder-to-shoulder way that the workers in the old society managed to get by." When he reached this point his rough face took on a dark expression. "I feel sure you're an innocent victim," he concluded.

From the plain words of this ordinary worker, I could see that the morality of the older generation of the proletariat had been passed down. Now, when evil influences were causing members of the same class to trample on each other indiscriminately, this dock worker's son suddenly appeared. He was like a glittering star rising over my gloomy spirit, giving me courage, letting me see light.

Thus began our very unusual relationship. We were neither relatives nor friends, but he still bore all expenses for me and my child. Each month on payday he came without fail to give me money. His salary was not high. He kept only $15 a month for himself; the rest he gave to me. He lived in the singles' dormitory at the factory. On Sundays he would come to visit me and my child. I ate sparingly and spent frugally, but I often prepared a nice meal on Sundays for my "benefactor." He would never eat it, though—he told me to give the food to the child. I asked him to put aside his dirty clothes until

Sundays so that I could wash them, but he only laughed and shook his head. He said his hands were used to work. He would never stay long but just played with the child a while and left. He gave us much but never wanted the slightest thing in return. Sometimes as I watched his sturdy silhouette hurrying away, I would become so sad that I would break down and cry.

In this unique way we passed two years' time. Each month when he brought my living allowance, he would quietly put it under the glass on the writing table. He never presented it to my face. I knew why he was so circumspect: he didn't want me to feel like a dependent. But each time after he left, as I took his hard-earned money from under the glass top and recalled that I was a "good-for-nothing," rejected by society, again I could not help weeping.

I don't know how I got through those two years. I once tried to find work because I wanted to be independent. But what work unit would take a "Counterrevolutionary Family Member"? All my efforts were in vain. I not only didn't find work, but also had to depend completely on Yimin's aunt, in her role as leader of the street association, to avoid being counted among the neighborhood's Five Black Categories[10] and suffering further political humiliation.

My child could already sing. He was clever like his father, and thoroughly lovable. He and Yimin were very fond of each other. As soon as Yimin arrived on Sundays, the boy would cling to him and beg him not to leave. One time the innocent child blurted out something like, "Uncle, don't go. Live together with Mommy." I was so embarrassed I had to run into the bedroom. "Don't talk nonsense," Yimin said to the boy, then picked up the child and carried him outside. I don't know why, but those chance words from my little boy became fixed in my mind as if carved there. They threw me into some confusion, but upon reflection I realized the idea was impossible. A person as good as Yimin deserved the most beautiful and happy love in the world, not a widow with an orphan.

Yimin never talked to me about his own life. It was only by accident that I learned his love life, too, had been unhappy. One day I encountered on the street another high school classmate who had been one of Yimin's better friends. He expressed deep sympathy for my plight. We talked and talked, eventually coming round to Yimin. He said Yimin had once been in love with a certain girl who was also our classmate. The two had become engaged but had postponed their marriage when the Cultural Revolution began because they were too busy being "rebels." After a while Yimin had withdrawn from the rebel committee, but his fiancee became one of the leaders of the rebel clique and then managed to squeeze into the ranks of the "chiefs" of her work unit. After this she had cast aside Yimin, a mere worker, to

10. See glossary.

marry a "top leader" whose position was even higher than her own. As if all this were not enough, she then trumped up some charges that Yimin was politically unreliable and brought them to his factory. Luckily Yimin's class background was good and he had also been a "rebel soldier," so the factory left him alone. But the incident had broken Yimin's heart; he swore that he would never marry.

At this point my schoolmate lost his temper right there on the street. "A woman like that is a disgrace to humanity! A calamity! A beast! If I ever run into her again I'll beat her up on the spot!"

Yimin's behavior gave every indication that he indeed lacked a girlfriend. I inquired everywhere about various female classmates from our high school days, hoping that I could help him find a mate. But all my efforts failed. No one knew where some girls were; others were already married; and a few, I heard, had even become those frightening "model" individuals. It was most frustrating.

By now three years had passed. It was 1971. I had gradually noticed a slight change in Yimin's feelings. As before, he brought us money every month. And every Sunday he would visit, play with my child for a while, and leave. But he stopped being as stubborn as he had been. When I once noticed that his jacket had a small hole in it and asked him to take it off and let me mend it, he did not resist. He watched bashfully as I sewed. When I raised my head and our eyes met, he suddenly blushed and looked away. There is nothing more sensitive than a woman's intuition. Yimin's actions made me sense that something new might be entering our lives. My face also turned red.

I was very frugal with the monthly allowance Yimin gave me. Beyond the food necessary for my son's growth, for my own food I was able to make two meals from a piece of fermented bean curd and some pickled vegetable. In this way I managed to save a little money each month. After three years, I had accumulated a considerable sum. I thought that if Yimin were to marry or to have some urgent need for money, then I would be able to give it to him. Now and then I sounded out the idea of buying him a bit of new clothing, but he refused. Once, though, when I noticed that his socks were worn out, I secretly bought him a pair of nylon socks. The next Sunday, when I gave him the socks, he cheerfully put them on. This change gave me a new feeling; I felt I should begin to take care of his personal needs. Surreptitiously, I noted his height and shoulder measurements and set about making him some clothing. One Sunday I placed before him a beautiful polyester jacket that I had painstakingly tailored.

"Where did you get so much money?" he asked, dumbfounded.

I laughed. "It's all your money, you know; it wasn't stolen. Try it on. See if it fits." I helped him put on the jacket, and he did not refuse. His face turned as red as a beet as I fastened the buttons.

"Thank you, Zijun," he said softly.

"If you have to thank me for this, how will I ever thank you?" I asked uncomfortably. "We've known each other three years, and you're still so polite." I don't know why, but tears started running down my face. When Yimin saw this, he was suddenly moved to hold my hand. My heart began to beat wildly. But Yimin regained his composure in just a few seconds. He hugged and kissed the child and then went out the door. He had great self-control.

I found myself in love. I loved him, really and truly loved him. I would have gone through fire and water for him. Life's sufferings and hardships had not ruined my looks, but I was, after all, a mother. From the time I noticed the change in Yimin's feelings, my soul had been calling out, struggling. I didn't know how to control my emotions.

Late in September, on one of Yimin's paydays, it had been raining steadily. I felt sure he would not come. But at eight o'clock in the evening, after the child was asleep, someone suddenly knocked on the door. It was he. He stood in the doorway wearing a raincoat; outside, the rain was pouring down. I rushed to welcome him in. As he took off his raincoat he said, "There was a big meeting at the factory today. That's why I'm late." His face beamed with joy as he continued. "Let me tell you the great news—Lin Biao is finished!"[11] Yimin was ecstatic. He pulled out a bottle of wine and said, "Tonight let's drink a farewell toast for those fascist bandits on their way to see Hitler!"

Throughout those months and years, I had been basically isolated from the world. This news came too suddenly for me; I didn't have time to think about its significance. But Yimin's wild joy was infectious. I rushed off to get wine glasses.

"The black clouds have passed! Soon the sky will be blue! We ordinary folk don't have to put up any more with the insults and persecution of Lin Biao and his fascist bandits! We can have a better life! Have some wine, Zijun!" He pushed a small wine glass, filled to the brim, in front of me. I was not a drinker but couldn't refuse when I saw how happy he was. In three years we had never sat face to face to drink a glass of wine or even to eat a meal. What a strange relationship!

I drank the wine and began to cough and choke; I coughed until my eyes watered. Yimin was looking at me intently. A passionate expression suddenly flickered across his face. "Zijun," he said in a soft voice, "you're really beautiful."

Embarrassed, I lowered my head; my whole face was ablaze. This was the first time in three years I had heard him make any comment about me. It was also the first time he expressed his love for me. Outside, the rain kept pouring down and the wind kept howling.

11. See glossary.

Mother Nature seemed swept away in boisterous celebration. It was a moment that could have touched anyone's emotions. I lowered my head and waited for him to continue talking. But instead he calmed down; he changed the subject back to his feelings about the evil deeds of the bastard Lin Biao and his accomplices. He kept drinking as he talked, obviously needing to release his pent-up feelings, and his happiness, before me. He talked incessantly for over an hour, saying more to me that night that he had in the past three years put together.

His mood affected me deeply. As I looked at the outline of his handsome lips and his clear bright eyes, I suddenly thought of my dead husband. No! Yimin was even stronger and more confident, his spirit even more generous. This worker had a kind of noble quality that commanded admiration and respect. He was the kind of person who, having set his goal, would fight for it against all difficulties. In the company of such a person, even the weak could gain strength.

I was losing myself in daydreams when he abruptly finished talking. He glanced at his watch, stood up, and looked at me. "I'm going back to the factory," he said softly.

Startled back to the present, I looked at my watch. It was nine-thirty. The rain had not stopped. How I wanted him to stay! The words were on my lips and my face was red, but I couldn't say anything. I only muttered to myself, "It's raining so hard—"

He hesitated a moment, then went for his raincoat. Slowly, he put it on and walked towards the door.

A rush of hot blood surged to my head. I leaned against the door; passionate feelings had turned my entire face bright red. Looking at my toes, I continued speaking. "Yimin, don't—don't go. If—if you need me." My voice was so low it seemed as though only I could hear it.

There was a brief silence. Suddenly, I heard the sound of his raincoat being dropped in the corner. Then, a pair of powerful muscular arms tightly embraced me.

6

Like a dream, my life began a new chapter. Yimin and I were married.

Our married life was as harmonious and blissful as could be. To clear off the debts that were weighing on my conscience, I devoted myself entirely to Yimin.

When I was cleaning the apartment in preparation for our new married life, I thought that I would remove the wedding picture of Liwen and me from under the glass table-top. I knew that some men resented such things. A man who marries a previously married women will often expect her to rid herself of every trace of her former husband, including his memory. I knew Yimin was not that kind of a man, but to keep my old wedding picture on the new table was just too conspicuous. Yet Yimin discovered me removing the photograph and stopped me. "Leave it. He had great strength and courage. I respect him and hope you'll always remember him."

"The child is getting old enough to understand these things," I softly protested. "If he catches on, it could leave an emotional scar."

"Don't deceive the child," Yimin replied. "We should let him understand love and hate right from the start. If he knows his father was persecuted to death by Lin Biao and his gang, he'll love the Party and socialism even more. He'll grow up even faster. You can't feel love unless you've known hate."

I was moved to tears. Yimin gently caressed my shoulders. "Don't cry, Zijun. Lin Biao and his gang were taking too much from the Chinese people these past years. What we need isn't tears, but study and struggle. Get hold of yourself! You're a technical expert; you'll be able to use your knowledge in the future." He fell silent a moment, then continued. "We've all been muddling along these past few years. Now we can set up a home study program. You can be my teacher—teach me math and science." He smiled charmingly. "You were the class monitor in high school and a top student. Then you hit the books in college for a while. You're more than qualified to be my teacher, don't you think so, Teacher Zijun?"

Yimin's teasing made me smile through my tears.

Not long after our wedding, Yimin really did go out and find some math, physics, and chemistry textbooks. We sat under the bright light of a lamp, close together, reviewing old lessons. A teacher-student relationship grew in addition to our husband-wife relationship. My gallant husband, as he listened to my explanations with rapt attention, turned as docile as a child. Sometimes I helped him with innovations he was working on. Our family life was never dull. My son loved his stepfather, and Yimin's feelings for the child exceeded the love most fathers feel for their own sons.

After this marriage my child and I were no longer considered "Counterrevolutionary Family Members." I got temporary work in Yimin's factory. My monthly salary was only about $20, but this was enough to improve our family's economic situation greatly. I went off to work and came home together with Yimin, and we respected each other completely. I assumed the household work myself; all of my mental and physical efforts went to ensure that Yimin and the child were comfortable and happy.

Yimin headed a squad in his factory's electrical repair section. His work was outstanding; he was a model in the factory's campaign to "Learn From Daqing."[12] Yet I worried about him because of his overly straightforward nature and his habit of commenting on polit-

12. Daqing, an oilfield in Heilongjiang Province, was a model for industry during the Cultural Revolution.

ical events. At home he often spoke of Jiang Qing in contemptuous tones: "Can't that rotten actress be satisfied being a member of the Party's Central Committee? Does she have to go around shitting and pissing on the old generals' heads? She's the same ilk as Lin Biao. China's going to the dogs at the hands of leaders like these." I frequently advised him that ordinary people like us were better off not taking too much interest in politics. Unwilling to agree with me, he would only heave a sigh. "There is too much that is backward and feudal about China, and it is too deeply rooted," he would say.

The year 1975 arrived. As the Party's new policies began to take effect,[13] some of the changes affected in our family. Yimin was promoted to section chief because of his outstanding work. One of his technical innovations, to which I too had made a contribution, was written up in the newspaper. Thanks to the concern of the factory's Party committee, I was transferred from a temporary job to a permanent position with the technical group in a mechanical workshop. After the twists and turns of the past years, the brilliant sunshine of Mao Zedong Thought once again shone warmly on my body and lit up my home. I lamented only the fact that Liwen and my aunt had not lived to see this day. If they had been alive during this marvelous time, when the people's economy was expanding under the guidance of the Three-Point Directive,[14] just think how much they could have achieved!

That autumn I became pregnant. I was elated and excited; Yimin was also as happy as could be. He insisted on taking over all the household chores so that I could rest. He was the kind of man who could show great consideration for his wife. At his suggestion we decided to name our unborn child Liu Aijun.[15]

With the coming of winter, the north wind began to rise and the climate changed. The so-called "Counterattack the Rightist Tendency to Reverse Correct Verdicts" movement began.[16] Once again a political struggle engulfed the country. In many places factories stopped work. The interruption of rail service caused coal shortages at factories, leading to further delays. Production declined day by day, dashing the people's hopes and aspirations. The masses felt anxious and restive. In January 1976 the country suffered a severe blow with the death of Premier Zhou Enlai. Yet every day the newspapers con-

---

13. The Fourth National People's Congress (January 1975) restored Deng Xiaoping to high position and seemed to signal a policy shift toward domestic stabilization.

14. Deng Xiaoping's Three-Point Directive gave lip service to (1) the importance of class struggle but emphasized (2) economic development and (3) stability and unity.

15. "Aijun"—literally, "loves (Zi)jun."

16. This movement arrived in 1975 after Deng Xiaoping, the second most prominent target of the Cultural Revolution, returned to power. Radicals running the movement charged that "correct" political verdicts rendered during the Cultural Revolution should not be reversed.

tinued to make oblique accusations against him. Deep sorrow and indignation weighed heavily in the people's hearts.

Yimin became very quiet during this period. I could easily sense the change. He often sat alone, lost in thought; at times he looked terribly depressed. I had a foreboding notion that something new was going to happen in our life. Sometimes I asked him what he was thinking about, but he couldn't explain. He would just use vehement language to comment on the political scene. Once, when he returned home very late, I asked him where he had been. Instead of answering my question directly, he pulled out some mimeographed material from his book bag and held it in front of me. I glanced at it and saw it was called "Collected Speeches of the Rightist Tendency to Reverse Correct Verdicts." It was a compilation, printed in Shanghai, of speeches by comrade Deng Xiaoping and other leading comrades of the State Council. "Look at this," Yimin said. "Uncle Deng's speech is the voice of the people, and the voice of the people will hold up under any criticism, any attack."

I read through without stopping this book of "lessons to learn from bad examples." It affected me deeply. The imposing image of an outspoken and frank old revolutionary, daring to speak out for the people, appeared before me, standing tall and upright like a monument. Without understanding everything, I could guess the nature of this struggle. As Yimin slept peacefully, I looked at his dashing eyebrows and handsome face. I silently pronounced a heartfelt wish—a wish that this struggle would not bring misfortune to my family. . . .

But, in the end, a terrible disaster befell me once again. On the third day after the Qingming Festival,[17] a black automobile from the Municipal Public Security Bureau drove up to the factory. I received a phone call from a worker in the electrician's section saying that Yimin had been arrested. At once peals of thunder seemed to rock my head; the receiver in my hand hit the ground with a thud. As soon as I recovered I ran desperately toward the factory gate. There I saw my beloved husband—handcuffed—being led away by two policemen in white uniforms. He was walking erect and unafraid. Behind him followed a big crowd of spectators.

I ran toward him, tears falling like rain.

Yimin stood as stern as a stone carving when he saw me. His voice was firm. "Don't be afraid, Zijun. I haven't committed a crime. Take care of your health, and look after the child. I'll be back!"

I fainted. When I regained consciousness Yimin had already been taken away. Several workers who often spent time with Yimin had also been arrested.

Later I learned that Yimin had been arrested because he had

17. See "Tiananmen Incident" in glossary.

participated in memorial activities for Premier Zhou at the Qingming Festival. He has posted in the center of the city a large banner reading "Overthrow anyone who has the audacity to oppose our beloved Premier Zhou." He had also written a poem about Jiang Qing entitled "Denounce the White Bone Demon."[18] These activities had constituted "counterrevolutionary crimes" and were the reason he was now locked behind bars.

Back at home, I gazed at the memorial niche to Premier Zhou that my husband had set up. "Where are you, Premier?" I cried in my heart.

I had once again become a "Counterrevolutionary Family Member"!

7

In October 1976, an autumn breeze dispersed the sinister mist that lay across the land. The Party central leadership, led by Chairman Hua, smashed the Gang of Four with one stroke, rescuing the Party, the country, the people, and my family. Before then I don't know how many tears I cried, worrying day and night about whether my husband Yimin was dead or alive. But once the Gang of Four lost power, I calmed down. My years of misery and misfortune finally received an explanation. It became clear that the heinous Lin Biao and Gang of Four had been responsible for the profound difficulties of thousands of ordinary citizens like me. I further realized, for the first time, the far-reaching significance of the Cultural Revolution: although the destruction and interference of Lin Biao and the Gang of Four had exacted a heavy and painful price from the country, the Party, and the people, the Cultural Revolution had also profoundly instructed and tempered us. The great masses of people, while captive in a confusing and complicated struggle, had developed keen vision and could now discern truth, goodness, and beauty. A fearless young generation, like Yimin but millions strong, who would dare go through fire and water for the revolution, had been created.

I believed that my innocent husband would soon be released and allowed to return home. Looking at the portrait of Chairman Hua, I was moved to tears.

Those days, when the entire country was given over to revelry, I was going through the month of isolation customary after a woman gives birth. I asked someone to take two bottles of wine to my imprisoned Yimin. I knew he would be especially eager for wine.

I waited anxiously as a month passed, but Yimin did not come.

18. White Bone Demon is a character in *Journey to the West* by Wu Cheng'en (c.1500–c.1582). The demon could change its outer appearance to disguise its wicked nature.

So I went to the prison, carrying our one-month-old daughter with me.

There I saw my husband. He was much thinner. Several months of life behind bars had turned his face pale. Yet he was full of vigor and in high spirits. The first time Yimin saw his own flesh and blood he was as happy as a child; he stroked his daughter's head and played with her legs. "You were born at just the right time," he said to her, beaming with joy. "Your generation probably won't have to endure all the misery and difficulty of your parents' generation." Turning to me he asked, "Why didn't you bring Sijun? I really miss him."

"I didn't want any wound to be left in his young heart," I replied softly.

Yimin smiled. "You should let the child understand more! Let him know that during the rampage of Lin Biao and the Gang of Four, some organs of the proletarian dictatorship temporarily became tools to institute a dictatorship over the proletariat. This is a lesson that not only our generation but also our grandchildren and later generations must remember!"

I wished that he would not continue with this kind of talk. But he only smiled and said, "What are you afraid of? The Gang of Four have finished reading their lines. Now it's time for the people to speak." Then, in a darker tone, "I know this period has been difficult for you, Zijun."

What he said caused me to weep again.

After my hoping day and night for several months, one bright and beautiful sunny afternoon Yimin was proclaimed innocent, released from prison, and allowed to come home. When he reached home he embraced the two children and kissed them madly. Then he grabbed an empty bottle to go out for some wine. "Today I'm going to buy some good wine, prepare some good food, and enjoy a reunion meal," he said, cheerfully making his way down the stairs.

Little Aijun was sleeping. Just as I was preparing to wash the clothes that Yimin had brought back from prison, there was a knock on the door. How could he have returned so quickly? When I opened the door, I found a stranger standing there. He was wearing a pair of thick glasses. His hair was prematurely gray. His face was covered with terrifying scars, and his upper lip was horribly split. If I had come across such a face some quiet evening on the street, I think I would have screamed in terror.

"Who do you want?" I asked with fear in my heart.

The person looked directly at me. Suddenly, his face twitched violently. "Zijun," he said, in a strained and indistinct voice. "I'm Liwen!"

I felt as though a bolt of lightning had passed over my head, as

Stubborn Weeds

94

though a peal of thunder had clapped in my heart. I was stunned. I leaned against the doorway. For a long time I couldn't say a word.

"Tell the truth, Liwen. Are you a person or a ghost?" I asked, trembling.

"What do you mean by that?" He was obviously confused and frightened.

"They said you committed suicide!" With chattering teeth, tears rolling down my cheeks, and a stammering voice, I briefly recounted the painful events that had transpired. His face resumed its frightening twitching. Having listened to my account, he gnashed his teeth and said, "They really did think I was dead. I'm a man who's clawed his way back from the netherworld. It all began when I exposed the criminal behavior of those murderers. Then the beasts trumped up charges against me, saying I was a counterrevolutionary. I was thrown into the 'cow shed' and tortured. I was beaten with chains; ice water was poured down my nostrils; I was forced to lie down with my feet on a stool while heavy poles were placed across my unsupported legs; I was burned with an electric soldering iron until my face and body looked as they do now. For a whole day and night I was unconscious. They thought I was dead, so the bastards carried me to the railroad tracks near the factory to make it look like I'd committed suicide. A kindhearted worker saved me and secretly brought me to the hospital. But when the factory found out, they took me from the hospital and put me in prison. I was in prison for eight long years. They didn't let me out until a few days ago."

I looked at the many horrifying scars on my first husband's face. The poor man! The whole thing was heartbreaking! Think of the torment and suffering he must have endured all these years!

"But why didn't you ever write me a letter?" I cried.

He sighed. "Eight long years! They deprived me of freedom of speech and movement for eight years. How could I write a letter? I sent a telegram to your unit as soon as I got out of prison. I didn't get an answer, so I came in person. I asked and learned you had moved to this place." Tears flickered in his eyes; the scars on his excited face glowed; he looked like a person who, having been stranded on a deserted island for a long time, suddenly sees a rescue ship.

Memories of the loving couple we once had been, which were memories I had treasured over eight difficult years, now combined with my great joy at seeing my husband return from death and created a huge wave of emotion in me. My entire body felt soft and light, as if I were in a small boat that was thrashing about on the spray of the churning sea, then was hurled toward the mountaintops by a gigantic wave. How I wished I could immediately run up to Liwen and with both hands heal the scars that had been cruelly left on his face by Lin Biao and the Gang of Four. I would gently wash away the

Short Stories

bloody wounds left on his heart and let his returned soul, which had suffered untold miseries, rest in my warm bosom.

"Eight years, Zijun! During those miserable years I never stopped thinking about you and the child. I might not have lived through it all if the two of you had not been in my thoughts. The heinous Lin Biao and Gang of Four broke up our family; but now, Chairman Hua and the central Party leadership are allowing this pitiable couple to be reunited!" He opened his arms excitedly. I could no longer control my emotions; choked with tears, I threw myself into his embrace.

The distinct sound of familiar footsteps came from the stairs. My other husband Yimin was back! The sound of his steps hit me with the force of an electric shock. I immediately struggled free from Liwen's embrace. My heart seemed to have been suddenly torn in two.

My God! What should I do?

JIN YANHUA and WANG JINGQUAN   *Cries from Death Row*

Stories of sex and violence of the kind readily available in the West are available in China only underground or, to coin a phrase, "over head"—in the restricted official strata where works from the West are allowed to circulate. Thus when the regular public press in China carries anything even mildly sensational, it has the potential to become very well known. The mention of rape in the present story, like bigamy in the last, is an example. To be sure, the authors are careful to attribute every deviance to the mistaken policies of the Gang of Four, but compared to what else was available, their descriptions are risqué.

"Cries from Death Row" and its authors are not particularly well known. The story is included here because it represents well a kind of fiction that was infectiously popular among youth in 1979–80. It has everything: romance, death, violence, intrigue, corruption, evil officials, the generation gap, banishment to the countryside, and many, many tears. While it is easy to fault such stories for farfetched circumstances, it would be wrong to conclude that they were spun entirely from fancy. Young writers in 1979–80 were often impelled to record them in order to "tell the truth" about cases they knew, and readers were quick to claim they were "typical" of other cases. The charge from political critics that stories like this were "nihilistic" also seems to misconstrue the way they were written and read by young people. In the authors' view, they were upholding ideals by condemning violations of them. Readers seemed to take the stories in this way and were not usually depressed by their reading. In fact, when a reader had personally experienced unhappy

Stubborn Weeds

events, he could be greatly cheered by seeing expression of his viewpoint in print. Nevertheless "Cries From Death Row" was sternly criticized in spring 1980, apparently because it was too strong and pointed its condemnation too directly at an authority figure.

Originally published in Guangxi wenyi *(Nanning), No. 1, 1980.*

Translated by Paul G. Pickowicz.

It's freezing here on death row. I'm a young woman barely twenty-six years old and also a prisoner sentenced to death. My dark cell is gloomy and terrifying, but my young heart is ablaze!

There are no calendars on death row, but the chilling winds blowing beyond the bars and the rustling of fallen leaves at the foot of the iron gate drearily remind me that autumn has arrived. Unless I'm mistaken, tomorrow is the Mid-Autumn Festival.

At midnight I am startled by the sound of a wild goose abandoned by its flock. Suddenly I feel a gnawing sensation in my stomach, followed by nausea that seems to bring my heart to a stop. Already eight months pregnant, I struggle to budge my swollen body, and then force myself to vomit several times over the side of the bed. Of course I want to sit up against the wall, but according to regulations the prison guards must punish anyone who fails to go to bed or get up at the required time. So all I can do is roll back and forth, waiting in pain for the morning bell.

It is said that on holidays one misses one's relatives more than usual. Certainly that has been true for me, all through this long night. I find myself gazing into the dark and empty sky and asking this boundless land whether, on a day like this, I still have any loved ones.

I am an only child and was loved dearly by my parents since childhood. But how I have wronged them! I have wronged my mother, who died from persecution during the Cultural Revolution, and my father, who was exiled for ten years to a "cow shed"[1] from which he emerged half-dead, judging from the brief glimpse I could get of him. If there were such a thing as regret medicine, I would take a thousand doses. If one could somehow undo past mistakes, I would repent a thousand times. I thought that what I was doing was separating myself from my "criminal" family and that by doing so I would become morally upright and pure. What has happened to reduce me to a convict awaiting execution? Whenever I reflect on the

---

1. See glossary.

Short Stories

past, the unforgettable events that have transpired become clearer and clearer—

It all began in the spring of 1969. After bidding a tearful farewell visit to my aunt's grave, I went to settle in Xiangyang Brigade, part of a mountain commune in a remote frontier region. Of the more than twenty classmates in my group, I was the only "reactionary bastard" to make the trip; the others were all from various categories of "red" families.[2] As soon as we got off the bus, they began whispering to the cadres of the brigade and commune who had come to welcome us. As I stood alone in the shade of a big tree, these classmates glanced scornfully in my direction from time to time. I thought I heard them say that they were unwilling to live in the same team with me.

I had come to this place determined to reform my thinking, to be reborn. I would need the warmth of the collective and the support and sympathy of others. I remember a time at the beginning of the Cultural Revolution when I wanted to join the Red Guards. I had agreed to burn publicly all the books and blueprints owned by my right-wing father, who was an engineer. At my father's struggle meeting, I had placed on his head a dunce cap of my own making. Not long after that, my mother had been taken away and investigated. After repeated criticism through seven days and nights, she died in a dark room! But not only had I shed no tears, I had actually hung a placard over our door that read: "To hell with them." It was on that day that I solemnly announced the severing of relations between my father and me. As I was walking out the door holding some clothes, my father had embraced me and cried, "Don't do this! Lu Di, my dear, don't—"

"Lu Yongxiang!" I screamed at him, giving him a violent shove. "From now on we don't have the same family name. My new name is Lu Chunxia—'Lu' as in 'Dalu'.[3] I'm like the spring clouds that rise from the rivers and plains of the motherland. I am a daughter of China, not your daughter!" I had fully expected that by acting in this way, taking the correct political stand and struggling so resolutely, someone like me, with good looks and able to sing and dance, would be accepted into a Red Guard propaganda team. But I continued to be called a bastard, and no Red Guard group would take me. I had become an orphan. So, with tear-swollen eyes, I could only go impose on my aunt—and now my aunt had died. With no one to support and care for me, the best thing for me to do was leave my aunt's

2. See "Five Red Categories" in glossary.
3. In the change from Lu Di to Lu Chunxia, the character for the family name Lu changes as well, although this is not clear in the English transliteration. Her new name is *Lu* (continent, mainland) *Chun* (spring) *xia* (rosy clouds), or something like "rosy spring clouds over the mainland"—a highly patriotic name.

Stubborn Weeds

grave behind and volunteer with this group of classmates to work in a remote mountain region. I believed that I would be entering a new world where everyone was equal. Little did I know that I once again would be placed in a "special category."

"Hey, Lu! I just told the Party secretary you can live in my house!" While I was still deep in thought, a pair of large warm hands pulled me away from that shaded area. When I lifted my head I saw that the commune and brigade cadres and the other young people from the city had already left. Standing before me was a kindly old woman of more than sixty years. She introduced herself in this way: "I'm the leader of the women's group in Team Five of Xiangyang Brigade; I'm the only one in my family, so why don't you keep me company?"

Once I moved into her house I learned that this woman—known as Aunt Shi—had been an activist at the time of Land Reform. Her husband had been killed in 1951 by local thugs because he had assisted the People's Liberation Army during a campaign to suppress banditry. This had left her to care for their two sons, three and five years old, by herself. Now, the eldest son worked in the trade bureau in the county seat. The other had joined the army the previous year. So Aunt Shi was both a martyr's wife and a soldier's mother, which made her highly respected in the village.

From that day on I lived with the old lady. I wasn't afraid of hard physical labor or the discomforts of life in the countryside. The only things I feared were the cold and scornful looks others gave me. Within two months I became rather good at hoeing, sowing, and transplanting seedlings. The old woman said I was clever, and she seemed to like me more each day. In time I came to regard her as my only relative and her home as my own.

Before I knew it, more than five years had passed. During this five-year period many of the urban young people who had fathers of good class background were recommended by the commune to enter a university or to begin work in a big city factory. Even the youngsters who sneaked back to the city were like "the Eight Immortals who crossed the sea, each with his own magic method"—meaning that they all found jobs one way or another. Many who had arrived only recently were already back in the city. I was the only one left. When I arrived I had been barely nineteen years old, and now I was suddenly a young woman of twenty-four. Every day after work, and especially in late-night solitude, I agonized over my situation. Wasn't it all because my father was a "rightist"?

Then something happened. A person who was at once both an acquaintance and a stranger came into my life. It was like a stone being thrown into still waters—suddenly the river that was my life began to swirl turbulently. For the first time in my life, the window to my heart had been opened by a young man—Shi Lei, Aunt Shi's youngest son.

Shi Lei's name had been familiar to me for some time. Since moving into his mother's home I had been writing to him for her. He was aware of my situation in the village and had already written to thank me for my concern for his mother. I had seen his photograph when I first entered their home. He had a round face, a pair of large, fiery eyes under bushy brows, a slightly turned-up nose, and a warm smile. Because of our correspondence we were on very good terms when he returned home on his first furlough from the army. Our meeting that night made a deep impression on me.

It was a breezy moonlit night, and we sat shoulder to shoulder on a grassy slope talking about every conceivable subject. I was surprised to learn that a junior officer in the army could adopt attitudes toward current events and life in general that were so similar to my own. He expressed sympathy for what had happened to my family during the Cultural Revolution. The soothing words he used to comfort me made my body warm all over. Then he told me a strange story. After several decades of service to the military, the political commissar of his division had been demoted to farm supervisor for those undergoing thought reform through labor. His only mistake was that he had expressed his own point of view about a poem that had appeared in the newspaper. (The poem said something to the absurd effect that the wisdom, bravery, and spirit of self-sacrifice that lead the People's Liberation Army to victory were reflected in a certain photograph of random clouds at dusk.)[4] Shi Lei waved his powerful arms as he spoke. There was anger in his voice. Under the moonlight I could see his eyes sparkle and hear his rapid breathing. His indignation and simple honesty moved me. Under the impulse of the moment I suddenly dared to extend my arms to him. Our hands locked together and stayed that way for quite some time.

From that night on we worked together by day and talked interminably about our feelings by night. The time we spent together was the happiest time of my life.

When Shi Lei's leave was over, his mother and I took him to the commune bus stop. When we arrived at the station, she found an excuse to wander away, leaving us with a couple of moments to say a few parting words. I gave him a small bag on which I had embroidered a red heart. The red heart encompassed a red star, and

4. The reference to "a certain photograph of random clouds at dusk" was very daring in the political environment of early 1980. The words "random clouds at dusk" come directly from a poem that Mao Zedong wrote on September 9, 1961, on a photograph of the Cave of the Immortals at Lushan. The photograph was taken by his wife Jiang Qing. Few Chinese readers would miss this implied criticism of the cult of Mao.

within the star were the characters for "eight" and "one."[5] He excitedly grasped my hands and blushed as red as a camellia in bloom. I blushed too, and for a few speechless moments all his warmth surged through his hands into my body.

As the bus began to roll, he leaned out the window and waved goodbye. The bus moved farther and farther away, finally vanishing into a clump of hills in the distance. When it disappeared, the deserted look of the road suddenly made me feel lonely and empty. It seemed I had lost something precious. Had we fallen in love? Was this what love was like?

Before long he wrote to me from his unit, and I immediately wrote back. Our letters soon became the bridge we used to communicate our love. If his first visit had sown the seeds of love, his constant letters now nourished and cultivated it, enabling it to grow strong and healthy.

Half a year later the flower of our love was about to bear fruit. Aunt Shi and I went on shopping expeditions to buy sheets, quilt covers, and pillow covers. I felt that if Shi Lei and I could really marry, I wouldn't mind spending my whole life here with his mother.

Two months later, between the autumn harvest and winter sowing, people began saying that a man sent by Shi Lei's unit had arrived to look into my situation. Before long, ugly rumors were circulating. "The Lu girl is OK, but it's a pity her father's a rightist"—"Young Shi has fallen in love with her, so now he'll have to come home, give up a promising career, and work as an ordinary sod buster." Perhaps people meant nothing by these things, but the words were like knives stabbing into my heart. I was bleeding! I feared that now the flower of our love might die before it could bear fruit!

One day at noon I received a letter from Shi Lei. He told me of a warning that his commanding officer had given him—if you continue your relationship with the daughter of a rightist, you'll have to resign and return home. But he said that he was willing to pay that price!

Shi Lei! You can't do that! You can't let me ruin your future! I wiped away my tears and drafted a return letter. I begged him not to resign and even lied to him. I said that I never did really love him so of course would never marry him. After I mailed the letter I ran home, shut myself in my room, and cried my eyes out. Aunt Shi, standing outside my door, tried to comfort me but to no avail.

For the first time in my six years there, I thought about leaving so that he could forget about me. Yes, leaving! The sooner and the farther away, the better! At that time I had heard rumors about a

5. The characters for "eight" and "one" mean August 1, the day in 1927 when the Red Army, later known as the People's Liberation Army, was founded.

factory in the city that had sent some people to recruit workers. The recruiters were living in the commune headquarters and periodically sent local people to the village brigades to scout around.

The next day I got up at dawn and slipped out, without Aunt Shi knowing, and headed straight for the commune headquarters. Liu, the commune head, was not there, but young Tan, the secretary, was in the office preparing some papers. I told him I wanted to leave the commune. He tossed up his hands and said it was a difficult matter, then gave me a little lecture on social responsibility. I was in no mood to listen to that and came right back at him with my own reasons, weeping like a fountain the whole time. Tan was flustered. "Now, now! Don't cry! I'll bring you to see Section Chief Shao, OK? He's in charge of recruiting the city factory workers, and he's also an old friend of Yu, the man in charge of urban youth in the commune. If we can get him to help, everything will be fine."

I brushed away my tears and went with Tan to see Section Chief Shao. We went to a special room at the commune's hostel. Through the doorway, we could see a tall, thin man leaning back in an easy chair, putting on his brightly polished black shoes. He stood up at once when we entered and greeted us with a smile. For some reason the man looked familiar to me. Below his narrow eyebrows were a pair of thin eyes, a straight nose, and thin lips. His long white face was topped off with a head of carefully combed black hair. He reminded me of the hoodlums that often appear in plays about old China. Then I remembered! He was Shao Xintian, one of the security cadres in the factory where my father had worked! I had heard that he had been promoted to section chief in some factory because of his contributions to the planning of armed struggle during the Cultural Revolution. He had one remarkable ability, which was to smile graciously in front of anyone, demon or saint. He really took good care of himself—after ten years he hadn't changed in the least.

Tan introduced us, explaining that Shao Xintian was the section chief of the Political Department of the Hongxing Iron Works. Then he explained my reasons for coming. I noticed Shao watching me carefully, but he said nothing. In order to make a good impression and achieve my goal of getting out, I called him "Uncle Shao" and reminded him of the days he and my father had worked together at the chemical factory. He lit a cigarette, blinked his eyes, stood up, and said, "So you are Lu Yongxiang's daughter? I was wondering who you were when you came in just now. You look like your mother! You've become quite the young lady in ten years' time."

When Tan realized I knew Shao, he found a convenient excuse and left. As soon as Shao saw that we were alone in the room, he handed me a form and asked me to sign. He then patted me lightly on the shoulder and said in a low voice, "I can get you into the factory, but there's a condition. I have to attend a meeting now, but I want you to meet me under the banyan tree by the river tomorrow night. We can discuss it then." I resented the pat on the shoulder but happily agreed just the same, since it was the only way I knew to get into the factory.

The next evening at dusk I went to the riverbank to wait under the banyan tree. The autumn fields were painted gold by the rays of the late afternoon sun, and the river, flowing east below my feet, sounded like sobbing. As the last glimmer of the setting sun faded from sight, Section Chief Shao suddenly appeared from nowhere. We sat face to face under that big banyan tree. As it grew darker, I began to feel frightened. I just wanted to hear his condition and get out of there. I had heard that young people who sought to enter universities or factories often had conditions imposed upon them. Those whose parents had power had to lend some of that power; those without power had to use money. Official posts were offered, special requests granted, banquets given, and presents bestowed; some even offered to make high-class furniture. No request was out of bounds. What might he want from a mere orphan girl like me? I had brought with me the few dozen dollars I had been able to save by scrimping on food and clothing over the past few years. Just in case he wanted to throw a banquet or give some presents, I'd give him the money. I was surprised, therefore, when he asked if I had found a boyfried in the countryside. I blushed and said no in a low voice. He laughed and said, "In view of the fact that your father and I are old co-workers, I'll do what I can to get you a job in my factory."

"But what about your condition? What can I do for you?"

"There's only one thing I want from you—"

Then he suddenly embraced me. I was terrified. I struggled desperately and tried to call for help, but he pressed his stinking mouth against my cheek and threatened me in a taunting voice: "Don't be a fool! You're forgetting that your father's a rightist. You're already twenty-five. If I don't get you into the factory, you'll never get in! Condition? Here's my condition—" His words sent shock waves to my heart. I suddenly went limp and slumped to the ground. My body trembled in the cold night air.

A week later I was instructed to report to work at the Hongxing Iron Works. When I left, Aunt Shi wept buckets, all the way to the bus stop. While I was waiting for the bus she kept clutching at my hands, as if unwilling to let me go. "Child!" she sobbed. "I have had only sons in this life of mine. I've never had a daughter. All I can hope for is a daugher-in-law like you. When you get to the city, don't forget to write to Shi Lei and me. . . ."

I couldn't hold back my tears. "I'll never forget you and Shi Lei," I stammered, squeezing her hands. "But I just can't go on being a burden to you."

The bus began to move. I wiped away my tears and said farewell to her. Suddenly a familiar figure appeared, running toward the bus. It was Shi Lei! The red military insignias had been removed from his hat and collar. Had he been discharged? The bus picked up speed, but he continued to run, waving his cap frantically and shouting something at the top of his lungs. All I could do was wave my hand-kerchief, but my heart was torn apart by conflicting emotions. In a moment tears blurred my vision. As the bus reached full speed, Shi Lei appeared smaller and smaller and finally disappeared in the dust.

I was too old to begin in the factory as an apprentice, so I was assigned to clean the molds in the casting shop. Because I was the only woman in this work group, I was allotted a small bedroom of my own. It measured about 65 square feet and was next to the stairwell on the second floor.

Before long I received a long letter from Shi Lei, saying that he had been discharged because he intended to follow through with his plan to marry me. He said he wanted me to do well in my work and to master some technical skills in order to contribute to the Four Mod-ernizations program outlined by Premier Zhou Enlai at the Fourth National People's Congress.

I felt terrible after reading his letter. First, cleaning molds in the casting shop was a boring job that had nothing to do with acquiring technical skills. Second, there was that unmentionable shame buried in my heart. I sent him a return letter sprinkled with tears.

The winter of 1975 was unusually cold. A severe north wind cut through the vast land of China like a knife. Dead leaves swirled about, and coal dust from the industrial section of town filled the air. People were upset because the political atmosphere was the same as the weather. Production at the Hongxing Iron Works often came to a halt. Political activists led campaigns to "Expound Legalism and Criticize Confucianism"[6] and sought to ferret out people who were still taking the "capitalist road." Shao Xintian was the most en-thusiastic activist in the factory and hence was promoted from the political section to the post of Vice-Chairman of the factory's Revolu-tionary Committee. Simultaneously, old man Li, who had been rein-stated as Party Secretary and Chairman of the Revolutionary Committee only half a year earlier, was reassigned to run study

6. The campaign to "expound legalism and criticize Confucianism" refers to a movement launched by radicals in 1975 in an effort to bolster Mao Zedong's power and reduce Zhou Enlai's.

groups in the city. This left Shao Xintian as the head man in the factory.

And this member of the new nobility—this beast in human form—sought to rape me once again.

It was a dark and dreary day. People across the nation were shedding tears. Loudspeakers played funeral dirges and repeated the devastating news again and again—our beloved Premier Zhou Enlai was dead! The rain made it seem that even heaven was weeping. Before the night was over, people had spontaneously fixed black mourning bands to their clothing and put up white funeral wreaths. But Shao Xintian was delighted. He called a mass meeting for all workers and staff members. "Premier Zhou is dead," he announced with a smirk. "The Party Central Committee has issued the following emergency instructions: the convening of memorial meetings, the wearing of black armbands, and the making of mourning wreaths shall not be allowed. In brief, the Four Olds[7] shall not be allowed. Everyone is to grasp revolution, promote production, work hard, and prepare for war." It was as if a bomb had been set off at the meeting. Some people discussed the matter in hushed tones, others shouted loud protests. Sobbing broke out, each sob louder than the last. Shao Xintian turned livid with rage. "These are the instructions of the Central Committee," he roared. "Anyone who fails to obey will be in big trouble!"

After the meeting he came looking for me. "My little Lu," he said, bubbling with smiles, "didn't you request a transfer to a job that required technical skills? Since tomorrow is a day off, why not come over to my house around eight in the morning and we'll have a good talk, OK?"

"Will your wife be home?" I asked timidly.

"Yes, her factory is off tomorrow too."

Having already fallen into his trap once, I was extremely wary about visiting him at home. But I felt better when I recalled Shi Lei's letter encouraging me to study technology. For Shi Lei's sake, I thought, I ought to pick up some technical skills. So I agreed to go.

The next morning I arrived at his home promptly.

He lived in a three-room apartment, nicely decorated and well furnished. As soon as I walked in he brewed a glass of hot malted milk for me. Then I noticed that the apartment was quiet—his wife and children were not at home! I was frightened—I knew I had fallen into his trap once again. As if reading my thoughts, he pulled an easy chair up next to the door, sat down, folded his legs, and slowly lit a

7. See glossary.

Short Stories

cigarette. He grinned as he puffed on the cigarette. But under the smile I could plainly see his despicable treachery and cowardice.

"I've become very fond of you, Miss Lu. But you must be careful not to tell others about that affair between you and me. It doesn't matter to me, but how would you be able to show your face? Understand?" As he glanced at me, I blushed and nodded my head.

"I'm glad you want to acquire technical skills. Naturally, doing technological work is a bit more respectable and less tedious than cleaning molds, so don't forget to put politics in command. You don't want to become a 'white expert'[8] like your father. That's why he can't go back to work."

This mention of my father sent shivers down my spine.

Shao Xintian came to my side and pretended to show concern. "We can't, of course, choose our family, but we can select our own path in life. I have faith in you. If you spot anyone spreading rumors or writing poems in memory of Premier Zhou, you must report it to me at once. I'll assign you to the technical department. You and I are alike—we are people of profound passion."

As he was speaking, he reached out to embrace me, but I jumped up as if jolted by an electric charge. Not only had he asked me to become a spy, he was trying to humiliate me once again! I picked up the glass filled with malted milk and threw it to the floor. This startled him momentarily and gave me the opportunity to shoot out the door like an arrow.

From that day I lost my ambition to study technology and did everything I could to avoid Shao Xintian. But within two months he twice entered my small room in the middle of the night and raped me. At first I thought I had neglected to lock the window, but I later discovered that he had secretly copied the key to my door. I was so terrified that I took to sleeping in the night-shift lounge. Even when I dared to sleep in my own room, I was constantly checking to make certain I had bolted the door.

I might have been the daughter of a rightist, but my love was pure. Shi Lei often wrote to me, expressing his true love and genuine concern. But how could I face him? All I could do was toil away at hard physical labor, somehow hoping that I could cleanse myself by bathing in my own sweat. But this was impossible. Horrible nightmares often interrupted my sleep. I felt dizzy and nauseous; I had no appetite and my limbs were weak. My pink cheeks turned ashen and gaunt. The only one who showed concern for me was Shao Xintian's driver, Yu Gang. He was over thirty years old but still had no girlfriend. He often brought me drinking water and food from the

8. A "white expert" was someone who possessed technical skills but did not have the proper revolutionary political consciousness. Technical specialists were expected to be "red" as well as expert.

Stubborn Weeds

canteen. When I was ill and confined to my bed, Yu Gang brought me my meals. Of course, none of this escaped the attention of Shao Xintian. After a few days I felt better and returned to work. I bumped into Shao Xintian along the way. When he noticed no one was watching, he put on a phony smile and said, "What do you mean, my dear Lu, by dumping your man for a new one?"

I spat in disgust and turned away.

Yu Gang was delighted when he saw that I was well. When I returned to my room after work that day, he came by with a movie ticket for me. I thought of Shi Lei's deep love for me and decided to find a convenient excuse to decline his offer. He looked rather embarrassed but said, "Is it possible for us to be friends?"

"You don't really know me yet."

"Then I'll wait patiently for you."

He had obviously misunderstood what I said.

Before I knew it, the Qingming Festival[9] had arrived. It was cloudy and a light drizzle was falling, but people worked through the night preparing memorial wreaths and writing elegiac couplets in memory of Premier Zhou Enlai. It was then I discovered I was pregnant. Terrified beyond words, I finally decided to tell Shao Xintian.

I waited for him after work on the road leading to his house. When he saw me he slid off his bicycle and smirked. Then I told him I was pregnant, and his expression suddenly changed. "It's not mine," he snapped.

"How can you deny it? You have to get me out of this mess—if you're not comfortable talking about it here, come to my room tonight; otherwise I'll come to your home—" I almost broke down under the strain.

"Shut up! I don't want you near my home, and I don't want you squealing about this. You better listen or you'll be sorry! I need time to think about what to do."

He gave me a dirty look, hopped onto his bicycle, and rode off.

Feeling both shame and humiliation, I could not keep tears from welling in my eyes. I hated Shao Xintian. I wanted to denounce him and rip him to shreds, but he had all the power. The head of the municipal Public Security Bureau had been a pal of his during the Cultural Revolution. I was nothing but the daughter of a rightist and a humiliated common laborer! These were chaotic times. Law had been trampled underfoot, democracy had been stolen away, and justice had been turned upside-down. His word would be worth more than a hundred accusations I might write!

From then on Shao Xintian simply avoided me. In the past it was I who had been in constant fear of him, but now he was afraid of me.

9. See "Tiananmen Incident" in glossary.

Short Stories

In the past I would double- and triple-check the bolt on the door before going to bed, but now I hoped he would come by to tell me he had a solution. Every day seemed like a year.

Then I received an unexpected letter from Shi Lei saying that his former commissar in the army, a man named Geng, had shown up at the commune to recruit workers for a state farm. Shi Lei had applied for a job and was accepted. He had to report to work within a week and would stop by to see me on the way. This should have been good news, but under the circumstances it was a disaster. What was I going to do? I had to tell him the truth. So I began writing a long, tear-stained letter. I told him everything that had happened from the day Shao Xintian arrived at the commune to recruit workers until the moment I learned I was pregnant. I begged him to forget about me and to cancel his visit, because I was too ashamed to face him. I worked on the letter through the night and lost consciousness several times before completing it.

One drizzly night, as I tossed and turned in bed, unable to sleep, I suddenly heard someone enter my room and shut the door. Thinking it must be Shao Xintian I sat up quickly, but before I could get my clothes on, the person was at the foot of the bed calling to me in a soft voice:

"Hey, Lu! Director Shao said you wanted to see me at ten o'clock—Here I am—why are you sleeping?"

I could tell from his accent that it was not Shao. "Who is it?"

"It's me, Yu Gang."

Yu Gang! What a relief. Stammering, he offered the following explanation: "Director Shao said he would help me find a girlfriend. He said he spoke to you, and you agreed to be my girlfriend. Look, here's the key to your door you gave him—"

When I heard this I knew something was wrong. Shao would not be so kindhearted. He was up to something.

"Get the bastards! Grab those shitheads! Don't let the fuckers get away!" I suddenly heard a screaming mob rush up the stairs, and I quickly bolted the door. Within seconds there was someone on the outside howling, cursing, and banging on it. Now everything was clear. Shao Xintian was trying to cover up his crimes by making his driver, Yu Gang, the scapegoat. That son of a bitch! "You've been set up!" I whispered to Yu Gang. "I never asked Shao to send you here. Now he's told his mob that we are sleeping together!"

Yu stared blankly for a moment, then caught on. He clenched his teeth. "He wants to frame me because I refused to drive for him at Qingming, when he wanted to track down the people who passed out poems in memory of the Premier. But I don't want you to get into trouble, Lu. I'm going to jump out the window!"

"Can you do it?" I gently placed my hand on his back.

Stubborn Weeds

"Sure! Three years ago when I was a fireman, I jumped out a third-story window. This is only the second floor. Nothing to it!"

He gave me a plaintive smile, stood on the windowsill, and jumped out. There was a thud followed by a shrill cry. I felt a sinking feeling in my breast, and then a pain like a knife puncturing my heart. Why had I agreed so quickly to let him jump? What if he were injured?

Suddenly the door crashed open and a mob of people rushed into my small room. Someone flicked the light switch, and the room was filled with eye-piercing light. I saw Shao Xintian standing to one side, looking like a monster. He slammed his fist on the table, pointed right at my nose, and began a verbal assault. "Lu Chunxia! I never would have thought it of you—"

Before I could say a word, the crowd pushed me down the stairs to the first floor. When we got outside, someone shined a flashlight on Yu Gang, who was lying in a pool of blood. I screamed and then lost consciousness.

When I awoke the next morning, I found myself handcuffed and alone in a small jail cell.

Several days later I learned from the public security officer who was interrogating me that after jumping, Yu Gang had hit the wire clothesline outside my window. Apparently he had lost his balance and landed on his head, cracking his skull on the ground below. He died on the way to the hospital.

The public security people questioned me in detail. They wanted me to admit that I had been having an affair with Yu Gang for some time. They also wanted me to say I had forced him to jump that night when the militia group caught us together and that I had caused his death. I replied that these things were not true, but I was still too frightened to say anything about Shao Xintian. So I just stuttered and stammered and finally said that Yu Gang had dropped by for a visit. When he heard the commotion downstairs, I said, he panicked and jumped out the window. But even I was ashamed of such a feeble story. As they continued their questioning, the humiliation and agony of the past became even stronger. All I could do was cry.

Two weeks later I was sent back to the factory for a public denunciation meeting. The assembly hall was packed. Shao Xintian was presiding. Granting himself the right to speak first, he took the stage and announced my "crimes" in a loud voice. He said I did not like to work and that I was intent upon becoming a "white expert" like my right-wing father. He charged that I wanted to see correct verdicts against right-wingers reversed[10] and that I was a moral degenerate who began by sleeping around with men and ended up committing

10. See "What Should I Do?", note 16, p.

murder in order to conceal my criminal activities. He spoke with conviction and promised evidence of my murderous crime! Several times I tried to raise my head to protest, but before I could speak the militia man standing at my side slapped me in the face and forced my head down.

I was furious by the time I was thrown back in my cell. Now I was determined to get revenge on Shao Xintian. So I took the pen and paper they had given me to write a "confession" and wrote a truthful account of how Shao Xintian had raped and persecuted me. I also described how he tried to shift the blame by tricking Yu Gang and thereby causing his death. Shao Xintian was the real murderer. Yu Gang and I were his victims. I never suspected that this document would later be used against me and regarded by the higher authorities as further evidence of my guilt!

When I stood trial again, the man who presided was Shao Xintian's old comrade-in-arms, the director of the municipal Public Security Bureau. Flanked by two police officers, this fat oaf lifted his head and barked out a question about my name. When I responded, he said I was under arrest and then showed me the "evidence" that Shao Xintian had mentiond at the denunciation meeting. It was a photograph of my fingerprint found on Yu Gang's back. He said the test had been carried out by a special institute in Shanghai and that it proved I had pushed Yu Gang out the window. I was speechless. At that point nothing I could say would have proved my innocence.

Within three months I was sentenced to death, although no public announcement was made. The sentence was to be carried out in two years.[11] My crimes were that I had inherited my father's reactionary outlook, that I wanted to see the reversal of correct verdicts against rightists, that I had engaged wantonly in illicit sexual activity, and that I had pushed my lover to his death in order to cover up my crimes. Furthermore, I had denied my crimes after arrest and had made false accusations against a revolutionary cadre, thereby slandering the dictatorship of the proletariat.

When I heard all this, my ears began to buzz and a dark curtain fell over my eyes. I collapsed to the floor.

Was there any truth under heaven—any justice in this country?

Before long I was sent to the Aishan thought-reform labor camp. It was dusk when I was thrown into a dark and clammy cell.

A dim light cast my lonely shadow on the wall. My solitude was broken only by the sound of a couple of crickets chirping sadly by the door. This made me feel even lonelier. Suddenly the crickets stopped chirping. I heard heavy footsteps moving toward my cell and then

11. It is standard procedure in certain capital cases in China to postpone the execution of the accused for two years. This permits commutation to life in prison if there is evidence that the accused has repented and has reformed in ideological outlook.

Stubborn Weeds

saw the outline of a familiar figure. I peered into the dim light with sadness and fright. First I saw the high nose and then the thick brows, large eyes, and firm lips. But the face was long and covered with a stubbly black beard.

"Shi Lei!" I cried out, throwing myself against the iron bars and bursting into tears.

"Lu! Don't cry, don't cry! Don't let them see you like this!"

I understood what he meant, as I closed my mouth and let the tears flow into my heart.

Shi Lei's eyes also became red.

"Did you get the letter I sent you before I was thrown into jail?"

"Yes, but I didn't tell my mother anything."

"I'm so sorry—please do what I said in the letter—forget about me from now on. Tell me, how is your mother?"

"She's—she's dead. She died a week before you were locked up. She wanted very much to see you when she was ill and told me she would come to the factory to visit you when she felt better."

Before he could finish, I began sobbing once again.

"Listen to me, don't cry," Shi Lei pleaded. "Do you remember my telling you about Geng, the old commissar of my military unit? He's now running our state farm. Well, several days ago I let him read your letter. He was furious! He's the one who asked me to come here tonight. Here's some paper. In the next couple of days you write an appeal and I'll deliver it to Geng. Keep your chin up, Lu! When your hair gets messy, comb it; when your clothes tear, mend them! I'm going to leave this sewing kit with you—it's the one you gave me when my furlough was over."

Then he left, heavy footsteps disappearing into the darkness.

I clutched the small sewing bag to my breast. In the dim light I noticed that a second red heart had been sewn on the bag beside the one I had originally embroidered. The two hearts were now snuggling together.

My heart had already begun to fade, but his was still a brilliant red.

More than a month passed after I gave my statement of appeal to Shi Lei, but I didn't hear a word. Like a clay ox falling into the sea, it disappeared without a trace. The anxiety was unbearable.

One day after the midday break, when our work detail was gathering, Shi Lei suddenly appeared and whispered something into the ear of the team leader. When I was called away from the work detail, I felt certain that my petition had been approved by the higher authorities. I asked Shi Lei, but he just shook his head and said, "No, it's your father. He's come to see you. He's brought some decent food for you. He's in the reception area now being questioned."

Totally confused, I stopped in my tracks and asked, "How can I

Short Stories

face him? Here I am, a criminal on death row. He's got his own problems. If he associates with a daughter like me, things will be even worse for him!"

"Your father has traveled hundreds of miles just to see you. Are you going to send him packing?" Shi Lei motioned for me to follow him.

I did so reluctantly. When I entered the reception room, I was shocked by the ghastly appearance of an old man with white hair. The wrinkles on his face were compounded by ugly scars. His contorted lips were trembling. His twisted body looked like an old willow that had been struck by lightning. Was this the father I had not seen in ten years? I stared at him and he stared back at me.

Shi Lei whispered to me. "Quick, say something to him!"

With tears streaming down my face, I instinctively threw my arms around him. "Father," I cried, using a word that had been alien to my vocabulary for many years.

"Di! So we meet again, I meet with my own daughter again! Even though we meet in a labor camp, I can die now without regrets! I don't blame you for what happened—" My father embraced me and caressed my head several times. "I've brought some nice things for you to eat," he said. "Please eat them! It's been ten years since you've eaten your papa's food. Eat some in front of papa, and then papa will be happy."

I had not been hungry in the first place, but now, with all the emotion and excitement, I actually felt a bit nauseous at the thought of eating the food he had brought.

My father became upset when he noticed my blank stare. "Papa wouldn't bring you poisoned food, Di! Just a moment ago the guard on duty said the food would have to be inspected. I told him there was no need and took one bite of everything just to show him. And look, nothing's wrong with me! You know Shao Xintian who was just appointed Party Secretary of the Hongxing Iron Works? Well, he may have given me a hard time during the anti-rightist campaign, but he never really forgot his old co-worker. The day after he became Party Secretary he recalled me from the May Seventh labor camp.[12] Not only was I reassigned to my old job, but I was also given all my back salary. He even asked the cook in the factory mess hall to fix up some nice food for you. Look at it—'appearance, aroma, and taste—it's got it all,' as they say. If you don't believe me, I'll eat some more for you!"

The words "Shao Xintian" sent a shock through my body. I felt numb all over. Shi Lei, ever astute, suddenly cried, "Don't eat it!" at

12. This "May Seventh" labor camp should not be confused with the many "May Seventh" cadre schools that appeared during the Cultural Revolution. Almost all cadres spent a year or two in rural cadre schools to reform their ideological outlooks. The labor camps, on the other hand, were used to punish people charged with political crimes.

my father, who was stuffing the food into his mouth. Shi Lei asked the guard to go have the food tested.

But it was too late. My father collapsed on the floor. His limbs twitched, his breathing became heavy, and his eyes began to roll.

"He's been poisoned! Get him emergency treatment!" As Shi Lei flew out the door I cradled my father's body and sobbed uncontrollably.

A moment later Shi Lei came running back with two public security officers. They placed my father on a stretcher and hurried over to the clinic. I tried to stand up and run with them, but I suddenly felt a sharp pain in my abdomen and collapsed on the floor.

When I regained consciousness, I found myself lying on a snowy white bed in the clinic, with Shi Lei sitting beside me. Geng, the old commissar with the thick and heavy beard, was angrily pacing back and forth in the corridor. His face was beet red, like that of a man who had guzzled down a pint of liquor. Doctors and nurses were popping in and out of another room in the clinic, desperately trying to save my father.

Geng suddenly threw open his shirt, put his hands on his hips, and strode into the room where I was recuperating. Then he spoke— half, it seemed, to Shi Lei and half to himself. "I knew all along that Shao Xintian was rotten. He's like a smiling tiger. When he eats people he eats them bones and all. During the Cultural Revolution when I went to the chemical factory to support the left, I heard that this son of a bitch had raped some of the Red Guards and had killed someone with his own two hands. Now here he is again, scheming to kill people who know too much! This poisoning incident must have something to do with Lu Chunxia's appeal."

"You have no news of her appeal?" Shi Lei asked.

"Yes, I have. I just got it. It says: 'We support the original sentence—carry out the sentence.' Shao was afraid someone would appeal to higher authorities, so he made sure he cleared the whole way for himself! Our socialist nation has been ruined by deadbeats like him. Framing and false accusations are stacked as high as mountains. It's almost hopeless. China needs people like Bao Gong and Hai Rui!"[13]

"Mr. Geng," interrupted Shi Lei, showing concern. "They're looking everywhere for democrats and capitalists these days, you'd better watch—"

"The truth must see the light of day! Shi Lei, I want you to help

13. Bao Gong (999–1062), an official who specialized in legal matters, is legendary for his incorruptibility. He was noted for exposing frameups of common people. Hai Rui (1514–1587), a high government official, was arrested and jailed in 1566 because he dared to criticize the emperor. Educated Chinese readers immediately associate the name of Hai Rui with Peng Dehuai, the Chinese Minister of Defense who dared to criticize Mao Zedong's Great Leap Forward in 1959 and was removed from office for his indiscretion.

me pull together the material on Lu Chunxia's case as soon as possible. I'll bring it to the provincial Public Security Bureau, and if they can't handle it, I'll go to Beijing! These people have gone too far. The Party and the people will never forgive them."

After Shi Lei left I gazed at the old white-haired commissar with gratitude and respect. I felt a pain in my abdomen and was reminded of the hateful Shao Xintian. I found that I hated the thing in my womb just as much as I hated Shao Xiantian. I just couldn't let it come into this world. I struggled to my feet and began wailing and furiously punching my abdomen! This hurt so much that cold sweat poured from my forehead.

Geng could see what I was trying to do and waved his hands frantically. "Lu Chunxia, it's the adult who's guilty, not the child! When the child grows up it will be like you, it will hate people like Shao Xintian—"

Before he finished speaking, I fainted once again.

The piercing sound of the morning alarm has shaken my cell and brought me back to the bitter reality of the present.

The scarlet sun is slowly rising in the east. The beautiful morning clouds seem headed toward me in this prison. I am convinced that the sunlight will one day make its way into this cell. My eyes no longer shed tears. Instead they reflect the burning intensity of the sun and the hope of the morning clouds.

Whenever I think about Shao Xintian and his ilk, the things old Geng said ring in my ear. "The people will never forgive them!"

But, the people—the people! When will we rise up and smash these monsters? Will a person like me, sitting here on death row, ever see people like Shao Xintian get what they deserve?

Outside the iron bars, the green bamboo is growing quietly and the wild chrysanthemums are slowly coming into bloom. Life could be so beautiful! There are thousands and thousands of people like Shi Lei and old man Geng in this world. I believe in life and I want to live! The day will come when I can attend the trial of Shao Xintian. That day will come!

BAI HUA *A Bundle of Letters*

Bai Hua (b. Chen Youhua, 1930) joined the People's Liberation Army in 1947 and the Communist Party in 1949. Since then he has worked primarily writing plays for the army, although he has also done poetry, fiction, film scripts, and opera. Ironically, he may eventually be known in Chinese political-literary history as the author of the film script "Unrequited Love" ("Kulian")—not because this is his best work, which it is not, but because political critics rather arbitrarily used this script in the spring of 1981, and again that fall, in order to send a signal to all creative writers in China about the dangers of "bourgeois liberalism". The true reasons for singling out Bai Hua for this purpose are unclear, but they probably are extraneous to "Unrequited Love." "A Bundle of Letters" is a more substantial example of Bai Hua's work in 1979–80, and was also much better known among readers until "Kulian" was attacked.

Originally published in Renmin wenxue *(Beijing), No. 1, 1980.*

Translated by ellen Yeung.

THE FIRST LETTER

Ming:

At the thought of going home I was dreamily spreading the wings of my imagination and soaring gleefully among layers of clouds in a sky crisscrossed with sunlight—

After journeying by car and train for three days and nights I finally arrived home. This is my first letter to you since my arrival. You don't really know too much about my family, even though we've been friends for over two years (starting from that day in the fall of 1976 when I arrived at the offshore oil rig to be a welder and you helped me with my luggage). Forgive me, but I can regard us as friends only, nothing more. Many of our young friends, when they meet someone of the opposite sex, assume immediately they have some special kind of relationship. That is such a rash conclusion. And it is why they so frequently change feelings and change partners. They end up eradicating sacred love at its source. While freely casting away love, like monkeys discarding corn husks, the real love in their hearts gradually withers and dies.

What is my family like? You've never asked me, and I've never felt the need to tell you. But now that I'm home, I can't help talking a little about my home and family. I wonder what you'll think of me after you've heard my story. But I'm sure you won't change your opinion of me, since you are, after all, *my* friend, not my family's. As you already know, I am a girl who has been used to living independently in a labor collective. You are my closest friend, and you must have been able to tell that the smell that comes from my hair and skin is not the scent of some perfume but the fragrance of the sun. My clothes—work clothes, actually—are always the same. I am already twenty-five years old and still have only work clothes. I have none of the kind of clothing that reveals feminine beauty. Of course, that's

Short Stories

not to say that I don't like to look nice, right? I'm sure you understand.

My family is what you would normally refer to as a revolutionary family. I can still remember my brothers and me wearing military outfits cut down from my father's old uniforms. In those days I called my parents "Comrade Father" and "Comrade Mother," the way I would call the guard "Comrade Uncle." On my father's rare days off, the whole family would march off to the countryside, to a little river called Orchid Creek, for a picnic. Comrade Father, Comrade Mother, and Comrade Uncle would join us children catching shrimp in the creek. Using a straight hook like Jiang Ziya's,[1] we would all lie in wait for those blithely ignorant shrimp in the shallow stretches, where the water was so clear you could see the bottom. Comrade Uncle would usually net the most and I the least. But I also ate as I fished and usually ended up stealing from the small pails of Comrade Father and Comrade Uncle, too. What a little brat I was!

Father was one of those "little red devils" who had joined the Red Army in the latter days of the Long March. Before joining, he had been a cowherd who had grown up on the back of a cow. He's sixty-two this year. After the Gang of Four was smashed, he came back as the deputy commandant of a military region. Mother was a reasonably well educated village schoolteacher in her youth. I understand that she was quite well known in the Taihang Mountain area during the latter days of the war. Besides being extremely capable, she was also surpassingly pretty. You've probably seen the same characteristics in the person of her youngest daughter—me (ha, ha!). She is now in her fifties and hasn't worked for years because of poor health. My eldest brother, Hesheng, was an honor student at a military engineering academy, and until recently was assigned to a research unit along the third defense line in Sichuan.[2] Now he's been transferred to work in the city where my parents are staying. My sister-in-law, Linyu, is a colleague of his. They have a two-year-old daughter, Kangkang. My other brother, who is two years older than I, is a soldier. And this is my whole family. If you want to know more, please be patient and read on.

Evening in the city is terribly noisy. As soon as I got off the train, I threw my drum bag[3] over my shoulder and headed down the sidewalk in huge strides that must have appeared strange to city people. I looked exactly the way I did when I leaped onto the ferryboat and

1. Jiang Ziya was a wise man who helped King Wu found the Zhou (Chou) dynasty in the twelfth century B.C. According to legend, the two men first met by a river where Jiang was fishing.

2. In Chinese military terms, the first line of defense extends north and south through Shanghai, the second line through Wuhan, and the third through Chengdu.

3. A drum bag is a hollow wooden cylinder with leather ends, used as a travel bag and also as a primitive drum in marches.

Stubborn Weeds

waved goodbye to you. I was wearing the same man's shirt, the same stiff, thick overalls, and the same plastic sandals. Since I hadn't been home for a while, I was stopped at the gate of the military compound. The guard didn't know me, nor did he believe that a suntanned girl like me could be the daughter of the Deputy Commandant. And there were other reasons for his suspicion—mainly that I had not been delivered in a limousine. I asked the guard on duty to telephone my father, but he only dallied about and walked around eyeing me as if I were a baby elephant newly imported from Africa. I was mystified. Was I so unlike a general's daughter? After questioning me for a full thirty minutes, he finally dialed a number, and I found myself talking to my mother. She let out a loud shriek. "You just wait there, Nannan! Don't move! I'll be right down!"

The guard immediately became very cordial. He brought me a chair, poured me a cup of hot water, and even extended both hands to offer me a cigarette. I sniffed at the cigarette. It smelled really nice, but unfortunately I don't smoke, so I returned it to him. Deciding not to wait for my mother, I picked up my bag and ran inside the compound.

Our quarters are in a small private courtyard. In order to avoid more unnecessary explanations, this time I adopted the methods of a burglar. Luckily our courtyard wall isn't too high, and with the aid of a parasol tree that stands just beyond it, I could reach the top of the wall. I took off my bag and threw it into the courtyard, then jumped and landed on the soft lawn. The joy of my success was quickly dispelled by the ferocious barking of a guard dog. In order to ward off the attack of this wolfish beast, I had to wave my heavy bag to and fro in mortal combat. You know what a stubborn, uncompromising, unrelenting whippersnapper I can be. Finally the cowardly barking and growling of my opponent attracted a group of guards and family members, including my elder brother Hesheng and his wife Linyu, who held little Kangkang in her arms. The guard dog must have thought he had amassed overwhelming support, because he now mounted an all-out attack, barking madly and spraying my face with saliva. It was then that Hesheng recognized me.

"Nannan!" he cried, and immediately ordered the dog to stop. "Kaidi! Scat!"

Mother had also arrived on the scene by this time. She looked as if she had gained in circumference again. Clapping her hands and shouting, she ran up to us, talking nonstop. "Nannan! Why didn't you listen when I told you to wait at the compound entrance? I went to the gate in your father's car, but the guard said you'd already gone in, so we came back here, but you hadn't gotten here yet, so back we went to the entrance, but the guard insisted that he had let you in— it's such a short distance—less than five hundred yards—how could you possibly lose your way? Who would have dreamed that a young lady of your age would be here fighting with a dog, of all things!"

At that, everyone present burst into laughter. Then Mother, Brother, and Sister-in-law led me into the house. I had barely sat down on the sofa in the living room when the family started fussing at me.

"You really are a first-class bumpsky!" said Hesheng. (Bumpsky sounds like a foreign word but isn't. It's something we made up in our childhood. It means "country bumpkin," except that it's even worse.) "Couldn't you have telephoned first? Or you could have gone to any regiment and just introduced yourself by saying 'I'm the daughter of the Deputy Commandant of such-and-such region. I'd like to use your phone—OK?' I guarantee you they'd have looked at you with respect and said, 'Please, help yourself!' Then, if we'd known which train you'd be on, naturally we would have driven to the station to pick you up—Look at you with that silly grin on your face! Imagine creating a spectacle like this as soon as you come home!"

Linyu led Kangkang up to me. "Kangkang, say to your auntie: 'What a narrow escape!' "

"What a narrow escape, Auntie!" said little Kangkang.

I laughed even harder and couldn't stop until Mother handed me a glass of chilled orange juice.

"I know exactly what Nannan is thinking in her little mind!" said Mother. "She's afraid that using public cars for private purposes looks bad. I used to feel that way too—but less and less frequently now. I learned a lesson from the Cultural Revolution: when you're in power, you're a good cadre even if you're extravagant; when you're out of power, you're a capitalist roader and have to be purged even if you're honest and frugal. Things are easy for us now that your father has position and power. Things are done for us even without our asking! A few years ago no one would have paid attention to us even if we'd bowed and scraped. The year I was so ill I couldn't even get out of bed, your eldest brother had to wheel me to the hospital on a bicycle. That kind of suffering—ai! One month your Uncle Jin lost his job and became a mere adviser. The next month his personal car was taken away. Your Uncle Wang, who had retired, always had to haggle with those junior clerks in the Administrative Bureau whenever he needed a car." Her tirade made me stop smiling. I stared silently at the translucent, gosling-yellow orange juice. Mother continued speaking with sincere emotion and conviction. Tears filled her eyes. She believed that all these were true lessons of life.

Just then Father came home, followed by a secretary with a big briefcase under his arm. I hadn't seen Father for two years, yet he somehow managed to look younger. Two years ago, suffering from

Stubborn Weeds

118

depression and boredom, his back had been bent, his face yellow and thin. Now he stood straight—his shoulders thrown back and his complexion much improved. I stood up and rushed to greet him as I had when I was a child.

"Father!"

He smiled and patted my head. "Let's eat!" he said.

At the dinner table my father unexpectedly asked for a cup of *maotai* liquor and raised his cup to me several times, always smiling. I returned his toasts with smirks of delight. Everyone in the family knew that Father was happy only because I was home and that he was drinking only because he was happy. His continual toasting of me alone made me so happy that my face turned red even though I myself was not drinking.

After dinner Hesheng and Linyu insisted that I visit their new house.

"What?" I asked. "Aren't you living with Father and Mother?"

"No, thanks to Mother's foresight," Hesheng answered with a conspiratorial smile.

"Why?"

"Mother was thinking of our future."

"Future?"

"Well, we still have to have a son, and little Kangkang will have to find herself a husband. As the Chinese saying goes, 'If a person doesn't worry about the future, he'll end up worrying about the present.'"

"She really *is* thinking ahead!"

I strolled along with them for more than half an hour before we arrived at a newly constructed tall residential building on a quiet street. They lived on the third floor in an apartment with a southern exposure. It had two bedrooms and a living room. They had obviously taken great pains to decorate it. The fine nylon print covering the walls, the custom-made sofa covers, the drawnwork curtains, the glass lamps hanging from the ceiling—all these created a sense of ease and comfort.

"Why did you transfer from your special research institute back to the city?" I asked.

"Others take care of the nation," Hesheng replied glibly. "I look after my family. But the purpose is the same—modernization."

He proceeded to exhibit the products of his rapid modernization over the past two years—a color television, a stereo tape recorder, streamlined furniture, a quartz digital clock, almost all things I had never seen before. "Without Mother's financial assistance, we'd never be where we are today," Hesheng said with obvious glee.

Little Kangkang punched a button on the tape recorder, and it answered with music that was extremely alien to me. It sounded like a woman singing, and yet it could have been a man's voice; it was sometimes gentle and soft, sometimes rough and wild. The singing had a weird appeal but also an irritating effect.

"What's that?" I asked with a shade of apprehension.

Hesheng laughed.

"It's music from Hong Kong. Before Liberation they called it popular music."

"Popular music?" I asked, baffled. "Why listen to stuff like that?"

"Oh, my, you really are a bumpsky! What's wrong with it?" So saying, he began singing along with the music, and Linyu and little Kangkang joined in.

Maybe I've become such a bumpkin that I'm simply beyond repair, but there's no way I can take this perverted music with its barely discernible lyrics about decadent living and cheap romance. It was particularly grating to hear it coming from their mouths. I stood up as if to leave but was pulled back by Hesheng, who then turned off the tape recorder.

Mother suddenly appeared, gasping and panting. "Nannan, come home right away!" And she dragged me home without letting me get a word in edgewise.

Behind me I could faintly hear Hesheng speaking to Linyu in his lazy tones. "Who would have thought that there still exist such Bolsheviks in this day and age?"

When I arrived home with Mother and went up to her room, she sat me down and gave me a long, frank, heart-to-heart talk. "Ai! I've worried myself to a frazzle over my sons and daughters! Hesheng and his family have finally been transferred back here near us. This old mother hen has to build nests for her chicks, you know. And not just for your generation. I have to think about Kangkang's generation—"

"And after Kangkang there'll be another generation, and another one after that," I said purposefully.

"Ai!" She heaved a great sigh and continued earnestly. "I've thought about that. As long as I'm still alive and kicking I'll do what I can. Now about your second brother. Seven years in the army and he still hasn't been accepted into the Party, nor has he been promoted to be a cadre. What's more, every year when discharge time rolls around, I have to patch things up with his unit. He's really a disgrace to the family!"

"Then why not let him be discharged?"

"That's easy to say! A two-bit soldier for seven years, neither Party member nor League member, does nothing but eat, drink, and smoke high-class cigarettes. What'll become of him if he's discharged? In a few days I'll have to go see him again and remind the cadres in the company—"

"Remind them of what?"

"Remind them that Jiangsheng is a pure child of the revolution! They mustn't stand in his way! And what about you? Are you planning to just drift on the sea for the rest of your life? The very thought of it nearly frightens me to death! A house like a chicken coop, a kerosene stove, a silly goose of a girl, greasy overalls year in and year out. No hope in high heaven of finding a high-ranking cadre's son! You tell me—how am I going to get you a good marriage while you're in a place like that?"

"Mom! According to that logic every man and woman on the oil rig would be doomed to be a bachelor or an old maid!" I stared hard at her. "Oil rig workers don't drift on the sea like mere fish, you know. And even if they did, fish get married too, don't they?"

"Don't be silly! What kind of marriages do fish have? They spend their lives swimming in schools—"

When she phrased it that way, I realized I was talking nonsense and rocked with laughter.

"Stop laughing!" Mother hugged me and continued in a more serious vein. "Marriage has been an important subject from time immemorial. Your brother Hesheng's marriage was arranged in haste because your father was jobless at the time. It's been a knot in my heart ever since. I feel I've failed your brother."

"They seem to get along great!"

"But I just feel so bad every time I see that old Shanghai!"

"Who's old Shanghai?"

"Linyu's father, that's who!"

"Oh, is Linyu's father from Shanghai?"

"I mean that old Shanghai brand car he rides in!"

"Oh!" It suddenly dawned on me that Mother's "old Shanghai" had a much broader meaning. Besides referring to his car, it also meant his background, which would include his job, rank, income, etc.—how very interesting! Following her logic, Ming, I ought to call your father "old Eternal" because old craftsmen like him ride Eternal brand bicycles. Right?

Mother continued: "At that time we couldn't afford to be choosy. The more I thought about it, the more incompatible they seemed, but by then the water was over the dam. And her father was, after all, a cadre "with smoke at his butt" [a cadre with a car] and already a department head. We knew that other people would understand if we just explained the situation. We once had a Zim [a Soviet luxury car] lined up for your brother Jiangsheng—" I couldn't help laughing as Mother's lament continued. "But when they saw that he never got into the Party and never got promoted, it just fell through. Lately I've been wearing myself out going around presenting our case, and I've managed to work things out with a Toyota. The father's a deputy chief of staff of a military district. The girl isn't much to look at, but she's an only child, so the whole chain of household keys is in her hands." She paused, then continued. "But if Jiangsheng can't get promoted or join the Party this year, and just leaves the army as an ordinary civilian, we may not even be able to land this Toyota—"

Try as I might, I couldn't keep from bursting into laughter. I laughed until I was rolling on the bed.

"Look at you! I don't see anything funny in this! Maybe your laughing nerves are out of order."

It took a supreme effort to calm down. Mother handed me a handkerchief to wipe my tears and kept on talking. "Over the past two years many people have asked about you, Nannan. Auntie Sun—you know, she's a Red Flag sedan!—said that her Dongping likes you in a special way—"

I knew that Mother was referring to the family of a deputy political commissar of a military region. I know Dongping, too. He's a big fool who loves to show off his knowledge. Once, in front of a lot of people, he bragged about the magnificent pyramids on the west coast of the U.S.A., which he had seen with his own eyes. When someone pointed out that the pyramids are in Egypt, not the United States, he said that person didn't know what he was talking about and almost got into a fight. From that incident he gained the grand nickname of "the American pyramid." Remembering this nickname, I couldn't help laughing again.

Mother looked at me bewildered. She couldn't understand the cause of my mirth.

"Your Auntie Li, a Benz 250, also likes you a lot. Her Shenshen has found a girlfriend, but the family is only a Pigeon [a bicycle], and their house is no bigger than the Li family's birdcage. Auntie Li plans to zap the affair. It's such a mismatch! 'Telephone me as soon as Nannan returns,' she said. 'I'll bring Shenshen over to see her.' " Mother was scrutinizing me as she talked.

I remember Shenshen well. He's worn glasses since he was very young, is very awkward in any social situation, and seldom says anything. But when he does speak, every sentence causes astonishment. People realize how well read he is, how strong his memory is, and how carefully he has thought over many issues. In the winter of 1969, when Lin Biao thought that he had cornered all his opponents in the political arena, and that he might be "crowned" at any time, we young revolutionary cadets found ourselves with nothing to do. We used to get together to chat about all kinds of things. One time we were discussing famous performers of the world. What our generation knows in this area is really quite pitiful. We did see some plays and movies when we were young, but only got to know the Soviet actors like Cherkasov, Tarasova, and Bondarchuk. We hadn't even

Stubborn Weeds

seen a Charlie Chaplin movie. Luckily someone looked for a chance during the campaign to Destroy the Four Olds[4] and copied information from library books about performing artists of the world. So we finally learned from the printed page about Western entertainers like Greta Garbo, Charles Laughton, Joan Fontaine, Laurence Olivier—all those bright stars who had never appeared in the skies of our youth. We also learned the names of some of the old masters of Peking opera—Yang Xiaolou, Gai Jiaotian, Mei Lanfang, Cheng Yanqiu.

Our little discussion group was the scene of spirited arguments in favor of this performer or that, as if we were old fans and knew what we were talking about. We used the jargon of the theater and argued until we were red in the face. Only Shenshen remained silent, now and then pushing his oversized glasses up onto the bridge of his nose. Finally everyone focused attention on him, demanding that he say something. Some of the boys pushed him with their fists until he began swaying from side to side. I couldn't bear this sight and rushed over to shield him.

"Let him talk!" I turned to Shenshen and spoke in a friendly manner. "Who would you say is the world's greatest performer?"

He pushed his glasses up one more time and then, in a soft voice, uttered a name that made everyone gasp.

"Lin Biao!"

I felt my hands turning numb. Everyone froze in place, eyes glazed. Finally one boy whispered his frank admiration. "Brilliant!"

Everyone who witnessed this was well aware that Shenshen, solely on the basis of those two words, could have sealed his own doom.

"I didn't hear anything," I said sternly.

The rest of the young people spoke up one after another: "I didn't hear anything either—"

But Shenshen persisted. "I said—"

I nudged him with my arm and pulled him away. But after September 13, 1971,[5] whenever the children saw Shenshen, they would raise their thumbs and say, "Brilliant! Wow!"

But Shenshen was displeased. "I didn't say anything," he would say.

To tell the truth, I was a little in love with him after that incident. Now, wait—I said "a little," so don't misunderstand. Besides, "was" means that it's past and over with.

All this time Mother was rambling on about a Volga, a Warsaw, a Dodge—but I was just too tired. My eyelids dropped lower and lower, and I had no idea what other automobile names she men-

4. See glossary.
5. The date on which the death of Lin Biao was announced.

Short Stories

tioned after that. Offended, she shook me awake. "How can you fall asleep like that?" she demanded. "Why don't you take a bath and go to bed?"

Rubbing my eyes, I got to my feet and walked away.

I stopped as I passed the open door of my father's bedroom. Father was writing at his desk, which was piled high with documents. He still behaved the same way he had at the forward command post during the war. His head was always filled with data about troop strength, ammunition, provisions, battle formations, the path of advancing troops. In front of him was a confidential telephone with volume control, which kept him in close contact with several hundred thousands of field troops. A question popped into my mind—how much contact does he maintain with his family? Brother Hesheng and his wife interest themselves in modernization in the form of popular songs. Mother interests herself in cars of various makes because she can measure a person's worth by his brand of car. But Father has remained dedicated to the goals he established for himself years ago. I stared for a long time at his thin back as an indescribable feeling of melancholy rose inside me. At least for now we must call it indescribable.

When I reached my little room that had been prepared for me, I found I had completely lost all desire to sleep. The room is my father's study. Besides deluxe editions of the Marxist-Leninist classics, his bookcases are crammed with books on military science. He has no books directly related to modern life, feelings, or thought. There isn't a single volume of classical or modern literature! This is such a perfect example of overemphasizing one thing to the neglect of all others. Most of the people of his generation are like that—well educated and yet ignorant. But writing this makes me astounded at myself. A small fry like me criticizing the older generation, with their dazzling war records? Sheer impudence!

Three days ago at this time, you and I were sitting silently on the pier, listening to the incessant rushing of the dark sea. The sea breeze kept brushing my hair against your face, making you uneasy. Ah, the cool, salty sea breeze—it nudged us, as if to urge us to fly away on its wings.

It's been an exhausting day, and now it's close to midnight, but I'm still not the least bit tired. At this moment my mind drifts back to that place, to thoughts of you and the sea. I'm deeply aware that I've grown accustomed to everything about that place—the air, the sunlight, the clouds, the aroma of crude oil, the scorching heat of the electric arc, our shared expectations of the future, and the hopes, worries, and frustrations that emerge from our conversations. Although I left only three days ago, I feel as though I've left one planet, both familiar and dear to me, only to arrive on a distant and alien one.

Stubborn Weeds

124

You can appreciate how strange it is that I should feel like this in the home I have dreamed about and in the company of my parents, my brother, and my sister-in-law. I knew I would have to force myself to go to sleep. I've never suffered insomnia before, but tonight, as I toss and turn, sleep will not come. Some people say that counting will bring sleep. But after counting up to 1,542 and still not feeling the least bit sleepy, I could only give up and stare irritably out the window at a pale blue star. My eyelids did eventually grow heavy. But then I experienced another kind of irritation. Beams of headlights appeared before me, more and more, and stronger and stronger, as cars of different brands surrounded me, their horns blaring. Red Flag, Zim, Benz, Warsaw, Toyota, Shanghai—I was like an acrobat taking a curtain call, dozens of beams converging on me. Then one of the cars made a sudden wild turn and headed straight toward me. I didn't have time to dodge and woke up with a scream. My body was soaked with perspiration, so I had to take another bath. I went quietly out to peek at my father. He was still up and writing at his desk. He probably hadn't stirred once from that spot.

I have spent the rest of the night writing this letter to you.

That pale blue star has already turned grayish white. Dawn has crept up on me. She has come from the seashore, from where you are—

Ya'nan

October 6, 1978

THE SECOND LETTER

Ming:

This is my second letter to you since coming home.

Let me tell you something about my father. Father is like most generals who have weathered long revolutionary campaigns. They have always been victorious, triumphant over all enemies, and accordingly have developed the assumption that their will prevails in their family life as well. Father thinks that each of his family members undoubtedly lives and thinks as he does and that this is so obvious that he doesn't even need to ask about it. A man who once served as his guard told us that when a battle began he would stand in open terrain on the front line. He wouldn't budge even when his cap was knocked off by the blast of a shell. When his subordinate commanders and his soldiers saw him standing there bareheaded, they would charge like an advancing tide, with no need for bugles to sound the attack. Today, he still looks on himself as that kind of exemplar for his family. That's what he thinks. But what is the reality?

Father always rises at the crack of dawn. He goes through a shadowboxing routine, then sits down at the dining table for a cup of green tea while he listens to the half-hour news broadcast of the Central People's Radio Station. Then he has a simple breakfast. Secretary Liu quietly brings in the most urgent military dispatches. Then the Red Flag sedan rolls out of the garage. The engine makes almost no noise—all we can hear is the crunching of the gravel under the tires.

Today I ate breakfast with Father in silence. When he rose from the table he took my hand and walked me to the door. He said nothing but stroked my hand lovingly. Secretary Liu ran ahead to open the car door. Father was about to climb in when Mother came running from the house.

"Junfeng!" she cried.

"What's the matter?" Father asked, his hand on the car door.

"I'm so worried about our little boy! And Nannan also misses her big brother Jiangsheng."

I thought it best to nod in agreement. In fact I did miss him a little.

Father turned to me and smiled. "Then by all means go see him."

Mother smiled happily, and out came the charming voice of her youth. "But that will mean leaving today."

Father nodded, then disappeared into the car.

"Secretary Liu!" Mother shot him a glance that meant, "You heard him, I trust."

Secretary Liu smiled and gave her a nod that meant, "Yes, I heard. And don't worry, I'll take care of things."

An hour later, train tickets were delivered to us. Then Mother went shopping in the car and brought back all of Jiangsheng's favorite foods. All of the food had to be the kind that would not raise too many eyebrows and would not require extensive preparation. When the food had been purchased it had to be repackaged. The liqueur-centered chocolate candies went into a paper box designed for bezoar pills. A label bearing the words "For External Use Only" was pasted onto the bottle of pastuerized milk. The fancy China brand cigarettes were repackaged in a box labeled Fragrant Mountain cigarettes. The expensive liquor was poured into a canteen, then resealed with wax. I really had to admire Mother for her patience and attention to detail. She was doing everything under the sun, as painstakingly as possible, to fulfill her mission of motherly love. "Jiangsheng has suffered so," she kept murmuring in a most solemn and touching way. "It's been so hard for him. Poor Jiangsheng!"

When she had taken care of everything and Secretary Liu had come, Mother dragged me into the car. Her arms were filled with all sorts of packages. Soon we were at the train station, where we stopped in front of the VIP lounge. Seeing our Red Flag car, the woman clerk immediately opened the door and ushered us into an air-conditioned waiting room. We had just finished a cup of tea when the train pulled into the station. Clutching our tickets, we boarded the train. Toward evening, we disembarked at the small station where my brother's regiment was located. The managing director of Jiangsheng's division, who had come from headquarters expressly to welcome us, and the Director of Political Affairs of the regiment were both waiting respectfully at the platform. They chauffeured us in a Beijing cross-country motorcar to a room that had been specially prepared by the regiment. Decorated in bright reds and greens and with brand-new furnishings, the room looked like a village bridal suite. There was even an oval mirror, festooned with tassels and engraved with the words "Double Happiness." Soon scurrying attendants arrived, carrying hot water bottles so that we could wash up. After that came the Commander of the Regiment and the Political Commissar to pay their respects. "Thank you, Mr. Commander," Mother kept saying, "for all your guidance and education of Jiangsheng." Yet I could detect uneasiness in both of them. There was tension in the air.

As we were dining with the Director of Political Affairs, Mother made an unexpected request. She wanted to see the political instructor in Jiangsheng's company before she saw Jiangsheng. The Director readily agreed and immediately telephoned the company.

Later that night, just after Mother had taken Jiangsheng's food out of her traveling bag, we heard a soft knock at the door. Mother hurriedly stuffed everything back into the bag. I opened the door and saw a slightly built, dark-complexioned young soldier standing there. He smiled, then immediately composed his face into a stern expression and saluted.

"Political Instructor Lian Yunbi from the sixth company of the second battalion."

"Please come in!" Mother said cordially. "Do sit down."

I found it hard to believe that this could be the political instructor of a whole company. He was so young! Could he command the respect and trust of a fighting unit of a hundred men?

Lian Yunbi sat down. I noticed that he was looking us over with particular care. Mother poured him a cup of tea.

"Please have a cup of tea."

"I just finished a big bowl of soup."

I almost laughed aloud at this graceless answer. Mother opened a pack of cigarettes and offered it to him.

"Please have a cigarette."

"I don't know how to smoke."

What a dumb answer!

"You really are an exemplary young man!" Mother was a bit put off.

"You—you wanted me for some reason?" Lian Yunbi was stuttering slightly.

"Well—" It was Mother's turn to be embarrassed. "I was thinking—"

"Comrade!" he said. "Please feel free to speak your mind."

"Good!" Mother was visibly relieved. "Then I won't beat around the bush. I want to ask you about Jiangsheng. I mean Deputy Commandant Zhang's son, who is also my son and this young woman's brother—"

"I am aware that you are the mother of Zhang Jiangsheng."

"I'd like to know why Zhang Jiangsheng has not yet been accepted into the Party."

Lian Yunbi smiled. It seemed clear he had anticipated the question. He seemed perhaps a bit intimidated.

"This question . . . should not be addressed to me—"

I sobered up in no time. It began to occur to me that there was more to this young instructor than appeared on the surface.

"Then to whom should I address the question?"

"To your son."

"To him?"

"Yes, to him. Ask him why . . . he still hasn't made himself fit for the Communist Party." Lian Yunbi managed to express a firm, no-nonsense attitude while maintaining a soft voice. Mother was a little ruffled but maintained her self-control.

"Where do you come from?" she asked, smiling. "Where is home?"

"I'm from Penglai in Shandong Province. Both my parents are mechanics."

"Then we ought to understand each other!" My mother acted as if she had found his weakness. "Being the son of two workers, you must surely have strong class feelings for the descendant of two revolutionaries. You should try your best to get him into the ranks of the proletarian vanguard."

"I agree! During his term in the army, Comrade Zhang Jiangsheng has changed companies twice. The Party branches in the two previous companies tried their very best, as have we, but unfortunately nothing has come of it." His eyes showed sincere regret.

"What exactly is his problem?" Mother asked.

"Well, for example, he has never returned from leave on time—even once."

"That's nothing!" Mother sneered.

"Comrade," Lian Yunbi countered, seeming a bit offended, "I cannot think of anything in an army more serious than breach of discipline."

"All you people know how to do is get excited over trivial mat-

Stubborn Weeds

128

ters! How will you benefit the Party by making things difficult for him?" My mother was bristling with indignation. "He will join the Communist Party to carry out the mandate of the older generation of revolutionaries and to fight for the realization of the glorious dream of Communism. How can you bear to reject such an idealistic and spirited descendant of the revolution?" My mother's outburst took me by surprise. Her voice was trembling slightly as she made this grandiloquent protest.

Lian Yunbi was astonished. Lowering his head, he stole a look at us, then spoke softly. "But that isn't what Zhang Jiangsheng himself says. He frankly tells us that you wangle a Party card so you can become a cadre, and you become a cadre so you can get rid of your uniform and transfer somewhere else in an official post. With position and influence, Party members and cadres can enjoy a comfortable life. At least your son is candid!"

This made me feel terribly embarrassed on Mother's behalf. My face was hot. But Mother only became more obstinate.

"My son, the Deputy Commandant's son, would never say such politically indiscreet things!"

"He did say such things," Lian Yunbi said in utter seriousness. "And the Party branch has just finished reviewing comrade Zhang Jiangsheng's case. Because he has already overextended his term of service, we felt it was only fair, both to the company and to himself, that we discharge him."

"Discharge him?" Mother could not believe her ears.

"We have already submitted the recommendation to the Party committee of the battalion."

"Will the battalion Party committee dare approve it? Listen to me!" Mother's tone of voice was enough to give me the shivers. "All we need to do—in order to get any old battalion or company cadre discharged, transferred, promoted, whatever—is to signal with our eyes. We don't have to utter a single word. Can you believe that, comrade instructor?"

"Yes, I can." Sadness appeared briefly in Lian Yunbi's eyes. "Even though it's unbelievable," he continued, shaking his head.

"Just you wait and see! First, my son not only is going to stay in the army, but also going to be accepted into the Party and promoted to be a cadre. If it can't be done in this regiment, I'll get him transferred to another. If it can't be done in this division, I'll get him transferred out of the division. It's my duty as a mother to uphold the honor of our revolutionary family."

I lifted my head to look at Lian Yunbi. He stood up, slowly put his army cap on his head, and in a barely audible voice said, "For the sake of the revolution, I—as a soldier, also need to uphold—the Party." Then, as if encouraged by the word "Party," he suddenly stood erect, saluted, and executed a smart about-face. He strode out with his arms swinging, as if marching with the advance troops of a regiment.

Mother collapsed onto the edge of the bed, tears rolling from her eyes. I had intended to give her my own views, but seeing her in such a state, I didn't quite know what to say. After three whole minutes of inaction, I couldn't stand the suffocating atmosphere and stole out of the room.

I could see Lian Yunbi in the distance, striding down the tree-lined road in the misty dusk. The poplar trees on both sides of the road were roaring in the wind like the waves of the ocean. For a long time I gazed steadily at his outline, which appeared especially small under the tall trees, until he disappeared into the night. I walked aimlessly around the drill ground for quite some time. When I returned quietly to the room I found Mother stuffing food and cigarettes, pack after pack, into an army duffel bag. Brother Jiangsheng was beside her, helping out. He had grown taller, to at least 5'9" by now, and his beautiful eyes glittered with a greedy light.

"Now don't you worry about anything, Jiangjiang," Mother was saying, as if coaxing a three-year-old. "Mommy and Daddy will stick up for you all the way."

Ming, you cannot possibly know how depressed and helpless this made me feel. Fortunately they had not seen me come in, so I was able to back out quickly. All the companies were taking evening roll call then. Commands and assembly whistles could be heard everywhere. As I listened to the soldiers counting off, I could imagine their boyish, animated faces, and I gradually calmed down.

I hadn't seen Jiangsheng for many years. How could I hide from him? I went back into the room and greeted him.

"Brother Jiangsheng!"

"Well, look at this!" He jumped to his feet and, grabbing a handful of my hair as he had when we were young, burlesqued the way he had used to speak to me. "Little rabbit! How are you?"

"Fine." I don't know why, but I can never put on a pleasant front. This time was no exception. He let go and stared at me, somewhat surprised. I stared back at him, this familiar-looking stranger. The uniform he was wearing looked as if it were borrowed. He didn't look right in a uniform, and to make things worse this one didn't fit.

"Well?" he asked. "Don't tell me that the barracks and the soldiers have you scared. We're that scary, huh?" He tweaked my nose to try to get a smile out of me.

"Not at all! I think that this kind of life is very vital."

"Vital? That just shows you're not telling the truth! Vital? It's not vital at all—just miserable and boring! You think I enjoy wearing this crummy outfit? I'm in a corner! Seven years as a two-bit soldier and I

Stubborn Weeds

130

still don't have my Party card. Once I get it and get my four pockets,[6] then it's 'au revoir,' everybody. I'll transfer out of here. Mother's already got everything lined up for me—job, fiancee, house—everything's waiting for me. We really have a wonderful mother! She has such foresight and really knows how to get things done."

The political instructor was right that at least Jiangsheng was candid!

"To tell the truth," he said, lowering his voice to a whisper, "the real commandant isn't Father, it's Mother."

"Jiangjiang!" Mother said in mock reproach. "Don't be ridiculous."

"Right. I can't say such things, but I can think them. My problem is right in this company. These hick soldiers can't get along with me, so they give me a hard time. Whatever I do is wrong. Too bad the Communist Party takes its members from the bottom levels and makes you work your way up. If you could start from the top and work down, Mother would have set everything up for me long ago. Gosh!" He sighed, then suddenly looked at his watch, alarmed.

"Mother, I'm going to be late again reporting back to the unit."

"Don't worry. Just tell them I kept you a little longer."

"Ah, but you don't know. My platoon leader is a real stickler! I have to go. Mother! Nannan!" So saying, he picked up his duffel bag and, grumbling about the injustices he had to suffer, walked out.

Ming, you know me well enough to imagine how badly I slept that night. Mother couldn't sleep either. All night we tossed and turned and sighed.

"Can't you sleep either, Nannan?"

"Um—"

"Because of Brother Jiangsheng?"

"Um, you could say it's because he—"

"This is maddening!" she said, "I've never come across such a hard problem!"

I didn't answer her but waited with open eyes for morning to come. Mother didn't say anything more. I tried to recall how Brother Jiangsheng had looked, but no matter how I tried, I could recall only a hazy image. Yet when I thought of that slightly built instructor, Lian Yunbi, I could see him very vividly—his salute, his properly executed about-face, his marching step. These images kept recurring. I had thought him a coward at first, Ming. How wrong I was!

Mother and I were to leave the regiment at noon to return home. At dawn, Mother went to say goodbye to the commanding officers. I have been alone, quietly writing to you in front of the window.

6. Jackets with four pockets—two breast pockets and two at the belt—are reserved for cadres and hence are status symbols.

Ming! It must be a beautiful morning by the sea. When I think of the expansive ocean waking from its dreams, I tremble with joy. At this time you must be out on the little motorboat speeding toward the oil rig. The sea breeze is running freely through your tousled hair, caressing your shoulders, and the salty spray is stealing kisses from your hands that are resting on the gunwale of the boat. I really admire the sea breeze and the waves, and I'm a little jealous of them, too. But just a little.

Ya'nan
October 8, 1978

THE THIRD LETTER

Ming:

When we got home from Brother Jiangsheng's regiment it was already late at night. Kaidi and I went into Father's office. (Kaidi, you probably remember, is the guard dog I battled so fiercely. We are now on excellent terms. This intelligent creature understands human nature. He seems to have discovered that the master who loves him loves me even more, so he is well disposed toward me. He wags his tail at top speed whenever he sees me.) When Father noticed that I was not my usual self and that my eyes were bloodshot from lack of sleep, he grabbed my hand. "Is something troubling you?" he asked. "The whole world is waiting for oil, little lady of the oilfield. So what are you worried about? A personal problem? Go talk to Mother. Go ahead. I'm busy. Besides, coming to me for advice about daily life is like using a rolling pin to fan a fire. I'm totally ignorant and completely helpless. But at least I know my own limitations, so I just don't concern myself with those things."

"I've come to see you, Father. I have to talk to you, no matter how busy you are—"

"Oh." He grew solemn. "Is it that important?"

"I don't know—"

"How much time will this take?"

"You ought to hear it no matter how long it takes."

"All right." He drew up a chair so that I could sit facing him.

I talked to him about my experiences and feelings since returning home, in the same frank and detailed way that I wrote my last two letters to you. At no time during the conversation did he interrupt me. He just sat listening with a glass of tea in his hand. Since he doesn't smoke, tea counts as his only addiction. He lowered his head and looked at the floor so that there was no way I could see his expression. I felt like an impassioned actor who can hear no response from the audience. But I kept on talking and held nothing back.

Stubborn Weeds

132

When I had finished, he kept his head down for a long time. There we were, sitting opposite each other, deep in thought. It was so quiet we could hear the ticking of the small clock on the desk.

Finally he lifted his head as if it were some immense weight. "Are you finished?" he asked softly.

"Yes."

"Go to bed, Nannan," he said affectionately.

I stood up and left the room. I had just entered my own room and sat down when I heard the sharp sound of shattering glass, followed by total silence—

The next morning I was the first to get up. I went to his office and carefully picked up the pieces of broken glass.

No one spoke at the breakfast table. Only Kaidi tried to soften Father. Mother's eyes, swollen from weeping, attested to the fierce and yet secret row they had had the night before. When he finished eating, Father slammed down his chopsticks, got up, and strode out. The sound of the car door closing was extraordinarily loud. Even Kaidi was frightened. When he recovered from his initial shock, he charged out in pursuit of the car.

Mother, obviously hurt, began weeping bitterly. Then she ran wailing up to her room. The whole house was engulfed in her sobbing. The houseboy and the old cook stayed huddled in the kitchen, not daring to venture out. After I cleared the table and went back to my room, I sat dumbly with my head in my hands listening to my mother's crying. Her door must have been open for the sound of her crying to be so loud. Gradually her loud wailing subsided to a kind of tearful lament that in a way seemed musical. It made me think of those women of the Tang Dynasty who worked as professional mourners. See how impossible I am, to make such weird associations? Rather as if she were singing, Mother began lamenting in an affected, drawn-out voice. "Why do I bother? Why? I wear myself out for my children, and all I get for it is blame—OK, from now on I won't lift a finger, even if a life depends on it!"

You see how foolish I am. One isn't supposed to air one's dirty linen in public, yet here I am, writing all this to you. It's because I believe you ought to know. You ought to know all there is to know about me.

While Mother was having a really good cry, her voice rising and falling in cadence, the phone rang and the weeping abruptly stopped. She picked up the phone and spoke like a different person. "That's right—speaking—how are you? What? The old man has transferred Jiangsheng's file? The company has recommended Jiangsheng's discharge?" Then she said with indifference, "I know, but the fact remains that a father is a father and a son is a son. I've never heard of a father who tries to block his own son's advancement. Sure, he'll say

Short Stories

anything when he gets steamed up, but don't pay any attention to that. We still have to rely on all you good people to watch out for the boy. The Commandant (she meant Father) has always praised you as an excellent subordinate, a reliable subordinate—really! Right now the most important thing is to give the boy a new chance, to let him transfer to another unit, a new environment. We're counting on you to be strict with him so he'll make fast progress—a Party member in two months, a cadre in half a year. That isn't asking too much, is it?" Mother laughed. "After all, a word from you will do it. So that's it!" Then she added, in the tone of voice used for army commands, "We'll consider this settled now!" She hung up the phone.

The rest of the day I shut myself in my room, lying on the bed but unable to read. From time to time I heard Mother speaking on the telephone, employing various tones of voice. I couldn't hear clearly and didn't really bother to listen. Her bedroom sounded like a battlefield command post.

Toward evening I heard a noise at the window. I got up to see Kaidi standing outside on his hind legs, his chin resting on the window sill. He had a letter in his mouth. I walked over to take the letter and reached through the window bars to pat his head. He looked at me obsequiously. The letter was from Father, of course, and only three lines long:

Nannan:
    I'm on duty tonight at the Underground Combat Readiness Head-quarters. Don't wait for me for dinner.

He didn't telephone and didn't tell Mother. He told only me. This was a sure sign he was feeling disturbed and depressed.

With Father not home, I felt at a loss the whole evening. Mother's telephone calls became even more frequent and continued long past midnight.

Ya'nan
October 9, 1978

The Fourth Letter

Ming:
    I have received your letters. You're an evil one. Right when I'm missing the sea so much, you have to describe it in such alluring terms. You make me remember the long dragon-like pipeline, the electric arc vying with the starlight at night, the smiles on the grease-streaked faces of the workers, the singing on the sampans, and the lights of the crabbers on the beach. I can close my eyes and see those little crabs darting sideways, burrowing into their little ready-made

Stubborn Weeds

holes as soon as they see somebody—the ones you have to reach all the way down in order to pull out, and if you're not careful, you get your fingers pinched.

Don't get the impression that my letters are always full of boring family matters. This letter is going to be different. At last I've had an experience I can be proud of. You would never have guessed I'd be lucky enough to see a massive joint land and air war exercise. Tanks were rumbling and planes roaring on that dusty battlefield. Infantrymen were charging, covered by guns and missiles, just as in a real battle. In order to let me see this "real battle," my father gave me a visitor's permit, and I squeezed in with some reporters on a command headquarters vehicle. I was surprised that Father would do this, since it was entirely at odds with his usual attitude of strict self-discipline. It may be because he thinks too highly of me, or he may have thought I needed a lesson in what war is like. In any case, I caught a glimpse in this "battle" of an entirely different Father.

In this mock campaign, pontoon bridge engineers were having trouble reaching a ferry crossing at the Huai River. A unit of infantry vanguards was bunched on the river bank with nowhere to go, and this stopped the troops that were following them. My father was speeding to the scene in the command car and immediately ordered a staff officer to summon the infantry commander. This commander was very young and a bit cocksure. I could tell that he was one of those "peace doves" who had never been in a battle before. ("Peace doves" is what the old cadres call the young commanders who have yet to prove themselves.) This one spoke both clearly and fluently. He stood before my father methodically reporting the various problems he had encountered. My father's eyebrows shot up. His eyes grew wide with anger.

"Shut up!" he roared, slapping the car's door handle. "You think the enemy artillery's going to stop and listen to your goddamn report? You want to end the lives of the whole regiment right here? Just because there's no pontoon bridge, you're not going to cross the river? Huh? I'm giving you half an hour to have your regiment digging in on the other side of the river. Now carry out the order!"

"Yes, sir!" The young commander, who had lost some of his self-assurance, saluted in a panic, turned and ran.

Father looked at his wristwatch, his face dark with anger. I felt terribly embarrassed. Why had he reacted so violently? How could he have been so harsh in reproaching a subordinate—a commander at that?

But in less than twenty-eight minutes, except for the heavy gear and artillery, that entire regiment had forded the Huai River and was digging in on the opposite shore. The pontoon bridge engineers had also arrived and made a speedy linkup so that the advancing troops could readily cross the river. I again felt embarrassed. This time I was embarrassed at the embarrassment I had felt half an hour earlier!

After three days of rapid marching during the same extended exercise, Father happened to notice Brother Jiangsheng sitting in an infirmary truck. Surprised, he ordered a staff officer to summon the political instructor of Jiangsheng's company. The slightly built instructor, whom I was now seeing for the second time, arrived with three carbines slung over his shoulder. Almost dropping from exhaustion, he came before Father and saluted, looking up at him with half-closed eyes.

"Hasn't Zhang Jiangsheng been discharged?" Father asked.

"We haven't received word from our superiors."

I saw my father's eyebrows rise again, but he was still able to control himself. "What's ailing Jiangsheng?"

"He says he has stomach pains, Mr. Deputy Commandant, sir," answered Lian Yunbi.

"*He* said? Bring him here!"

In a moment Lian Yunbi reappeared with Brother Jiangsheng, who was overjoyed to see Father. When Jiangsheng caught sight of me, he came bouncing over to shake my hand.

Father signaled to Brother Jiangsheng, who said softly, "Father!"

"I hear that you're suffering from stomach pains." There was a slight tremor in Father's voice, and Brother Jiangsheng interpreted this as a sign of Father's concern.

"Not really," he whispered into Father's ear. "But you know, of course, how tiring this rapid march is. I just found an excuse to rest in the infirmary truck. As long as I can be there, let them go three hundred miles a day—see if I care! Hey, Dad! Do you have any sausages with you?"

Father's face was ashen. Pursing his lips tightly, he paused for a long while before addressing Lian Yunbi. "Instructor! Soldier Zhang Jiangsheng is pretending an illness. What kind of punishment should he get?"

"Aw, come on, Dad," Jiangsheng said with a cheeky smile.

Lian Yunbi was silent for a moment.

"Comrade instructor?"

Lian Yunbi looked into my father's face before replying. "With the Deputy Commandant's permission, sir, he should be criticized. If he doesn't take the criticism, his punishment could be stepped up." Unperturbed, Brother Jiangsheng said to Lian Yunbi, "Maybe you don't know, comrade instructor, but this is my father."

"That's the kind of attitude that calls for stepped-up punishment," Lian Yunbi said softly.

"He shall be given a public reprimand and returned to his unit!" Father said sternly.

Stubborn Weeds

Lian Yunbi answered clearly, "Yes, sir! Publicly reprimanded and returned to his unit."

Blustering, Brother Jiangsheng protested. "But, Father!"

"Carry out that order!" Father angrily barked at Lian Yunbi.

"OK, on your way, Zhang Jiangsheng!" said Lian Yunbi, quietly but very firmly.

Brother Jiangsheng shot a look of resentment toward Lian Yunbi, then turned and left.

All of Father's excellent qualities, refined by long years of battle, resurfaced during this war exercise. Firmly and decisively, he was always leading the charge. Whenever any part of the total plan developed a problem, he was able to come up with an astute solution. For victory and for progress, his cheeks had grown thin, his throat hoarse, his eyes red, and his lips cracked in these few days. The maneuver ended as a resounding success.

On the final evening of the exercise, all the troops were camping on the steep riverbank. The battlefield, which had been filled with gunfire and dust, returned to being pleasant and peaceful farmland. Birds circled in the sky and dogs of all sizes, which had been too frightened to venture out during the past few days, came around in groups to visit one green tent after another. They looked as if they were delegations sent to convey greetings and appreciation, but actually they spent most of their time circling the steaming cooking pots.

Father and I strolled along the bank, a guard following us at a distance. We walked side by side for half an hour without speaking. Suddenly he stopped.

"Nannan! Do you think you can help me?"

"What?" I nearly jumped out of my skin. Glancing at the reflection of his face on the river, I could see he was very solemn. What kind of help could a general who commands vast armies possibly want from a daughter who was a mere worker? "Father, you—?"

"Can you give me the answers? These problems—how am I to deal with them?" He was gesturing as he spoke, but still I couldn't understand what problems he was referring to.

"What—what problems do you mean?" I asked.

"I mean the problems you raised with me the other night. Plus another one. Here I am, the deputy commandant of a military district, who can command a whole regiment of troops to carry out an attack, and yet when I give an order to discharge an unqualified soldier, every level of every department either does its best to delay the order or doesn't dare carry it out—just because the soldier is my son. Why does this have to be?" Thoroughly miserable, he knit his brow.

I didn't reply but continued quietly listening.

Father heaved a sigh and began to speak again, very slowly, as we walked along. "Heavens! This family is my own creation, and yet I

Short Stories

don't understand it at all. Certain attitudes shaped by family and society are harder to destroy than a fortified enemy defense line. By comparison, the efforts of any individual, no matter how wise, moral, or highly placed he may be, are tiny indeed. I have realized only recently that I've been surrounded for many years. Socialist construction has been going on for thirty years. Thirty years, Nannan! But those attitudes—those burdens passed down to our people by history—are still there. They are the very things we've tried to shed in all of our massive revolutionary campaigns. We've given rivers of blood and mountains of corpses in this cause! Yet we're still bearing the burdens! The only difference seems to be the color of their wrapping. Whose fault is this? Is it the fault of us old-timers? No, it would be unfair to make such a generalization, terribly unfair—"

Why was Father talking about philosophy and sociology to me? His eyes looked particularly bright in the dusk, except that they were tinged with regret. "What do you say, Nannan?" he asked in a hoarse whisper.

I don't know why, but I began shivering under his inquiring gaze. I replied carefully, enunciating every word. "Let me think, Father, let me think. It doesn't seem like the kind of problem one individual can analyze or solve. It must go much deeper. Let me think, Father. At least I can say this for the time being—you and your generation of revolutionaries have contributed greatly to the history of our people's advancement. But, Father, why are you asking *me* these things?"

"Why? Because you're young."

"But, it's a pretty difficult question, Father!"

"Would I ask you if it weren't? The future doesn't belong to us, Nannan. It belongs to you!"

Ming! You're young, too. Can you help me think? Let's figure it out together. The times have left us with too many issues to consider, but I don't feel discouraged. On the contrary, I feel a strong spiritual responsibility.

The future is ours!

Ya'nan
October 25, 1978

THE FIFTH LETTER

Ming:

You probably won't believe this, but I have lost my freedom. I'm writing to you from captivity. This will shock you, and you will certainly insist on knowing the reason. It's a long story.

As soon as Father returned from the war exercise he went directly to the Underground Combat Readiness Headquarters to write

Stubborn Weeds

138

his report. I returned home alone, where Mother was very affectionate toward me. She brought out three suits of clothes and five nylon scarves she had recently bought for me, and proceeded to explain, item by item, how they had not come easily, how they had been purchased at stores limited to foreigners and the families of a very few high-ranking officials, and how they were both high in quality and low in price. After a lengthy commentary on the quality and the stylishness of the clothes and scarves, she insisted that I model them for her. She oohed and aahed, then hugged and kissed me. When I said that these things were of no use to me at all, she tweaked my nose and called me a silly goose. When I told her that my leave was almost over and that I would be going back to the oil rig the next day, her expression changed. "Is it because there's a 'Ming' waiting for you by the sea?" she asked.

I immediately realized that she had intercepted some of the letters you sent me. What did you write in those letters that caused her to look with such fear on our relationship? She insisted that I report your background in detail—your political attitude (actually, she only wanted to know whether or not you're a Party member), education, work history, family income, resources (including savings, personal property, real estate). Of course my report didn't satisfy her. I did fairly well on your background, political attitude, education, and work history, but had to plead ignorance on all the other details. Mother's breathing grew heavier as she listened. Finally she burst out with a scornful pronouncement: "He's just a common citizen—that's what you mean, isn't it?"

Mother has no definition for "common citizen." Like people in the families of many high-ranking cadres, she puts everyone who isn't a high official or peasant into the category of "common citizen."

"You have no self-respect at all!" she shouted at me.

I was flabbergasted. Mother had never spoken to me in that way before. What had I done? What was my crime?

"You don't even know the difference between high class and low class."

What? Since when had I become a high-class person?

She stamped her foot when she saw my continued stupefaction. "The blood in your veins is the blood of a *general!*"

I had never before thought about the fact that the blood of generals does indeed flow in my veins, just as the blood of poor peasants flows in my father's veins. But what does that have to do with high class and low class? Aren't we supposed to be materialists? In the eyes of materialists, there are only different blood types, no high-class or low-class blood. Of course my very simplistic, elementary, and naive way of looking at things infuriated my mother.

"Tomorrow afternoon," she announced, like a diplomat deliver-

Short Stories

ing an ultimatum, "Auntie Sun will be coming in a Red Flag with Dongping—to look you over!"

The words "look over" struck me as funny, and my face must have showed a fleeting smile. Mother mistook this as a sign of acquiescence. Moderating her tone of voice, she said, "You must do something about your looks. Don't go around with that rumpled hair and dirty face."

"Mother," I said earnestly, "I'll be leaving early tomorrow morning."

But Mother cut me off. "Your mother means what she says." Then she closed the door.

"We'll see!" I thought to myself. "If I say I'm leaving, I'm leaving. I too mean what I say!" I assembled my meager luggage, then flopped down on the bed without a second thought. The last few days have been exhausting, and I fell asleep as soon as I lay down.

When I awoke, the morning sunlight was already streaming in. I hurried to wash up and then reached for the doorknob. That's when I discovered I'd been imprisoned! At first I wasn't at all disturbed and actually found the situation comical. Had I become the Zhu Yingtai[7] of the 1970s? The more I thought about the situation, the funnier it seemed. I actually began to laugh out loud. All the windows downstairs have bars on them, so escaping that way was impossible. But I found on the window sill a cup of milk that was still steaming, a dish of pickled vegetables, and two steamed buns. I devoured the food and felt a bit stronger, but I no longer felt like laughing.

As time passed, I began to feel the misery of confinement. I called for my mother, but there was no answer. I called for the houseboy, but again no answer. Then I called for the old cook. Still no answer. Mother had obviously left strict instructions. I tried to calm myself and to analyze what had happened. But I just couldn't figure it out. If I were not wearing a man's shirt but had on an embroidered satin blouse with wide sleeves, if my hair weren't all rumpled but was bedecked with jade hairpins and other gold and silver ornaments, if I weren't a coarse female welder but a delicate, storybook beauty— then the present situation would be understandable. I would accept it as my fate and await the sound of the *suona* horn that heralds the arrival of a bridal sedan chair. I would submit to having a red cloth thrown over my head and to being pushed into the sedan chair. Then, for the rest of my days, I would learn to swallow my blood and tears until I became pale and wan, finally to die before my time. The "weeping at the grave" and "transformation to a butterfly" for which

---

7. Zhu Yingtai, said to have lived in the Eastern Jin dynasty (317–419 A.D.), is the heroine of "Liang Shanbo and Zhu Yingtai", a popular traditional story and drama in many versions. Obliged by her family to marry someone she does not love, Zhu Yingtai and her true love Liang Shanbo turn into butterflies at the story's end.

Stubborn Weeds

Zhu Yingtai is so famous are mere fiction. No such thing ever happens in real life.

But what can I make of this? My father is a general in the People's Liberation Army and a member of the Communist Party. Although my mother hasn't worked for a long time, she is a cadre of World War II vintage and also a long-standing Party member. In her youth she was very progressive. She taught school, led a district Women's Relief Association, and after Liberation was for many years General Secretary of a Party branch at one of the institutes of the Chinese Academy of Sciences. And me? Even as a child, I followed my brothers around as a Red Guard and sang quotations from Chairman Mao to destroy the Four Olds. Is there some organic connection between all of that and my present situation? The connection is more tragic than comic! It is tragic enough to make me weep.

Ming! I have always been a "toughie." I was resettled in the countryside when I was very young, and no matter how tired I was, how distressed, or how abused, I never shed a single tear. But here I am now, weeping. Am I weeping over my own fate? No. In the final analysis, I am still in command of my own fate. There is no "suspense"—as they say in the theater business—in Mother's locking me up here. Nobody need get excited over my situation. I'm hardly a candidate for suicide.

I have quite forgotten what "the American pyramid," who is coming to view me, looks like. In my mind right now he resembles the famous wastrel sons of high officials in Peking opera—with a streak of white on his nose, waving a folded fan, and walking with a swagger. The thought of him makes me break out in laughter through my tears. Weeping and laughing at the same time! A crazy world is driving me a bit crazy, too.

A moment ago Kaidi appeared. The clever creature had quietly put his front paws on the window sill. I went to the window and reached through the bars to caress the silky hair of his head. He looked at me innocently, as though he wanted to ask, "What happened? Can I help?" This gave me an idea. I scribbled a note to Father.

> Father: Please hurry back and rescue me.
> Your Nannan

I drew three feathers on the note to signify "urgent," then folded the note into a small triangle and gave it to Kaidi. Without wasting a second, he took the note in his mouth and sped away as if he understood the idea of "do or die." This once bitter enemy of mine had become my loyal and reliable messenger. But immediately I had regrets about having written such a terse note to Father. What would he think when he received it? It would really be something if he came

Short Stories

with a whole regiment of guards ready to break an encirclement. Ming, never in my wildest dreams would I have imagined that in October 1978 I would lose my freedom and have to be rescued by an experienced old general. Yet I am feeling secretly proud of myself, especially when I imagine Mother and Auntie Sun discovering that I have sprouted wings and flown away, and discovering the note I am leaving on the table for them:

> Let the Red Flag limousine go "look over" another Red Flag limousine. All their parts will be perfectly matched.

I would love to see the expression on their faces and even more the expression on the face of the American pyramid.

A car horn is blaring. Ah yes, that's the sound of Father's car. He's coming. I can hear a car door opening, and now the front door opening, and now Father's footsteps gradually approaching. I'm listening intently, my ear to the door—

At the thought of leaving home, I am dreamily spreading the wings of my imagination and soaring gleefully among layers of clouds in a sky crisscrossed with sunlight. How strange that I should feel now exactly the same way that I felt then about coming home. Why is that? It has finally dawned on me—this is not my home!

Ya'nan
October 26, 1978

JIANG ZILONG *Foundation*

Jiang Zilong (b. 1941), who for many years was a genuine "worker writer" in the Tianjin Heavy Machinery Plant, was unusual in 1979–80 for his ability to please both political critics and large numbers of readers at the same time. Generally speaking, readers were attracted by his satire of bureaucratism and power abuse, and his willingness to raise pointed questions. The critics appreciated his upbeat endings and his keeping wholly "correct" characters at the centers of his stories. His most famous story, "Manager Qiao Assumes Office," received most votes in the 1979 reader preference poll conducted by People's Literature *and also won first prize from the National Short Story Prize Committee. But "Foundation," except for the melodrama in part 7, is superior to "Manager Qiao" in its critical realism. It is also a favorite of the author.*

Originally published in Shanghai wenxue, *No. 12, 1979.*

Translated by Denis C. Mair.
Stubborn Weeds

It was shortly before National Day, and many workers in the forging shop were gathered around their director Lu Yongcun to demand overtime for the holiday. By working three days at double wages, a Grade 3 worker could end up with $5 or so, a Grade 4 worker could get $7 or more, and workers of Grade 5 and above could do even better! But what could they do for overtime work? There was nothing that needed to be done. Everybody pointed out that since the concrete foundation for the 500-ton rapid press—which was the most important piece of equipment in the shop—had already been poured, the press could be installed ahead of schedule over the holiday. But Lu Yongcun emphatically disagreed, arguing that the foundation would have to last well into the next century. He said it was essential to insist on quality as the top priority and to proceed carefully according to the established installation schedule. The workers who were hoping for overtime looked at each other and masked their disappointment as well as they could. But they did not walk away.

This man Lu was tall and thin, with a back that hunched forward and a head of fluffy white hair. His age was difficult to discern—it must have been somewhere between fifty and sixty. His rough, kindly face bore evidence of the tumultuous half-century he had lived through. There was not a trace of guile in his character; he always handled things bluntly. He had a reputation for sometimes passing things up that were there for the taking. The problem now wasn't that he could not see what was on everyone's mind but that he refused to compromise on matters of principle.

The workers expressed their opinions in a clamor of voices, saying it wasn't true that installation ahead of schedule would affect quality, declaring that they might as well just give up and go find odd jobs instead, and tossing unsavory language in old Lu's direction. But Lu Yongcun did not get flustered or angry. He was always earnest, if somewhat preachy, in standing up for his ideas. Once he had decided something, it was hard to make him budge. He remained trapped in his office by the nagging workers until Kang Tongyan, clerk of the forging shop, came to extricate him.

Kang Tongyan was also over fifty, but his hair was still lacquer-black and glossy with oil. The smooth, soft flesh of his face gleamed a childlike pink. His short frame carried an especially protuberant belly which had bent his spine into a bow. But this awkward build belied a great nimbleness. Pushing his way to the center of the crowd, he addressed them in solemn tones: "OK, everybody, don't just stand around yakking. Get back to work, I've got something important to discuss with Director Lu." His keen eyes swept over the group. Then, suspecting they did not believe him, he added, "The main office has decided to withhold all bonuses in this shop starting this month. I've got to see the director right away so I'll know what to do when I take the matter up with the paymaster."

Not only failing to get the overtime pay they wanted, the workers now saw their bonuses being withheld. Realizing that things were not going their way, they unhappily left the office.

Kang Tongyan's eyes crinkled in amusement. This was his specialty—every time Lu Yongcun was stuck with a problem too hot to handle or when people pestered him and he couldn't get free, Kang would fabricate a yarn that contained enough truth in it to convey a sense of urgency. He would say that Lu Yongcun had an urgent phone call from the factory manager or that something had gone wrong and required the director's attention. No one could tell that he was making it up. Sometimes old Lu himself could not detect that Kang Tongyan was secretly covering for him. Artless person that he was, old Lu sometimes took Kang Tongyan's fantastic improvizations at face value, thus obliging Kang to act them out as if they were real.

The workers dispersed, leaving Kang alone with Lu Yongcun, who looked very serious. "Who says the bonuses for our shop will be withheld?" he asked.

"I heard it on the grapevine," Kang Tongyan said with a mysterious laugh.

Lu Yongcun's mood brightened. "Hah! The 'grapevine' again! If that's where you got it, why'd you announce it in front of everyone? You made it sound so convincing, like hard fact! Things like that cause trouble, you know!"

"My grapevine is at least 95 percent reliable. And when I picked up the news I had to get it straight to you. Otherwise, when the main office really does withhold the bonuses, how would you explain things to the workers?" Kang Tongyan was thoroughly displeased at having been reprimanded, yet smiled apologetically as he spoke. His friendship with Lu Yongcun went back more than thirty years. Before Liberation, Kang had been the boss's son in the Kangji Iron Works, where Lu Yongcun had worked as a craftsman. Now the craftsman had become the shop director and the boss's son an errand-running clerk.

After a moment Kang Tongyan offered old Lu some honest advice: "You must not ignore the workers' demands, Mr. Director. I've had my ear to the ground and know that all the other shops are giving overtime. Isn't it up to the individual shop whether there's work? Forget about the foundation for now. Just find them some work— anything—and they'll have their overtime, right? That'll at least keep them from swearing at you. Why make them resent you?"

"What can I do? If we pay out an extra 20 percent in overtime when there's really nothing to do, who suffers? The country, of course! No, we cadres just have to put up with the insults, that's all."

Stubborn Weeds

144

"You have to take insults just because you're a cadre?" Kang Tongyan shook his heavy, mallet-like head but kept the reasons for his disagreement to himself. If the factory belonged to you, he was thinking, then it would be worth taking insults. But, no—they give you the thankless task of directing this shop and only about $50 a month for doing it. Is it worth all the flak you get? So what if the workers get their overtime? It's not coming out of your own pocket, so why resist? Besides, if they get overtime, so do you. You could pick up $6 or $7 for yourself and go have a good time. Why not? Why be so obtuse? Kang figured he understood Lu Yongcun—Lu was a naive straight arrow. No wonder he had never been promoted and probably never would be. Opportunity could hit him on the forehead and he would let it go by.

Suddenly Lu Yongcun remembered something. "Oh, yes, Kang, the Office of Policy Implementation just called and asked you to stop by."

Kang Tongyan's eyes flashed and widened to twice their normal size. His heart was pounding rapidly as he turned to leave, but an afterthought stopped him. "Mr. Director!", he admonished. "Don't forget to go to the paymaster's office to ask about the bonuses."

"I'll go in a minute. On your way tell Xiaoqing I'd like to see her, OK?" Old Lu was turning something else over in his mind.

2

Xi Xiaoqing hung up the telephone, her mind as unsettled as a potful of water at a rolling boil. Her boyfriend Lu Jie, Lu Yongcun's son, had just called to invite her to his house for the holiday. This was called "making acquaintance with the house," which meant that she would formally pay respects to his parents and, more importantly, let all his close friends get a good look at her. Lu Jie had also told her over the phone that he had brought her some fashionable clothes and high-class cloth from Nanjing. This put Xiaoqing in an awkward position. They had known each other only a few months, and she had not expected that Lu Jie would already start making such substantial preparations for their marriage. After seeing Lu Jie a few times, she had discovered that he was not the one for her. The two of them nearly always talked at cross-purposes, and his integrity was a far cry from his father's. Now Lu Jie had invited her to spend National Day at his home. If she went, wouldn't it mean their relationship was definite? On the phone she had neither agreed nor refused but promised to give him an answer before they got off work that day.

Then Kang Tongyan, who had introduced them, arrived to tell her that Director Lu wished to see her. Kang, his face beaming, lowered his voice to say, "I have good news to tell you a little later. Lu Jie says you're still short a television set for the bridal chamber. You just leave that to me!"

With that Kang Tongyan flashed her a mysterious smile and slipped away, his squat body as agile as a bighead carp's.

Xi Xiaoqing's looks were not extraordinary, but she did have an unassuming and wholesome beauty about her. She was quiet by nature and spoke in a subdued, steady voice. She had depth. But the reason she stood so high in Lu Jie's estimation was probably that she was secretary of the shop's branch of the Youth League.

When she walked into Lu Yongcun's office, her heart was pounding like a small drum. Lu Yongcun gestured for her to sit down. "Morale has been pretty low among the workers these days," he began. "They don't work very hard during regular hours, and now they want overtime during the holiday. You people in the Youth League need to do more ideological work among the League members." Xi Xiaoqing breathed easier when she realized Lu was not bringing up her relationship with his son. She nodded her head.

"Are you having difficulties? Has your branch held its new elections yet?"

"Yes, we have," answered Xiaoqing, "but no job assignments have been made. Nobody's willing to be a League cadre. The ones who've been chosen, and who can't get out of it, will serve only on the organization committee. Nobody wants to be on the propaganda committee."

"Why not?"

"Propaganda committee members have to do propaganda, write reports on the blackboard, print up materials, and drum up motivation. It's a thankless job. Organization committee members only have to collect League dues—a snap!"

"What? They really have that kind of attitude?" Lu Yongcun was shocked.

The branch secretary smiled wryly. "I don't know what's going on either, Director Lu. The prestige of our League branch seems pretty low right now. We can't get people to rally around us. The members' sense of honor and responsibility isn't very strong. We still have more than ten League members in our shop, but now more people are quitting than joining. The young ones just don't come. The apprentices won't even fill out a membership application unless you give them a few pep talks."

Xi Xiaoqing was raising questions in Lu Yongcun's mind. As he thought about the problems this branch secretary was facing, he stood up and walked toward her. He looked at her and felt a burning agitation inside his chest. In both work performance and character, Xi Xiaoqing was one of the best young people in the shop. But old Lu had always felt that she was holding something back, something she

Stubborn Weeds

146

dared not reveal to him. He picked this moment to ask, "Well, we have to keep our own thinking on firm ground. Is something on your mind?"

The girl's face reddened and she lowered her head. After a moment she lifted it again and met Lu Yongcun's eyes. "May I ask you a few questions, Director Lu?"

"Sure. What questions?"

Doing her best to suppress her intense feelings, Xi Xiaoqing said, "When the *Communist Manifesto* was first published, Communism was only like a disembodied spirit, yet it gave the capitalist world a terrible fright. They were really afraid of it. But now that there are so many socialist countries in the world, capitalism is no longer afraid of—and even looks down on—socialism. Why is this? If the socialist system is incomparably superior, why don't its productive forces develop as quickly as those of capitalism? Why can't socialism catch up with capitalism in economic and technical development? I might believe, as a matter of faith, that Communism will triumph, that it will eventually win out over capitalism. But whenever I listen to scientific reports or read technical magazines, capitalism is always ahead of socialism. How can we explain this?"

Lu Yongcun, a practical man who usually stayed away from theory, was quite taken aback. These questions might not be immensely difficult, but neither were they easily answered on such short notice. He never would have guessed that Xi Xiaoqing would pose such questions.

Xi Xiaoqing had obviously been doing some deep, hard thinking. She had run these questions through her mind many times. Her voice had started to quaver as she asked them. When she saw the shop director's usually crinkled eyes grow wider and wider, she changed the subject to old Lu himself. "Director Lu, you took part in unions and strikes before Liberation. Was your faith in Communism the same then as now? Revolutionary martyrs used to die for Communism with smiles on their faces, with no doubt that the revolution would be victorious. But how many people have such faith now? And what weight do Communist ideals have in the minds of certain old cadres, even though they lived through those times? How much of their lives is still devoted to the future?"

Lu Yongcun was truly dumbfounded. He simply could not connect these bizarre questions with the League secretary who was usually so enthusiastic and optimistic. His first impulse was not to address her questions but to feel sorry for her and to worry. She'd be better off if her thinking, rather than being so complex, were like that of all those feather-headed girls who wore flowery, bright clothes and talked incessantly of food and fashion. A serious look came over his face.

Short Stories

"What crazy things you think about!"

The girl did not protest, but fixed old Lu with a stubborn gaze as if to say, "You're just as perplexed as I am, aren't you?"

3

Lu Yongcun ran squarely into a brick wall when he went to negotiate bonuses with the Bonus Evaluation Section. As he walked back to the shop, the argument he'd been having with the head of the section was still running through his mind. "Your shop ruined its equipment and stopped production for several months. You've operated at a loss month after month, and you still want bonuses? What a nice dream—"

While listening to this, old Lu had stared angrily for some time without knowing what to say. But now the words came to him: "Of course, by all rights a shop that stops producing and loses money should not get bonuses. But why did our shop stop production? Who is to blame for losing money? Where in the world was there ever a rapid press that went all to hell, including its foundation, only three or four years after being mounted? As soon as the rapid press stopped working last February, we made an urgent report to the main office. Right from the start no one took notice; no one gave a damn. When the cement was there, the reinforcing rods were not. When we got the reinforcing rods, we were short on gravel. We had a terrible time getting the materials together, and then nobody would do the construction work. Things dragged on for more than half a year. You can assemble and mount a whole new press in that much time, but we had to wait eight months just to get the foundation. How could we avoid losses? Am I, Lu Yongcun, to blame? Is it the fault of the shopworkers? Why do you have to withhold the bonuses? And another thing—all the other shops are giving bonuses. Only the forging shop is being left out. How am I supposed to go on as shop director? What will I say to the workers?"

There were plenty of good arguments, but he had been upset at the time and anger had tied his tongue. Now, as he calmed down, the arguments came to mind one by one. Old Lu was annoyed at himself. He was not actually dull-witted, and was perfectly articulate as long as he was allowed to speak in his slow, judicious manner. He never interrupted when others were talking, and he could not present his opinions well when others interrupted him. When he got involved in buck-passing squabbles and red-faced shouting matches, people needed only to butt in when he opened his mouth, and he was speechless. No matter how right he was, everything stayed bottled up inside. As a consequence he was always the whipping boy at the meetings of middle-level factory cadres. Even the factory manager,

Stubborn Weeds

148

when feeling out of sorts, would swallow his anger at the other shops and take it out on Lu Yongcun by picking on the forging shop. Lu Yongcun was a sure bet not to get irritated or give any trouble. But although people pushed him around, everyone throughout the factory admitted that he was a great guy and a conscientious, down-to-earth workhorse.

The people in the forging shop were all waiting for the good news their director would bring back, but when they saw the way Lu was hanging his head and muttering as he walked, they cooled off right away. To them, those five or six extra dollars were no laughing matter. People began tossing off insolent remarks, deliberately raising their voices so old Lu could hear.

"Nice guys get the short end of the stick, and that's the way it's always going to be. Our boss Lu's a loser! He's the only flaming soldier in that bunch of flaming generals, and we all take it on the chin with him!"

"You can tell a good horse by how it walks, and a good man by how he talks. Our Director Lu can't pull anything off!"

Honesty is supposed to be a virtue—an expression of Party spirit—but these workers were equating it with foolishness, incompetence, and dullness. When the badgering continued for several days, old Lu pretended not to hear. The sorry state of the forging shop was due to his own failures in leadership. He could hardly blame the workers for their insolent remarks. But the longer he remained silent, the more insistent the complaints became, until some people even stopped working. This made him lose his temper.

"So you're going to stop work just because of a few lost dollars in bonuses? Money's the only reason you work, huh? Your consciences feel comfortable with that?"

Seeing the change in the director's countenance, the workers fell silent. Everyone knew he was suffering too, and was just as powerless as they. But one young fellow would have no part of this mood. "Conscience?" he blared. "My conscience tells me to take pay for work, to eat food, and to wear clothes."

"If everyone thought like you, could this country ever modernize?"

"I'm a worker. I can't be concerned with all that."

Old Lu's lips were trembling with rage. The workers prevailed upon the rash young man to leave, and old Lu went back to his office. He was being pressured from above and jostled from below. Caught in the middle, how could he keep doing his job? If things kept dragging on like this, the forging shop really would go to pieces. He would just have to put up with the workers' abuse and proceed with arrangements for the work they would have after the holiday. He suddenly wondered whether Lu Jie, who was supposed to have re-

Short Stories

turned many days ago, had in fact come back. He reached for the telephone.

An impact cushion was needed in order to install the 500-ton rapid press. Twenty days ago the Supply Section had sent Lu Jie south on a purchasing trip. Before his son left, Lu Yongcun had instructed him in no uncertain terms that he must get the impact cushion and come back with it immediately. Now old Lu was dialing the Infrastructure Construction Section, where Lu Jie himself answered. When he heard his son's ebullient voice, old Lu felt better right away, assuming Lu Jie had succeeded in buying the impact cushion. But Lu Jie casually told him that he had not bought the cushion because the source factory had none. A buzz sounded in Lu Yongcun's head. If Lu Jie had been standing before him, old Lu would have smacked him. His son had ruined it! Meanwhile Lu Jie, failing entirely to perceive his father's irritation, prattled on about how he had brought a load of good lumber back from the south. He asked his father to leave work early to help him bring the lumber from the station to their home. When old Lu refused, Lu Jie's tone changed immediately. He complained that his father showed no concern for his affairs and pressed his point with some glib reasoning. When has there ever been a father who did not make arrangements for his son's wedding? He answered his own question with numerous examples: so-and-so's father had bought such-and-such furniture for his son; so-and-so's father had managed to get a certain kind of house for his son. The point was that Old Lu was singular among fathers in his disregard for his son's welfare.

Old Lu, furious, hung up on his son. Preparations, preparations! Lu Jie and Xi Xiaoqing had seen each other only a few times, but most of the things for the wedding had already been rounded up. What about the arrangements for the shop? What about arrangements for the factory?

Lu Yongcun was at the end of his patience. He was itching to do something, but there was nothing he could do. He stormed out of the office and, without thinking, found his way onto the new foundation for the rapid press. He was suddenly aware that the shop was uncommonly quiet. How could a forging shop lack the sounds of steel hammering against iron? Where was the rumble of the overhead crane? Even the wheezing, bellowing furnace stood silent. How he wished he could still hear the familiar, deafening sound of heavy impact! Such stillness in an ironworking shop was not a good thing. It was the sort of silence that could strangle a person.

Old Lu had been working with iron most of his life. The conditions and equipment in his line of work had steadily improved, but the work itself had become more difficult and less profitable. Back when he had started as an apprentice, the factory owner had earned piles of money with nothing more than workers swinging heavy hammers. With the money rolling in, the owner had bought a press with upper and lower dies, and this had brought in even more money. After a time the hammer became worn, and its stem had begun to crack around the edges. So they bound it tight with wire and went on using it, and the money kept gushing in. Who ever heard of losing money on an ironworks? How could it be that this mining machinery plant, which employed thousands of people, and this forging shop, with hundreds of workers, would lose money? What was the root of the problem?

Lu Yongcun was squatting on the foundation, hands clasped behind his head. He stared fixedly at the mass of reinforced concrete as he thought about these questions. He could not answer them, but he did notice a place on the foundation that was not very solid. He knocked at it with an iron bar, and off came a big piece of concrete like a lump of bean curd. This gave him quite a start. He immediately went over the whole foundation very carefully. What he found was hardly reassuring. Old Lu was not a mason, but he was an experienced ironworker, and he was sure something was wrong. The Construction Section was responsible for the rapid press foundation. He went back to his office and called the head of the Construction Section.

"Supervisor Yu? There's something wrong with the foundation of the 500-ton rapid press! I poked it with an iron bar and a piece fell off. How's it going to take 500 tons of pressure?"

"Well of course if you poke it with an iron bar you can poke some pieces loose!" the supervisor replied sarcastically. "Why don't you try using explosives? Maybe you can blast it sky high!"

"That foundation is nothing to joke about, Yu! The first time we installed this rapid press, we had to dig up the foundation and replace it after only four years! What other country does things that way? Other people use these things for decades or even a century. A foundation is supposed to outlive two or three presses. If we go on like this, our country will lose so much money it's not funny! Why don't you take a sample from the foundation and run tests on it!"

"No need for that. If anything's wrong with the foundation, we here at Construction will take responsibility. It'll be quite enough if you just mind your own shop!" The supervisor angrily hung up the phone.

This was rubbish. Was there no end to the wrangling, the accusations, the anger? "Just keep on wrangling," Lu Yongcun muttered to himself. "Wrangle, wrangle, wrangle. Wrangle your hair white! Wrangle the factory to the brink of ruin! But don't stop wrangling!"

Kang Tongyan was prancing along as if there were springs under his feet. The Policy Implementation Office had just absolved him of his "reactionary capitalist" label. What an immeasurable relief! He opened the office door at the forging shop to find Lu Yongcun staring vacantly at the telephone. "Old Lu!" he called out crisply.

Lu Yongcun raised his head to see the look of satisfaction on Kang's face. "What's up, Kang?" he asked.

Kang Tongyan laughed. "Don't play games, old Lu. You were the one who did it all for me, weren't you?" Kang was a smooth talker. He knew it had been Party Central's decision to press the new policy, but he chose to direct his appreciation to Lu Yongcun. Lu Yongcun had indeed been good to him these past years. Even after Kang had been pinned with a bad label, he had not been treated as a reactionary element in the forging shop. When he got older and could no longer stand physical labor, Lu Yongcun had appointed him clerk of the office. This allowed him to make use of his special abilities and also put a bit of authority into his hands. From then on, he had been willing to scamper everywhere, serving as the big talker for the forging shop. In his heart he was grateful for Lu Yongcun's consideration.

Lu Yongcun finally understood what Kang was talking about and handed him a cigarette. "You should thank the Party for removing your label," he said. "If you want to think about something, think about how to get the forging shop back on the track."

For a moment Kang Tongyan didn't see what Lu Yongcun was driving at. "Well—how am I supposed to do that?"

"What if I were to turn the forging shop over to you, as if it were your privately owned operation; what would you do?"

"Turn it over to me?" In his surprise Kang Tongyan's blood coursed into his head, and his blood pressure seemed to rise. He was confident of his own abilities and was also sure that Lu Yongcun knew he was no slouch. He had pulled the director out of many sticky situations in the past. Could it be that Lu Yongcun wanted to promote him to vice-director of the shop now that his label had been removed? Good heavens! Would glad tidings really come twice in one day? His appetite for authority, suddenly revived, burned his face red and sent waves of heat through his body.

Seeing that Kang's thoughts had taken him elsewhere, Lu Yongcun came back to the point: "In the old days when your father opened the Kangji Iron Works, he had only those few hearths and a few dozen men. I remember you never came to work. You were always out in the country hunting rabbits and trapping birds, and in the evenings you visited brothels. You'd show up at the shop only if you felt like it. But the place did earn lots of money. These days working

Stubborn Weeds

conditions are much better. We have more equipment and more people. So why do we operate at a loss?"

Kang Tongyan understood. He clearly realized the shop director's difficulties and frustrations, and replied in an acrimonious tone that he had not dared to use in over ten years. "I think you've done a respectable job just to get the forging shop to run as well as it does," he said. "After all, it's not your private operation."

"What do you mean by that? You think I'm not giving it everything I have?"

"You've done all you can but in a blind effort. If you owned the shop and it sank to this condition, you'd have to close up. You and yours would have to commit suicide or else go begging in the streets. The unemployed workers would have to look elsewhere to feed themselves. They sure wouldn't have it as nice as they do now, earning money while they gossip all day. The Communist Party is generous and tolerant. The superiority of socialism is in sharing the available food with everyone."

"The shop is going bad because of my inability—"

"What inability? The shop isn't yours, so you don't have complete authority over it. And therefore you have no prestige with the workers. They can listen to you or not, as they choose. Instead of controlling the workers by getting a grip on their basic interests, you have to control them through political campaigns. And after too many campaigns, you find there are certain side effects, just like the side effects of too much medicine. Party members are even less obedient than the activist nonmembers. Remember a few years ago when everybody was competing to get workers of the Four Black Categories, just because they were more obedient and hardworking than people from the Five Red Categories?[1] If the person in charge of a factory doesn't consider the factory his own, do you think he'll run it well? If the truth were known, there *is* no boss in our factory now. It doesn't belong to the factory manager; it doesn't belong to you shop directors; and of course it doesn't belong to the workers. You'll probably say it belongs to the Party or the country. But since when can the head of a national government concern himself with every single factory?"

"There you go talking nonsense again." Lu Yongcun stared furiously at his former boss's son. What really made him furious was that Kang Tongyan's words were not entirely nonsense. In fact they made him think of what Xi Xiaoqing had been saying. These two people—completely different in their experience, political background, and age—had expressed some of the same things. This was so uncanny that Lu Yongcun's fury gave way to a shudder.

1. See glossary.

Short Stories

But Lu Yongcun's remark had sent a chill through Kang Tongyan and had brought him quickly back to his senses. "What an ass I am," he thought to himself. "I get pleased with myself and forget who I am. Good thing Lu Yongcun is a decent, kindhearted sort. If he were somebody else I could get reported, and that label I just got rid of would be pinned right back on me." He broke out in a cold sweat. Wreathing his face in an apologetic smile, he hurried to say, "I was just letting my mouth flap, Mr. Director. Don't take me seriously."

"You didn't have to feed me that line. Look at the act you put on!" Lu Yongcun said, showing disgust. "There's a problem with the quality of the rapid press foundation, but the Construction Section won't run a check on it. Can you do something?"

Kang Tongyan perked up. He was always ready to help Lu Yongcun with a problem and was confident that there was nothing in the factory he could not handle. He pulled a pack of cigarettes from his briefcase and turned it over in his hand. "Leave this to me," he said with a laugh. "I'll find a way to get somebody over there to do it." As he finished speaking, Kang Tongyan turned to go. Then something else occurred to him. He pulled a wad of money from his briefcase and put it in Lu Yongcun's hand. "This is for Lu Jie," he said solemnly.

"Where'd this money come from?"

"He's still short a television set for the bridal suite. As the person who introduced them, I thought this was the least I could do."

Old Lu lost his temper. "I'll have nothing to do with this!" he roared.

Kang Tongyan took the money back in chagrin. "All right, then I'll give it directly to Lu Jie."

5

When Lu Yongcun read the test results that Kang Tongyan brought back, he stood shaking helplessly in anger. The entire foundation for the 500-ton rapid press was below standard. The design had called for a strength rating of 200, and the actual rating was only 90. Production had been halted for seven months, and this was what they had waited for! Over a hundred tons of cement and over thirty tons of steel reinforcing rods had been wasted. Even worse was the great waste of time. Once again they would have to hack the huge foundation to pieces with picks and put in another foundation. There was no telling how many more months *that* would take!

In all this misfortune one thing was very fortunate. Imagine the consequences if Lu Yongcun had not checked for problems with the foundation and had not asked Kang Tongyan to have secret tests done. If they had gone their merry way and mounted the press anyway, the result could have been genuinely catastrophic. The factory manager, as enraged as Lu Yongcun, called an urgent meeting. All supervisors and directors were to be present.

The supervisor of the Construction Section had started out as an allotment clerk. Though gaunt and monkeylike, he had a stentorian voice. Known as one of the factory's "four iron mouths," he led the Construction Section with great flair and was reputed to be one of the cleverest and most capable middle-level cadres at the plant. But today the manager's interrogation left him dumbfounded. He had not had the slightest warning of it. He asked to see the report Lu Yongcun was holding. One look told him the tests had been done by someone in his own section. This made him seethe inside. "The bastards sell out their own people to help outsiders. They do sneak tests for others and don't even let me know when they find trouble!"

But by the time he had finished reading the report, he had already formulated a reply. He lifted his head and, with a sincere and comely smile on his face, spoke in a confident and unapologetic tone. "This is not our fault. There was nothing wrong with the way we did the job. The failure in quality is due to lack of bonding strength in the cement. And I have to point out here that the residence hall now under construction is being built with the same batch of cement. If something goes wrong there in the future, my department can accept no responsibility."

See how cleanly and lightly he shifted the blame? These days personal power, and success as a cadre, require nothing more than the gift of gab. Lu Yongcun was flabbergasted. Before he could think of a reply, someone else answered for him. This was the supervisor of the Supply Section, a tough-looking middle-aged fellow whose lips were stained from cigarettes. The factory's Supply Section was like a department store or grocery store elsewhere. People often needed its help, but it seldom needed anything from others. Because of this, people involved in supply work were puffed up with a sense of their own importance. This supervisor, who was well known throughout the factory as Lin the Big Taker, now abruptly lifted his head from the sofa and addressed the supervisor of the Construction Section coldly.

"Look, Yu," he said. "If you can't take the heat, don't try to shift it to others. You can't just bite whomever you like with that iron mouth of yours, you know! All of our cement is certified for quality. What do you mean 'low bonding strength'? Why didn't you run your tests before you started the job? It was obviously good cement, but your people ruined it, and now you turn around and lash out at me!"

Immediately the meeting was in an uproar as the two antagonists went at each other. Listening to this verbal battle, a person who did not know the true story would have felt quite torn. Both sides had mastered the key to effective prevarication—if one can speak with

Short Stories

self-righteous assurance, the validity of one's position is halfway established. The truth counts for nothing.

The factory manager's towering stature and ruddy complexion gave the impression of an expansive heart housed in a generously proportioned body. He wanted to fix the blame and wrap the case up. But when he pointed at the Construction Section, Iron Mouth Yu glibly weaseled out of it. When he pressed the Supply Section to admit error, Big Taker Lin was even firmer in his denial. The manager's anxiety to settle the matter was useless; angry stares alone would not resolve it. The situation was most peculiar—a factory manager is supposed to have control over his supervisors, but certain things were now clearly beyond his control. And a supervisor's authority is supposed to be less than a factory manager's, but when these supervisors discovered areas beyond their manager's control, they ran wild. Each exploited the other's vulnerabilities. It seemed that sometimes everyone had authority and sometimes no one had it: when doing their jobs, it seemed that everyone lacked authority, or did not choose to use it; but when they were out for their private advantage, they had plenty of authority and were only too ready to use it. The complex of "connections" among the cadres was based on an interlocking, hopelessly tangled maze of utter balderdash.

Lu Yongcun sat off to one side, helpless with anxiety.

Seeing that there was really nothing he could do, the manager had no choice but to wave his hands and put a stop to the battle of tongues. "All right, enough of this baloney. We'll look into the problem of responsibility later. First let's decide what to do about the foundation."

Lu Yongcun winced inwardly, knowing that the manager had given in. He would not get to the bottom of a mistake even this big.

Big Taker Lin lay back on the sofa. "Deciding what to do about the foundation doesn't involve my department," he remarked casually.

"What do you say we should do?" the manager enquired of Iron Mouth Yu.

"Beats me," said Yu nonchalantly.

Lu Yongcun could no longer restrain himself. "Somebody's going to have to go back to work, hack the bad foundation apart, and put in a new one!"

"Who?" asked Iron Mouth.

"Your people, of course. It was your job in the first place, and you were the ones who botched it."

The supervisor of construction glowered. "Who cares what you think? The problem hasn't been analyzed yet. Responsibility hasn't been determined. The manager hasn't even ruled on the case. So what right does somebody like you have to jump in?"

Stubborn Weeds

156

"Well—" the question alone was enough to fluster Lu Yongcun. His philosophy of life was that honesty would always win out over dishonesty. But others held exactly the opposite philosophy—that dishonesty overcomes honesty. When these two philosophies crossed blades, old Lu always lost. All he could say was, "If you don't do it, who will? Maybe you can afford the delay, but the rest of us can't. And in the long run the country will suffer."

The supervisor of the Construction Section answered him sarcastically. "You think you're the only one worried about our country's modernization? I'm even more wrought up than you. It's just dandy to say we should do it, but right now I don't have any men free. If I'm going to hack apart the foundation, I'll have to stop work on the residence hall."

"Impossible!" interrupted the manager, worried by this threat.

"I have an idea," Iron Mouth Yu said with a laugh. "Old Lu, aren't the people in your shop standing around all day with nothing to do? Maybe you should hack it apart yourselves."

So the burden, having been shunted everywhere, was finally shunted onto the forging shop.

"That isn't our job," spluttered an outraged Lu Yongcun. "We are iron-workers. We can't do this work!"

"What's all this 'you' and 'us' stuff? It's all for the sake of our country's Four Modernizations!" Iron Mouth Yu lay back on the sofa, pulled a filter cigarette from the factory manager's pack, and held it between his lips. "Hey, don't think only of yourself!" he said, holding out his hand.

Big Taker Lin pulled out another cigarette and tossed it to Iron Mouth. "Look at you," he chuckled. "So stingy you ought to be called Iron Rooster[2] instead of Iron Mouth. Whenever there's a meeting, you smoke nothing but 'Extended Hand' brand cigarettes."

Iron Mouth Yu, never one to let someone get the better of him, returned the compliment. "I hear from your men that you can teach an honest man to cheat his father in only three months!"

The two men lit their cigarettes and burst out laughing. The fierceness of their argument a moment ago had been bogus. The mock antagonism would be forgotten immediately after the meeting and would have no effect on their personal relationship. Old Lu simply was not in the same league as these two supervisors. Feeling greatly pained, he suddenly recalled the question Kang Tongyan had raised not long before. Who *did* this mining machine plant belong to? Among the manager and supervisors sitting before him, there was not one man who regarded the factory as his own. A serious problem had arisen, and they were not even worried! "Don't tell me this plant

2. The feathers of an iron rooster cannot, of course, be plucked; thus it can pluck things from others with impunity.

has become mine by default!" old Lu mused. No, the plant belonged to the Party. But where was the Party? Was the Party a real thing or an illusion? The Party had been deceived. These people were taking advantage of the Party! Not one of them viewed the Party as more important than himself. It was the Party that had entrusted them with their positions, but they had played games with the Party and had ruined the foundation. They had turned into out-and-out liars. Oh, Xiaoqing, weren't these the very answers you were looking for?

Lu Yongcun had always lacked the ability to make quick, penetrating judgments, but today he suddenly understood many things he had not dared to confront in the past. He realized that when the social environment calls for certain characteristics in people, those characteristics will naturally develop. If there were no need for buck-passing and wrangling, society would not produce slick characters. But when the need is there, people naturally learn the ropes. Just look at his own son, Lu Jie, who was right in there learning to be like Big Taker Lin.

The factory manager thought things over for a moment, then settled the matter. "It's probably best if your shop goes ahead and tears up the bad foundation," he said to Lu Yongcun. "You can send your men over to the Construction Section to learn how it's done."

6

Lu Yongcun returned to his shop, called the workers together in front of the 500-ton rapid press, and assigned duties for demolishing the foundation. The workers were indignant, not only because tearing apart the foundation was dirty, tiring, and extremely difficult work, but also because it was so absurd that they were the ones to do it. The Construction Section had committed an error so grave that their supervisor should have been dismissed and their bonuses withheld to compensate the forging shop for its losses. But look how things had turned out! Not only had the Construction Section evaded all responsibility; they had even ended up being bailed out by the forging shop. First the forging shop's bonuses had been withheld, and then this highly undesirable job had been assigned to them. Were the shopworkers supposed to accept this gleefully?

Lu Yongcun understood the workers' dissatisfaction but had no power to change anything. The basic problem had been developing over the past ten or even twenty years, and now it all seemed to become old Lu's personal burden. The workers were complaining angrily when someone suddenly noticed that Director Lu was sitting white-faced and crumpled over inside the foundation pit.

"Director Lu!" The workers rushed to his side. Lu Yongcun himself did not know what had happened. At first there had been only a

Stubborn Weeds

158

feeling of distress, then difficulty in breathing, then a series of wringing chest pains that gradually overcame him. Xi Xiaoqing and a number of young workers hastened to prop him up. His blood pressure and heart had never shown any signs of abnormality, but today he was suddenly being stricken by a heart attack. A frightening shadow passed across his face. Spasm after spasm contorted his facial muscles as he forced himself to bear the intense pain.

Old Lu urged everyone back to work, saying that he would be all right. But Xi Xiaoqing, who wanted to stay and take care of him, refused to go. Suddenly thinking of his son's marriage, old Lu felt he had to draw the girl aside. "My boy Lu Jie is an ass," he whispered. "He's not good enough for you—" Old Lu wanted to go on, but when he saw the color rush to Xiaoqing's face and the tears well in her eyes, he could not.

A moment later old Lu, obviously fighting pain, spoke to Xiaoqing as firmly as he could manage. "I want you to organize a Youth League rush squad who will set themselves a goal of hacking this ruined foundation apart within one month." As he spoke he pulled a roll of bills from his pocket and pressed it into Xiaoqing's hand. "Use this money for bonuses. If it's not enough, I'll give you more on my next payday—"

Xiaoqing felt a lump in her throat and could not hold back her tears. She handed the roll of bills back to old Lu. "Don't worry, Director Lu," she sobbed. "I promise we'll finish the job on time without a cent of bonus money."

"No, take it. This is tough work. And it's all my fault. I didn't do my job well, and everybody else has to suffer for it!" Old Lu insistently stuffed the money into Xiaoqing's hand.

When the ironworkers heard about this, they flocked around old Lu in consternation. They spoke in quavering voices. "You still don't really know what makes us tick, Director Lu. What we say is just a lot of talk, but when there's work to do, we do it. We were shooting our mouths off just now but not because of you. What we can't stand is this crazy business where right and wrong is for the birds and all that matters is somebody's goddamn mouth. Please don't take it personally! If it'll help get production going, we'll do the job even though the Construction Section won't. And when we finish we'll drag them to the authorities and get justice! All of us'll join the rush squad, and we'll hack in shifts around the clock! We'll do just fine without bonuses. We don't work just for money, you know!"

Lu Yongcun laughed in delight and kept laughing until teardrops rolled down his face. Then another terrible burst of pain nearly made him pass out. For the workers, the sight of great beads of sweat on their director's drawn face was as painful as a whiplashing. The workers were starting to lift him up to take him to the hospital when

Director Lu struggled to raise his head and fixed them with a wide-eyed angry stare. "Put me down, you numbskulls!" he roared. "I'm not sick. It's our shop and our factory that are really sick—sick at their very foundation!"

A flurry of voices rushed to comfort him. "Take it easy. We'll tear apart the bad foundation, Mr. Director!" Someone brought a canvas-backed chair, and they helped him to sit down in it. "Watch us start in right now; we'll take care of this foundation!"

A ray of hope swept across Lu Yongcun's face. "The factory is our country's foundation; we can't go on mismanaging it this way." He was pronouncing each word slowly and solemnly. "We must not plant the seeds of future disaster for our country. The foundation—the foundation—"

When the workers said they would work, they meant it. The forging shop leaped instantly into feverish activity. Strange though it seems, on that day the ironworkers were doing construction work more efficiently than experienced construction workers. Xi Xiaoqing rounded up young workers from the Youth League, who looked like little tigers as they busily carried heavy loads on shoulder poles. When Kang Tongyan came along carrying his briefcase, he could not believe the bustle before his eyes. He glanced sheepishly at the director. Old Lu pointed to a crowbar on the floor. "What are you waiting for?" he shouted rousingly. "See that crowbar?" With a quizzical squint of his small eyes, Kang Tongyan separated his thin lips just enough to pronounce the words, "OK, OK." Then he threw down his briefcase, picked up the crowbar, and without a backward glance strode toward the people who were attacking the bad foundation.

Two Stories from the
Unofficial Press

From 1978 to 1980, a number of literary magazines appeared in China that did not have official sponsorship.[1] The best known of these, Today (Jintian), thrived in the ferment around "Democracy Wall" in Beijing. (Two poems from Today appear on p. 184 and p. 187). Most of the others were run by literary clubs at universities, where they had semi-official status at best. In fall 1979, thirteen student literary magazines from China's leading universities launched a project to publish a national quarterly called Our Generation (Zheiyidai). *The political critics, fearing that such activity could get out of hand, felt ambivalent from the start, and the first issue confirmed their fears: it was too audacious—both artistically, which was irritating, and politically, which was unacceptable. Only half of the first issue (which proved to be the only issue) was actually printed. A last minute message to readers, mimeographed on the inside front cover, explained, "For reasons that everyone can surmise, and which are understandable, the printers with whom we have contracted suddenly ceased printing this journal of student literary compositions. Hence we must gather our fragments and greet our readers in the present incomplete form."*

The two stories that follow were published in Our Generation. *Xiao Yi's "The Little Egg Girl" is similar in theme to Liu Zhen's "The Girl Who Seemed to Understand." While its young author lacks the maturity of vision that Liu Zhen commands, he represents well the characteristics of his generation of writers. He faces reality directly and writes with little care for face-saving circumlocution.*

An Dong's "The Sea Does Not Belong to Us" is about the malaise of urban youth, especially former Red Guards. The story is noteworthy less for its theme than for its experiment with form. With China's reopening to the West in the late 1970s, many writers and readers, especially youth, looked eagerly to discover what the West had been doing in literature. What they found and fixed upon, rather too narrowly, was "stream of consciousness." Yet some of the works that appeared under this banner were interesting, and were certainly refreshing additions to China's literary scene. Their importance as innovations in China can be measured, ironically, by the sharp backlash of conservative opinion against them. According to some critics,

---

1. The evanescent unofficial publications of 1978–80 are often called "underground literature," a designation that is inappropriate. The unofficial publications of those years were not formally illegal, and were edited, produced, and distributed rather openly. Besides, to call them "underground" obscures an important distinction from a very different kind of truly underground, and formally illegal, literature that was usually hand-copied, string-bound, and passed around secretly. During 1979–80 most of this underground literature consisted of love stories, detective stories, and other kinds of entertainment fiction.

anything that was not plainly expository and understandable by a majority of readers on first reading was either frivolous or pretentious, and thus unfit for publication in a socialist country. Yet some young and middle-aged writers persisted, and experiments with literary form continued after the demise of the unofficial press.

XIAO YI *The Little Egg Girl*

I am writing this story certainly not because of its mystery or wonder, or because it will shake heaven and earth. If the historic incident which occurred on that day[1] was like a landslide, my story is only like a little spark from a fire. Yet I feel impelled to record this because it is like a thorn in my flesh, whose nagging pain leaves a permanent impression in my consciousness.

The weather that day was not as writers often depict it, with evil winds howling and turbid clouds obscuring the sky. At least in X county, the bright sunshine of April had already brought the hint of spring to the branches of the trees and was spreading through the path-laced fields. The gentle southerly breeze that brushed my face gave me a faint sensation of headiness. It was our last afternoon on the work project, and while everyone else was taking a nap, I slipped out alone to take a stroll up the main street.

X county, worthy of comparison to Dazhai,[2] did not fit very well the common image of a county town. It had no clamorous markets, and it lacked the congestion of oxcarts and pack mules. On one side of the neatly made asphalt road were the shiny glass display windows of a department store; on the other was a great billboard advertising a model play [3] at the movie theater. A large hotel and a new county office building were under contruction. On the office building the names of the county Party organs were mounted in rows of large and small red characters. As I casually surveyed the beautiful fields and gardens under a cloud-dotted blue sky, and let my thoughts turn to the epic struggle for sustenance that I had been witnessing over the past few days, the poet in me was suddenly brought to life. Yes! The

1. See "Tiananmen Incident" in glossary.
2. A commune in a barren and remote area of north China, Dazhai was held up as a national agricultural model during the Cultural Revolution.
3. During the Cultural Revolution, eight model plays dominated China's theater and film.

working classes were drowning poverty and backwardness with their own sweat. They were the masters of nature and, more importantly, the masters of their own destiny.

"Buy some eggs?" The timid voice shattered my daydream. I halted to discover that I had unwittingly strayed into a small alley. Following the voice, I met the cautious, searching eyes of a little girl of ten or eleven years, who was squatting near a pitch-smeared electric pole. She was completely enveloped by an excessively large black padded coat, the front and shoulders of which were spotted with blackened pieces of encrusted rice gruel. A fine layer of yellow dust coated her elegant face, which obviously hadn't been washed for days, and lusterless hair tumbled about her forehead. A piece of dried phlegm was clinging to her tightly pursed upper lip. I gave her a sweeping glance but didn't see any eggs.

"Are you selling eggs?" I asked. She nodded slightly and lifted the hem of her coat, which was dragging in the dust, to expose a black, warped bamboo basket. I moved closer and lifted the yellowed cloth that covered the basket. Wow! Huge hen eggs! Each egg, chalk-white in the sunlight, revealed the yellowish fluid moving within, as though encased in frosted glass.

"How much a pound?" I asked, fingering the eggs. Considering the present egg supply in Beijing, I might as well take some home to counter my mother's impression of me as a hopeless bookworm whose awareness was limited to the world of academics.

"Ten cents," she said in a flat voice.

"Ten cents a pound?" I asked, opening my eyes wide in surprise. That was too cheap to believe.

"Hah," she laughed, "ten cents *each.*"

My cheeks reddened. We hidebound intellectuals do not even know the basic unit of exchange in the countryside, and yet we come out to "audit the situation." To cover my blunder, I stood there pretending to compare the sizes of two eggs.

"Isn't—isn't that too expensive?" I asked.

"Hens lay less in the spring," she replied, taking the eggs from my hand and replacing them in the basket. Thinking she was about to leave, I took my wallet from my pocket.

"I'll buy two pounds—I mean, twenty eggs." Although I'd never been in a rural market before, I had heard that if you were too straightforward with the peasants they would take advantage of you. And, sure enough, these eggs got smaller and smaller the farther down I dug in the basket. After I had managed to pick out eighteen eggs, the rest seemed mediocre. I glanced at her and felt, to be honest, a bit of resentment. Where did she get the cunning and guile of a merchant at such a tender age? Perhaps sensing my suspicion, she turned her face away. Oh, well, what can you do? There is a maxim

Short Stories

among teachers: "the ingenuity of the small producer is the hotbed of capitalism."

I placed the eggs, one by one, securely in my book bag and handed over $2. She fixed her eyes on the bills with a hesitant look and waited until I stood up before calling out in a singsong voice: "Won't you buy two more?"

"Why?" I asked, puzzled at first. "Mm. No, the ones at the bottom are too small."

"Buy two more; I don't have any change," she said in a more subdued voice, hanging her head. So that was it.

"All right, I'll buy another two," I replied, made vulnerable by a wave of sympathy.

When she raised her head slightly, I expected to see a faint smile of gratitude, but she was as expressionless and indifferent as before. I squatted down again and had just placed the eggs in my bag when a thin, dirty hand reached into the basket and snatched two eggs. Startled, the girl and I turned in unison to look.

A young fellow was leaning on the opposite side of the electric pole. Tufts of long, thick, unkempt hair hung down in his eyes. Not a single button was left on his black padded coat, and he had only a piece of rope tied about his waist. As though no one were watching, he broke the eggs, tipped back his head, and poured the light yellow liquid between his dry, cracked lips.

I sprang to my feet, grabbed his arm, and glared at him; although he looked young, his face bore the traces of having weathered many a storm.

"What's the big idea? What's the big idea?" he demanded, stiff-necked and struggling.

"Pay up," I snapped harshly. "Twenty cents!"

His expression changed in an instant. "Hey, old buddy!" he said. "You're from Beijing! I can tell by your accent. We're all in the same boat here—sent down to the countryside to work—'educated youths' supposed to 'build revolution'—ha!—so let's not make a big deal over a couple of dimes, huh? Look at this." He lifted his lapels, which were shiny with grease. "I own nothing but the clothes on my back!"

"If you don't have any money, why do you steal people's eggs? If you're from Beijing—"

"—get together and pool our poverty, huh? The officials rip people off by the basketful and truckload. You mean us regular guys can't grab a bit on the side?"

"What the devil are you talking about?" I shook his arm.

"What are you doing? You really want to get tough? I'm telling you, I'm ready for you!"

"Mister!"

The little girl was calling from behind me in a low voice. Turning

Stubborn Weeds

164

around, I was puzzled to see her imploring expression. Then I suddenly felt a sharp blow on the back of my hand. My fingers were jolted loose, and the young man pulled his arm from my grip. He scampered several paces away and stopped with his hands on his hips.

"Go order the big shots around, if you're so smart," he shouted. "Why get your kicks picking on the little guy? Look at the great hero!"

A wave of anger welled inside me. I put down my book bag intending to pursue him but was stopped by the pitiful voice of the little girl.

"Let him go, mister. I don't want the twenty cents." Perhaps it was because I looked so astonished that she explained in a quiet voice, "They—they've got it pretty tough, too."

Oh—people are so complicated! Every padded coat conceals a heart—some saintly and beautiful, some coated with dirt. Not knowing how to comfort the girl, I silently took out two of the largest eggs and put them in her hand, but in the same silent manner she handed them back.

"No, little girl, I'll take the twenty cent loss." She shook her head and sighed.

"Mister, if you have any more money—buy a few more eggs," she said, raising her long eyelashes. Without waiting for my response and almost as if speaking to herself, she added: "Nine cents each will be enough." In that subdued utterance from that small thin frame, I realized how heavy the burdens of life were for her. I don't know if it was from pity or curiosity, but I asked her about herself. At first she gazed woodenly at the clumps of dried grass on the wall across the way, wringing the white cloth cover in her hands. Then she just stood there like a carved stone figure. She didn't begin to talk until I promised to buy the rest of her eggs.

She lived in Y village, about a mile and a half east of town. Her parents, still young and sturdy, were considered hard workers on their production team. But unfortunately they were descended from a rich old farming family and according to the policies of X county could draw only 70 percent of the pay which otherwise would be their due. For most people, working overtime at night was considered "striving hard for socialism," but for them it was "thoroughly re-educating themselves," for which they earned no work points. She had two younger sisters, but the youngest couldn't be officially counted because she was "number three."[4] This little angel, sent by mistake into the human world, had already consumed four years of

4. Population control policy at this time called for two children per family. Third and subsequent pregnancies were discouraged by denying regular rations for such children. Families with too many children had to eat less or use grain which otherwise they were allowed to market.

Short Stories

marketable grain. The family pigsty had been empty for the past two years, and her father had long ago intended to fill it with a pair of piglets. But with what money? With the arrival of spring, her mother wanted to give the children a seasonal change of clothes, but where could she get the cloth? And the house had needed new roof tiles for a long time. They just could not survive another year under their present conditions, the five of them squeezed together in a corner of the *kang*[5] with a tile basin set out to catch leaks. But—money! Money!

Then yesterday her mother had gone into difficult labor. The pain was so great that she rolled on the *kang* and invoked heaven. The production team leader, observing that this was a fourth birth, adamantly refused to allow a midwife to assist. Her father's frantic beating at the team leader's door was enough to make the mountains rattle, but only after one of the old-timers repeatedly pleaded on their behalf did the leader finally allow a midwife to come. Then father did everything he could—poured tea, passed around cigarettes—but the team leader would not let the midwife go into the labor room.

"You haven't paid this year's premium on the cooperative medical plan," he said to the father. The father begged him to save the mother and child, but the leader tossed his head and refused to listen. At length, pointing straight at the father, he delivered a warning: "Remember that you've lost another day of work, which will be entered on the monthly ideological report." With a shrug of the shoulders, the leader left.

The midwife merely shook her head and quietly slipped two packages of sterilized cotton to the father. Holding the two packages in his hands, this six-foot man cried helplessly. He had no idea how to assist at a birth. Fortunately a neighbor, Third Wang's wife, rushed over to help. The mother had suffered terribly and had lost a lot of blood, but finally a little life emerged into the world—another daughter.

When Third Wang's wife announced the good tidings and asked the father for $3, he roared like an angry lion. Carrying the infant, his eyes bloodshot, he started for the door. The mother crawled across the floor and grabbed his pant leg in an attempt to stop him. But she fainted.

At this point the little egg-seller buried her head in the crook of her arm and stopped talking.

The imprint of my sweaty fingers remained on the handle of her basket. I looked up to see the massive form of the "Learn from Dazhai Exhibition Hall" which loomed at the end of the alley. It was then that I realized why I had not seen this crumbling dirt wall or these filthy

---

5. A *kang* is a large raised area kept warm by circulating smoke trapped underneath. It is used for sitting and sleeping.

Stubborn Weeds

rotting thatched eaves from the main street. The great Dazhai Hall blocked one's view.

We said nothing else to each other. I placed the remaining eggs in my book bag, thirty-seven in all, and gave her $3. She counted the bills one by one, totaled them, then figured it all out once more. Finally she gave me a half-dollar bill in change. Holding the bill, still wet from her spittle, I was gripped by an indescribable sensation. It was like the stab of an icicle, yet also like the kiss of soft lips. While she was stuffing the bills into her coat, I stealthily placed several eggs back into her basket.

By the time I got back to the guest house, it was already dusk. Feeling extremely ill at ease, I paced up and down in my room. In the conference room next door, the county Party secretary was sharing his valuable experience with the chairmen and vice-chairmen of various visiting delegations. I could hear their intermittent talk and laughter. I was opening the door, hoping to find a quiet place to collect my thoughts, when the glass doors of the conference room burst open and out rushed a young steward in a white cap and jacket. On the wooden tray at his shoulder were two big platters of a cabbage dish which had hardly been touched. I stood there gaping, my eyes fixed unseeing on that pair of multi-colored porcelain platters, until the steward vanished around a corner.

The little girl's big, dull eyes and long lashes reappeared before me, along with the bills smeared with saliva, the empty basket, and even the rope which had been cinched around the waist of that unruly youth. Could it be that what he said was really—I couldn't let myself think it. Another round of laughter came from behind the glass doors as Secretary Li's sonorous voice floated out, mixed with the aroma of wine and prepared dishes.

"OK, everybody, dig in! This is nothing compared to what you get in Beijing—come on, have some—" Feeling as though all my energy had been suddenly siphoned away, I staggered back to my room and threw myself onto the bed.

The next day was April 5, when that political volcano erupted in Beijing and cast its warm lava over all of glacial China. The whole world heard that mighty roar, but X county was as calm as the day before—tranquil, in fact. Carrying my simple baggage, I walked into the bus station. The fresh air was fading my nightmares. Before I would be able to eat all the eggs I was carrying, I would have forgotten their little owner.

"Mister, take pity, take pity. Give me some money for steamed bread," said a little girl behind me, but my hands were loaded with things, and I was anxious to board.

"I don't have any," I replied blandly without turning around. The girl didn't speak again, but the light patter of her footsteps followed me to the bus. Somewhat impatiently I twisted my head around. "Didn't I tell you—what?" There were those big, listless eyes, the thick tufts of hair, the black padded coat not quite reaching the knees.

It was she. She recognized me and turned to run away.

"Little girl, what are you doing here?" I knew she was begging, of course, but had asked anyway. She hung her head without replying. Following her gaze I saw the bamboo basket of yesterday still over her arm, but it held only a crude china bowl with some aluminum coins in the bottom.

"What made you do this?" I asked impatiently, putting down my luggage and shaking her frail shoulders. "Where's the money from yesterday's eggs?"

"Secretary Du took it from me."

"Why?" I heard my own voice tremble.

"Yesterday—"

Yesterday, just as she had reached home, she had chanced upon Party Secretary Du, who was leaving her house after one of his lectures to her parents. The secretary had looked suspiciously at her basket and had begun questioning her about its contents. The naive child had shown it to him. How could she have foreseen—

At a mass meeting of commune members last evening, Secretary Du had held up the basket. "A typical example of capitalism," he had announced with a steely face. "An ironclad case of the enemy class secretly scheming to restore the old order." The egg money had been confiscated and the girl's father driven through the streets with the basket around his neck.

Afterward the father had stumbled home and had pulled his daughter from her hiding place by the stove. As he had started swinging his hoe handle, she had bitten her cheek to keep from crying out. The mother had left her bed to restrain him, but he had struck the mother too and had called her a worthless woman who could produce only girls.

I cupped the little girl's face in my hands and noticed a black and blue bruise on her forehead.

"Papa drove us three girls out of the house," she continued, "and wouldn't let us back in. We squeezed under the window sill. My sister said she was cold, so I covered her with my coat. My other sister said she was afraid of the dark, so I hugged her and cheered her up. In the night a stray dog came and bit her on the leg."

"OK, stop, that's enough," I urged her as I squeezed her cold hand tightly and closed my eyes in agony. I felt the way I do when I see the pain-wracked face of an honest peasant or the shriveled breast of a pale farm woman or a child stomping its feet and crying for something to eat or a festering wound crawling with flies. I handed

Stubborn Weeds

168

the basket of eggs to her and also pulled out a ten-dollar bill which I stuffed into a hole in her padded coat.

"Here's money to pay the doctor's fee and to buy some rice for your sisters. Take these eggs home to your mother to pep her up."

She observed my somewhat nervous movements without any change of expression. Her dull eyes showed neither pleasure nor surprise.

"What? You don't want it? Not enough? What can I do to help? Tell me!" Then I saw the extraordinary flash in her eyes.

"Mister, are you going back to Beijing?"

"You like—Beijing?"

"I like—Beijing." She gripped my arm and begged me with all her heart. "Mister, take me back to Beijing with you."

"Take you to Beijing?" I didn't know how to react.

"I can do anything. I can cook, wash clothes, cut grass, weave mats. I don't want anything. I don't want your money. I won't be a bother to you. Just don't beat me, and give me rice to eat. Say yes, mister, please?"

"Well, let me think. Listen, little one, your mama has just had a baby girl, and she'll need help caring for her. And your sister is lying on her bed waiting for you to bring some bread. If you go away like this, they will be anxious and worried. Don't you like your village? Don't you love your family, your mama, and your poor little sisters?" I was holding back the tears as I spoke. I thought anyone would be moved by the word "mama," but she shook her head.

"I don't love her. Mama and Papa won't let me go to school. All the village kids go, but I have to stand at the school gate and watch them play. If I don't bring home enough firewood, Mama beats me worse than Papa does. I don't dare cry, because they turn me out without any supper. The team leader's daughter Shunzi calls me 'rich peasant brat.' She throws dog scraps at me and makes me lick them up. Mister, I know you are a kind person. Take me to Beijing with you. Save me!" She knelt to the ground, big tears running down her cheeks. I couldn't restrain the urge to grab her and hold her. My tears wet those tufts of thin hair as the morning wind tugged at them.

"I'll—take—you. I'll take you. You take the eggs home and in a few days I'll come back to get you."

"Really?"

"Real . . . ly."

Her dispirited eyes suddenly brightened at this first spark of hope. Yet I felt totally wretched. Friends, what would you have done? I was filled with a deep inner despair at having done the shabbiest thing in the world—I had deceived a helpless child. But what else could I do? I hadn't the heart to refuse her. I lightly brushed the dust from her coat and arranged the straggled hair at her forehead, then followed her with my eyes as she walked out the main door of the station.

In a daze I boarded the bus and took a seat. My peace of mind had been torn to shreds. Every fiber of my being was quivering in tune with the engine of the bus. I just wanted to get out of X county quickly. As Secretary Li had said, it was nothing compared to Beijing.

As the bus slowly drove out of the station, I saw her again through the windowpane, her lonely image dwarfed by the big red-character banner on the gate of the Tax Bureau: "Block the Capitalist Road." Suddenly a stocky man in official garb appeared at her side and snatched her egg basket. I could see his lips opening and closing. But there was no trace of fear on the girl's face. She was gazing into the distance as if she saw a rosy sunrise in the eastern sky. This apparently angered the official, who began to search her roughly.

A wave of fury swept through me. Without thinking, I thrust my head out the window just in time to see the ten-dollar bill, freshly snatched from her, clutched in the man's hand.

"Thief! Thief!" I screamed, pounding wildly on the window, oblivious to the stunned gaze of the other passengers. But through the yellow pall which was churned up by the bus wheels, all I could see were those eyes with their long lashes, suspended somewhere between pain and expectation.

And whenever people reminisce about the great event that occurred on April 5, my thoughts turn instead to the road at the entrance of that village, where a little girl stands waiting.

Originally published in Zheiyidai.

Translated by Dale R. Johnson.

AN DONG   *The Sea Does Not Belong to Us*

His tan wasn't dark yet. His skin was about the color of the dazzling sandy beach, and mine was no different, of course. Compared to the others, the white skin of those who had just arrived at the seashore was funny-looking indeed. But, my, how my little brother had grown the past two years. He was so sturdy!

"Hey, sis, watch me!" His youthful voice had reverberated in the open street. His skinny arms and legs were flailing as he scrambled onto the base of a stone lion and stood under its belly. The street lights were quietly twinkling, as if winking at that oversized head of his. He was only five years old then! Fourteen years have passed.

"God, is it pretty!" my brother said, slapping his big feet and neatly concealing his face in the shadow cast by my legs. His stylish Japanese sunglasses, looking like the black eye-patches of a panda, flashed amber. "Look at that sea, will you?" he said, using his foot to shield his eyes from the strong setting sun and turning his long-haired head around.

"Too bad! It's not yours!"

"Huh? What do you mean? I *wish* it were mine. What? Don't you like the sea? Want a smoke?"

"Ah, no, thank you, monsieur, not right now—because neither of us is a coastal person."

"Then—you mean it's *theirs?*" He blew a smoke ring, squinted, and propped one leg up on his knee, like positioning a rifle, to eye the brown-bodied beach people through the ring. They had nothing to do with us as they dashed into the arms of the blue sea, swinging their baskets.

"Do you—envy them?"

The sun was golden fiery hot. As it struck the sand it shot back dazzling white rays. A group of people in a dozen shades of tan were laughing loudly as though they hadn't a care in all of this gold, blue, and white world. It was really hot! The sun on our backs was almost unbearable. (Why isn't life as fiery hot for us?) A little girl in a red swimsuit, playing in the spray, stooped to gather seaweed. The tide was going out.

"Come off it! Does that bother you? We're better than they are."

I closed my eyes. "Hmm, of course you come here only for vacations—of course. Does that bother *you?*"

Outside the bus window the long, lonely sea coast flew by. The tires hissed evenly on the gray road surface, and the fluttering brown nylon curtains at the window flapped in my face. My brother turned around in his seat in front and casually offered Father a cigarette.

"You little rascal, what are you up to?" Daddy forced open my brother's hand and reached into his own pants pocket. My brother stuck out his tongue at me.

"Ha!" I laughed out loud.

Huge bundles of translucent kelp—shoulder poles—several human backs glistening with perspiration—

Strauss's magnificent "Spring Sonata" started to play in stereo as the people began to twirl, lightly and gracefully. My brother led Feng-

feng onto the dance floor. The two of them well knew how refined and beautiful they looked and were delighted to be in the limelight.

"Allow me—coffee," this one said as he approached me with an elegant air and a teasing look on his face. Huh! Just fine!

Music is indeed a wind that lives.

"Don't!" I ducked his lips.

"What's the matter?"

"Look over there."

"What do I care about them?"

"Nonsense! What do we care about them? My father is over there!"

Funny thing! Without even opening his eyes, the team leader said: "This morning you two go to the threshing floor and grind grain. When you finish, get some gunnysacks from the threshing boss, load it up on a cart, and haul it to the pigpens." Then he turned his head to spit and continued to smoke his pipe.

I had to arch my neck in order to swallow the corn cake. This was breakfast. It scraped my throat going down but felt good just the same. But would it last until noon?

The team leader's spittle seeped into the dirt and dried up in no time, crystallizing an unfortunate ant.

"Hey—does it really matter to you?"

"What? What do you mean by all this?" My brother rapped my hand in astonishment.

"Your head is—like an empty tin." I opened my eyes as I spoke. It was true. My little brother had grown up, but his bright eyes concealed nothing. All I could see in the black pupils of his eyes was myself—as small as an ant.

The militant song "Sailing on the Seas Depends on the Helmsman" was playing over the loudspeakers on the station platform at ear-splitting volume. Why? Every time I hear it, perhaps out of habit, I always get a feeling of "conclusion." Everyone on the platform was weeping, their faces furrowed in frowns, their eyes reddened, their spastic hands frantically waving. Red Guard armbands. Little red books—some people losing their footing—wave after wave of voices like an ebb tide.

"Fellow Red Guards! You have resolved to answer the wise call of the Great Helmsman, Chairman Mao, to go up to the mountains! Down to the countryside! Out across the whole wide land! You are the great new generation!"

Ah! Little Jia! He was squeezed down amid the throngs, biting his lips, his eyes seeming filled with ice crystals—

Stubborn Weeds

It was a human sea of crowding, surging people. At that moment they all looked light and weak enough to be swept away in the flood of tears. The mainstays of their lives—their hopes, their treasures— were all on board the train with us. Their only wish was that we not go, that we come back to their sides. By this time no one could tell where their own loved ones were. People gazed randomly at the windows, calling constantly, inaudibly. No one could hear anything clearly. They seemed all to be staring miserably in my direction. Yes. Because I was one of their children and was about to leave. I felt as if my heart, cold and shriveled by the pain, was snuggling up into the embrace of their hot, flowing tears.

Wave after snow-white wave rocked the swimmers, laughing with them in unison—

"I see—OK, true enough—" My brother impatiently dropped to his hands and knees again, his voice becoming more deliberate. "You had your ten rough years, your so-called ten years of glory. So what of it? You know all about the 'grass roots'—them! But I was too young to go, right?"

"Look, Jia, forget it! Don't let it bother you. Do you know what people think of us now?"

"OK, OK, there you go again! What of it? I don't want to start arguing with you again—who cares, anyway? Everything that hap- pened—you asked for it, right? So you deserve what you've got now too!" My brother pushed at his sunglasses with complete indiffer- ence.

"Yes, damn it, you bastard," I said, getting angry, gnashing my teeth and spitting out the syllables.

"Right, so long as people flatter you—"

"Yeah—look who's talking! Didn't you head for the coast to see Daddy too? To have fun! To use Daddy's pull!" We were warming up for another argument, but what could I say? My brother just looked at me with that expression of his.

The afternoon of Mother's accident, my brother came in—and what a look he had in his eye! What was he up to? He closed the door and walked slowly toward me. Slowly—why was he walking so slowly? He had never acted that way before. He suddenly smiled silently. A six-year-old boy! Smiling like that! Like a malicious little wolf. His eyes were like—like two black caves! I was afraid of falling into them.

A thick puff of smoke enveloped my brother's face. He was an- gry, and smoking with a vengeance. I—spoke.

"I know I'm not—'they.' That's why I'm lonely. But for them, it is

Short Stories

as though the sea—" I broke off when I felt a purple shadow cover us. In front of me were a pair of handsome muscular legs, covered with curly hair.

"What do you think you're doing?" I sat up instantly.

"My dear young lady! Could you please tell us, which way to the water?" A group of boys in swim trunks had surrounded us.

"Get out of here! What do you think you're doing?" I stood up and adjusted my swimsuit.

The voices and mannerisms of these boys were peculiar. Each of them was wearing a girl's straw hat with flowers on it. Their hair was all tangled and disorderly, and they seemed to be trying to pick a fight. My brother didn't move. He squinted coldly at the boy who had spoken.

"Watch yourself, buster!" the boy said, casting a scornful eye toward my brother. "You better lead the way." My heart was pounding so hard it threatened to choke me. We're in for it now! If there's a fight, we're outnumbered.

My brother slowly got to his feet. There was a faint mocking smile at the corners of his mouth. The gang of boys were looking us up and down with provoking gleams in their eyes. A crowd of excitement-seekers had begun to gather. Their number gradually increased as they coolly observed the first stages of what promised to be an ugly battle.

"If you want to play with the girl," said my brother, putting his hand on my shoulder, "you have to check with the boss!" Of all the nerve! There was a roaring inside my head—

A truck drove between us, separating me from Jiajia for an instant. I was so frightened I covered my mouth with my red neckerchief. But then Jiajia was standing before me again, alone and small, his monthly pass hanging around his neck.

"Sis!" He dashed to my side and grabbed me tightly by the hand, screaming for all his might at the truck as it hurtled away. "Lousy truck! You—scram!"

I wrenched free from his grasp and flung his hand away. "Disgusting!"

My brother, without so much as a glance at me, removed his glasses, nodded toward the boy with the clenched teeth, and walked over to him. "OK, buddy! Let me show you how to make it with a woman." Before anyone could stop him, my brother had struck the ringleader full in the stomach with his fist. The young man doubled over, gasped once, and fell to the ground. Then the iron fist of a boy on the right nailed my brother in the face. The blow arched his body like a drawn bow and knocked him about two yards backward. Then the others pounced on him, panting and shouting like madmen.

Stubborn Weeds

I pressed my chest with both hands to restrain my pounding heart. Of course I had seen this kind of thing many times before. Some people fight like crazy wild pigs—they don't know how to fight at all. But I was worried about my little brother! He was really taking a beating this time. To tell the truth, though, those first two blows that had opened the fighting were really beautiful. Yes, and I seemed to remember—

Daddy was sitting at the table. He was thinner. He couldn't be ill, could he? There was one subject he had never mentioned to me. He never mentioned—Mother. What's this?—his hand was trembling. I knew he was worried about my brother.

"Prison visiting hours are up," said the man, rapping impatiently on the table. Daddy just looked at me, frowning slightly, saying nothing.

The crowd, aloof and indifferent, stood watching the crazed gang of boys. Some were even laughing. They were all staring at me in the same way—with cold indifference. I was just a girl in a swimsuit. I'd become the helpless object of their unbearable cold stares. They all despised me. They did!

Fortunately Jia, resilient little beast that he was, managed to struggle to his feet. He retreated a few steps while throwing off one attacker. Then he warded off a flurry of fists and feet that were aimed at his head and abdomen. But he took several vicious blows before slinking away.

There was a crash, and some people began to yell. The crowd was jeering and hooting. An ear-splitting whistle rang out. A policeman came rushing from nowhere and stopped one of the young toughs who wanted to chase my brother with a rock. Meanwhile several bystanders had gone to drag my brother back. He had a bloody nose—of course. But no matter—his arms and legs were all right. The guy really knows how to take care of himself!

"What's going on here?" asked the policeman. His jaw was set as he slowly scanned the crowd with a piercing gaze. His eyes finally came to rest on the ringleader whom my brother had knocked to the ground. The youth was covered with sand and dirt, sprawled on the ground out cold.

"Him!" cried one of the hoodlums, red in the face and panting as he brushed the sand off his body. My brother said nothing but merely wiped at the blood on his upper lip and eyed the policeman with a half-jesting look.

"Who are you?"

My brother looked straight into the policeman's steely face but did not open his mouth. I pushed my way to the front and said,

Short Stories

"We're not from around here. I'm his sister. They came here trying to pick a fight, and they—" I couldn't go on. The cold eyes all around me felt like sharp knives. I was afraid.

"Is that so? Well, all of you come along with me—including you." The policeman was pointing at me. He abruptly turned on his heel and walked away. Two armed soldiers came to take us away.

"We've done nothing wrong! Everybody saw what happened!" I began to feel anxious.

"Oh?" The policeman turned to face the crowd—

Uh—no. I was afraid! Afraid of their eyes! I'd seen absurdly malicious scenes before, but nothing so frightful as—as these good, simple people staring at us in this way. Hate, disdain—they showed everything but a willingness to speak on our behalf. But they were such *good* people. Ah! Why did we have to be wearing clothes that made people stare at us? Why did we have to be recognized as—They say heaven guarantees just deserts. Maybe it does. But no simple syllogism can apply to all of life. Life may be the antithesis of all formal logic.

What did all this mean? My composure had deserted me. I hugged my shoulders, trying with all my might to keep from shaking.

I really was shaking. My heart was shaking. The blood-red banners on the stage glowed in the ghastly lamplight, their color so deep that they seemed likely to drip. The crowd was slightly restless. A piercing female voice blared over the loudspeaker like a dagger with a saw-toothed blade, sawing at my childlike heart: "Down—with—"

Daddy was up front. They were yelling, "Ride an airplane!"[1]

Someone was pushing me from behind. A low murmur of voices began to swell in the audience. I couldn't hear what everybody was saying but suddenly was aware of many flashing eyes staring at me. A cluster of twinkling stars had suddenly appeared from this blue-black universe and had come showering down over my trembling, empty little heart. I was only thirteen then. I cried, but the tears were just as hot as my heart. This deeply sympathetic and public-spirited crowd—they may have had a solemn look in their eyes, but it was most warming, like the warmth of a spot of earth that has been bathed in sunshine for hours.

The people were silent. Their cold eyes were scanning us, stabbing at us. It was then that my brother arrogantly raised his head and

1. A common method of persecution during the Cultural Revolution was to interrogate a victim while forcing him or her to "ride an airplane"—to lean forward at the waist with arms stretched backward, parallel to the ground, so that the torso and arms resembled a jet airplane.

Stubborn Weeds

said to the policeman, "Can I have a word with my father before we go?" He looked up the road and pointed to a white Mercedes.

I felt my face turning white, probably as white as the Mercedes. The policeman turned and looked over his shoulder, squinted, and sneered. The crowd stirred ominously.

"What is your father's work unit?" the policeman asked coldly and very slowly.

"Jia!" I was on the verge of trembling again.

"The Changtan Sanitorium," my brother replied, paying me absolutely no attention. He seemed fully self-assured, even indignant.

A soldier was on duty behind the desk, absent-mindedly toying with his cigarette holder.

"Please let me in, sir. My brother has a fever, and I don't know what to do. Tomorrow I have to go on countryside duty in Shanxi. My father doesn't know. Honest!"

"The prison has no visiting hours today. I can't do anything about that. Go back home and return day after tomorrow."

"Sir!— Sir!—" I pleaded again and again, but he picked up his cigarette holder and walked out the door.

My brother sat at the table and slowly took a photograph from his tattered brown book bag. He placed it on the table and stared at it blankly. It was of Daddy and him when he was five. The Jiajia of that time was leaning on his father's shoulder, smiling out at his future. Now Jiajia slowly tore the photograph into two halves, then tore the half with his image into shreds—strip by strip by strip. Maybe his future had already been transfixed on that frozen face.

Jiajia—

I lay on the narrow wooden bed, tears running into my mouth, feeling regret and hatred. Why did I have to go and tell my brother? Why didn't I just say Father had been too busy to see me off? Why did I have to make my brother—I'll never be able to get it off my conscience. I have wronged him! It was at this point that our lives began to take their separate courses.

The sun's glare was making me see black. My god, now I'm weak in the knees!

Naturally, what my brother said was effective. The crowd was growing a bit restless. Amid the mocking jeers and whistles, I could hear someone cursing. The policeman had lowered his head, and two tendons stood out on his neck. His cold gaze fixed on my brother and me as though we were his mortal enemies. He stood there without moving, as though he wanted to stare the blood right out of his eyeballs. I could see he wanted to punish us. The crowd was jostling him, cursing him, baiting him, but he wouldn't give the order to arrest us. It was as if he were gripped from behind by a pair of huge formless hands.

The young tough on the ground came around. His eyes were bloodshot, dark, and listless. "OK, scram!" the policeman finally hissed at us through clenched teeth. No one could hear him clearly, but I knew right away what he meant.

The soldiers on duty then took away the hoodlums who had started the fight. The crowd dispersed after one final cacophony of wagging tongues. I remember putting up with pushes and shoves from every direction. Everything else I have forgotten—forgotten—

"The sea! Daddy! Mommy! Quick, look! Look at the big waves!" I was tugging hard at my parents' hands, jumping up and down in the back seat of the car. The sea! Blue as the eyes of a foreign doll! At age six, I was seeing the seashore for the first time. (That was before I had a little brother.) I have now completely forgotten how it was that I first splashed into the water or even whether I was afraid to go in. I remember only that the hot sand burned my feet. The seawater may have been brackish, but it was clear and transparent—like moist eyes—like Mama's, and Daddy's too—the great sea—

Suddenly a voice as heavy as steel and carrying an icy, hollow echo rang down from the heavens: "Our fathers' generation endured all manner of hardship. But truly they were like infants and cannot be blamed. As the Big Dipper turns and the stars revolve in their courses, a group of natural-born leaders has fallen into place. Perhaps before these leaders were aware of it, a new generation rose behind them in the track of history and inherited everything—all the suffering, the power, the status, the general nature of things—everything that was viewed as 'property' to inherit. But in the limited conceptual system of this younger generation, the full and precise implications of the term 'subordination' were lacking. What they understood was only the acceptance of 'domination.' In accepting the positions thus assigned to them, they considered themselves the natural heirs of those old men who had shaken the earth. This view of things sprouted in their minds when they were young and grew when they saw the heroes of their fathers' generation being beaten into the ground. Seeing them lose their just deserts only etched the concept deeper and more forcefully into these narrow, intrepid, innocent young minds—"

No! This is too frightening. I—I really want—to pray—to heaven—

Stubborn Weeds

"Wait up. I'll go wash off in the sea and be right back." My brother stood before me, facing into the sunlight that was so cold it was bluish. The sea breeze was blowing that conspicuous, offensive long hair of his. At some point he had retrieved his sunglasses and put them on again. He was still covering his nose with one hand.

"No, let's go! Daddy will be waiting." I felt weaker than I'd ever felt before. I tried to take his hand.

He ducked away. I looked at this balky, stubborn brother of mine and out at the boundless, deep, stern sea behind him. I suddenly felt a bitter taste and puckering feeling in my throat. I never would have imagined it possible, but I then used a tone of voice that was nearly a beggar's. "Don't wash off. Let's go back, Jiajia—the water's cold."

Originally published in Zheiyidai.

Translated by Dale R. Johnson.

POETRY

Not many poems in 1979–80 attracted national attention and controversy in China. The most famous example of one that did was Ye Wenfu's "General, You Can't Do This!", which was published in the August 1979 issue of Poetry (Shikan) and expressed outrage and a sense of betrayal about a report that a high-ranking military official had diverted several hundred thousand dollars from construction of a nursery school to construction of his mansion. But in general, poetry was not the favorite genre in the excitement over truth-telling literature in 1979–80, among either readers or critics. In the Ministry of Culture an internal report summarizing the achievements of 1979 found that drama had been most successful and that short stories had been second. Poetry was near the bottom of this list, on which music ranked lowest. Such broad-scale rankings might seem absurd if it were not true that readers also were remarkably consistent in expressing the same basic preferences.

But when the dust settles from the politically and socially based controversies that surrounded many stories and plays of 1979–80, it will certainly emerge that the poetry of these years was not as ordinary as many had supposed. Even measured in terms of political boldness alone, few literary journals exceeded Poetry. More important, some young poets were experimenting with artistic language in ways that will likely prove more significant to the development of Chinese literature than all the reports of social ills in the fiction and drama of the time. Accordingly we brave the inherent difficulties of translating Chinese poems into English in order to provide a modest sampling that includes elements of both social protest and literary experiment.

Gong Liu (Liu Renyong, b. 1927), while belonging to the "older" generation of poets, commands special respect among youth. His poem here speaks of a "petitioner," a term that had a specific sense in 1979–80. It meant someone who had suffered for years as a "rightist," a "counterrevolutionary," or the like, and who by rights should have had his oppressive label removed after the Gang of Four fell; but local officials were often slow to expedite these changes of status (some had gained their positions precisely by putting the labels on), and victims had no alternative but to "petition" higher authorities. This sometimes meant walking miles to capital cities and living on the streets until one's case could be heard.

Other than Gong Liu and Huang Yongyu (b. 1924), who is renowned as both a painter and a poet, the poets represented here are young and have young reputations. Luo Gengye (b. 1951), whose poem challenges the conservative view that discontent is akin to subversion, was a dancer with an arts troupe in Sichuan from 1976 to 1980, and in 1981 went to Beijing to study song writing and music at the Chinese Institute of Music. Qiu Xiaolong (b. 1953) is an Assistant Research Fellow at the Academy of Social Sciences in Shanghai and is writing a thesis on T. S. Eliot.

Gu Cheng (b. 1956) and to a certain extent Shu Ting (b. 1952) have become controversial as practitioners of so-called "obscure poetry," i.e., lines with imagistic or oblique messages that some critics feel to be insufficiently pellucid for a socialist society. Gu Cheng, who is son of the elder poet Gu Gong and started writing poetry at age twelve, lived in Beijing in 1981. Shu Ting worked in a bulb factory in Xiamen, Fujian Province.

GONG LIU *The Petitioner and His Dependents*

For heaven's sake don't curse me. I'm not a troublemaker.
A starving man isn't interested in fooling around.

THE PETITIONER SPEAKS:

> I am the blood oozing from extensive burns,
> I am igneous rock. My home is Purgatory.
> Look. All around is jagged granite;
> Here there is no amethyst or jade.
>
> As the tides of life surge past,
> Holding God's special files of steel,
> They wear me away for all they're worth,
> Each with less mercy than the one before.
>
> I was thrown into the yard of the local Party office.
> "Where are you from, you clod?
> You're an eyesore and a pain in the neck. Get lost!"
> With curses the security squad sent me on my way.
>
> I was swept into the reception room of the district Party
>   committee.
> "He's got lice," shrieked a female official,
> Getting rid of me and then going to wash her hands
> As if she had just got rid of toilet paper.

Poetry

In the provincial capital the leaders were busier still,
Building paradise for the people.
Being an ill-mannered lout I wrote my address as Purgatory.
"Nonsense! There's no such place in China."

The tide of anger swept the land once more,
Carrying me to Beijing's Xinhua Gate.
Take a look at that dried-up, shriveled crowd—
They could be made into a mat of human straw.

Chang'an Boulevard, accept my apologies:
Ugliness has sullied your beauty—
These fingers like sticks of charcoal,
These rags that barely cover our bodies.

But injustice is even more unbearable than shame.
I remember once two iron-trees grew here.
Are they both dead by now?
I dreamed that they had a second flowering.

Comrade, I don't complain, let alone curse.
Don't, I beg you, refer my case back home.
If you could grant me just half an hour,
You'd save me half a lifetime's suffering.

HIS DAUGHTER TALKS IN HER SLEEP:

I am the petitioner's daughter,
I am wild by profession.
I go around counting telegraph poles;
Everywhere are the beds where I've been sold.

I sell myself off cheap, a bit at a time,
For food and drink and a yard or two of cotton.
Mother knows what I'm doing,
But still calls me a good girl, with a sob in her throat.

A good girl, indeed!
One dark night, twelve years ago,
They took my father away,
Putting out the stove and hope.

The lost world of beauty,
The lost innocence, schoolbag, and songs
Were left in a place far, far away,
Shrouded in mist, where I'll never return.

Here there is degradation,
Here there is grief.

Stubborn Weeds

Only my young brother's innocent shouts
Remain to link the present and the past.

I am the petitioner's daughter.
People mock me and jab me in the back.
Of course, I wasn't qualified to join the political brothel—
I didn't know the Gang of Four.

I'm only good enough to be their target.
I'm not allowed to talk so fine, even if I could,
Or plant chaste blossoms to hide debauchery,
Or set up my memorial in the shrine of filth.

I'm too weak now, like a broken spring.
I'd fly away, but have no wings of my own.
The police have warned me: "Classification unchanged.
Besides, your father has disappeared again."

HIS WIFE ARGUES:

People take me for a widow.
In fact I have a husband.
But he's hitched a ride on a train to Beijing;
I dare not think how all this will end.

I spend my days with rubbish,
Digging out tins, plastic, paper, and rags.
My conscience is clean:
Tears wash away the dirt from everything.

Sorting through rubbish doesn't make you rubbish.
Don't you believe me? Dirt sometimes hides jewels.
All the red-scarfed youngsters used to salute me.
By what right did I lose my textbooks, chalk, and dais?

Now I silently roam the streets:
I know where the filthiest places are.
But I am the outcaste, the untouchable,
As if this were not China but India.

"Clear off! Out of the way!"
Shouts a loathsome student I once taught.
He treats the whole town as his rubbish bin—
He has the right father and the right father-in-law.

But still I take home the old newspapers I pick up,
To read and reread, not knowing what to believe.
Then my poor crippled boy starts crying:
"Mum, why did you ever learn to read, you fool?"

THE SICK BOY'S INVOCATION:

I hate my father,
I hate my family,
I hate this bloody polio,
I hate doctors and their long white coats.

I hate this damp basement
That drags me down with it.
I hate the murky skylight;
It's half-blind and so am I.

I hate those busy men and women
Whose heels are always drumming at my head.
I hate their busyness.
Why does no one think of me or give me something to do?

That wild plant growing in the dirt by the window
Is the only thing I like. I love it. It's watered
With my tears. Perhaps the sun one morning
Will notice it. There could even be a flower.

Originally published in Qingming *(Hefei), No. 1, 1980.*

Translated by W. J. F. Jenner.

GU CHENG *A Short Stop*

The train was tired
The delegates climbed out
Still wearing their best clothes

Under the eaves of the signal box
A girl
Mechanically crushed stones
She never looked up

Originally published in Jintian *(Beijing,
unofficial press), No. 8 (1980).*

Translated by W. J. F. Jenner.

GU CHENG *One Generation*

The black night has given me black eyes,
Yet I use them to search for light.

Originally published in Xingxing *(Chengdu),*
March 1980.

Translated by William Tay.

GU CHENG *Curve*

A bird in the gusty wind
Deftly changes direction

A boy tries to pick up
A penny

The grapevine in fantasy
Stretches its tentacle

The wave in retreat
Arches its back

Originally published in Shikan *(Beijing),*
No. 10, 1980.

Translated by William Tay.

GU CHENG *Feeling*

The sky is gray
The road is gray
The building is gray
The rain is gray

In this blanket of dead gray
Two children walk by,
One bright red
One pale green.

Originally published in Shikan *(Beijing),*
No. 10, 1980.

Translated by William Tay.

Poetry

GU CHENG *A Walk in the Rain*

Clouds that are gray
Can no longer be washed clean.
So we open the umbrella
And simply paint the sky black.

In the slowly floating night,
Two pairs of twin stars
Move with no trajectory,
Now distant, now near—

Originally published in Shikan *(Beijing),*
No. 10, 1980.

Translated by William Tay.

SHU TING *"?.!"*

Then it's true
You'll wait for me
Wait till all the seeds in my basket have been sown
Wait till I've taken the lost bees home
Wait till the oil lamps and torches have been lit
      under boat awnings, in cottages, in workers' shacks
Wait till I've read all the windows bright or dark
      and talked to all the bright and dark souls
Wait until the highways become songs
Wait until love can walk in the sun
When the vast Milky Way forces itself between us
You will still await me patiently
And make a faithful little raft

Then it's true
You'll never break your word
Even when my soft hands crack
      and the bloom fades from my cheeks
Even when my flute gives out blood
      and still won't melt the ice and snow
Even with the lash behind and the precipice ahead
Even if the darkness catches me before the dawn
      and I sink with the earth

Stubborn Weeds

Before I can release a lovebird
Your waiting and faithfulness
Will be
The reward for my sacrifice

Now let them
Shoot at me
I shall walk calmly across the land
Towards you, towards you
My long hair blowing in the wind
I am your wild lily in the storm

Originally published in Shanghai wenxue, *No. 9, 1981.*

Translated by W. J. F. Jenner.

SHU TING *Perhaps*

Perhaps our cares
    will never have readers
Perhaps the journey that was wrong from the start
    will be wrong at the end
Perhaps every single lamp we have lit
    will be blown out by the gale
Perhaps when we have burned out our lives to lighten the darkness
    there will be no warming fire at our sides.

Perhaps when all the tears have flowed
    the soil will be richer
Perhaps when we sing of the sun
    the sun will sing of us
Perhaps as the weight on our shoulders grows heavier
    our faith will be more lofty
Perhaps we should shout about suffering as a whole
    but keep silent over personal grief.

Perhaps
Because of an irresistible call
We have no other choice.

Originally published in Jintian (Beijing, unofficial press), *No. 8 (1980).*

Translated by W. J. F. Jenner.

FENG YU   *Two Cents*

Bureau head, factory manager, Party secretary,
When you meet the
Withered, begging hands
Of an old man, a woman, or a child.

Please don't bring out
Two cents.
That won't quiet your conscience.
For in your hands
Is the power
They gave you.

Originally published in Shikan *(Beijing), No. 12, 1979.*

Translated by W. J. F. Jenner.

HUANG   *The New Face of Judas*
YONGYU

If he has no friends
An informer starves.
The better his friends,
The fatter he grows.
The ghosts of his victims
Follow him through the streets.

He has to be a perfect actor.
If you feel good
He is happy for you;
If you are down
He shares your grief.
Once set in his sights
An honest comrade is defenseless.
When you're confused, he'll counsel you.
If you forget, he'll jog your memory.
Gently, patiently, he leads you
Across the bridge of no return
To the place of execution.

Originally published in Shikan *(Beijing), No. 9, 1979.*
A final group of lines that refer to Jiang Qing and her associates has been omitted.

Translated by W. J. F. Jenner.
Stubborn Weeds

WANG ZHONGCAI   *Desert Scenes*

PATHS

I've walked no end of roads—busy ones, dull ones, grim ones, pale ones.

I've had enough of roads.

In the deathly desert I could make out a faint path, a whitish line disappearing over the horizon—

Like a child falling down a well who grabs at the thin bucket-rope, I have followed that path with fear and joy.

I know that at the end of the path lies an oasis of life.

THE WHITE CLOUD

In the vast desert the sunlight scorches and blinds. I dare not look up.

A white cloud drifts across the sun, obscuring it. At last I can raise my head. The cloud is an even purer white, like a gentle smile. Even the sunlight is softened, like a tender caress.

The white cloud drifts on, and the desert world is filled again with scorching, blinding sunlight. I have to bow my head; a tear falls into the hot sand at my feet.

I don't know whether the tear came because of the scorching sun or because the white cloud has drifted away.

THE DRY WELL

In the searing desert noon I am thirsty. My throat is on fire.

As I stagger forward I notice a little well nearby.

In ecstasy I run toward it. But it is only a dry well, with no trace of moisture in the cracked mud at the bottom.

Am I angry at it?

No, I thank the well.

Think of all the people who have sucked its sweet liquid. They have survived, while the well died because it saved not one drop for itself.

Survivor, as you sip your iced soda and champagne, do you still remember this dry well in the desert?

Originally published in Shikan *(Beijing), No. 10, 1979.*

Translated by W. J. F. Jenner and Perry Link.

Poetry

LUO GENGYE *Discontent*

> From any fruition of success. . . .
> shall come forth something
> to make a greater struggle necessary.
>
> —Walt Whitman, "Song of the Open Road"

Like flowers longing for sweet fruit,
Like cinders nursing a wish to burn,
My heart is pregnant with a "terrible" thought,
I want to proclaim to the present situation:
—"I am discontent!"

Who says discontent is heresy?
Who says discontent is revolt?
Can a swelling wave be confined in a mountain gulley?
Can a hawk chick rest in the darkness within the egg?

Discontent stimulates fascination with the seas!
Discontent revives thirst for the skies!

The creation of life is so anguished and mighty,
Please grant mothers the favor of sweet content;
"No! Wish that your child will grow with all speed,"
The infant entering the world implores its mother's discontent.

Oh, who can say that discontent is not love?
Oh, who dares say that discontent is plaint?

Discontent with the old printed charts of the seas,
Columbus found the ocean's farther shore;
Discontent with the Holy Bible's writ,
Copernicus revealed the marvels of the universe;
Discontent with the doctrine of heliocentricism,
      Kepler discovered the truth;
Discontent with Plato, Aristotle surpassed his own teacher.

Oh, who says discontent is the abandonment of the great men of the
      past?
Oh, who says discontent is a desecration of the noble and the wise?

Discontent: turned ape-men away from raw flesh and blood to the
      kindling of fire;
Discontent: led our footsore nomadic ancestors to fumble at tilling
      the land;
Discontent: substituted magnificent bridges for rude wooden planks;
Discontent: made artful stone axes give way to casting in bronze;

Stubborn Weeds

190

Discontent: produced Hua Tuo,[1] whose miraculous cures could
    restore the dead;
Discontent: trained Lu Ban,[2] whose brilliant craft put nature to
    shame.

Oh, discontent is a hope for change;
Oh, discontent is the beginning of creation.

I am electric current, I am discontent with rivers' waste,
What you idly let flow by is the milk of my subsistence;
I am a blast furnace, I am discontent with the earth's miserliness,
What you hoard deep within you is my life's flame;
I am crops, I fear the wantonness of Mother Nature,
Whose unpredictable winds and rains disturb and shake me;
I am markets, I yearn for dazzling displays of riches and beauty,
Drab shopwindows make my head bow in shame;
I am ancient cities, my finery old and faded,
Please deck me with ribbons of expressways
And crown me with a coronet of skyscrapers;
I am a reserved life-style, disturbed by decadent habits,
Please don't be too critical of clothing and dancing,
Please don't meddle too much in young love;
I am low-yield land, I am discontent with hobbled oxen;
I am bruised shoulders, I am discontent with two ropes;
I am discontent with rifles, with waterwheels, with sailboats;
I am discontent with mud, with noise, with pollution.

Discontent is like the whistle blast of a fleet leaving harbor,
Discontent is like the cock crowing to the dawn.

I am plans, locked up tightly in a safe,
I want to step down from the blueprint and join the construction
    site;
I am reform, ashamed to rest on my laurels,
I want to seek new ways, scale record heights;
I am policy, I am discontent with Bo Les[3] who hesitate,
Why not put into immediate effect legacies public and private?
I am creation, I am discontent with Yelang's[4] provincial conceit,

---

1. Hua Tuo (?–208 A.D.) was a master of medicine, and a cultural hero roughly
equivalent to Hippocrates in the West.
2. Lu Ban was a renowned craftsman of the Spring and Autumn period (770–476
B.C.).
3. Bo Le was a skilled judge of horses in the Spring and Autumn period. According to legend he once alighted from his carriage to weep over a thoroughbred that had
been crushed under a salt cart. The horse's groans reached to the heavens, but Bo Le
was unable to relieve its agony.
4. Yelang was a tiny kingdom in south China during the great Han Dynasty (206
B.C.–220 A.D.). The king of Yelang, in his provincial ignorance, once asked whether
the Han was as large as Yelang.

Poetry

Quickly destroy the barriers that cut me off from the world;
I protest marathon meetings, in the name of time,
That willfully fritter away the days of my life;
I denounce religious-style inquisitions that inhibit the search for
    truth;
I am flowers, I want to grow, I want to contribute my honey,
I beg the help of the gardener's solicitous shears.

Oh, discontent is like the stirrings of the fetus in its mother's womb,
    discontent is like a mother's anguished and mighty parturition!

I am discontent with bureaucracy,
Lightly brushing aside our martyrs' heritage;
I am discontent with our cultural level,
Too shallow to support today's Four Modernizations boat;
I am discontent with the weak legal system,
The ground before the Heroes' Monument is stained with the blood
    and tears of democracy;
I am discontent with boasting and fantasy,
Painting vague tomorrows in their castles in the sea;
I am discontent with grudges and resentment,
Lurking behind the embankment of the age, finding fault with the
    rushing waves—

Oh, discontent is an excellent daily agenda,
    discontent is a fine new proposal for action;
Discontent has already hastened the birth of a great shift in strategy!
Discontent has already hastened the hoisting of war banners for a
    New Long March!

Ah, the riverbed in discontent straightens out its course,
    oil in discontent wells up from the sea surface;
    science in discontent breaches forbidden zones,
    production in discontent overtakes rockets;
    thought in discontent develops keen insights,
    truth in discontent extends the line further;
    poverty in discontent presses on the heels of wealth,
    the present situation in discontent is swiftly rising!

Oh, discontent is like a bridge spanning two contradictions,
    discontent is like fission produced in an atom;
    discontent is the force that discovers, creates, advances,
    discontent is the way to prosperity, happiness, perfection!

Like flowers longing for sweet fruit,
Like cinders nursing a wish to burn,

My heart brims with a deep and earnest love,
I want to proclaim to the present situation:
          —"I am discontent"!

Originally published in Shikan *(Beijing), No. 5, 1979.*

Translated by Bonnie S. McDougall.

HE XIANQUAN *Blossoms on a Frosted Pane*

Every day when I awake
I open my curtains
To see what sort of prints the night has left
Upon the windowpane.

And just for this I love wintertime,
For such lovely scenes are never seen in spring, summer, fall.
Windowpanes are so many canvases
With crystal paintings redone day after day.

Breath inside the window, wind outside the pane,
On the boundary between warm and cold
The breath of man and the breath of winter clash,
And hot and cold breed crystals, uncountable, incredible.

No. I would rather use a fairy tale to explain this happening—
There must be a lovely spirit who comes to do these paintings every
     night.
With translucent colors
She takes the painting into a realm of immaculate dreams.

Ah, I do believe
These frosted window blossoms are patterns from my own dreams,
For no two days have they ever been alike,
Just as I have never dreamed the same dream twice.

Originally published in Shanghai wenxue, *No. 8, 1980.*

Translated by Jan W. Walls.

Poetry

QIU XIAOLONG *Lost Identity*

Accustomed to stand
On a high-rising scaffold
His spirit exulted
His heart grew bold
Though the scaffolding swayed
As rot spread and took hold.

Now he is back
His feet on the ground
Lost and bewildered
He feels his heart pound
Thrown into a panic
By gravity bound.

Original publication unclear.

Translated by Qiu Xiaolong and Bonnie S. McDougall.

QIU XIAOLONG *Thinking of You
on New Year's Eve*

*One night I was reading Bian Zhilin's "New Year's Eve Reverie." The mood
and setting seemed to fit my own, so I wrote this poem after his:*

I opened the curtain to gaze at the moon, but in the lamplight the
    windowpane
Is a mirror; the solitary image in it is hard to bear,
But the even deeper emptiness in my heart
Is a mirror that reflects your troubled eyes.

"I can't take you with me in my nightmare"—
I recall fragments of a broken watch.
I in the moonlight, the moon in your dreams,
Distance disappears only on television screens.

Originally published in Qinghaihu (Xining), *May 1981.*

Translated by Qiu Xiaolong and Bonnie S. McDougall.

Stubborn Weeds

QIU XIAOLONG *Temptation*

Soft are the arms
That press me to your bosom:
"Stay—listen—here is your still haven,
Embrace me, and no harm can come to us."

Sweet are the lips
That pout to mine:
"Stay—look—a bud that blossoms for you,
Kiss me, and we'll get drunk on joy."

But when I lift my head, I hear
The speedboat churn the waves across the boundless ocean, I see
The white trail left by the jet that roars across the sky, and I feel
That there are many things beyond my knowing, that I would
      know.

Originally published in Xingxing (Chengdu), June 1981.

Translated by Qiu Xiaolong and Bonnie S. McDougall.

QIU XIAOLONG *Five Sketches of Student Life*

STUDYING THE NIGHT

The stopped clock complains in silence
Of its neglect—with a thirsty ink bottle,
The desire to sleep is as distant as camel bells in the desert,
While our land's oases draw near beneath the pen.

BROWSING

Perhaps this small shell I find, and those two,
Are only other people's discards, now abandoned,
And yet the inexhaustible bounty of the ocean spreads before me,
Only unending sublation can produce a collage of pearls.

Poetry

In the Library

The water bottle that never had any water
Found a spring at last, only to
Leave it behind, to press forward
Into the desert, the mist, and know no bounds.

Dawn Watch

Clasping her books she appears with the dew,
Her figure slender, her voice clear and sweet,
The dew rises and merges with the clouds in the sky,
To become tomorrow's rain that will nourish the earth.

The Old Professor

Stooped back, shuffling steps,
But with a smile he spreads out his pile of papers;
The students listen, take notes, and recall
An old peasant bearing the harvest home in the setting sun.

Originally published in Xingxing *(Chengdu), June 1981.*

Translated by Qiu Xiaolong and Bonnie S. McDougall.

QIU XIAOLONG   *Street Scene*

A red wall by the bus stop
A poster proclaiming "Advance to world heights!"
A ramshackle shoe mender's stall
A fashionably dressed young woman
Sitting on a small rusty stool
Dangling a dainty white leg
Asking the shoe member to fit
High heels on her new leather shoes.

A few rusty nails
A number of idlers gazing at who knows what,
As if the rhythm of the shoe mender's hammer
Were at the top of the pops this year.

Stubborn Weeds

Under the willows by the bus stop
Another solitary young girl
Draws out a page from a foreign language dictionary
To read in the headlights of an oncoming bus.

Original publication unclear.

Translated by Qiu Xiaolong and Bonnie S. McDougall.

DRAMA

SHA YEXIN,
LI SHOUCHENG,
and YAO MINGDE

What If I Really Were?
(A PLAY IN SIX SCENES)

*"What If I Really Were?" was reportedly written over
a period of fifteen days and rushed into production in
August 1979 by several members of the Shanghai
People's Art Theater, inspired partly by the arrest of a privilege-seeking youth
five months earlier on charges of impersonating a high-ranking cadre. Yet the
play is certainly the product of a more substantial social and artistic ferment
than either its topical nature or the impressive swiftness of its creation might
imply. Because of its form and substance, "What If I Really Were?" for
several months became a central document in Party-led discussions of what
was to be considered responsible and permissible in literature.*

*In the context of the esthetic doctrines prevailing through most of the
1970s, one of the boldest strokes of "What If I Really Were?" is to place its
negative and morally flawed characters at the center of attention, departing
from the accepted practice of emphasizing positive characters. While this is
fundamental to the art of satire, the authors felt compelled to defend their
decision by prefacing the script with a quotation from Gogol to the effect that
the portrayal of the immoral can suggest moral purpose just as effectively as
direct portrayal of positive moral action. To be sure, "What If I Really Were?"
is not the first play since the founding of the People's Republic to trace its
lineage to Gogol, but it comes closer than any previously published play to
Gogol's style of satire (especially that of* The Inspector General*) in its
closely observed and bitingly satirical attention to its negative characters.*

*Lao She's "Looking West to Chang'an" ("Xi wang Chang'an"), first
published in 1956 and republished in July 1979 just prior to the appearance of
"What If I Really Were?," is also based on a real incident in which a man
posed as a war hero wounded in Korea. But all we finally learn of this
cowardly swindler is that he wanted to use his faked record to eat well and to
live in comfort. He is mistakenly helped by others out of their well-meaning
consideration for him and their desire to see him as the ideal hero.*

Following the Cultural Revolution, as satire grew more pungent, a one-act play appeared in Shanghai entitled "The Artillery Commander's Son" ("Paobing siling de erzi"), in which a hypocritical, social-climbing timeserver in the Party under the Gang of Four attempts to steer his daughter into an alliance with the son of a high-level cadre at the expense of her desire to marry a common worker. This rotten apple is tricked by a conspiracy of young people into agreeing to his daughter'ss choice. Such an assertion of the egalitarian spirit over a venal Party cadre set the stage for "What If I Really Were?," which expanded considerably on the satire of Party cadres and the issues at stake. It presents a basketload of cadres as so much overripe fruit nourished on the branches of bureaucratic hierarchy and the soil of a privilege-oriented mentality, juggled and manipulated in scene after scene by a saddened and cynical young picaro, until the circus of corruption and hypocrisy is finally quashed with the arrival, deus ex machina, of a leading cadre with social authority and personal integrity.

Official critics, who sometimes lauded the principle of hard-hitting social criticism, found its execution in "What If I Really Were?" to be disturbingly unbalanced.[1] The central action of the play was considered typical enough to be significant, but the context created for the action was too exaggerated to count as an accurate portrayal of Chinese society. Similarly, the play was too cavalier in its treatment of negatively portrayed cadres, reducing them to a mere parade of acquisitive clowns rather than distinguishing them as individual characters more fully representing varied aspects of social failure. As for the cadres who were positively portrayed, Zhang Senior was given inadequate attention, and Director Zheng was unduly despairing over the fate of his state farm. Whether true or not, these points disregard the play as literary satire, a form by nature rooted in distortion, exaggeration, and general unfairness, the more impartially unfair the better.

"What If I Really Were?" is not altogether a satirical work, however, and it is not impartial when it makes the young swindler largely a sympathetic figure. In the eyes of Party critics, this character's concerns are a reflection of petit bourgeois individualism. As one authoritative critic said:

Situated as we are now in a period when the new is replacing the old and when the new is still interlaced with the old, all kinds of thought either can appear or are now making an appearance. Currently there is quite a market for petit bourgeois thinking among a portion of the people, not only because China in the past was a nation dominated by the petite bourgeoisie but also for social, political, and economic reasons which have accumulated over a long period of time. Presently, while the vast majority of youth may belong to the worker class, many

1. The critical views cited here are found in Chen Yong, "Realism and Political Inclination in Literature As Seen from Two Plays" ("Cong liangge juben kan wenyi di zhenshixing he qingxiangxing"), Renmin ribao (March 19, 1980), reprinted in Zhonghua yuebao, no. 5 (1980), pp. 187–93; and Li Geng, "Opinions on 'What If I Really Were?'" ("Dui juben 'jiaru wo shi zhedi' di yijian"), Renmin xiju, no. 3 (1980), pp. 7–11.

Drama

among them have been influenced by all kinds of petit bourgeois thinking or have never had their petit bourgeois thinking reformed.[2]

The social problems depicted in the play are linked to the misrule of the Gang of Four, but it is also made clear that two years have passed since the Gang was toppled. This careful identification of time clears the way for the dangerous inference that some problems are attributable either to the present leadership or to socialist society in general. Political critics were always quick to challenge works that did not associate social failures strongly enough with the Gang of Four, and it was probably for this reason that "What If I Really Were?," despite its great fame in the People's Republic, was never published there except in restricted-circulation publications for cadres. It was performed in major cities, but not for the public except very briefly in Shanghai and Guangzhou. The present translation is based on the script published in the Hong Kong magazine The Seventies (Qishi niandai), January 1980. This text has been checked against restricted-circulation texts from China and is entirely accurate.

Introduction by Edward M. Gunn.

Translated by Edward M. Gunn.

Cannot positive and negative serve the same end? Cannot comedy and tragedy express the same sublime thought? Is not the dissection of shameless souls of some aid to outlining the image of the virtuous? And cannot all that which violates law and constitutes depravity tell us what the nature of law, duty, and justice should be?
Nicholas V. Gogol, "At the Theater Entrance"

Characters
ZHAO—managing director of a drama company.
QIAN—director of the political office of an organization department; wife of Secretary Wu.
SUN—chief of a bureau of culture.
LI XIAOZHANG (ZHANG XIAOLI)—an educated youth[1] assigned to a state farm.
ZHOU MINGHUA—worker in a cotton mill; Li Xiaozhang's girlfriend.
WU—secretary of the Party municipal committee.
ZHENG—director of a state-owned farm.
JUANJUAN—daughter of Bureau Chief Sun.
ZHANG LAO—cadre in charge, Party Central Commission for Inspecting Discipline.
PUBLIC SECURITY OFFICERS A AND B.

2. Chen Yong, p. 189.
1. An "educated youth" is one of the 17 million urban young people sent to the countryside in the 1960s and early 1970s to teach and learn from the peasants.

Stubborn Weeds

200

Spectators A, B, C, D, E, F.
Theater attendants.
A middle-aged man answering the telephone.
Restaurant waiters.
Educated youths A and B.
Presiding judge.
Assistant judicial officers A and B.
Prosecutor.

Prelude

Plays have their origins in life. And this play of ours also is taken from actual lives as they really occurred. So before the curtain goes up, why don't we start this play with an actual scene from life?

Fine. Then, before the performance begins, let's have a look at this beloved and faithful audience of ours pouring into the theater from all directions. Naturally, they know nothing about the play which they have come to see, save for its title. And so some of them have taken their seats to leaf through the program notes they just bought, hoping to glean in advance some understanding of the plot. Others stand in the lounge amid the noise of the crowd, talking with their companions, guessing what happens in the play. Still others are smoking cigarettes or eating ice cream contentedly, with no desire to tax their brains in such pursuits.

Shortly, under the urging of bells, the audience files in toward their seats. They wait, some attentively and some casually, for the curtain to part.

At last the time has arrived for the play to begin! The houselights dim, the music begins, and the eyes of the audience widen, concentrating on the stage. Suddenly the music stops, the houselights go back up, and from behind the curtain is heard the voice of the managing director of the company, Zhao, shouting, "Hold it! Hold it! Close the curtain!" Thereupon the stage curtain, which has barely parted, is again closed. After a moment, Managing Director Zhao walks from behind one edge of the curtain onto the stage.

Zhao (to the audience): Comrades, my apologies to you all. The play was scheduled to begin by now; however—however, we are expecting two leading comrades and their guest who have not yet arrived. Therefore I am obliged to request that you wait a bit longer. Things like this happen frequently; there's nothing unusual about it. Still I must ask you to bear with us. The play will go on in any event. If you will wait just a little longer, when they arrive we'll begin without delay. My sincerest apologies. I'm most sorry—

Her speech concluded, Managing Director Zhao walks back behind the curtain. And what of the audience reaction to this? Are they filled with helpless resentment? Do they give voice to their dissatisfaction, heatedly

Drama

201

protesting, loudly hissing or swearing? The only answer is that the audience is bound to react with many varying, individual attitudes to this pre-show inconvenience. And this is as it should be.

The initial wave of commotion having subsided, Managing Director Zhao again pokes her head out from the edge of the curtain and scans the front entrance of the house. Suddenly her face expresses surprised delight. The audience, of course, is certain to follow her eyes to the entrance.

At this point, under the gaze of the audience, there arrives at the front entrance a woman of uncommon appearance. She is Director Qian of the Political Office of the Party Municipal Committee Organization Department, and wife of the Secretary of the Party Municipal Committee. She is accompanied by the dignified Bureau Chief Sun, head of the Cultural Bureau. While the audience is certain to regard these two as the distinguished patrons for whom they have had the honor of waiting, this is in fact not so. Rather, notice that they are also ushering in a youth—he is the distinguished visitor. His name is Li Xiaozhang, but he presently calls himself Zhang Xiaoli.

Director Qian and Bureau Chief Sun are speaking to him with great deference in hushed voices: "After you, please. Please!" Escorting him forward, they walk straight to three empty seats in the front row near the center aisle. Once they are seated, Managing Director Zhao's voice can be heard from behind the curtain; "Let's go! Let's go! Curtain, ready. Curtain, now!" And the music resumes.

Abruptly, however, two public security officers enter, carrying guns; they move rapidly to where Li Xiaozhang is sitting.

OFFICER *(to Li Xiaozhang)*: Li Xiaozhang, you are under arrest!

QIAN *(startled)*: What? What's going on? His name is not Li Xiaozhang. What makes you think you can go around arresting anyone you feel like?

OFFICER *(producing the arrest warrant)*: Here's the warrant!

(The other officer handcuffs Li Xiaozhang.)

SUN: Get your hands off him! You've got the wrong man. Do you know who this is?!

OFFICER: You tell me.

SUN: This is Zhang Xiaoli!

QIAN: He is the son of a leader in Party Central.

OFFICER: No, he is an impostor!

QIAN AND SUN: What?!

(Managing Director Zhao has just dashed from the edge of the curtain to the front of the stage.)

ZHAO: Hey! What's going on here? How can we begin the show with this going on? *(to the public security officer)* Comrade, please be so kind as to explain just what's going on here!

OFFICER: All right!

Stubborn Weeds

(The two public security officers, Li Xiaozhang, Director Qian, and Bureau Chief Sun mount the stage.)

OFFICER: Comrade spectators, I'm very sorry to have interrupted you! This is an impostor by the name of Li Xiaozhang, calling himself Zhang Xiaoli. He is an educated youth assigned to a state farm. He has impersonated the son of a leader in Party Central and has engaged in fraudulent activities in this city. Because there is a danger that he will flee, we have had to take urgent measures to secure his arrest.

ZHAO: What? *(to Li Xiaozhang)* Is this true?

LI: Aren't you acting out a performance? I also acted out a performance for all of you. Now that my performance is over, you can go on with yours.

ZHAO: What?

QIAN: You?

SUN: Oh!

(The spotlight focuses in succession on the faces of Li Xiaozhang, Managing Director Zhao, Director Qian, and Bureau Chief Sun. Blackout.)

SCENE 1

Early evening during the first half of 1979.

The front entrance to a theater. (If this play has the good fortune to be performed in a theater, then the stage setting should resemble as closely as possible the front entrance of the theater where it is performed.)

Along one wall of the theater are large posters reading: "The XX Spoken Drama Company presents the Russian satirical comedy The Inspector General.*" Also on the posters is a portrait of the play's central character, Khlestakov.*

The theater is obviously full, and many people are clustered at the front doors waiting to buy unwanted tickets. With currency clutched in their hands, they hastily ask everyone they see: "Are you returning your ticket?" If someone has a ticket, the crowd surges forward instantly, every man for himself. The lucky purchaser, wildly delighted, utters a string of thank-yous and gleefully enters the theater. The unsuccessful—disappointed but not resentful—resume their search. This scene must be played in a thoroughly lifelike, natural fashion to make the spectators feel that it is realistic, just as though the performers were the spectators themselves or the members of the audience had themselves mounted the stage to perform.

Li Xiaozhang enters wearing an old army uniform, with an army satchel slung over his shoulder. He lets his cigarette dangle from his lips and blows smoke rings, impassively watching the crowd and the doors of the theater. Then he tosses away his cigarette and reaches into his pocket. Spectator A quickly comes forward to intercept him.

Drama

SPECTATOR A *(eagerly)*: Got a ticket?

LI: Ticket?

SPECTATOR A: Uh-huh.

LI *(in a slow drawl)*: Ye-e-es!

SPECTATOR A *(overjoyed)*: Great!

> (When the crowd around them hears that Li Xiaozhang has a ticket, they instantly surround him, crying out: "Let me have it!" "Give it to me!" "I'll take it! I'll take it!" Li Xiaozhang is pressed helplessly back against the wall.)

SPECTATOR A: I should get it! I was here first!

SPECTATOR B: I'll trade you ten movie tickets for one of yours!

SPECTATOR C: Give it here! Over here! Three dollars a ticket, how about it?

LI: Don't fight now! Don't fight! Everybody will get one! Everyone form a line! Form a line!

(There is much commotion as everyone forms into a line in front of Li Xiaozhang.)

LI: Don't worry, don't worry! I've got plenty of tickets, enough for everyone. From all over the country, from this area, too. I've got them all!

SPECTATOR A: What?

SPECTATOR B: All over the country and around here too?

SPECTATOR C: Just what kind of tickets are these?

LI *(takes several ration tickets from his wallet)*: Look, ration tickets!

SPECTATOR A: Huh?

SPECTATOR B: Is this some kind of joke?

LI: What do you mean? Ration tickets are tickets, aren't they? These are the most important tickets you can have. Without these you'd starve!

SPECTATOR C: Damn!

SPECTATOR D: Jerk—punch him out!

LI *(coolly, impassively)*: You want to try? Eh?

SPECTATOR B: All right. Forget it. Let's go, now, let's go.

(They disperse sullenly.)

SPECTATOR A: Comrade, you shouldn't trick people.

LI: It was just a joke. So what if I trick people? Putting on plays is tricking people too, isn't it? You people ignore the real drama taking place all around the world and instead have to come here to watch make-believe drama. Don't you think you're being tricked here too?

SPECTATOR A: What do *you* know? Today's play is world-famous! *The Inspector General!*

LI: Oh? *The Inspector General?* Any good?

SPECTATOR A: It's really good! It's about this grade 12 Russian civil servant from St. Petersburg who stops off in a town. The mayor of this town thinks he's the Inspector General, so he really flatters and fawns over him, gives him money and gifts, and then wants to marry his daughter to him. It's hysterically funny.

Li: Oh? The inspector general is a fake?

Spectator A: A swindler!

(Li Xiaozhang quickly walks over to a poster and examines it with great interest. After a moment he looks at his wristwatch, glances off into the distance, then continues reading the poster. After a moment, Zhou Minghua rushes in carrying a handbag.)

Zhou: Li Xiaozhang!

Li: Minghua! Look at you, late again!

Zhou: Dad wouldn't let me go out.

Li: That old stiff.

Zhou: How can you—

Li: He *is* an old stiff! I was just over at your place, and he ignored me completely!

Zhou: You mustn't be that way about my dad. (*She produces a bottle of* maotai *liquor from her handbag.*) Here! Dad told me to return it to you.

Li (*taken aback*): Ah! Did he drink it up?

Zhou: Drink what up? He doesn't drink.

Li (*taking the bottle*): Oh.

Zhou: What are you doing buying fancy *maotai* liquor like this for my father?

Li: Trying to get in good with my future father-in-law.

Zhou: But you're really extravagant buying a fancy brand like this!

Li: It's fake.

Zhou: What? Fake liquor?

Li: Could I have bought the real stuff? Oh, the bottle is real enough. Bought it at a secondhand goods stall where they were going for twenty cents apiece. But then I filled it with ordinary $1.20 *baigan* liquor.

Zhou: Ah? Weren't you afraid my father could tell the difference?

Li: People always go for appearances, and your dad is no exception.

Zhou: What made you want to do that?

Li: To get your dad to like me—what do you think? I did it for us.

Zhou: If that's what you really want, then hurry up and get yourself officially transferred back from the farm! Nothing else—no gift or anything is going to make him approve of us being together. You've just got to get transferred, and fast!

Li (*annoyed*): Whew, what a pain!

Zhou: I'm working on a solution for you. But you're smart and you're capable yourself; *you* have to be thinking of a solution too! All these

Drama

other people have been transferred back to the city, so why can't you be? Didn't a lot of my old classmates just get transferred back a little while ago?

LI: And what do their dads do?

ZHOU: One is Party secretary in a factory, and one is a deputy fleet commander, and then there's the girl in my class whose father is chief of the Bureau of Culture.

LI: Then of course they could get transferred! But what does my father do? *(sarcastically, raising his thumb)* A worker, a worker who never thinks of himself, a member of what they call the "vanguard" social class! Not worth a fart! The year before last when it was my turn to be transferred, wasn't my name cut from the list and passed over?

ZHOU: Yeah, if you had a good father, things would be fine.

LI: Before my next reincarnation I'm going to check first to see if my father is a high-level cadre; and if he isn't, I'd sooner die right in the womb and never come out!

ZHOU: Don't be silly. You'd better think of a way to get transferred soon. You can't put this off any longer—you know?

LI: All right, all right. There's no use getting upset! I'd better get us a couple of tickets so we can get in to see the show.

ZHOU: See a show?

LI: I hear this play is pretty good.

ZHOU: No, I can't. I sneaked out to see you.

LI: You won't come with me?

ZHOU: I'm afraid Dad will find out.

LI: Suit yourself.

(Zhou Minghua hesitates but finally decides to leave nevertheless and exits.)
(Li Xiaozhang starts to follow Zhou Minghua but is blocked by the arrival of a limousine. The glare of the limousine headlights is followed by the sound of braking. Simultaneously Managing Director Zhao runs out the front door of the theater, dispersing the surrounding crowd of onlookers. A moment later Bureau Chief Sun and his daughter Juanjuan enter. Zhao hurries forward to greet them. Li Xiaozhang stands to one side, eyeing them coldly.)

ZHAO *(with enthusiasm)*: Ah! Bureau Chief Sun, you're here! *(shaking his hand)* How are you!

SUN: How are you!

ZHAO: How has your health been recently?

SUN: Not bad.

ZHAO: But who do we have here! Is this Juanjuan?

SUN: This is Auntie Zhao.

JUANJUAN: Auntie Zhao!

ZHAO: My, my, what a pretty one! Transferred back from the farm?

Stubborn Weeds

JUANJUAN: Some time ago.

ZHAO: And your young man?

JUANJUAN: Still up in the northeast.

ZHAO: Oh, a young couple separated like that! That won't do, will it?

JUANJUAN: Dad is working on it.

SUN: Who said that? Nonsense!

JUANJUAN *(whispering to Zhao)*: I'm not talking nonsense. *He* is!

ZHAO *(with a laugh)*: Please, come on in! *(She takes out two tickets.)* Here are the tickets we've held for you.

(Another limousine arrives with the glare of headlights and the sound of braking. Zhao and Sun stop and look toward the car.)

SUN: Who's that in that car?

ZHAO: It looks like Director Qian from the Organization Department.

SUN: Director Qian?

ZHAO: The wife of Secretary Wu in the Party Municipal Committee.

SUN: Oh, sure, sure!

ZHAO *(showing off)*: We were buddies back during the war. We go way back together.

(Director Qian enters.)

ZHAO *(instantly going up to greet her)*: Sister Qian, to what do we owe the honor of your presence?

QIAN: My dear Zhao, have you so completely forgotten about me that you don't invite me to your shows anymore?

ZHAO: I wanted to invite you several times, but I was afraid you'd be busy. You want to watch this evening?

QIAN: Are there any tickets?

ZHAO: You think there wouldn't be a ticket for you? Just tell me how many you want and they're yours.

QIAN: Just one is all I want.

ZHAO: Isn't Secretary Wu coming?

QIAN: How can he take time to watch plays? He's busy all day and into the night. I tell him to relax and take a break, but he's so obstinate he won't do it—talks about regaining all the time that was squandered by the Gang of Four.

ZHAO: Secretary Wu really works hard. That's quite a heavy burden he has, eh!

SUN: Director Qian, let's go in. They're starting the show.

QIAN *(not recognizing Sun)*: This gentleman is—?

SUN: I'm in the Bureau of Culture.

ZHAO: This is Bureau Chief Sun. You've never met?

QIAN: Oh, yes, of course, your immediate superior. Why, it's been ten years, and look at how that hair is all white now!

ZHAO: Bureau Chief Sun, why don't you escort Director Qian and go on in—I still have to wait for Director Ma.

Drama

QIAN: Which Director Ma?

ZHAO: The one who heads the Party Municipal Propaganda Department.

QIAN: Oh, old Ma! He's going overseas tomorrow for a visit, so he won't be showing up.

ZHAO: Oh? Then let's go in!

QIAN: Please!

(Qian and Sun exit into the door of the theater. Zhao is stopped by a call from Li Xiaozhang, who has been standing off to the side listening surreptitiously to their conversation.)

LI: Comrade!

ZHAO: What?

LI: Any tickets?

ZHAO: No, none!

LI: What're those in your hand?

ZHAO: These tickets are reserved for leading cadres!

LI: Didn't they just say that Director Ma wasn't going to come?

ZHAO: Even if he doesn't, I can't sell the tickets.

LI: But there are plenty of them. Why can't you sell some?

ZHAO: They are reserved for leading cadres.

LI: That young woman who just went in—is she a leading cadre too?

ZHAO: Her father is. Is your father?

(Zhao exits into the theater.)

LI: Damn. Even to see a show you have to have a good father. (Li Xiaozhang starts to leave but then walks over to the poster and again pauses before it. He dawdles there, unwilling to leave. He thinks for a moment, then walks to the left edge of the proscenium, where, on the proscenium arch, a telephone appears. He picks up the receiver and dials.)

LI: Hello. I want backstage. I'm Director Ma, Party Municipal Propaganda Department . . . Right, I want your Managing Director Zhao on the phone. OK. *(a pause)* Right, right, it's me . . . Is this Managing Director Zhao? I'm going on a visit overseas tomorrow, so I can't get over to see your show this evening . . . Secretary Wu's wife told you? Good. I was wondering if I could trouble you to do something for me . . . The son of an old war buddy of mine is here from Beijing, and he's really eager to see your show. He just gave me a call and said he couldn't pick up any tickets at the door. Can you help him out? . . . No problem, eh? Good. He only wants one ticket . . . His name is Zhang Xiaoli—*Zhang* as in "stretch"; *Xiao* as in "small"; *li* as in "ideals." . . . You'll wait for him at the door? Fine. He's in the vicinity of the theater; I'll tell him to get right over and find you.

(Li Xiaozhang hangs up and stands at the proscenium leaning against the wall, observing the theater entrance. After a pause,

Zhao runs onstage carrying theater tickets and stands watching among the crowd. Before long, Spectator E approaches her.)

ZHAO: What's your name, comrade?

SPECTATOR E: Wu. So what?

ZHAO: Oh, I'm sorry.

(Zhao now approaches Spectator F.)

ZHAO: What's your name, comrade?

SPECTATOR F: Ji. Got any tickets?

ZHAO: No, no. None. None at all!

(Zhao anxiously looks at her watch. Now Li Xiaozhang walks over to her.)

LI: Comrade, are you Managing Director Zhao?

ZHAO: Yes, yes. And you are—

LI: I'm Zhang Xiaoli.

ZHAO *(with a start)*: Ah! It's you?

LI: Yes. Did Director Ma call you?

ZHAO: Yes. Yes. Goodness, why didn't you tell me before when you were just here? I misunderstood, simply misunderstood! You don't have to bother Director Ma for something as trivial as this. From now on, if you want to see a show you just come straight to me, OK?

LI: Oh, that's so much bother for you! Too much bother!

ZHAO: No, not at all! It's the least we can do for someone introduced by Director Ma. Your father and Director Ma were—?

LI: My dad and Director Ma are old war buddies!

ZHAO: Well! Please—right this way! Please!

(Zhao invites Li into the theater. From here on, Li Xiaozhang becomes Zhang Xiaoli.)

SPECTATOR B: Hey, how did that jerk get in?

ZHAO: His father is a leading cadre. Is yours?

SCENE 2

That evening, after the performance.

The VIP lounge in the theater. To the left and right are doors, one leading to the house, one leading backstage. Cushioned armchairs and sofas are arranged along the walls. Photographs of the production of The Inspector General *hang on one wall; a poster advertising* The Inspector General *is stuck on another wall.*

As the curtain rises, the sounds of enthusiastic applause from the audience and the commotion of their leaving are heard offstage. After a moment, Zhao enters the VIP lounge from the door to the house, leading Zhang Xiaoli (Li Xiaozhang) by the hand.

ZHAO *(eagerly)*: Come, come. Let's go in and relax. Have a seat. Wher-

Drama

ever you like. The facilities in our theater are pretty backward com-
pared to Beijing, eh?
*(A theater attendant enters carrying two cups of tea; gives one to Zhao and
one to Zhang Xiaoli, then exits.)*
ZHAO: Well, how did you like the play? Give us your opinion.
ZHANG *(sincerely)*: Good. Very good. I've really never seen a play as
good as that before.
ZHAO: Your real opinion now, come on!
ZHANG: Really. It was really good. Well, I'd better be on my way.
ZHAO: Relax a minute! What's your rush?
ZHANG: I ought to get back.
ZHAO: Don't leave, don't leave! I was just telling Director Qian and
Chief Sun that they have to come and meet you.
ZHANG *(with a start)*: They're coming to meet me?
ZHAO: Yes, they're backstage right now meeting the actors, but they'll
be here shortly.
ZHANG: No, no. Leading cadres are extremely busy, and I wouldn't
want to take up their time!
*(Zhang Xiaoli stands and starts to leave. Zhao quickly and solicitously pulls
him back. Theater attendant enters bringing hors d'oeuvres and then exits.)*
ZHAO: Wait a little. Come on, have a little something to eat. *(passing
the tray of food to Zhang)* Have some, have some. How can you
refuse? Go ahead! *(Zhang reluctantly sits and eats, still a bit uneasy.)*
ZHAO: Is the weather still holding up well in Beijing?
ZHANG: Fine. It's snowing.
ZHAO: Snowing in summer?
ZHANG: No, it snows in winter. Everywhere in the country it's the
same—it snows in winter.
ZHAO: Right, yes. Did you come from Beijing on business this time?
ZHANG: No. I can't stand business trips; they bother me no end.
ZHAO: You've come to see a friend?
ZHANG: Yes, to see a friend.
ZHAO: Did you have any other purpose in mind?
ZHANG *(alarmed)*: No, no other purpose. When I came to look for you
this evening I just wanted to see a play, that's all.
ZHAO: No, I mean besides seeing your friend, do you have anything
else to take care of?
ZHANG: No. Just to relax and take in some shows.
ZHAO: Shows? Well, I have plenty of tickets. Oh, yes. *(takes out some
tickets)* Here are tickets to some restricted-audience films[2]—
American, Japanese, French. They're all showing next week. Here,
take them all.
ZHANG *(delighted)*: Great! How much do I owe you?

2. Usually these are foreign films that may be seen only by people in certain jobs,
or by officials of certain ranks and their families.

Stubborn Weeds

ZHAO: Here you've come all the way from Beijing. How could I take your money?

ZHANG: How can I let you do this?

ZHAO: Oh, come on, can't I afford to invite you to some shows?

ZHANG (*accepting the tickets*): It's awfully embarrassing to impose on you this way. (*A sudden thought occurs.*) Oh, right. (*drawing out the bottle of* maotai *liquor from his shoulder bag*) I don't have a thing with me—all I can offer Auntie Zhao is this—

ZHAO: *Maotai?*

ZHANG: It's just a token.

ZHAO: I'm not much of a drinker.

ZHANG: Then give it to someone else. Here, take it. From now on if I want to see a show, I'll have to come bother you!

ZHAO: (*accepting the liquor*): Now I'm the one who's embarrassed. Did you buy this at your hotel?

ZHANG: No, you can't get it at the hotel. This is a special grade, for export only.

ZHAO: Oh? So it must be in a class above the standard *maotai?*

ZHANG: Well, at least it doesn't taste quite the same.

ZHAO: Does your father always drink this high-class *maotai?*

ZHANG: All the time—at least thirty bottles a month!

ZHAO: My! Your father, is he—

ZHANG: You want to know who my father is?

ZHAO: Is it a classified secret?

ZHANG: No, it doesn't have to be secret from you.

ZHAO: Then who is he?

ZHANG: Guess. My family name is Zhang.

ZHAO: Is your father Zhang Jingfu?

(*Zhang smiles mysteriously and shakes his head.*)

ZHAO: Zhang Qiling?

(*Zhang shakes his head.*)

ZHAO: Then—is it Comrade Zhang Tingfa?

(*Zhang shakes his head.*)

ZHAO: Oh, Zhang Wentian! Oh, no. No. That's not right, he's dead. Zhang—right, Vice-Chairman of the General Staff Zhang—Zhang Caiqian!

(*Zhang shakes his head.*)

ZHAO: Then who?

ZHANG: Guess. In any case you know it can't be Zhang Chunqiao![3]

ZHAO: Of course, of course. Now which high-ranking cadre is it?

ZHANG: No, he's an ordinary cadre.

ZHAO: No, it can't be. It can't be. He's a high-ranking cadre for sure! (*in a burst of enthusiasm*) Oh, it's got to be—

ZHANG: Who?

3. Zhang Chunqiao was one of the Gang of Four.

Drama

ZHAO: He's—(*leans to whisper in Zhang's ear*) Right?

ZHANG: What do you think?

ZHAO: It must be; it's got to be!

ZHANG (*laughing*): Just as you say!

ZHAO (*gleefully*): Ah! Is it really him? Oh, dear, what a good father you have! How lucky you are!

ZHANG: It's true. And it's sad everyone can't have such a good father.

ZHAO: For that matter, your father is more than Director Ma's former superior—he also knows our Secretary Wu pretty well!

ZHANG: Secretary Wu?

ZHAO: You don't know who I mean? Secretary Wu of the Party Municipal Committee.

ZHANG: Oh, Secretary Wu of the Party Municipal Committee! I've heard my father talk about him.

ZHAO: I've heard Sister Qian, Secretary Wu's wife, say that in the summer of 1953 Secretary Wu was in Beijing for a conference and went to see your father at your home. You were still a baby then, weren't you? And Secretary Wu gave your dad a rare cactus plant. Your dad saw how much Secretary Wu smoked, so he gave him two cartons of imported State Express cigarettes. Sister Qian says it's been twenty years since your dad and Secretary Wu have seen each other. Right, I'll go tell Sister Qian right away. When she knows you've come she'll be thrilled! Wait just a minute.

(Zhao exits through the door to backstage. Zhang Xiaoli shakes his head at the departing Zhao. Then he takes one cigarette out of a pack on the table and puts it in the pocket of his jacket, intending to save it for later. He gently opens the door to the house and is just starting to go out when, after a single look, he hastily retreats back inside. Director Qian and Bureau Chief Sun enter. Zhang goes up to greet them with great poise and confidence.)

ZHANG: Auntie Qian!

QIAN (*nonplussed*): Who—?

ZHANG: I'm the one introduced by Director Ma to come see the show.

QIAN: Oh yes, I heard, I heard. Where's Managing Director Zhao?

ZHANG: Auntie Zhao said she was going to look for you.

QIAN: Have a seat, have a seat!

ZHANG: How is Uncle Wu?

QIAN: Not bad.

ZHANG: Does he still smoke like a chimney?

QIAN (*surprised*): How'd you know that, you clever little thing?

ZHANG: I heard my dad say so. My dad has quit smoking. He said to tell Uncle Wu to cut down a little.

QIAN (*stumped*): Your dad? Oh, uh, how is he?

ZHANG: Fine. It's just that his work keeps him too busy, and he doesn't have any time to raise flowers. But he's always enjoyed that

Stubborn Weeds

212

rare cactus plant Uncle Wu brought him when he went to the conference in 1953.

QIAN (*beside herself with joy*): Oh, so you're—oh, my, why didn't you say so before! No wonder you even know about Secretary Wu's smoking!

(*Bureau Chief Sun questioningly approaches Director Qian, who whispers in his ear.*)

SUN (*startled*): Oh? (*Sun hastily sits down on one side.*)

QIAN: This is wonderful. Wonderful! Come, come, come over here! Over here! (*pulls Zhang over to sit next to her*) Are you the youngest or the oldest?

ZHANG: In 1953 when Secretary Wu came to Beijing I was still a baby.

QIAN: Oh, then you must be the fifth.

ZHANG: That's right, I'm the fifth.

QIAN: What's your name, cute little thing?

ZHANG: Zhang Xiaoli. *Xiao* as in "small"; *li* as in "ideals." You can call me what you like—Zhang, or little Zhang, or Xiaoli—whatever.

(*Zhao enters quickly from the door to backstage.*)

ZHAO: Sister Qian—oh, you already know each other?

QIAN: Of course, why not? Secretary Wu knew his father twenty years ago. And Secretary Wu held him in his arms. You know whose child he is, don't you?

ZHAO: Yes, I do. I even guessed it!

QIAN: You had to guess? Why, I would have known him at first sight! Look how much like your dad you are!

SUN: Yes, yes. Looks just like him! A chip off the old block!

QIAN: He'll be a guest of mine and Secretary Wu's, so from now on, Zhao, you'll have to invite him to see plenty of shows!

ZHANG: Auntie Qian, you have other things to take care of—I'll just be on my way.

QIAN: Relax!

ZHANG: I'm taking a flight back to Beijing early tomorrow morning.

QIAN: Stay and enjoy yourself a while longer!

ZHAO: Next week you have to see the restricted films, remember.

ZHANG: I'll take a flight back when the time comes. Let me visit you next time, Auntie Qian.

QIAN: Stay a few more moments, just a few more moments. (*pulls Zhang over to sit next to her*) I haven't had a chance to chat with you yet. What brings you here from Beijing?

ZHAO: He's come to see a friend.

QIAN: Male friend or female friend?

ZHAO: The same as I—male, that is.

ZHAO: Little Zhang, you mustn't fool people!

ZHANG: *People* I have never fooled.

QIAN: Where is your friend?

Drama

ZHANG: At the Haidong State Farm.

QIAN: Oh? Sill not transferred out?

ZHANG: His father is an ordinary worker, so he has no way out. I've been worried to death about him.

ZHAO: You can use your father's connections!

ZHANG: But my father doesn't know the director of the farm.

ZHAO (with sudden recollection): Bureau Chief Sun, aren't you an old war buddy of Zheng at the Haidong Farm?

SUN: Mm. Yes, that's right.

ZHAO: Well, little Zhang, why don't you ask Bureau Chief Sun to look up Director Zheng and ask him to give it some consideration?

SUN (with an embarassed expression): Well, this—

(Zhao signals to Zhang to talk to Qian.)

ZHANG: Auntie Qian, do you think this would be a bother to Uncle Sun?

QIAN: Why don't you take a run out there, Sun?

SUN (hastily agreeing): Sure, sure. I'll give it a try. Hm, what's his name?

ZHANG: His name is Li—Li Xiaozhang—in the 57th Company.

SUN (jotting it down in his notebook): Fine.

ZHANG (delighted but restraining himself): Wonderful. If Uncle Sun can really help him settle this transfer problem, then for the time being I'll put off my plans to return to Peking tomorrow!

QIAN: Right, and you can stay here for a few days and relax.

ZHANG: Uncle Sun, when do you think I can hear from you on this?

SUN: Hm, why don't you come over to my house in a week?

ZHANG: Fine! I'll be over to see you in a week for sure!

QIAN: Right. Where are you staying now, little Zhang?

ZHANG (blurting it out): The Nanhu Guest House.

QIAN: What room number?

ZHANG: 102.

QIAN: Since you're not going back to Beijing for the time being, why not stay at our place?

ZHANG: No, no, no. The hotel is just fine.

QIAN: You won't find my home a letdown!

ZHANG: But then I'd have to cancel the room and create a lot of bother and all, so let's just let it go!

QIAN: What's so hard about canceling a room? (She picks up the telephone receiver.) I'll speak with them.

ZHANG (hastily snatching the phone receiver): I'll take care of it. Have a seat, have a seat.

QIAN: Do you know the number?

ZHANG: Yes! (Zhang dials a number at random. To one side of the stage appears a telephone answered by a middle-aged man.)

ZHANG: Hello. Nanhu Guest House?

MIDDLE-AGED MAN: What? The Nanhu Guest House? No, no, this is a mortuary.

ZHANG (*nodding to Qian to indicate his call has gone through*): I'm Zhang Xiaoli in Room 102.

MIDDLE-AGED MAN: Wrong number! What is this? Who are you?

ZHANG: Hu Eryu? Listen, Comrade Hu, I won't be back this evening.

MIDDLE-AGED MAN (*to himself*): How come I'm Comrade Hu? (*into the receiver*) Name's Lei Te!

ZHANG: Letters? None from my father? What about a telegram?

MIDDLE-AGED MAN (*with a wry smile*): You're a case!

ZHANG: My case? No, don't worry about it. I'll come back for my bags in a few days.

MIDDLE-AGED MAN (*losing his patience*): You got nothing better to do or what? What do you mean playing practical jokes in the middle of the night! You're nuts! (*He slams down the receiver. Fadeout.*)

ZHANG: Thank you. Yes, thank you so much. Sorry to trouble you. (*hangs up*) Really courteous service!

ZHAO: It's a high-level hotel!

QIAN (*standing*): Let's go, little Zhang!

ZHANG: Okay. Uncle Sun, I'll hear from you in a week.

SUN: Fine, fine.

(*Zhang enthusiastically pats Sun on the shoulder until, suddenly recalling that he's an impostor, he quickly withdraws his hand and smiles with embarrassment.*)

SCENE 3

The morning of a day the following week.

The living room of Bureau Chief Sun's home. There are doors to the left and right—one leading to the bedroom, one to the kitchen. There is a door in the center leading to a corridor and the courtyard. The living room contains a color television set, radio console, sofa, cane chairs, tables, telephone, and so forth.

When the curtain rises, Zhou Minghua is kneeling down scrubbing the floor, her pants rolled up and her feet bare. She has clearly been scrubbing for some time, as she is perspiring heavily. She suddenly feels nauseated and wants to vomit but struggles desperately to control herself. After resting for a while, she continues to scrub the floor. Bureau Chief Sun enters the living room through the door to the corridor.

SUN (*dissatisfied*): But this floor should be waxed! How can you put water all over it? (*Astonished, Zhou Minghua doesn't know what to do.*)

SUN: And I'm having guests over today! Look at this, will you! Look at it! Agh! All right. That's enough.

Drama

(Zhou Minghua picks up her mop and pail and exits through the door right. Juanjuan enters through another door, carrying a book.)

JUANJUAN: Dad, you're back?

SUN: Did you just get up?

JUANJUAN: No, I woke up at nine o'clock. I was just reading this novel in bed.

SUN: You really have it easy! Juanjuan, did you hire a woman to work here after your mother left?

JUANJUAN: No.

SUN: Well, then who was that washing the floor just now?

JUANJUAN: Oh, she was in my class at school.

SUN: You were classmates?

JUANJUAN: She can do anything. Rough work, delicate work—it's all the same to her. Look *(pointing at her own skirt)*—this is a skirt she made for me yesterday. And she says she's going to knit some wool things for me, too.

SUN: Oh? Why haven't I seen her over here before?

JUANJUAN: She's here because she wants you to help her.

SUN *(annoyed)*: I'm already busy enough as it is!

(Zhou Minghua enters, her arms wrapped around a large basket of laundry.)

JUANJUAN: Minghua, come on in. Come in. I'll introduce you. This is my father.

ZHOU: Uncle Sun, how are you?

JUANJUAN: Her name is Zhou—Zhou Minghua. She was transferred out of a state farm last year and assigned to a cotton mill as a worker.

SUN: Oh, I'm sorry, I was under the impression—*(indicating the basket of clothes Zhou is carrying)* Set it down, set it down. Let Juanjuan wash them!

JUANJUAN: Hey, how am I going to wash all that? I've asked you and asked you to get a washing machine, and to this day you haven't bought one. Oh well, I'll just send these out to the laundry!

ZHOU *(worried at missing her opportunity to wash the clothes)*: No, no. I'll wash them.

JUANJUAN: Minghua, hold on! Dad!

SUN: What is it?

JUANJUAN: Minghua has a boyfriend still on the farm. They've known each other for years now, and they want to get married. Only her father won't agree to it and he won't give his consent unless her boyfriend is transferred back to the city. Dad, poor Minghua is really desperate. You've got to figure something out for her.

SUN: You're her classmate, so you should go to work on her father's ideology. Tell her father that such thinking is incorrect. In our country there's no such thing as high or low status. Any job, whether on a farm or in a factory, serves the people and has a bright future.

Stubborn Weeds

JUANJUAN: Spoken like a simpleton. *You* go say that! Who listens to that babble nowadays?

SUN: So let the marriage be set back a couple of years, that's all. I imagine her boyfriend will be transferred out sooner or later.

ZHOU: Uncle Sun, we can't put this off any more—

SUN: You're still young. Right now you should be putting your energy into your work and your studies.

JUANJUAN: Dad, don't be that way! Don't you know Director Zheng at the Haidong Farm? Go give him the word—you can just telephone him!

SUN: How can you tell your father to do such a thing? I'm a state cadre—you want me to do something that violates principle?

ZHOU: That's all right, Juanjuan, forget it. Let's not make things awkward for Uncle Sun!

JUANJUAN: He's putting on an act! All right! *(She takes the basket of laundry held by Zhou and with both hands stuffs it into Sun's arms.)* You go wash these clothes! Here someone's helped us so much these last two days, only to find out it's for nothing!

SUN: You—you! All right, all right, we'll talk about it later, not now. Later! *(pulling Juanjuan to one side)* I've got company coming in a little while, and these Beijing people like steamed rolls. So go buy some steamed rolls for me.

JUANJUAN: That's a long way. I'm not going all the way over there!

SUN: You can take the car!

JUANJUAN: I want to read this book.

ZHOU: Juanjuan, what's going on?

JUANJUAN: He told me to go buy some steamed rolls.

ZHOU: Uncle Sun, you don't need to buy them. I can make them.

SUN: Oh? That's fine, fine. You'd better go get to work in the kitchen. They've got to be ready before noon.

ZHOU: Uh-huh.

JUANJUAN: Minghua, you're amazing!

(Zhou exits through the door right.)

JUANJUAN: That's really rotten, Dad. Here other people help you, but you won't do anything for them!

SUN: Juanjuan, when you're talking in front of other people, from now on pay attention to what sort of impression you're making.

JUANJUAN: Everything I've said is true!

SUN: Now that also depends on what you're talking about.

JUANJUAN: Telling the truth depends on what you're talking about? What about telling lies?

SUN: Who tells lies?

JUANJUAN: You do. Day after day I hear you telling lies!

SUN: You! You're getting more and more outrageous! Wait till your mother gets back. I'll have her rein you in!

JUANJUAN: I'm not afraid of Mom. It's *you* who's afraid of her!

Drama

217

SUN: Ah, you—you! I'm through with you! That's it!

(*Shaking his head in despair, Sun exits left. Juanjuan reads on the sofa.*)

JUANJUAN: Minghua, what are you up to?

(*Zhou Minghua's voice: "Kneading the dough!"*)

JUANJUAN: Come out and join me!

(*Zhou Minghua enters carrying a bowl of dough.*)

JUANJUAN: With my mom away everything falls on you, Minghua!

ZHOU: It's nothing—so long as you and your father can get my boyfriend transferred back from the farm, I'll do anything to help your family!

JUANJUAN: Relax. My father is faking this straight-arrow act. Right now he's busy with my case. When he's done with that, I'll talk to him again about yours.

ZHOU: What's the problem with you? Weren't you transferred back here a long time ago?

JUANJUAN: It's my husband. He's up in the northeast. Mom went up there a few days ago carrying a letter that Dad got someone to write. She looked up the head of my husband's unit to try to get him transferred back.

ZHOU: Is there any hope it'll work?

JUANJUAN: Well, in any event, I have Dad to rely on.

ZHOU: I really envy you!

JUANJUAN: Your boyfriend will be transferred too. Minghua, I've never seen your boyfriend. Is he good-looking?

ZHOU (*embarrassed*): Average.

JUANJUAN: Do you really love him?

ZHOU: I loved him so much to begin with—

JUANJUAN: To begin with?

ZHOU: When he first came to the farm, he was terrific—idealistic and clever. He could do any work he put his mind to, and he was a talented actor. But later, when the farm went from bad to worse, people found all kinds of ways, legitimate or not, to get out. Under the policy the year before last, he could have been transferred back to the city, but before we suspected anything he was squeezed out by others. His name was cut from the list, and he got really depressed. Later he started to smoke, and then drink and got more and more—

JUANJUAN: So you don't love him now?

ZHOU: Oh, yes. He'll get better.

(*Managing Director Zhao enters the living room from the corridor.*)

ZHAO: Juanjuan!

JUANJUAN: Auntie Zhao! (*Zhou Minghua exits.*)

ZHAO: Here, I brought some tickets for you!

JUANJUAN: Oh, wonderful!

ZHAO (*taking out a number of tickets*): They're all for restricted films from overseas.

Stubborn Weeds

218

JUANJUAN (accepting the tickets): Do you have any more?

ZHAO: What an appetite! I've got a list of over three hundred people, and only ten tickets for each film. So every time I distribute the tickets I have to divide them up carefully or I get into some real squabbles. Now I've given you two tickets for *each* film. How about it—is that still not enough for you?

JUANJUAN: Thank you, Auntie Zhao!

ZHAO: Your father?

JUANJUAN: He's in there. (calling) Hey, Dad! Auntie Zhao is here!

(Juanjuan exits. Sun enters left.)

SUN (indifferently): So, what's brought you here today?

ZHAO: Didn't you say that after a week you'd have something to tell that young Zhang from Beijing?

SUN (displeased): You have your mind on that too?

ZHAO: I thought I'd see what I could do to push it through. Everyone knows what a warm heart I have. (takes out the bottle of maotai liquor from her bag) I've pulled some strings to get this for you.

SUN (delighted but instantly assuming a somber visage): What are you up to?

ZHAO: I don't drink, so there's no point in having it take up space in my house. I knew you like to drink, so I brought it over.

SUN: I don't like it when people do this!

ZHAO: Yes, I know, and if it were any other kind of liquor I wouldn't have brought it. But this isn't ordinary *maotai*. It's a special grade, for export only. It's probably fortified with medicinal ingredients.

SUN: Oh, a special grade? Not the ordinary *maotai*?

ZHAO: It sure isn't! I had to go through a lot of people before I could get it, and it wasn't easy even then.

SUN: Then—then why don't you leave it here! But I can't let you bear the expense!

ZHAO: If you try to pay, I'll take it back.

SUN (smiling): You? Fine, fine, fine. We'll settle it later. (Sun puts the bottle of maotai in a cabinet.)

ZHAO: How are you doing on young Zhang's problem?

SUN: We'll talk about it when he gets here.

ZHAO (probing): Has Juanjuan's husband been transferred back from the northeast?

SUN: Don't listen to Juanjuan's nonsense. I'm not getting involved in that business!

(pause)

ZHAO: Bureau Chief Sun, about my housing problem—

SUN: Didn't I tell you that I can't do anything about it?

ZHAO: You're a bureau chief!

SUN: You have a fine place to live. Why do you want to be transferred to a larger place? You're a Party cadre; you ought to keep your life a bit on the plain and rugged side.

Drama

ZHAO: But some of the people who joined the revolution when I did already have over 750 square feet for their living quarters.

SUN: Disparities are inevitable.

ZHAO: Bureau Chief Sun—

SUN: You'll have to go try the Party Municipal Propaganda Department!

ZHAO (*producing a formal petition letter*): I've written out a formal request. I wanted to ask you to forward it on to Director Ma.

SUN: Director Ma is out of the country.

ZHAO: Then give it to his secretary before he returns.

SUN: That's out of the question. If I forward it for you, I'll be implicated. I think we'd better wait a while and see.

ZHAO: But isn't young Zhang's problem getting taken care of?

SUN: It's being arranged personally by the wife of the Secretary of the Party Municipal Committee. Now, in your case, if you also get a nod from upstairs, I can work it out for you.

ZHAO: Bureau Chief Sun—

(*The telephone rings, and Sun starts to answer it. Juanjuan runs in from the right.*)

JUANJUAN: I'll get it, Dad! (*picking up the receiver*) Right, yes, good. (*excitedly to Sun*) Dad, it's Mom calling long distance from the northeast!

SUN: Stop shouting! You'll drive me to an early grave with your ranting. (*to Zhao*) Let's go. We'll go sit in there.

ZHAO: Fine. (*She rises slowly, then suddenly and deliberately twists her ankle.*) Ouch! (*Taking advantage of this, she sinks back onto the sofa.*) Ouch!

SUN: What's wrong?

ZHAO: I twisted my foot!

SUN: Great timing!

JUNAJUAN: Is it serious?

ZHAO: I've got to rub it some.

(*Zhao makes a deliberate show of rubbing her foot. Sun fumes.*)

JUANJUAN (*continuing her phone conversation*): Mom! It's me, Juanjuan! What? That letter Dad arranged for was very effective? Wonderful! They've agreed to transfer him? (*excitedly to Sun*) Dad, did you hear, did you hear?

ZHAO: Chief Sun, Juanjuan is asking if you heard.

SUN: Hang up, hang up!

JUANJUAN (*continuing on the telephone*): OK, OK. (*hangs up and speaks to Sun*) Mom said they've agreed up there to let him go. She says for you to arrange the transfer order from this end and send it up there on the double.

SUN: I'm not taking part in this. I'm not taking any part in any of the stuff you two cook up!

JUANJUAN: You won't do it? Hmph!

(*Juanjuan exits right. Sun, in a rage, starts to exit left. Outside a car horn honks.*)

SUN (*turning toward Zhao, hastily*): What else is on your mind?

ZHAO (*with a show of pain*): Oh, my foot!

(*Sun exits through the door to the corridor. After a moment Sun enters together with Zhang Xiaoli, who is carrying a basket of fruit.*)

ZHANG: Uncle Sun, Auntie Qian had me bring over this basket of fruit for you.

SUN: Oh! Please thank Director Qian for me when you go back!

ZHANG: It's just a token, no thanks necessary!

ZHAO: Young Zhang!

ZHANG: Auntie Zhao, you're here too?

ZHAO: Have a seat.

(*Zhang sits on the sofa.*)

SUN (*passing cigarettes to Zhang*): Have a cigarette!

ZHANG: No thanks. (*takes out a pack of State Express cigarettes*) I smoke these! (*Zhang passes them to Sun and Zhao.*)

ZHAO: Did you come by car?

ZHANG: Uh-huh, Secretary Wu's car.

ZHAO: Oh? Secretary Wu's car.

ZHANG: Uncle Wu went to a conference at Huangshan.[4] I got to his house late at night and he left early the next morning, so Auntie Qian is letting me use his limousine.

SUN: Then you still haven't met Secretary Wu?

ZHANG: He still doesn't know I'm here.

ZHAO: Auntie Qian has really looked after you, eh?

ZHANG: She has no children, and it's as if she's adopted me as her own. Uncle Sun, Auntie Qian told me to ask you how my problem was coming along.

SUN (*uneasy*): It hasn't been coming along very well!

ZHANG (*attentively*): What seems to be the matter?

SUN: I was over at Director Zheng's yesterday. He said the last time they carried out transfers and urban job assignments, they made a mess of it. The Party Municipal Committee criticized them, and they are just now straightening things out. So for the time being they've stopped handling such cases.

ZHAO: That's the official line he's putting out.

ZHANG: Didn't you tell him that there were special circumstances surrounding the transfer of Li Xiaozhang and that the wife of the Secretary of the Party Municipal Committee was personally interceding?

SUN: I told him. It was no use. Director Zheng said that it was Secre-

---

4. A famous mountain resort in southern Anhui Province.

tary Wu's own order to close the door on this, and if anyone wanted the door opened, no matter whether it was the front door or the back door, they'd have to have an order written by Secretary Wu himself.

ZHANG: We have to have an order from Secretary Wu?

SUN: Zheng's afraid that if it's not in writing he'll have nothing to fall back on, and if there's an investigation later he'll get in a lot of trouble.

ZHANG (indignant): You mean when the Municipal Committee Secretary's own wife speaks it doesn't amount to anything? What? All right, I'll go see Auntie Qian!

SUN: Little Zhang, wait!

ZHANG: I've already waited a week!

SUN: But without his order, no one can risk the responsibility for this!

ZHAO: I've heard Sister Qian say that Secretary Wu can really be a stickler for principle. Are you afraid he won't write the order?

SUN: Exactly!

ZHANG: What do you say we should do, then, Auntie Zhao?

(pause)

ZHAO (thoughtfully): It looks like you'll have to bring your father into it!

ZHANG: How?

ZHAO: Tell Secretary Wu that—that Li Xiaozhang has a special relationship with your dad.

ZHANG: What relationship?

ZHAO (suddenly inspired): He rescued your father!

ZHANG: Rescued my father?

ZHAO: Right! (thinking it up as she talks, with mounting excitement) You can say that at the outset of the Cultural Revolution, Li Xiaozhang went to Beijing as a Red Guard. Hm. And it happened that when he saw your father under attack, Li Xiaozhang rescued him and hid him. Hid him for several months even. Later, when your father was exonerated and sent back to work, he never forgot that episode and always felt deeply grateful. So now he has sent you here especially to ask Secretary Wu to resolve the matter of Li Xiaozhang's transfer. When Secretary Wu hears that your father has entrusted this to you and that Li Xiaozhang once rescued your father, who can tell? He might write the order after all! (with satisfaction) How's that?

ZHANG (having nodded his head constantly while Zhao was speaking): Uncle Sun, what do you say?

SUN: Hm. There's no harm in trying. No harm in trying.

ZHANG: Fine. Auntie Zhao, my thanks to you for thinking up such a good scheme. I'll definitely get Secretary Wu to write that order!

SUN: That'll make the whole thing easy!

(A restaurant attendant carries in containers loaded with cooked food.)

Stubborn Weeds

SUN: Put it there!

(The attendant arranges the dishes and then exits.)

SUN: It's nothing lavish, little Zhang. Just help yourself here. I'll go see if the steamed rolls are ready. Just sit and relax. *(Sun exits right.)*

ZHAO: It's a shame my place is so small; otherwise I'd definitely invite you over for some home cooking.

ZHANG: How big is your place, Auntie Zhao?

ZHAO: Oh, it's impossible! It's tiny—540 square feet for three people.[5] I've sent up a request to exchange the place for a larger one, but I'm afraid the comrade in charge is too busy to pay any attention to it. Say, you could help me forward my request to Director Ma—ah, no, to Secretary Wu, okay? And then when you see him, you can help again by letting him know the trouble I'm having with housing. Just get him to put in a word for me and that will do it.

ZHANG: Sure, no problem! Leave it to me!

ZHAO *(giving her request letter to Zhang):* I really appreciate this!

ZHANG: And I appreciate what *you've* done!

(Sun enters right.)

SUN: The steamed rolls will be ready any minute now. Just hang on!

ZHAO: Chief Sun, you'll have to excuse me.

ZHANG: What, are you going?

ZHAO: My foot is better now, so there's no point in staying, is there?

SUN: Then I won't keep you!

ZHAO: Goodbye! Goodbye!

(Zhao exits through the corridor.)

SUN: Young Zhang, what request did Managing Director Zhao bring up with you?

ZHANG: Only a minor thing—to help her pass on a request to solve her housing problem.

SUN: Well, now, you're from cadre stock and you must take care what impression you make. When people don't go through proper channels and just ask you for whatever they like, you mustn't give in to them!

ZHANG: Oh, it doesn't matter. I help whenever I can.

SUN *(delighted):* Oh? Really?

ZHANG: That's right, Uncle Sun. If there's anything I can help you with, just let me know.

SUN: There is—*(stops before he can get it out)* oh, no, no. How can I trouble you about it? It's too embarrassing.

ZHANG: Say it. I'm not a stranger. What's there to be afraid of?

SUN: I—I have a son-in-law stuck in the hills in the northeast. His unit has already agreed to let him come back here, but they still want us to issue a transfer order from our end.

ZHANG: Nothing to it. Nothing to it. You write the request, and then

---

5. This in fact would strike the audience as unusually large.

Drama

I'll say a few words on your behalf when I see Secretary Wu. It's sure to go through!

SUN: Good, good. I'll write it right away.

(*Sun happily exits left. Zhang admires the furnishings in Sun's home. Zhou Minghua enters carrying the steamed rolls. She puts the steamed rolls on a table and is about to exit when she sees Zhang Xiaoli with his back to her. At this point she stops and observes him, trying to identify him, until she realizes it is Li Xiaozhang.*)

ZHOU: Li!

(*Zhang gives a start.*)

ZHOU: Li!

(*Zhang slowly turns his head.*)

ZHOU: Li, it's you!

ZHANG (*amazed*): Minghua! (*instantly rushes to her*) What are you doing here?

ZHOU: For *your* sake!

ZHANG: My sake?

ZHOU: I was in the same class with Sun's daughter.

ZHANG (*understands*): Oh. (*He sizes her up. Filled with emotion, he takes her hand passionately.*) Minghua, you— (*Zhang takes out a handkerchief and lovingly pats the perspiration on Zhou's forehead.*)

ZHOU: How come you're here too?

ZHANG: Don't ask me now. I'll tell you later!

(*Juanjuan enters left.*)

JUANJUAN: Minghua!

(*Zhang and Zhou move rapidly apart.*)

ZHANG (*warmly greeting Juanjuan*): You must be Juanjuan, no?

JUANJUAN: Right. How are you? Minghua, do you two know each other?

ZHOU: He's my boyfriend—

ZHANG (*quickly interrupting*): Her boyfriend's *friend*, Li Xiaozhang's friend.

JUANJUAN: What? You know Li Xiaozhang too?

ZHOU: He—

ZHANG (*quickly interupting*): What do you mean "know him"? Li Xiaozhang is an educated youth at the Haidong Farm. We graduated the same year, and we even look a lot alike. I've known him for a long time. I'm here now from Beijing to figure out a way to have him transferred from the farm!

JUANJUAN: Oh? That's wonderful! Minghua, this guy's father is a high-level cadre. He's got a lot more pull than my dad.

ZHOU: His father is a high-level cadre?

JUANJUAN: Don't you know? I just heard Dad say so.

ZHOU: Ah?

ZHANG: You never imagined it, eh?

Stubborn Weeds

224

ZHOU: You—

ZHANG: I'll look after you and Li Xiaozhang!

JUANJUAN: Oh, that's wonderful. I'll go tell Dad there's a way to settle this!

(Juanjuan runs off left.)

ZHOU *(indignantly)*: Li! How can you trick people like that?

ZHANG: They're tricking people too, Minghua. Don't be naive!

ZHOU: This is no good!

ZHANG: Don't you want me to find a way to be transferred from the farm?

ZHOU: But you can't do this!

ZHANG: Then what can I do? Didn't you tell me you wanted to get married as soon as possible? Didn't you say we can't put it off any longer?

ZHOU *(softening, mumbling)*: Yes, we can't put it off any longer—

(Sun and Juanjuan enter left.)

JUANJUAN *(handing a request note to Zhang)*: Dad just wrote it. You really know how to get things done—kill two birds with one stone! No wonder Dad wanted to invite you to lunch!

SUN: Come on, come on! Have a seat!

(Sun, Juanjuan sit down. Zhou starts to exit right.)

ZHANG: Zhou Minghua!

(Zhou stands still.)

JUANJUAN: Right, Zhou Minghua should join us, too!

SUN: Juanjuan—

ZHANG: Uncle Sun, she's Li Xiaozhang's friend. She's my friend, too.

SUN: Oh, then let's eat together. Everybody eats together!

ZHANG: Move the table over here, Uncle Sun. Juanjuan, you sit here. Uncle Sun, you sit here. *(walking up to Zhou and pulling her over)* Come on, Minghua, you sit here!

(Zhou sits down at the table, her body rigid and motionless.)

ZHANG *(passing a steamed roll to Zhou)*: Eat while it's still hot.

(Zhou looks up blankly at Zhang Xiaoli.)

SCENE 4

Morning, one week later.

   The home of Secretary Wu.

   Just what are the exterior and interior of a Party Municipal Committee secretary's house like? Unfortunately, the authors of this play and the great majority of any audience seeing this play have never been to one, so there's no way to know. If the homes of today's Party Municipal Committee secretaries were not so heavily protected and hidden behind walls and gates and if the Party Municipal Committee secretaries would open their homes to welcome ordinary common people as their guests, then when it came time to describe

Drama

*what the home of a Party Municipal Committee secretary looks like, we
wouldn't be reduced to guesswork as we are now.*

(*When the curtain rises, Zhang Xiaoli is sitting in the living room
reading a book. Director Qian enters.*)

QIAN: Morning, Young Zhang!

ZHANG: Auntie Qian! Is Uncle Wu up yet?

QIAN: Not yet. After a two-week conference at Huangshan he and his
throat are both worn out. He just got back last night, so I'm letting
him sleep late this morning.

ZHANG: Have you talked to Uncle Wu about Li Xiaozhang?

QIAN: Yes.

ZHANG: How did it go?

QIAN: He said there's a temporary halt on transferring educated
youth and on children of factory workers replacing their retiring
parents. The Party Municipal Committee made the decision, so he
can't go against it.

ZHANG: Ah? Didn't you tell him how Li Xiaozhang protected my
father and about his special relationships with my father?

QIAN: I told him. I told him all about how noble he was in saving your
father's life and how he was wounded protecting your father, too. I
made it even more vivid and moving than when you told me.
(*laughs*) I was so good I even convinced myself.

ZHANG: So what did Uncle Wu say?

QIAN: He just said your father may have a special relationship with
this Li Xiaozhang, but he can't let his personal feelings ruin Party
policy.

ZHANG: It's not that serious!

QIAN: Yeah, but that's just the way the old man is. He does everything by the book. It's always some policy. He's that way with me,
too. When he went to Huangshan this time I asked him to bring me
back a monkey, one of those rare golden monkeys they have there.
But he adamantly refused to. That's not all. Party Central is just
about to send a big delegation overseas, so I asked him to get me a
place on it—better yet, two places. Then we could go overseas
together. But he wouldn't agree to it! I think he's a bit ultra-leftist in
his thinking. I mean his thought isn't liberated one bit!

ZHANG: If that's so, Li Xiaozhang's case is hopeless!

QIAN: Too bad. If you'd come a month or two earlier, before the Party
Municipal Committee's decision came down, it would have been
easy to take care of.

ZHANG: How was I to know that? One moment the policy's tight; the
next it's loosened up! Now they let people out; now they keep
everyone in! I've already written a letter to Li Xiaozhang, got him
travel tickets and ration tickets, and told him things definitely look
hopeful. But now I'm told— (*suddenly covers his face and weeps*)

Stubborn Weeds

226

QIAN: Don't worry, sweetie! Don't worry, Auntie will figure something out!

ZHANG: The only trouble is that if my father hears that this hasn't been taken care of, I'm afraid he'll have something to say about it!

QIAN: You musn't say anything to your father for the time being. Right now there's just a temporary delay in the transfer. When this interval is over I'll have him transferred out first thing.

(Secretary Wu enters from an inner room.)

WU: What's going on?

QIAN: Look, you won't agree to write an order and you've got the little guy so upset he's crying.

ZHANG *(wiping his tears with a handkerchief)*: Uncle Wu!

WU: Can't see the problem, can you? Something like this is risky business. It could easily mean big trouble for that farm youth Li, for you, *and* for your father!

QIAN: Come on, Wu, if you act this way about it, aren't you afraid of what his father might think?

WU: We're in a bind! If I have to, I'll call him this evening and explain.

ZHANG *(alarmed)*: You're going to call my dad?

WU *(beginning to pay closer attention to Zhang)*: How about it? I haven't seen your father for twenty years. As long as I'm calling him up I can take the opportunity to find out how he's doing. *(observing Zhang's expression)* Is that OK with you?

ZHANG *(quickly restoring his composure)*: Of course it's OK. That way he won't blame me or think I can't get anything done. Let's just do that, Uncle Wu. I won't take more of your time now.

(Zhang starts to exit.)

WU: Where are you off to, little one?

ZHANG: These last few days I've been to shows every evening. I'm really tired, so I thought I'd sleep for a while.

WU: Sit down and stay for a while. Come on, come on. Do you smoke? *(He passes Zhang a cigarette.)* Have a smoke!

ZHANG: Thanks, I will.

WU: Have you always lived in Beijing?

ZHANG: Uh-huh.

WU: No wonder your Mandarin is so good. Where's your father from?

ZHANG: My father?

WU: Uh-huh.

QIAN: You old half-wit. His father is from Sichuan. Everybody knows that.

WU: I was just asking, talking about home life, nothing special.

ZHANG: Auntie Qian is correct. My father is from Sichuan.

WU: Your father joined the revolution back in 1934, didn't he?

QIAN: How could he have joined in 1934?

WU *(interrupting Qian)*: So you know it all!

Drama

227

ZHANG: You're wrong there, Uncle Wu. It wasn't 1934. It was 1924. He joined the Party in June 1925. Went into the Jinggang Mountains in October 1927. Promoted to platoon leader in 1928; regimental commander in 1929; wounded in 1930; then in 1931—

QIAN: My gosh, what's the old goat asking all these questions for? *(hands Wu the book Zhang was just reading)* Here's a book of memoirs his father wrote, with all the details he was just talking about.

ZHANG: Anything else, Uncle Wu?

WU: Nothing, just chatting. I'll give your father a call and explain this matter to him. Go ahead and take a nap.

ZHANG: OK. *(Zhang exits.)*

QIAN: Are you really going to call?

WU: Just to get things straight. But look what *you* did! Without even checking any details on him, you just gave him my car to use. What if something had gone wrong? It would've made a pretty bad impression!

QIAN: What's so special about your car? In Beijing he rides in a big Red Flag limousine. I bet you're suspicious of him, aren't you? No wonder you were giving him the third degree!

WU: But you kept interrupting so I couldn't question him.

QIAN: I tell you he can't be a fake! If he were fake, would Director Ma have given him an introduction so that he could see a show? And how would he know that you were at his home in 1953 and gave his father a cactus plant?

WU: It never hurts to double-check.

QIAN: There's nothing wrong! What impostor would ever have the nerve to stay in our home? impossible! I think you should get this matter settled for him.

WU: No. We'll see about writing this order later, but not now.

QIAN: Enough! You—you're just looking for an excuse because you basically don't want to do it for him. Every time I ask you to do something you're like this. Why didn't you bring me a golden monkey?

WU: Me, a Party secretary, getting off the plane leading a monkey on a leash? Quite a picture, huh?

QIAN: Then what about my request to join the overseas delegation?

WU: There aren't any vacancies!

QIAN: Can't you ask Party Central for a couple of places?

WU: As easy as that?

QIAN: You don't care about me. Some people asked for a bunch of places and they had no trouble getting them. But you can't get one or two even?

WU: You're the director of the Political Office in the Organization Department of a Party Municipal Committee; what do you need to go overseas for?

Stubborn Weeds

228

QIAN: For the Four Modernizations—to observe and study!

Wu: Go to a capitalist country to study Party political ideology? That's ridiculous!

QIAN: You're the one who's being ridiculous! People who've been cadres only since 1938 have already taken their wives overseas. And you? Have you taken me? Hm? Let me add that for the last ten years I've suffered through plenty with you, been accused of all kinds of crimes, and just about paid for it with my life! Now that the Gang of Four has fallen, why can't I go overseas with you to restore myself and relax a bit?

(Qian sits down to one side in a pique.)

Wu (placatingly): All right, all right. Wait until there's another opportunity and we'll see.

QIAN: How many years do I have to wait? Until you retire? Until your funeral?

Wu: All right. All right. I'll look into it some more. If we can go, then I'll be sure to let you go. Will that be okay, dear? Heavens! You— you just—

(Wu exits. At the same time Zhang Xiaoli rushes on from the edge of the stage, riding his bicycle to the proscenium, where a telephone appears. He picks up the receiver and dials. Inside Secretary Wu's house the telephone rings. Director Qian answers it.)

QIAN: Hello. Who's this?

ZHANG: Is this the residence of Secretary Wu?

QIAN: Yes.

ZHANG: This is the regional garrison command. You have a long distance call from Beijing. Hold on, please. (changes to a Sichuan accent) Who's this?

QIAN: This is Secretary Wu's wife. Who's this?

ZHANG: I'm Zhang Xiaoli's father.

QIAN: (delighted): Ah! It's the venerable Zhang!

ZHANG: You're Qian, aren't you?

QIAN: Yes, yes. That's right!

ZHANG: We've never met. Should I use "senior" or "junior" to address you? What do you think?

QIAN: Of course you should call me "junior"!

ZHANG: Well then, junior Qian, my boy Xiaoli wrote me that he's staying with you. I disapprove! You're busy with your work as it is, and you can't have people bothering you like this. You shouldn't let him stay—just send him out the door!

QIAN: Oh, no, no! It's fine for him to stay here. It was my idea for him to come, so don't worry about that!

ZHANG: This toddler doesn't understand anything yet, and he doesn't know how to behave. When he gets out of hand you'd best show him who's boss; you have to be a bit strict with him!

Drama

QIAN: Not all all. He's been fine. Secretary Wu and I both like him. Has your work kept you pretty busy recently, Mr. Zhang?

ZHANG: Awfully busy. There's a large delegation getting set to go overseas, and the preparations are my responsibility.

QIAN (overjoyed): Oh? Are there a lot of people in this delegation?

ZHANG: Of course there are; I said it's a *large* delegation!

QIAN: Have they settled on the members?

ZHANG: There are still some that are not certain yet. Are you interested?

QIAN: Naturally I'm interested! Going overseas is good for study! And old Wu is interested, too.

ZHANG: Good, I'll put down your names.

QIAN: That's wonderful.

ZHANG: Is Wu there?

QIAN: Yes, yes he is. Hold on a minute. (calls in to Wu) Wu! (exuberantly as Wu enters) Mr. Zhang is on the telephone; he wants to speak to you!

WU (curious): Oh? (He answers the phone.) Is this Zhang?

ZHANG: Right, right. This Wu?

WU: Speaking.

ZHANG: How are you?

WU: Fine. You?

ZHANG: Just now I was talking to Comrade Qian. Party Central has decided to let you two join an overseas delegation.

WU (with a start): Oh? (addressing Qian) You!

QIAN: It's Party Central's decision.

ZHANG: How about it?

WU: I'm just afraid I might not be able to get away!

QIAN (snatching the receiver): No, no! He can get away, he can get away!

ZHANG: You can hand over your work at the Municipal Committee to another person.

WU: I'm afraid that might not work out.

QIAN (crowding in): It'll be fine, fine. It'll work out just fine!

(Wu and Qian silently argue with hand gestures.)

ZHANG: This is an organizational decision, after all. You'll just have to bear with the hardship for a while.

QIAN (crowding in at the receiver): Good, good. We're not afraid of hardship.

ZHANG: Then it's settled. How's your health, Wu?

WU: Still holding up. How's yours?

ZHANG: Just a problem with my leg.

WU: How'd that happen?

ZHANG: It was when I was being "struggled against" in the Cultural Revolution. Somebody pushed me off a platform and I broke it.

Fortunately a young man protected me, or this leg of mine would have been done for.

QIAN (*crowding in*): Was that young man's name Li Xiaozhang?

ZHANG: Exactly, that's him. I like him so much, he's just like a son to me. I hear he's still on a farm, hasn't been transferred out yet.

WU: Eh—

(*Qian gestures desperately to Wu to answer him.*)

WU: Don't worry. This can be taken care of.

ZHANG: Good, then I can relax! How's production where you are?

WU: It's a lot better this year than last! We're right in the middle of carrying out the Four-Word Plan.[6]

ZHANG: How about the discussion on "practice is the sole criterion for testing truth"?[7] How is that coming along?

WU: We're studying up on it now. It's coming along very well.

ZHANG: That's good. Well, best of luck to you in your work. If I have time I'll come visit!

WU: Fine, fine. You're welcome here. Always welcome!

ZHANG: You can never tell, I might be there real soon!

WU: Splendid! Splendid!

ZHANG: Goodbye!

WU: Goodbye!

(*As soon as he hangs up, Zhang mounts his bicycle and pedals off stage. Simultaneously, lights on the telepone at the proscenium fade out.*)

QIAN: That's wonderful. I never imagined old Zhang cared about us so much.

WU: I suppose you're finally satisfied!

QIAN: Huh! As if *you* had anything to do with it! I still had to get it from someone else, like Mr. Zhang. And here you were so suspicious that the younger Zhang was a fake!

WU: I was just afraid of being taken for a ride and left with the responsibility!

QIAN: I told you I'm an infallible judge of people! How could he be a fake? If he's a phony, then I'd say this phony is more genuine than the real thing! Not a chance he's fake! Now, quick, get Li Xiaozhang transferred out of there! Besides, it's such a small, insignificant request from a man like Zhang, who marched and fought all over this country for decades. You're going to honor it!

WU: OK, I'll write the order.

QIAN: That's more like it. Write it *now!*

(*Bureau Chief Sun enters.*)

SUN: Director Qian!

6. An economic policy of Party Central to "adjust, consolidate, develop, and improve"—rather than trying to go too fast.

7. A 1979 slogan summarizing Deng Xiaoping's pragmatic approach to solving China's problems.

Drama

QIAN: Hello, Sun. Secretary Wu has agreed to settle this. See, he's writing the order.

SUN: That's great! (*He takes out the bottle of* maotai *from a bag.*) Director Qian, I hear Secretary Wu enjoys *maotai*. So I have a bottle here for you.

QIAN: He has more than enough. Keep it for yourself!

SUN: But you may not have this kind of *maotai*. It's not your ordinary grade of *maotai*. This is made especially for export. The ingredients aren't the same at all.

QIAN: Where did you get it?

SUN: From an overseas trading firm.

QIAN: (*accepting the* maotai): Then we'll put it here! Have a seat. I'll go see our little Zhang.

Having put the maotai *in a cabinet, Qian exits. Secretary Wu has finished writing the note and stands up.*)

SUN: Secretary Wu!

WU: Go take care of this Li Xiaozhang affair, Chief Sun!

SUN (*receiving the written orders*): Fine, I will.

(*Qian enters.*)

QIAN: Ha, that little fellow really sleeps soundly. I shouted for ages before I woke him up. When I told him his father called he grinned from ear to ear. He really is a kid!

(*Zhang runs on, buttoning up his clothes.*)

ZHANG: Uncle Wu, did my dad call?

WU: Uh-huh. The order is written. I gave it to Bureau Chief Sun.

ZHANG: Great!

QIAN: Be sure you get this taken care of correctly for him, Sun.

SUN: Okay, I'll go out to the farm immediately. Young Zhang, do you want to go out there with me to see Li Xiaozhang?

ZHANG: Huh? No, I'll go see him tomorrow.

SUN: OK, I'm off!

ZHANG (*walking up to Sun*): Uncle Sun, this is quite an imposition on you.

SUN: Not at all. (*whispering*) Have you worked anything out for me?

ZHANG: Give it time. Secretary Wu just got back yesterday.

SUN: OK, I'm on my way! (*Sun exits.*)

ZHANG: Uncle Wu, may I borrow your car for a while?

WU: You want to go out?

ZHANG: I have some personal matters to take care of.

WU: All right, tell Auntie Qian to notify the driver.

ZHANG: Thank you!

WU: What a little operator!

(*Wu exits. Zhang jumps for joy.*)

QIAN: Well, my little one—don't you look happy!

ZHANG: Auntie Qian, now that Li Xiaozhang is taken care of, I ought to return to Beijing.

QIAN: Stay a few more days!

ZHANG: I've been away quite a while now.

QIAN: I bet you're homesick, aren't you? All right, next time you come, you must stay with us again. Consider this your own home!

ZHANG: No, this is a lot better than my home!

QIAN: When you go back to Beijing, little one, I want you to take your dad a present—something Uncle Wu brought back from Huangshan. *(takes out the* maotai *from the cabinet)* It's a special grade. *(Zhang receives the* maotai.)

ZHANG: Thank you. *(laughs)*

SCENE 5

The afternoon of the same day as in Scene 4.

The office of the director of the Haidong State Farm is in complete disarray. Every utensil used at work or in the office seems to be set out in some improbable location. An aging silk banner hangs near the floor on the battered wall. A broken broom has been tied onto the cord to a light switch. It seems certain that any order emanating from such an office cannot have much effect, and probably no sooner does it get past the door than it dies an early death. Several tufts of grass are sprouting arrogantly at the corners of the room. Through them the audience can imagine the sort of spectacle the farm fields must present.

As the curtain rises, Director Zheng enters carrying a canister of pesticide spray on his back. He then sits despondently on top of a desk and drinks some wine.

Youth A enters running.

YOUTH A: Director Zheng!

ZHENG: What is it?

YOUTH A *(taking out a telegram, with a sad face):* My grandmother is critically ill! A telegram came from home, asking me to return immediately!

ZHENG: What's her illness?

YOUTH A: Cancer!

ZHENG: Don't try to scare people, OK? If you want time off, then ask for time off. What's the point of crying that your grandmother has cancer—

YOUTH A: But she really does have cancer!

ZHENG: So? You're not a doctor. If you go back, will that cure her cancer? If it will, then when I get cancer I won't go to the hospital. I'll come and see you every day instead, and all the cancer cells will vanish.

YOUTH A *(pleadingly):* Director Zheng!

CHENG: All right, all right. Have you spoken with your company commander?

Drama

YOUTH A: The company commander's father is ill. He went home a few days ago.

ZHENG: And the assistant company commander?

YOUTH A: The assistant company commander's mother is ill. He just left yesterday afternoon.

ZHENG: How come everybody is ill? Oh, yes, they've probably all caught a contagious disease. All right, how many days do you want?

YOUTH A: That depends on when my grandmother is cured.

ZHENG: When you have a relative like this who's ill, they never get cured quickly. It will take at least half a month, maybe even half a year. So how many days do you want?

YOUTH A: A month, to start with.

ZHENG: OK. Leave the telegram here.

YOUTH A: Director Zheng, you're all right!

(Youth A exits gaily on the run. Youth B enters running.)

YOUTH B: Director Zheng!

ZHENG: Is your father ill?

YOUTH B: No, no.

ZHENG: Then it's your mother?

YOUTH B: No. My older sister is getting married. Here *(taking out a letter)*, a letter just arrived.

ZHENG: Do you want to ask for time off to go back?

YOUTH B: Un-huh.

ZHENG: If you don't go back, then your sister will refuse to marry her fiance, is that it?

YOUTH B: No, no, no. I want to attend the wedding!

ZHENG: Have you talked with your company commander?

YOUTH B: The company commander's brother is getting married, and he's gone to attend the wedding.

ZHENG: And the assistant company commander?

YOUTH B: His sister got married, and he hasn't come back yet.

ZHENG: Good. The contagious disease has passed, and everyone's back to collective weddings. How many days do you want?

YOUTH B: Not many. Just a week.

ZHENG: All right. Leave the letter here.

YOUTH B: Oh, Director Zheng! I'll bring you some of the wedding sweets when I come back!

(Without looking up, Director Zheng dismisses Youth B with a wave of his hand, and Youth B exits running. With mournful nostalgia Director Zheng hums a tune from the era of the "Resist America, Aid Korea" campaign [1950–52]. The sound of an automobile horn is heard from a distance, and Director Zheng leans out the window to take a look. The sound of brakes is heard, and after a moment, Bureau Chief Sun enters.)

ZHENG: I've been expecting you for days now. I just knew you'd be

234
Stubborn Weeds

back.

SUN: Good grief, are you drinking?

ZHENG: What about it—would you like a shot or two?

SUN: You're drinking on the job. Maybe you're not worried about creating a bad impression, but I am.

ZHENG: There you go again, putting on the straight-arrow act! What do you mean "on the job"? At this point there isn't any job to do! Take a look out the window at those fields. Who is on the job? Who's working? Come on, come on. Have a drink!

SUN (*taking a swig while he talks*): Then you shouldn't be drinking. You should be going around to each company, working on their ideology, immersing yourself among the masses!

ZHENG: The masses? They're all gone with the wind, back to the city—to replace their parents at factories, or by transfer orders, or through back door connections. They've all been let go.

SUN: What are you complaining about? You can thank your own mismangement for this!

ZHENG: Mismanagement? You try managing this place. I'll kiss your feet if you'll take over this post!

SUN: All right, you've made your point. (*He produces the order written by Secretary Wu and hands it to Zheng.*) Here!

ZHENG (*takes it, then reacts with a start*): So Secretary Wu has actually put an order in writing?

SUN: Before I came here, I also went over to the Labor Bureau and used this to get a transfer order from them. So let's hurry up and get Li Xiaozhang and his files transferred out of here. Secretary Wu says the sooner, the better.

ZHENG: But it can't be done. You've just missed the boat.

SUN: What do you mean?

ZHENG: The Party Committee here has decided that for the present we're going to review the whole problem of transfers for educated youth. We have to make every effort to reduce back door connections. The decision was that for the second half of this year, the roster of people getting out through the back door will be strictly limited to twenty.

SUN: Secretary Wu's intervention in this case does not count as the back door!

ZHENG: My dear old Sun, don't be embarrassed. (*giving Secretary Wu's note a shake*) This is a back door connection through and through, 100 percent!

SUN: You've got nerve saying the Party Municipal Secretary uses back door connections.

ZHENG: Why, there are heads of ministries and members of the Central Committee who use the back door! Why should I worry about a municipal secretary?

SUN: You're drunk! This is not using the back door!

Drama

ZHENG: It *is* using the back door!

SUN: It *isn't!*

ZHENG: It *is!*

SUN: It *isn't!*

ZHENG: It *is!*

SUN: It absolutely is not. We didn't go to Zhang for favors: he came to us! *(realizes his slip)* Ah, no, that's not it. That's not what I mean. I'm drunk too. All right, all right. What do you think—is there any way to work this out?

ZHENG: Not unless you push someone else off the list.

SUN: What do you mean "push someone else off the list"? This isn't pushing, this is "applying proper priorities." Let me see that list!

ZHENG *(handing the list to Sun)*: The names of the twenty people are all at the top. Whom do you want to drop?

SUN *(pointing on the roster)*: What about this one?

ZHENG: Can't cut *him!* He's a nephew of Feng, the Chief of Staff for the regional garrison!

SUN: My god! *(pointing on the roster)* This one?

ZHENG: Daughter of a nephew of the sister of the Vice-Minister of Health.

SUN: Wow! *(pointing at the roster)* What about that one?

ZHENG: Grandson of the son-in-law of a cousin of the Vice-Premier.

SUN: They get bigger every time! *(pointing on the roster)* Is this one also related to a high-level cadre?

ZHENG: No, not a high-ranking one.

SUN: Oh, terrific!

ZHENG: But that's no good, either. She's the girlfriend of the son of the Party Secretary at the farm.

SUN: Shoot! Isn't there one related to some ordinary cadre?

ZHENG *(pointing on the roster)*: This one. His father is the eighth Assistant Bureau Chief of the Housing Bureau.

SUN: An assistant bureau chief, and the eighth, at that? That's the one, all right. Ask him to be patient till next year, and put Li Xiaozhang in his place. How about it?

ZHENG *(with a wry smile)*: Can do! A municipal Party secretary naturally has right-of-way over a mere eighth assistant bureau chief! The higher the rank the more the clout. Right-of-way! Right-of-way! Get the rights, and you've got the ways! This is "truth," according to some, and it *has* passed "the test of practice!"[8]

SUN: So it's settled.

ZHENG *(opening drawers and taking out files)*: Li Xiaozhang's dossier, his ration documents, his change of residence certificate—they're all here. Take them.

8. See note 7.

Stubborn Weeds

SUN: Oh! So you've already arranged all the departure procedures for him?

ZHENG: With all this high rank and strong backing, could I afford not to bend with the breeze?

SUN: So you were putting me on after all?

ZHENG: No. I was waiting for the order from the Municipal Party Secretary.

SUN *(picking up the dossier and other materials):* You're going to get in touch with Li Xiaozhang now and let him go as soon as possible, right?

ZHENG: OK. I'll call him right now. *(picks up the telephone receiver)* I want the 57th Company. *(pause)* 57th Company? Is this Company Commander Chen? This is Zheng. Is Li Xiaozhang there in your unit? . . . He just came back at noon today? No, don't criticize him, he's leaving right away! . . . Transferred back to the city, right! What? You don't approve? Well, good, so we still have a little of the old spirit of rebellion! What—you're asking if it's all according to proper procedure? Using the back door? Hold on a minute. *(He hands the receiver to Sun.)* Here, you answer him, please!

SUN *(taking the receiver, slightly tipsy):* Hello. You're asking who I am? I'll tell you: I'm the Municipal Party Secretary—

ZHENG *(surprised):* You're the Municipal Party Secretary?

SUN: —'s deputy!

ZHENG: Oh—that's really enough to scare the daylights out of them!

SUN: That's right! You're asking if I'm acting with proper procedures? I can tell you for a certainty that I'm not—

ZHENG: Huh?

SUN: —in any way violating proper procedures!

ZHENG: Hah!

SUN: All cadres have special privileges and the back door is perfectly legal—

ZHENG: What?

SUN: —only according to the Gang of Four!

ZHENG: OK. Enough. Enough. I'll take it. *(taking the phone receiver out of Sun's hand)* Chen, old man, the Municipal Party Secretary has written an order specifying that he wants Li Xiaozhang transferred immediately—right, right. You want to turn it down? That's all very well, only I'm afraid we can't! Go tell Li Xiaozhang to get up to headquarters. Right, and immediately! *(He hangs up.)* Do you want to wait for him and take him back with you?

SUN: No, if he has packing to do and so on, who knows how long I would have to wait for him? I'll go now. Actually I seem to be a bit drunk. No, no, I'm not, no, I'm not! See you.

ZHENG: See you. You know the way out.

(Sun exits. After a moment the car is heard starting up. Zheng

Drama

looks out the window at the departing Sun. He shakes his head and goes back to drinking. Suddenly he reaches for a piece of paper on the desk and hastily jots something down on it. Zhang Xiaoli enters, having reassumed his original identity as Li Xiaozhang. First he cautiously inspects the building, then goes inside. He has completely reverted to his original habits of speech and behavior.)

LI (*with more than a hint of mischievous wit*): Li Xiaozhang, 57th fighter of the 57th Company firmly struggling for the glory of the Haidong Farm, reporting as ordered!

ZHENG: So you're Li Xiaozhang?

LI: The real thing in person, I can guarantee you. Height, five feet, nine inches. Weight, 146 pounds. Age, 26. And in just 66 days—

ZHENG: What?

LI: It will be the eighth anniversary of the start of my struggles at Haidong Farm. Let me join you in a toast now.

ZHENG: Cut the act. No need to pretend you're such a jovial guy. You've been miserable all along.

LI: Good for you, Director Zheng, you're discerning.

ZHENG: Has your company commander told you? You've got a transfer.

LI: I heard something like that.

ZHENG: We've carried out all the procedures for you. I've given Bureau Chief Sun your file and verification documents to take with him. You're free to leave our farm.

LI: Thank god.

ZHENG: Should I offer my congratulations to you, or should I express my apologies?

LI (*puzzled*): Apologies?

ZHENG (*his bitterness accentuated by the alcohol*): Why not? The farm has been a failure. It's been a waste of land, and—and yes, it's been a waste of your youth, for all of you. So—so everyone just wants to get out and forget it. And each time one more person goes, I—I just can't take it. It's like I've owed you a debt. But then what else— what else is there for me to do? Even municipal Party secretaries— municipal Party secretaries are pulling rank and using their influence. They don't care about the farm—they don't care. How are we supposed to devote ourselves to the revolution any more? It's hopeless no matter what we do. Now it's not—it's not just you young people on the farm who want to get out through the back door—even the cadres—the cadres who run these farms, don't they want to pull strings and get out, too?

LI (*not without sympathy*): And you?

ZHENG: Mi—miserable. (*points to the wine*) This here is what I rely on to forget, to escape. I wanted to make something of this farm, but the way things are it's absolutely impossible. If things go on like this, then I—I don't want to rot here any more either. The way I'm going, the more I feel I'm—I'm just about fed up.

LI (*surprised*): So you want to get out too?

ZHENG (*with a show of grievance*): Put in a memo—for a transfer order. There is a son of a high-level cadre; Zhang Xiaoli is his name. You know him, don't you? Ask him—to help me—to put in a word for me with the Municipal Party Secretary and have me transferred.

LI (*nonplussed*): But—but how can I do that?

(*Youth A enters.*)

ZHENG: Why not? Why can't you do it? (*producing the note written by Secretary Wu*) Tell him that if he can write an order to transfer you, why can't he write an order to transfer me? (*picking up the transfer request statement which he has just written*) Here's my request for transfer, based on two reasons—the first, my grandmother has cancer; the second, my sister is getting married!

(*Zheng hands the transfer request to Li, who stands motionless in stupefaction. Abruptly, Zheng withdraws it, shakes his head in sadness, then waves Li out the door. Li exits. Slowly but vehemently, Zheng tears the transfer request to shreds. Youth A, standing behind Zheng, slowly tears up his own leave request form.*)

(*Curtain.*)

SCENE 6

An afternoon several days later.

    The home of Secretary Wu as it was in Scene 4. No one is on stage when the curtain rises. After a moment, Zhang Xiaoli's voice is heard from offstage: "Let me show you what it's like over this way." Zhang enters leading Zhou Minghua.

ZHANG (*standing by the doorway with a show of refinement*): This way, please.

(*Zhou views the room dumbstruck.*)

ZHANG (*imitating a tour guide*): This is the living room of the Municipal Party Secretary. Please note that there are two stories, electric lights and telephone, steel frame windows, built-in cabinets, carpeting, padded sofa and chairs, television, phonograph, and, last but not least, air conditioning. (*opening the door to an adjoining room*) Here we have a bedroom. Please, step in.

ZHOU (*to Zhang, as she stands at the bedroom door*): Ah!

ZHANG: How often do you get the chance to go in? Go on in!

ZHOU: No, no.

ZHANG (*opening a cabinet*): Have some orange juice! (*pours a glass and offers it to Zhou*) Have some!

Drama

ZHOU: This is not your house; how can you just go around taking what you feel like and inviting people in when no one is home?

ZHANG: No problem. I have these special privileges. Have some juice!

ZHOU: No. I've never gone around taking what belongs to other people!

ZHANG: I do all the time. And the more I take, the happier they are.

ZHOU: You've been living here for over ten days now?

ZHANG: Sure. Aren't you envious?

ZHOU: No.

ZHANG: Minghua—every time I take advantage of all this stuff, I can't help picturing you. I see you at Chief Sun's house, barefoot and sweating, washing clothes and mopping the floors—

ZHOU: Did you ask me to come over here today to let me see how you now live in the lap of luxury?

ZHANG: I wanted to show you how different life can be when you have a good father! But I also wanted to show you something else!

ZHOU: What's that?

ZHANG: Guess!

ZHOU: How can I guess when you've got so many tricks up your sleeve?

ZHANG (*producing a notification of job reassignment*): Look at this!

ZHOU (*looking it over, wildly delighted*): What? You got it? You!

ZHANG: I've got it! Chief Sun has already made all the arrangements, and now that I have this, I can report tomorrow to the very best factory in the whole city!

ZHOU: I—I'm dreaming, aren't I?

ZHANG: No! The dream's over!

ZHOU: It's fantastic!

ZHANG (*mimicking Zhou*): "It's fantastic!" And you've been scolding me all along for impersonating a cadre's son, haven't you?

ZHOU: It isn't right.

ZHANG But if I hadn't (*indicates the notification*), would I have gotten my hands on this? Besides, I should have been transferred two years ago, but those cadres' children managed to squeeze me off the list then, and that wasn't right either, was it?

ZHOU: But that still—

ZHANG: Minghua, I'm not a villain. I haven't stolen or robbed, I haven't killed anyone, or set fire to anything. I didn't conspire with the Gang of Four to seize power. I haven't tried to start World War III. All I've done is pull a pretty harmless joke on some privileged cadres.

ZHOU: But I've been worried sick about you every day.

ZHANG: Sure, I've been scared stiff myself most of the time. So, all right, starting tomorrow, Zhang Xiaoli, the crafty confidence man, will become honest, law-abiding Li Xiaozhang. I don't want to take any more risks. This was the first time, and it will be the last.

Stubborn Weeds

ZHOU: Do you mean that?

ZHANG: I do. You're not happy with me the way I am now, are you? *(with a seriousness he has not displayed before)* That's because I've felt so miserable and empty. I've felt desperate. I couldn't see any future ahead, I couldn't stand myself, and so I just wanted to put something over on people. But starting tomorrow, you'll be happy with the way I'll be, I promise you.

ZHOU: Well, then, I, ah, I have—some good news to tell you too!

ZHANG: How can a luckless waif like you have any good news?

ZHOU: You haven't noticed at all?

ZHANG: Noticed what?

ZHOU *(bashfully):* We're going to have—

ZHANG: Have what?

ZHOU: Oh, you! *(Zhou whispers in Zhang's ear.)*

ZHANG *(delighted):* What? Really? Minghua, oh, you! *(He hugs Zhou close to him.)* Thank you, oh, thank you! Why didn't you tell me earlier?

ZHOU: Didn't I tell you that we couldn't put off getting married?

ZHANG: Oh!

ZHOU: So tell me when we're going to.

ZHANG: Hm. I report for work tomorrow, otherwise next month—

ZHOU: Next month? No, no, we can't put it off any more!

ZHANG: Then what do you say?

ZHOU: We'll get married tomorrow!

ZHANG *(excited):* OK, tomorrow! Minghua, from tomorrow on, for sure—for sure I'll make you happy.

ZHOU *(controlling her feelings):* I've hoped so much you will! You're not happy with the way you are now, and for that matter, I'm not happy with the way I am, either. I've been unhappy with everything you've been doing recently, and still I've gone along with it and forgiven you. I suppose it's just my selfishness, thinking only about our getting married and having children. It would be fairer to say I've been forgiving myself.

ZHANG: Why are you telling me this?

ZHOU: Maybe it's to try to rekindle all the feelings and the idealism that we've lost. Xiaoli, we ought to remember always what this chance means for us. From now on we should work and live and be as we were meant to be—as we used to want to be. Promise me now, from tomorrow on, you'll stop smoking!

ZHANG *(agreeably):* Uh-huh.

ZHOU: And stop drinking!

ZHANG: Uh-huh.

ZHOU: And never fool people again!

ZHANG: For sure.

ZHOU: For us and for our children—

ZHANG: Don't worry, I'll be a good father!

Drama

ZHOU: I know you will!

ZHANG: *(moved, he takes Zhou's hand)*: Minghua!

ZHOU: Xiaoli, why don't we get out of here now!

ZHANG: I can't. My performance isn't finished yet. There's still one more act to go this evening.

ZHOU: What are you up to?

ZHANG: When I told them I was taking a plane to Beijing first thing tomorrow morning, Director Qian insisted on taking me to see one more play this evening. So it'll be tomorrow before I can say good-bye—forever—to all this and the bogus Zhang Xiaoli.

ZHOU: Then I'll go back now.

ZHANG: Stay a while longer.

ZHOU: I have to go back and tell my father about your transfer and about tomorrow, too—

ZHANG: Will that old buzzard—I mean, will Father-in-law still object?

ZHOU: He shouldn't, any more.

ZHANG: Well, if your dad agrees to it, come in the prettiest clothes you have. That will tell me the answer without a word spoken.

ZHOU: Good!

(Zhou exits. Zhang follows her with his eyes, filled with tender concern. Director Qian enters, rushing excitedly.)

QIAN: I have some good news for you!

ZHANG: More good news? What is it now?

QIAN: There's someone here to see you.

ZHANG: Who?

QIAN: Guess!

ZHANG: Do I know this person?

QIAN: Of course.

ZHANG: Auntie Zhao?

QIAN: Wrong!

ZHANG: Chief Sun?

QIAN: Wrong!

ZHANG: Well there's no one around here I know well except Li Xiao-zhang. Oh, it's Director Ma?

QIAN: I'll tell you. Your father is here!

ZHANG *(startled)*: Father? What father?

QIAN: Huh? You've forgotten your dad? You've been away too long!

ZHANG: No, no. I said, "What, Father?" I was so surprised!

QIAN: Of course you were! He didn't tell anyone he was coming.

ZHANG: Ah—

(Zhang goes limp and falls on the sofa.)

QIAN: What's the matter?

ZHANG: I—I'm just overwhelmed with joy, just overcome.

QIAN: You scared me.

ZHANG: Where is he now?

QIAN: He'll be here right away.

(Zhang Senior enters. He spots Zhang at a glance. Zhang Xiaoli rises from the sofa and stands. Zhang Senior and Zhang stand at opposite ends of the room silently staring at each other. As Zhang Senior inspects him, Zhang waits for the storm to break.)

QIAN (chattering on): Hm? Have a seat, Mr. Zhang. Please, have a seat. Why not have a seat? Young Zhang, why are you looking at your dad as if he were a tiger? (She looks them both over, as they continue to stand silently confronting each other.) Look at you two—one old, one young—how interesting! You see each other, and you just stand there without saying a word. Oh, I understand. It's probably like what they have in plays where two people have been apart for so long that when they see each other they're too moved to say anything!

ZHANG SENIOR: No. I do have something to say to him.

QIAN (still chattering and babbling): Oh, it's easier for you to talk if I'm not here? Sure, sure, I ought to let father and son have a good talk all by themselves. Young Zhang, you take care of your dad. We still have a play to see this evening, remember. Well, I'm off. Bye-bye. Have a nice chat. (Qian exits.)

ZHANG SENIOR: Don't go on standing. Sit down.

(Zhang sits and so does Zhang Senior. A pause.)

ZHANG SENIOR: Is your name also Zhang?

ZHANG: No, my name is Li.

ZHANG SENIOR: Well, it really looks like you've "put Zhang's hat on Li's head" [confused one thing for another], as the saying goes. What is your full name?

ZHANG: Li Xiaozhang.

ZHANG SENIOR: So he was you yourself after all. How old are you?

ZHANG: Twenty-six.

ZHANG SENIOR: Haidong Farm?

ZHANG (surprised, nods his head): That's right.

ZHANG SENIOR: What were you doing pretending to be my son?

ZHANG: I wasn't being treated fairly. I wanted a transfer.

ZHANG SENIOR: And besides this you haven't done anything wrong?

ZHANG: I could have, but I didn't.

ZHANG SENIOR: Did you get your transfer?

ZHANG (hostile): You ruined all that by coming here. Ruined my hopes and my happiness—the happiness of three people!

ZHANG SENIOR: Three people?

ZHANG: My girlfriend and I were planning to be married tomorrow.

ZHANG SENIOR: That still leaves one.

ZHANG: We're going to have a baby.

ZHANG SENIOR: Having a baby before you're married?

ZHANG: It was partly because of love and partly because we've been miserable.

ZHANG SENIOR: Why didn't you get married at the time?

Drama

ZHANG: Once you're married, you can't get transferred. You're stuck. (*pause*)

ZHANG SENIOR: Why did you want to impersonate my son and fool people?

ZHANG (*emotionally*): You can't say I'm the only one fooling people, can you? No. Everyone is in this game. Aren't the people I was fooling all going around fooling others? They not only provided me with situations and opportunities and helped me commit my fraud; some of the people I fooled even *taught* me how to fool others. I don't deny that I've used your identity and your position to get what I wanted for myself. But you can't tell me they haven't also tried to use the identity and position I pretended to have in order to achieve even bigger goals for themselves.

ZHANG SENIOR: "They?" Who are "they?"

ZHANG (*taking a sheaf of documents from his pocket*): See for yourself. This is Managing Director Zhao's; she wants a larger house. This is Bureau Chief Sun's; he wants his son-in-law transferred back from the northeast. This was written by Director Qian herself yesterday for me to give to you personally, asking for your support in pulling strings for her and Secretary Wu to join an overseas delegation. They all wanted favors from me, but whom could *I* turn to? And they all tried to charm me so that I would help them solve their problems, but who was there to solve mine?

(*Zhang Senior leafs through the documents. His brow knit, he paces slowly in thought, almost oblivious of Zhang's existence.*)

ZHANG SENIOR (*softly but forcefully*): This stinks! Were you planning to help them?

ZHANG: They're insatiable! I held on to these papers precisely because I wanted proof—proof that they aren't always as idealistically Communist in their hearts as they are with their mouths!

ZHANG SENIOR: Did you intend to keep these to bring charges against them?

ZHANG: No, to keep them from bringing charges against me!

ZHANG SENIOR: You thought of everything.

ZHANG: With no privilege and no influence, it's the only way I could take care of myself.

ZHANG SENIOR: But you do understand that you've committed the crime of fraud?

ZHANG: Because I've impersonated your son?

ZHANG SENIOR: You can't impersonate *anybody's* son.

ZHANG: But why did I impersonate *your* son? It was because I impersonated your son that they were so responsive, so flattering—offering me all kinds of convenience and allowing me to do certain things I simply had no other way of getting done. If I had impersonated the son of a ordinary worker or peasant, would they have

Stubborn Weeds

244

hovered about me like that? Would they have opened their doors and made things so easy for me? Of course they wouldn't! And why is that? Isn't it because you, or other people with status like yours, have enough privilege that whatever you say goes, whatever you want done gets done? If you didn't have that kind of privilege, then neither I nor anyone else would impersonate your son.

ZHANG SENIOR: Are you trying to tell me that this constitutes a legitimate reason for fraud? That since privilege exists, you should exploit it? That since other people commit fraud, you also should commit fraud? That's the logic of a hustler; it's not the intellectual integrity that an upright youth ought to have. Yes, the cadre system we have at present does provide a lot of unwarranted privileges, but that doesn't mean that all cadres exercise, much less abuse, those privileges!

ZHANG: What you're trying to say is that you are wise old Uncle Zhang, the honest official, eh?

(Zhang laughs sarcastically. Zhang Senior stares at him with such force of dignity that Zhang is reduced to silence.)

ZHANG SENIOR: You may have impersonated my son, but you don't understand *me* very well. And it looks as though you also don't understand our Party or the basic situation among the rank and file of our cadre. I hope you will hand over those documents to me.

ZHANG: Why should I give them to you?

ZHANG SENIOR: Because I have a responsibility to understand these things and do something about them.

ZHANG *(handing the documents over to Zhang Senior)*: All right—are you—are you going to arrest me now?

ZHANG SENIOR: The department concerned will take the appropriate actions.

ZHANG: OK. I'm waiting.

(Bureau Chief Sun enters.)

SUN: I've come over to pick you up, young Zhang. Let's get over to the theater right away.

ZHANG *(to Zhang Senior)*: You see how considerate they are toward me. They've even sent a car around especially to take me to the show.

ZHANG SENIOR: Who is he?

ZHANG: Chief Sun of the Bureau of Culture.

SUN: Young Zhang, is he—

ZHANG: My father!

SUN *(tongue-tied with awe)*: Ah! Zhang Senior!

ZHANG *(to Zhang Senior)*: May I go to the show?

SUN: Tonight is the last showing, Mr. Zhang! Let him go!

ZHANG SENIOR *(to Zhang)*: You must take responsibility for your own actions.

Drama

(Secretary Wu and Director Qian enter.)

QIAN: Your friend Wu is here, Mr. Zhang!

Zhao: Wu: Zhang! How are you?

Zhao: Wu: Sit down, sit down. I really had no idea you'd be here so soon.

QIAN: Sun, you're here to fetch young Zhang for the show, aren't you?

SUN: Yes, it's time for us to be going!

QIAN: Right, we'll be on our way and let them chat. Come on, young Zhang, we're leaving.

(Qian warmly bundles Zhang offstage as Sun follows.)

WU *(to Zhang Senior):* Well, to what do we owe the pleasure of—

ZHANG SENIOR: Party Central sent me to investigate the state of discipline in the Party.

WU: Oh?

ZHANG SENIOR *(producing a letter):* This is a letter of accusation sent by the director of a state farm to the Party Central Commission for Inspecting Discipline. There is an order written by you attached to it.

WU *(takes and reads it):* You—you didn't know about this before?

ZHANG SENIOR: What did *I* know? You've been swindled!

WU: How's that? *(suddenly understands)* Oh, Zhang Xiaoli—

ZHANG SENIOR: He's not my son.

WU: But he used your name—

ZHANG SENIOR: Look, even if I had sought you out myself, you know you should have refused this. *(takes out the orders and letters written by Qian and the others)* Take a look at these, they're even more outrageous!

WU *(taking them in astonishment):* Managing Director Zhao, Bureau Chief Sun—and even my wife?

ZHANG SENIOR *(upset):* It's a pain in the neck! Our Party wasn't always like this; it's a Party with an outstanding revolutionary tradition! Remember back during the war years—how you lost your children? Back then we really devoted ourselves to nothing but the revolution! And when we entered the cities, we wore straw sandals, slept in the streets, shared every hardship and every bit of joy with the common, ordinary people. But where has that old tradition gone today? Of course, we aren't denying that this is an evil created by the Gang of Four, but the Gang of Four was toppled two years ago, and there are still comrades as dishonest as this. It's a tragedy for our Party! We've been with the Party for decades, Wu—shouldn't we be upset about this?

WU: Yes. I'll do a self-criticism for Party Central. For the other comrades we'll arrange some intra-Party education.

ZHANG SENIOR: Intra-Party education should be done, yes, but these comrades have also been caught up in a criminal case. The judiciary may well decide to prosecute Li Xiaozhang, and then the comrades connected with this case will probably have to appear in court.

Wu: I'm not opposing that, but I am a bit concerned that with the credibility of the Party in decline as it is now, if this case is tried publicly, won't it—

ZHANG SENIOR: That's the problem, right there. We can't cover this up. Sooner or later the masses will know about it. If this isn't confronted openly, then people will talk behind our backs; it's as simple as that. And if things go on this way, the public trust in us will be eroded even more. But if we dare to expose openly the privilege-oriented mentality of Party cadres and their dishonest behavior, if we show that our Party is forthright, that it can be openly criticized, and that it is fully able to overcome these flaws, then there is hope, plenty of hope!

(Zhou Minghua enters running, dressed in beautiful clothes.)

ZHANG SENIOR: A public trial of Li Xiaozhang will educate not only our cadres but—at the same time—our youth. It will rescue them, help bring them around, so that we won't have more and more Li Xiaozhangs passing themselves off as Zhang Xiaolis.

(Zhou turns pale with fright.)

Wu: Very well, I'll telephone Public Security!

(Wu walks over to the phone and starts to dial.)

ZHOU *(crying out):* No, don't—*(Zhou gives a piercing shriek and faints.)*

(Zhang Senior and Wu immediately rush toward her.)

EPILOGUE

Someone (unfortunately we've forgotten who) once said that the stage is a chamber of parliament. However this stage is now a courtroom in which a public trial is in progress; our beloved and faithful audience, sitting below the stage, have become spectators in court. And we hope that they, having witnessed firsthand the entire course of events in this case, will express their own opinions on the fairness of the court's verdict.

A chief judge and two assistant judicial officers sit at the judge's bench. The accused, Li Xiaozhang, sits in the prisoner's dock. Two guards stand behind him. Witnesses Wu, Qian, Sun, Zhao, and Zheng are sitting in the witness box. Zhang Senior is sitting at the defense counsel's desk. The prosecutor sits at the prosecutor's desk. As the curtain rises, the prosecutor is reading the indictment.

PROSECUTOR: —based on investigation, the evidence is irrefutable. Accordingly, we have instituted court proceedings. That is all.

JUDGE: The prosecutor has just read the indictment which details the culpable activities of the suspect Li Xiaozhang. Does the accused Li

Drama

Xiaozhang regard the statements of the prosecutor to be true or false?

LI (standing): They are all true.

JUDGE: Do you regard your activities as constituting a crime or not?

LI: I am not familiar with the law. But I acknowledge that I was wrong.

QIAN: What? You were "wrong"? Is that all?

ZHAO: What kind of "wrong" was it? Tell us!

JUDGE: Order!

LI: I was wrong to be a fake. If I really were the son of Zhang Senior or another leader, then everything I've done would be completely legal.

ZHAO: What do you mean?

QIAN: More arrogance!

SUN: He should be dealt with severely!

JUDGE: Witnesses must not speak without the Court's permission!

LI: At this time, I would like to express my appreciation to the witnesses in this case. That I was able to perpetrate this act and nearly be transferred from the farm, I owe to all the helpful advice Managing Director Zhao offered, and to all the avenues Bureau Chief Sun cleared for me, and to the directives Director Qian and Secretary Wu wrote for me, and to the transfer forms Director Zheng issued on my behalf. (makes a deep bow to the witnesses) Once more I would like to thank you for your kindness, thank you for the conveniences you provided me, and thank you for your strong support!

(Director Zhao is thoroughly flustered; Director Qian is beside herself with anger and shame; Bureau Chief Sun gapes, speechless.)

ZHAO: Your Honor, please allow me to speak.

JUDGE: Proceed.

ZHAO: What the accused has just said is irrelevant to this case, and I ask Your Honor to silence him.

ZHENG: No! Your Honor, I ask for permission to speak.

JUDGE: Proceed.

ZHENG: I consider what the accused just said to be completely true and of the utmost relevance to this case.

JUDGE: What is the opinion of the other witnesses?

WU: (rising to his feet): I agree with Director Zheng. The accused should be allowed to offer the whole truth. This, ah, would be most—beneficial.

JUDGE: The accused, Li Xiaozhang, is there anything more you wish to say?

LI: I would like to ask why Zhou Minghua is not present in court.

(The judge and the two judicial officers whisper to each other.)

ASSISTANT JUDICIAL OFFICER: Zhou Minghua cannot be present due to her confinement in a hospital for illness.

Li: What's wrong with her?

Assistant Judicial Officer: She is in critical condition.

Li (speechless with astonishment): Huh?

Judge: Do you have any further questions?

Li (weakly): No—None—(he sits, his head folded in his arms, sobbing)

Judge: At this time the counsel for the defense will please proceed with his defense.

Zhang Senior (stands): I hardly expected that the accused would entrust me to be his defense counsel. But prior to the trial I obtained a detailed knowledge of the facts in this case, and after several discussions with the accused, I finally accepted the trust he has placed in me. First, it is my view that the accused did in fact perpetrate fraud and that the Prosecutor's Office should bring charges against him. Without this we cannot ensure social order, nor can we educate and save youth who have gone astray. However, I wish to raise two issues which I ask the judge and judicial officers to take into consideration during their deliberations. First, why did the accused take a wrongful and dangerous path? Aside from such subjective causes as his own thought and character, are there other, deeper, social and historical causes? I believe that more than ten years of rampant madness from Lin Biao and the Gang of Four completely destroyed our campaign to send youth to the countryside and made these young people cynical. This was an important factor in motivating the accused Li Xiaozhang to commit a crime. In this sense, the accused Li Xiaozhang is also a victim, and I ask you to consider extending leniency to him. Second, the accused was able to conduct his fraud with such ease not because of any particularly brilliant method on his part. Rather, it was because a society that still maintains special privileges and has flaws in its system provides fertile soil for fraudulent activities. Some of our "swindlees," who are Party cadres, handed the accused his opportunities and even helped him to carry out his fraud. One reason these comrades behaved this way is that they acted from habits that are rooted in a feudalistic, privilege-oriented mentality. But there is another reason—they wanted, through the accused, to satisfy their own individual selfish desires. Given this fact, it is clear that they are not only victims but also collaborators. In the political sense, they should also be held responsible! While carrying out its deliberations o the sentence of the accused, should the Court also confront this reality? I ask your consideration.

Zhao: What? We are collaborators in the swindle?

Sun: We must also assume political blame?

Qian: Zhang Senior, you're being too harsh. I don't understand this, and I won't take it either! We are *all* persecuted by the Gang of Four.

Drama

ZHANG SENIOR: You don't mean to tell me that we are the only ones who were persecuted by the Gang of Four, do you? I would say our Party, our nation, and our people suffered even worse persecution! Why do you take into account only your own advantage and neglect to consider what is best for our Party, our nation, and our people? We ought to think hard for a moment and recall when we were suffering persecution under the Gang of Four, longing for the day when we would be free—what were we thinking of? Didn't we hope to be restored to our work, and once restored, to work even harder for the revolution? In the past the masses gave us their unbounded sympathy and devotion. They thought we could save the nation. They hoped we would benefit the people. But today you have forgotten all that! You have told the people to make allowances for the difficulties of the nation, to show self-restraint and obedience, to take the "big picture" into consideration, while there you are—grabbing your housing and calculating your own self-interest. You tell everybody else's children to "put down roots on the farm," while you use every means at your disposal to have your own sons and daughters transferred back to the city. And you want the masses to suffer privation and live simply while you yourselves crave a life of even greater luxury! If we cannot share in the lot of the masses, then how can we ask the masses to make common cause with us? I am really afraid for our cadre system, which, having survived the Gang of Four, may be brought to ruin by its own corruption.

Beware, comrades, or else—though some of you may now be sitting in the witness box of this court of law—in the court of Party discipline you will just as surely be standing in the dock of the accused!

(The end.)

POPULAR
PERFORMING
ARTS

Comedians' Dialogues

Comedians' dialogues or xiangsheng (literally, "face and voice") is a lively popular entertainment form that is especially well loved in northern Chinese cities such as Beijing, Tianjin, and Shenyang. Although from one to five performers may participate, usually there are two, a "joke cracker" and a "joke setter." The two can conjure scenes involving several people by cleverly switching roles as they proceed. They joke, pun, sing, tell stories, do imitations, and above all satirize.

Traditionally, comedians' dialogues were set routines about well-known stories. Audiences watched more to savor the performance than to discover what happens. But in the People's Republic the emphasis has shifted to creation of new pieces and to finding new objects for satire. For example, after the fall of the Gang of Four in October 1976, comedians' dialogues were among the first art forms (along with cartoons) to satirize the Gang of Four. Their quick appearance was possible partly because they were based on jokes that had been circulating underground well before the arrest of the Gang, and partly because they were so simple to stage and perform—requiring two willing actors and little else. The closeness of comedians' dialogues to popular concerns and their quickness in reflecting these concerns contributed greatly to their popularity during the relaxation of 1979–80. The satire of red tape, buckpassing, and overstaffing (as in the three examples collected here) brought great cheer to audiences who encountered such problems in daily life and sought release through comedy. Because appreciation of comedians' dialogues requires no literacy, and because performances were frequently broadcast on China's most pervasive medium of radio, this art form has enjoyed the largest of audiences.

Comedians' dialogues are also published in written form as literary works, and the roles of writer of these texts and performer of the dialogues have grown largely separate since the 1950s. "The Multi-Level Hotel" is exceptional in this sense, because its author, Ma Ji, is also a famous performer. Liu Ziyu, author of "The Tyrant Bids Farewell to His Mistress," was a young editor at the magazine Tianjin Performing Arts (Tianjin yanchang) in 1979–80.

WEI QIPING Bureau Chief Bureau

A: Do you know anything about apple-polishing?
B: I do not!
A: Do you know how to set up a stool pigeon?
B: I do not!
A: Do you know how to handle a telephone call?
B: I do n— Of course I do! Anybody can answer a telephone!

Stubborn Weeds

252

A: Well then why can't I?

B: At your age, you still can't handle a phone call?

A: It's not that easy where I work.

B: Where do you work?

A: At the Bureau Chief Bureau.

B: Bureau Chief Bureau? I've heard of the Industry Bureau, Agriculture Bureau, Transportation Bureau, Commerce Bureau, Supply Bureau, Personnel Bureau, Construction Bureau, Culture Bureau, Education Bureau, Sanitation Bureau—since when has there been a Bureau Chief Bureau?

A: Anyway, that's where I work—the Bureau Chief Bureau.

B: What do they do at this Bureau Chief Bureau?

A: Beats me, but if you work there, I guarantee you, everything will be—

B: Soft and cushy?

A: One frustration after another! I'm a full-grown man, and I can't even handle a phone call without problems. I'm on duty the other day, for example. The phone rings. I pick up the receiver and put it to my ear, and then the trouble starts!

B: Who's calling?

A: The new deputy secretary of the Municipal Committee.

B: Who does he want to talk to?

A: "Bureau Chief Bureau? Let me talk to your bureau chief."

B: What's so hard about that? All you have to do is get your bureau chief to answer the phone.

A: Sounds easy, doesn't it? "Oh, the Bureau Chief? He's at a meeting with the provincial government."

B: He's unreachable.

A: "Well, then I'll talk to the deputy bureau chief."

B: Easy enough. Get the deputy bureau chief.

A: "Deputy bureau chief? Um, which deputy bureau chief do you want?"

B: Got to have a name!

A: "Well, let's see. How about a deputy bureau chief named Ma?"

B: Deputy Bureau Chief Ma.

A: "Do you mean Elder Ma, Big Ma, or Junior Ma?"

B: Three of 'em!

A: "Well, then, how about Deputy Bureau Chief Hu?"

B: Now we'll see who's Hu around here!

A: "We've got two Hu's. You want Big Hu or Number Two Hu?"

B: Hu ever! Why does he have to talk to a bigwig, anyway? Why not just talk to the person left in charge?

A: Below the bureau chiefs there are only two section members.

B: And below the section members?

A: Two office personnel.

Popular Performing Arts

B: And below them?

A: The door man.

B: That's five personnel. And how many chiefs and deputy chiefs?

A: One bureau chief and nine deputy bureau chiefs—exactly ten altogether.

B: Twice the number of workers?

A: Why do you think they call it the Bureau Chief Bureau? Lots of officials with hardly any workers!

B: Even with the "iron rice bowl" [guaranteed job] mentality, somebody has to do the work!

A: That depends on the situation! The deputy secretary of the Municipal Committee still hasn't hung up. "Bureau Chief Bureau? The Bureau Chief is out, you say? Well, if I can't talk to Number One, then give me Number Two."

B: The number two man!

A: "Number Two is very old and weak. He's resting at home on extended leave." "Well, then, how about Number Three?"

B: That's it; work your way down.

A: "The number three man is on family visitation in Hangzhou and hasn't returned yet."

B: Try Number Four, then.

A: "Number Four is a soccer star. If you throw the ball to him, he'll kick it right back to you."

B: How about Number Five?

A: "Number Five is a female deputy bureau chief. She got herself transferred here last month through marital connections. She hasn't come to work since she first reported in."

B: Whew! Try Number Six, then.

A: "Number Six is in a bad mood at the moment. He objects to the order in ranking of the deputy bureau chiefs."

B: Well, from the looks of it, we'll have to settle for Number Seven.

A: "Number Seven, you say? He can't answer the phone either. Says he's under too much pressure. Afraid Number Eight will accuse him of having 'long arms'—reaching for power."

B: Then all our hopes are pinned on Number Nine, aren't they?

A: "Number Nine has made it very clear that nobody in his position dares to make a decision about anything."

B: I see what you mean about your telephone being hard to answer.

A: The fellow on the other end of the line was getting desperate too. "Bureau Chief Bureau? Why can't anyone handle my phone call? We're going to have to do something about this, you know!"

B: Ah, things are looking up!

A: "You tell those people—"

B: Here comes the solution!

Stubborn Weeds

A: "Tomorrow I'm assigning the Bureau Chief Bureau another deputy bureau chief!"
B: Another chief—just what you need!

Originally published in Quyi *(Beijing), March 1980.*
Translated by Jan W. Walls.

MA JI *The Multi-Level Hotel*

A: I recently went to perform in your hometown.
B: You did? What was your impression?
A: Great! If I ever get the chance I'll do everything I can *not* to go back.
B: Huh? You call it "great," but you don't want to go back? What happened—cold audiences?
A: The audiences greeted my performance with enthusiastic applause. They were as warm as could be.
B: Could it be that the climate didn't suit you?
A: The climate was wonderful. "Four seasons like spring"—neither hot nor cold—and the scenery was delightful. It suited me just fine.
B: Could it be that they didn't treat you properly?
A: Who says? The leading comrades received me personally. The director of the Bureau of Culture accompanied me to every performance. And the hotel I stayed in was too beautiful for words. The rooms had thermostats. The bathroom had piping from the hot springs, and there was hot water twenty-four hours a day.
B: Which hotel did you stay in?
A: The Multi-Level Hotel.
B: The Multi-Level Hotel? How many levels did it have?
A: More than two hundred!
B: More than two hundred? There're no buildings that tall!
A: No, no. Not that kind of level. There were over two hundred levels of *formalities* at this hotel.
B: Oh, I see. What you're saying is that the hotel had a swollen bureaucracy—endless regulations—*that* kind of multi-level hotel.
A: But the room charges were comparatively low.
B: How much a day?
A: One dollar!
B: Only a dollar for such nice rooms? Really cheap!

Popular Performing Arts

A: Well—in addition to that, there were some service charges.

B: Couldn't have been too much, could it?

A: Oh, no? There was a fee for raising and lowering the heat, a management fee, a sanitation fee, a water and electricity fee, a furniture depreciation fee, a fee for repairing doors and windows, a fee for laundering the bedding, a fee for pillow slips, a fee for pillowcases.

B: Wouldn't it have saved trouble to add it all up as a one-time charge?

A: Can't do that! Too many departments in the hotel! They've got an elaborate division of labor. Everybody handles his own job and takes his own fee.

B: They couldn't be very efficient, then.

A: The day I registered, for example, I was bounced back and forth so much that it almost put me in the hospital.

B: What happened?

A: I took my letter of introduction to the Municipal Party Committee to get a chop [official stamp] put on it. They sent me to the City Service Corporation to get a chop. From there I had to go to the Primary Level Headquarters for a chop. Then from there to the District Primary Level office for a chop. All this before I even got to the Multi-Level Hotel.

B: That's quite a few levels already!

A: The minute I entered the hotel, an elderly attendant asked me, "Are you registering to stay in this hotel?"

B: Right!

A: *(continuing as the attendant):* "You have a letter of introduction?"

B: *(now assuming the role of the arriving guest):* Of course.

A: "Let me have a look at it. What's it say in the letter?"

B: You can't read it clearly?

A: "I can't read at all."

B: If you can't read, what're you looking at it for?

A: "Procedures required by my superiors. All letters have to be looked at. What's your occupation?"

B: Performer.

A: "Oh, well, then! Go in this door, and go to Business Office Number Six.

B: Wow! So many business offices?

A: "Uh, Business Office One handles officials of the Party, government, and military. Office Two is in charge of industry. Three is in charge of agriculture. Four handles communication and transport. Five does finance and trade, and Six does culture, education, and public health."

B: That's dividing it too fine!

A: *(in his own role):* When I got to Office Six and took a look around,

Stubborn Weeds

there were quite a few personnel there—at least six or seven—all sitting along two sides of a table, concentrating completely on what they were doing.

B: Having a meeting?

A: Playing chess!

B: Playing chess on the job?

A: Well, they didn't have very much to do, so why not play some chess to kill time?

B: A typical case of overstaffing—more hands than needed.

A: One of the attendants greeted me warmly: "Who're you looking for?"

B: *(taking the role of "A")*: I've come to handle the formalities.

A: "OK. How about filling out a form?"

B: If you say so.

A: *(himself again)*: There was no way I could fill it out.

B: How come?

A: It was a postal money order form.

B: He must've given you the wrong form. Better exchange it!

A: *(in role of attendant)*: "They're all the same. To remit a hundred dollars you pay one dollar."

B: No, no. The man's here to register in the hotel!

A: "Oh, I'm sorry. My specialization is postal money orders. For hotel registration you'll have to wait for Comrade Xiaoman." [pun: *Xiaoman* = "little slow"]

B: Where's Comrade Little Slow?

A: "You'll have to wait a little while. She's gone out to lunch. She'll be back at 2:30."

B: Guess you have to wait, eh?

A: *(in his own role)*: I must admit that Comrade Little Slow had an acute sense of time. At exactly 2:30 on the dot she came in doing shadowboxing.

B: Shadowboxing?

(A *stretches and simulates a yawn.*)

B: Must've been sleepy from her noon nap.

A: "Which comrade wants to complete formalities?"

B: *(as "A")*: Me!

A: "You have a letter of introduction?"

B: Sure.

A: "How about filling out an application?"

B: What is all this filling out of applications?

A: "Right. A nation has its laws. A home has its regulations. A hotel has its rules. In our hotel everybody has to fill out a form—no exceptions! Have to be three copies. Writing brush or pen only. Invalid if altered. Attach a one-inch photo of self from waist up. No hats."

Popular Performing Arts

B: *(in own role):* That's just great! More trouble than applying for a passport!

A: I took the application and looked it over. Two large sheets of tiny scrunched-up characters. Over forty items to be filled out.

B: What were they?

A: Name; any other name or alias; previously used names; sex; age; place of birth; date of birth; family background; class status; purpose of visit; introduced by; approximate length of stay; whether carrying any important documents, letters, maps, secret documents, and if so what is written therein—

B: Wow!

A: Just plain impossible!

B: That's what I say.

A: —was I carrying in my suitcase any of the following: checks made out to cash; valuable objects, such as gold, silver, jewelry, bicycles?

B: Bicycles? In a suitcase?

B: There was more. Was I carrying any combustibles, explosives, or dangerous perishables such as gasoline, gunpowder, nitric acid, sulfuric acid, hydrochloric acid, banana oil, orange juice—?

B: Wait! Wait! Orange juice? A dangerous substance?

A: That's not all. How many boxes of matches was I carrying into the hotel? How many cigarette lighters? Any firecrackers such as sizzlers, fizzlers, double-bangers? How many strings of mini-firecrackers? How many concussion bombs and cherry bombs? How many rockets? How many boxes of "rat droppings"?[1]

B: Good god! You had to fill out all this?

A: It took over half an hour to fill it all out. When it was finally done, "Little Slow" took a big stamp and stamped the application. "OK, comrade."

B: What room number?

A: *(as the clerk):* "Don't be in such a hurry. I have to ask you where you're from."

B: It's all on the application."

A: "Just to be on the safe side I want to ask you orally."

B: *(aside):* Like a college entrance examination?[2]

A: "Where'd you come from?"

B: Beijing.

A: "Where're you going?"

B: Here!

A: "This your destination? Or passing through?"

B: This is my destination.

1. "Rat droppings" is the nickname for a kind of small firecracker.
2. In some Chinese universities, departments such as foreign languages or performing arts require an oral entrance examination after the written one.

Stubborn Weeds

A: "What did you come here to do?"

B: Perform.

A: "Going back this evening?"

B: *(as "A"):* Going back this evening? Why would I be going through all these registration procedures if—

A: "Don't get excited, comrade—"

B: I'm *not* excited, but staying in a hotel is simply a matter of registering. How come all these tedious formalities?

A: "One has to be secure in business matters. Remember—'First stop, then look, and only then proceed.'[3] 'Better three minutes too late than one second too early.' "

B: *(aside):* What'd she think she was doing? Driving an automobile?

A: *(continuing):* "Did you just get off the train?"

B: Hah! I've been here over three hours!

A: "Where'd you have lunch?"

B: I haven't yet.

A: "Oh. Not had lunch yet? Well, that's no problem—"

B: How come?

A: "Combine it with dinner!"

B: *(aside):* How absurd!

A: "OK, take your applicatin and go to the Security Section to register."

B: Ye gods! Now I have to go to the Security Section. Where's the Security Section?

A: "Go out here—Building Two—"

B: *(in own role):* Better hurry up.

A: I went around Building Two three times and couldn't find the Security Section.

B: How come?

A: That's what I asked her. "You're in too big a hurry," she said. "I wasn't finished—"

B: You said Building Two.

A: "Right, but I was saying, 'Building Two will get you nowhere—' "

B: I see. Then where *should* I go?

A: "Building Three—"

B: *(own role):* OK, then go to Building Three!

A: I did but still couldn't find it!

B: *Still* not there?

A: I asked her again. "You don't learn, do you?" she said. "I wasn't finished speaking—"

B: You said Building Three.

A: "I was about to say, 'Building Three has another building diagonally opposite—' "

3. This a widely used warning to pedestrians.

Popular Performing Arts

259

B: *(aside):* This gal must've had some heavy noodles for lunch. So where was it, anyway?

A: "In Building Four—"

B: *(own role):* Don't go yet! Wait and see if she has anything to add to that.

A: Right, that's what I did. I lit a cigarette and waited. I'd almost finished the cigarette when she added a word: "—alongside—"

B: Oh, boy! This Comrade Little Slow really was too slow.

A: I found the Security Section, went in, and took a look around. There were four comrades there. One was reading the newspaper, one was working on some furniture, and one was listening to the radio. Only one was sitting at the desk, not making a sound.

B: Hard at work?

A: Nope. Fast asleep.

B: Nothing to do, eh?

A: "Comrades, I've come to register for a room." "I see," one said. "Fill out this form."

B: Another form!

A: This one was even more complicated than the last.

B: What kind of a form was it?

A: A questionnaire on the safety of guests.

B: What'd it ask?

A: Name; any other name or alias; names used in the past; sex; age; place of birth; date of birth; family background; class status—

B: Same old junk as the other one!

A: —facial appearance; characteristics; height; weight; girth; length; wearing what clothes? Any facial blemishes? Any moles? How many whorls and loops in fingerprints?

B: What were they trying to do? Arrest a wanted criminal?

A: There was more—year, month, and day of arrival in the city; list all activities; was death from sudden illness, vehicular accident, suicide, assassination, or murder? Caused by slashed throat, hanging, jumping in a river, jumping down a well, swallowing DDT—?

B: What utter nonsense!

A: The comrade said to me: "If 'yes,' fill in the reasons. If 'no,' mark with an X. We always prepare for the future in our security work. What if we waited for something to happen to you before we asked you to fill out the form? Could you?"

B: Since when do guests fill out this kind of questionnaire?

A: "Comrade," he said, "we're simply carrying out the wishes of our superiors. We hope you'll comply. Isn't this also a contribution to the Four Modernizations?"

B: OK, OK! Let's all contribute!

A: I decided just to fill out whatever they wanted me to. I completed the form, and, bang! He whacked it with a big chop. "Okay, comrade—"

B: What room number do I get?

A: "Take it easy. Bring this form to the Health Protection Office and register."

B: Where? Health Protection?

A: Come to think of it, this hotel really shows great consideration for its guests.

B: How's that?

A: For safety's sake they issue everybody a double-edged sword.[4]

B: Whaaat?

A: Oh, dear! When I entered the Health Protection Office I saw their staff was bigger yet.

B: Yeah, but still no work.

A: What do you mean? The people in this office were all so worn out that sweat was running down their necks.

B: Doing physical exams?

A: No, propped on pillows playing poker!

B: That's really loafing.

A: "Comrades, I've come to register at the hotel." "Fill out a form!"

B: Wherever you went they wanted a form filled out. If you'd known in advance you could've had a dozen printed up and saved yourself a lot of bother.

A: I took a look at the form. "Survey of Guests' Physical Condition."

B: What did it ask?

A: Name; alias or any other name used; sex; age; place of origin; date of birth; family background; class status—

B: All over again.

A: —condition of appliant's health? Any disease? How being treated? History of past illnesses; family history of past illnesses; illness history for three generations back. Ever had any of the following diseases: gallstones; colitis; skin disease; communicable diseases; high blood pressure; hypoglycemia; severe colds; blood fluke (schistosomiasis); vasculitis; vitiligo; kidney stones; tracheitis; psoriasis; epilepsy; paralysis; lack of proper care after childbirth; fatal heart attack; hyperplasia of the bones? Normal reaction to type O blood? Ever had X-rays? Ever had an electrocardiogram? Ever had any preventive inoculations? Vaccinated for smallpox? Ever admitted to a hospital? Ever admitted to a crematorium?

B: No!

A: . . . How well do you sleep? What sleeping habits? Do you sleep on your side? On your back? Across the bed? Standing up?

B: I've never practiced that particular skill!

4. This is a word play on *baojian*—"health protection" and "double-edged sword."

A: . . . Do you snore? Sleepwalk? Sleeptalk? Have any quirks during sleep such as grinding the teeth, passing wind, or smacking the lips?

B: What's all this got to do with staying at a hotel?

A: "That's not up to us," he said. "We're assigned to investigate, so we investigate. Hurry up and complete the form! How're we going to raise efficiency with a slowpoke like you?"

B: Look who's talking about "raising efficiency"!

A: When I finished filling out the form, another big chop landed on it. "Okay, comrade."

B: What room number do I get?

A: "Don't be in such a hurry—"

B: Where else did they send you?

A: "Take this form to the Cashier's Office and pay an asker."

B: Asker? You mean a teller.

A: "Nope. Our whole bureaucracy can't tell you a thing. We only have askers."

B: At least he was right about that! Where was the Cashier's Office?

A: "Go out the main door, get on the Number Eight bus, take that to the Number Nine electric bus, go three stops, get off and walk back in the direction you came from, go two short blocks and then turn north. It's on the east side of the street, facing west. A big red gate."

B: Good god, dispatched again!

A: "We're expanding, comrade! We're increasing our office space and the size of our staff. We don't have enough space in the hotel right now, but in a year the Cashier's Office will move back here."

B: I see—you'll be streamlining the bureaucracy.

A: "No, we're going to cut down on the number of guests."

B: With that kind of expansion there'll soon be nothing left but offices.

A: "I can't be bothered about that. You just hurry on over to the Cashier's Office and register—"

B: Off you go!

A: When I got there two people jumped to their feet. "Let me handle this, Zhang. You better finish *Count of Monte Cristo* before you have to give it back." "No, no," said the other one, "I haven't done anything for days. Let me do it." "No, don't bother with it," said the first one. "I don't have anything else to do." "No, you take it easy." "OK, OK, I'll let you do it." "Well, have it your own way then, you take care of it."

B: So who finally took care of you?

A: Neither. They entirely ignored me.

B: Gosh!

A: Another fellow sitting at the side stood up and said, "If you won't handle this, I will, and this month's bonus will go to me again!"

B: Huh? The guy was concerned about a bonus?

A: "What can I do for you?" he asked.

B: I've come to register.

A: "Oh, so you want to register—"

B: Fill out another form, I bet. What kind of form this time?

A: "Appetite Survey."

B: Looks like this hotel has to take more people. They survey everything!

A: I hurried to fill out the form, which started out—

B: I know it by heart! Name; alias; names previously used—

A: After that I had to fill out "Family's Financial Condition and Circumstances": How many people in family? How many brothers? How many sisters? How many children? How many spouses?

B: What?

A: "Sorry, there's a printing error on the questionnaire. Just do the best you can."

B: That's outrageous!

A: Then it asked: Who provides for your parents? How much do you give them every month? Does your spouse object to this?

B: Is that any of their concern?'

A: What level of board are you buying at the hotel? The fifty-five-cent rate? Sixty-nine-cent rate? Eighty-five? Dollar and six cents? Are you vegetarian? Do you prefer rice or wheat? Do you like stuffed buns, dumplings, or noodles? Buckwheat noodles? How much do you eat at one sitting? Do you drink? White wine? Colored wines? Beer? Sparkling wines? Sweet rice wine? Medicinal liquors? Do you act crazy after drinking? Do you hit people or merely curse them? Do you cry or laugh? Just talk or cause a disturbance? How many times might you drink while staying at the hotel? How many times might you cause a disturbance?

B: What a crock of nonsense!

A: When I came out of the Cashier's Office I went back to the service desk, filled out a form, paid the service charge, and then headed for the Meals Office. There I filled out another form to buy meal tickets before going to the Secretariat to fill out a form for my identity pass. Finally I made it to the Room Allocation Office.

B: What room did you get?

A: Don't be in such a hurry.

B: More forms,eh?

A: There was no point filling out any more forms. They were out of rooms!

B: Great! After all that tearing about, you filled out all the forms for nothing!

A: From there I went layer by layer through all the responsible persons, explaining my situation. Finally they took care of me. They gave me Room One on the ninth floor.

B: So you finally got a room!

A: I went up to the service desk on the ninth floor. "Can you open the door for me, comrade?"

B: What did the attendant say?

A: "First please fill out this form."

B: Not again!

A: "Comrade," he said, "these are procedures stipulated from above. But first step into the room."

B: So go in!

A: I could see at a glance the room was a total mess. A layer of dust covered everything.

B: Why hadn't they cleaned it up?

A: "Please excuse us, comrade. We're short of help. There are more than ten guests living on the ninth floor, and we have only thirty-four people in our service department."

B: That's "short on help"?

A: "But comrade, that thirty-four includes the department chief, the assistant department chief, the section chief, the assistant section chief, the team chief, the assistant team chief, the group chief, and the assistant group chief."

B: Quite a few cadres, eh?

A: "We've also set up a service office for seventeen unemployed cadres."

B: Is that so?

A: "Then there are two cadres in charge of personnel matters, two cadres in charge of security, two in charge of the labor union, two in charge of the Communist Youth League, two in charge of women's affairs, two in charge of family planning, and two in charge of education. How many does that leave?"

B: Everybody's a cadre!

A: "There's a few things I must ask you to attend to yourself."

B: OK.

A: "—make your bed, and fold your quilts—"

B: That I can do.

A: "—get your own tea water—"

B: No problem.

A: "—clean up your own room—"

B: OK, OK.

A: "—sweep up the corridors, mop the floors, polish the mirror, clean the toilet, nail the leg onto the bed, put up the mosquito netting, fix the electric light switch, clean out the sewer lines, plaster the back outside wall—"

B: You mean I've come here to repair the whole building? There should be specialists for all these things!

A: "There are. Somebody's in charge of each thing, but to handle all

264

the procedures would take from three to five months. Can you wait?"

B: No.

A: "—I must also tell you there's no electricity in the room."

B: What happened?

A: "The light bulb blew."

B: So? Change it!

A: "Right! I made a report a year and a half ago, but it hasn't been approved yet."

B: Too complicated for words.

A: It's only for three days, I thought to myself. I'll just make do.

B: Right.

A: "But," I said to the comrade, "there's one thing I must trouble you with. I have to go perform in the evenings, beginning tonight. Could I possibly eat an hour early?"

B: Shouldn't be any big problem.

A: "For that," said he, "you'll have to check with the Dining Room Bureau. It's not our department."

B: Off to the Dining Room Bureau!

A: In the Dining Room Bureau a woman comrade with long braids was most friendly. "So you want to eat a little earlier, do you? I'm sorry, but there won't be time to cook up anything special. How about some noodles?"

B: Yeah, OK.

A: "Well, would you mind filling out this form?"

B: Good gosh!

A: "What's your room number?"

B: Ninth floor, number one.

A: "Surname?"

B: There they go again—!

A: "Age?"

B: Forty-three.

A: "Occupation?"

B: Entertainer.

A: "How many years have you been married?"

B: Mar—what?!

A: "Just fill out whatever they ask, OK?"

B: Hah!

A: "Take this slip and get the supervisor to approve it."

B: Layer after layer of approvals again?

A: The supervisor signed it and wrote, "Waiter Work Team approves—transfer to Kitchen Work Team for approval."

B: What?!

A: The supervisor of the kitchen team approved it with the notation, "Pending approval of the Section Chief"; and the Section Chief

Popular Performing Arts

wrote, "Awaiting approval of the Department Chief"; and the Department Chief wrote, "Request certification by the Bureau of Culture."

B: Was one bowl of noodles worth all that?

A: When I saw the way things were going, I went straight to the hotel manager.

B: To the manager for a bowl of noodles!

A: He wasn't a bad type at all—very straightforward. "Secretary Liu!"

B: I hope he's told them to cook the noodles—

A: "Check the documents for any possible guidance on the question of noodles!"

B: Since when are there documents on noodles?

A: "Better go back to your room, comrade. I can't approve this on my own."

B: The noodles stumped even the manager!

A: "Comrade! We leaders must not be autocratic! Can we let a single pushy person decide things? Let's just wait for the assistant manager to come back. He and I will discuss it as quickly as possible."

B: Where was the assistant manager?

A: "On business in Guangzhou."

B: God! I can't wait that long.

A: "Can't wait? Then let me request instruction from the municipal Party secretary."

B: Yeah?

A: "Forget it," I said. "Before you know it, this'll go to the province level. I can do without the noodles."

B: What did you eat, then?

A: I bought a loaf of bread and made do. When my three days of performances were over and I was on my way back, I was getting onto the train when the hotel manager came running down the platform.

B: He'd come to see you off—

A: "Comrade," he said, "your bowl of noodles has been approved!"

Originally published in Tianjin Yanchang, *No. 5, 1979.*

Translated by Robert N. Tharp.

LIU ZIYU *The Tyrant Bids Farewell to His Mistress*

A *(a young man's voice):* Do you like traditional Peking opera?

B *(an old man's voice):* Most people my age do.

A: We young people feel—ah—a certain way about it.

B: What's that?

A: We don't know what they're talking about!

B: My goodness! Peking opera is an ancient folk theater, full of distinctive national artistic character—the singing, recitation, acting and fighting all have to be just right. Traditional Peking operas dramatize a great many splendid historical stories and have real educational significance.

A: Right! Right! I saw a scene the other day that I did understand and learn a lesson from.

B: Which opera?

A: "The Tyrant Bids Farewell to His Mistress."

B: Oh, that's a great play! It's about the despotic arbitrary rule of Xiang Yu, the Tyrant of Chu. He clung obstinately to his course and in the end fell into General Han Xin's ambush on ten sides. He bade final farewell to his beloved concubine, Yu Ji, and then slit his own throat at the Wu River.

A: That's the story, all right. Where do you think Xiang Yu's common sense went?

B: Well, he was a tyrant, after all. What can you expect?

A: He wouldn't listen when his advisor Fan Zeng told him to kill Liu Bang.

B: He thought he was the only one who was ever right.

A: And in the end he couldn't face the parents of the boys who died for him.

B: He brought disgrace and ruin upon himself.

A: But you know, that guy really did have talent.

B: Enough to move mountains!

A: And he had a lot of people under him too.

B: Eight thousand followers in the camp!

A: And he fought victorious battles.

B: He was invincible!

A: He was also a Party branch secretary.

B: A leading cadre—huh? Party secretary?

A: But he didn't study quite hard enough.

B: Hold on there! *Who's* a Party secretary?

A: The tyrant!

B: The Tyrant of Chu was a Party member?

A: Uh—nope! I'm talking about the Tyrant Wu.

B: Where did you come up with Tyrant Wu?

A: You don't know Tyrant Wu? He's the Party secretary in our unit. Name of Wu. He can be benevolent or very highhanded. Everyone calls him Tyrant Wu. Come to think of it, he looks a lot like you!

B: Now wait a minute! How can you be talking about Xiang Yu and suddenly drag your Party secretary into it?

A: As I see it they're pretty similar.

B: Xiang Yu was despotic and arbitrary.

A: He's arbitrary and despotic.

B: Xiang Yu wanted to hear only good news and ignored the bad.

A: He ignores bad news and wants to hear only the good.

B: Xiang Yu wouldn't listen to opposing views.

A: Opposing views plug his ears.

B: Xiang Yu pulled off a "Tyrant Bids Farewell to His Mistress."

A: He pulled off a—uh—a "Party Secretary Bids Farewell to His Missus."

B: Farewell to his missus?

A: Yep. His old lady filed for divorce.

B: OK. Just how does this guy act most of the time?

A: He can do nothing, and nothing is what he does. All he can do is give arbitrary orders. What he says goes; his every word is a profound truth, and there's no room to object. Try and go against him and he'll make things tight for you. If you obviously wear a size 40 shoe, he's sure to give you a 34½.[1]

B: Really puts the pinch on you?

A: And then ties the laces as tight as possible.

B: Ouch!

A: Then he'll go stamp on your toes.

B: Wow, is he mean!

A: He has a pet phrase.

B: What is it?

A: "First democracy, then centralism."

B: Good. We need to "let everyone have his say" and get rid of "what I say goes." We must centralize the correct opinions of the masses. Then we'll have centralism on a democratic foundation.

A: Oh, no, with him it's "you do your democratizing, and I'll do my centralizing."

B: Huh? He's got it mixed up.

A: Just take the last time our unit had some housing to divide up. The leaders wanted to give special consideration to families that

1. In contemporary slang, when a leader deliberately gives someone a hard time without acknowledging that he is doing so, he is said to make the person "wear small shoes."

especially needed it. So they set some places aside. Well, he got wind of it and came hotfooting right over. "I hear you're going to divide up housing?"

B: —eyes popping right out of his head?

A *(continuing to imitate the tyrant)*: "How're you gonna do the dividing?"

B: We're discussing it with the masses right now.

A: "OK! First off, let me remind you that the basic principle is, 'first democracy, then centralism.' When everyone is through talking it over, the Party branch will discuss it and I'll centralize. The homes must go to those households that are truly in a bad way."

B: Yes. Our idea exactly.

A: "Like mine, for example."

B: Yes—huh? You have four people in a five-room flat. You call that hardship?

A: "You've got to take a long-range view. As of now we have four people, but when my son gets married, there'll be five."

B: Oh, so that's how he looks at it!

A: "And when he has a child, there'll be eight."

B: He just got married and he has a child?

A: "Premature."

B: Even if it's premature, that's only six people. How do you get eight?

A: "Maybe there'll be triplets."

B: So that's how he's got it figured!

A: "My demands are nothing much. Just a few more rooms, OK? A little wider corridor, hm? And—heh, heh—somewhat better living conditions."

B *(ironically)*: And slightly reduced rent.

A: "Thank you! That's fine!"

B: Come off it. Where can you find a deal like that?

A: "I hear you've also got your hands on a few other items?"

B: They allocated a few TV sets to us.

A: "Oh, some TV sets?"

B: There go those eyeballs again.

A: "Now when we allocate them, we first need democracy, then centralism. If they're really quality merchandise at a low price, then our family will take one first."

B: They'll be first, I see.

A: "What else have you got?"

B: We have some—imported curtains.

A: "Hee! We'll have some!"

B: And some limited-circulation books.

A: "One set for us."

B: And five ration coupons for full-sized wardrobes.

Popular Performing Arts

A: "We'll take a coupon."

B: And two giant hot water vats.

A: "We'll take one."

B: You want a whole vat?

A: "Uh—we'll share it with everybody!"

B: You call this allocating?

A: "We have the best interests of the masses foremost in our minds."

B: Right—when something the size of a water vat comes along he finally thinks of others.

A: But we analyzed it afterward, and it turns out that his method of allocation fully accords with his principles.

B: First democracy, then centralism?

A: Yeah! Something good comes along, we have a go at democracy, and then everything is centralized at his house.

B: Oh, *that* kind of democratic centralism! This guy really is a first-class tyrant.

A *(imitating the tyrant again):* "What? What'd you say?"

B: I said you are a tyrant.

A: "A tyrant? What the hell are you driving at? Who's a tyrant? How am I a tyrant?"

B: Isn't it obvious?

A: "Where'd you get this attitude toward the Party? Let's get one thing straight—the battalion has a commander, the nation has a head of state, the work unit has a chief, and the family has a—head of household."

B: You count the head of a household too?

A: "You can't be absolutely egalitarian; that's what the Gang of Four tried to push. You criticize every little thing; just what the hell are you driving at? You may think you're quite a rebel, but I'll show you a thing or two."

B: Don't you touch me. *You* are acting like the Gang of Four.

A: "What the hell are you driving at? What're you up to? Let's get one thing straight—I'm the secretary! I'm not mixed up with the Gang of Four one bit. Wherever I'm transferred I'll be the secretary. What've you got to say to that? If I don't serve here, I'll serve there. What've you got to say to that? I can't be fired, I've got an iron rice bowl. What've you got to say to that?"

B: He really is blustery and pugnacious.

A: "What do you mean I make people's blood boil and pinch their feet? Who pinches? When have I ever pinched you?"

B: He certainly heard *that* wrong.

A: "*Your* blood is boiling, you say? Serves you right! Hope you die of it."

B: Boy, it's really enough to burn you up!

A: When he acts this way, what can the masses do?

Stubborn Weeds

B: All they can do is get angry.

A: The most annoying thing is the way he turns everything into an issue of Party leadership.

B: Even when it's irrelevant?

A: Yeah. Now take a small example from last Saturday. Our unit's dining hall got hold of some pig's head from a slaughterhouse—really cheap, thirty cents for a big helping. Everyone was divvying it up. When Tyrant Wu got wind of it, he came hotfooting it over to the kitchen. "I heard there's some pig's head?"

B: There go his eyeballs again.

A: "Not bad. Great! Hurrah!"

B: So what happened?

A: Tossed a piece into his mouth.

B: Pretty greedy!

A: "Hey, you! Pack me up a few portions."

B *(taking the part of the meat seller):* "Hold on there. 'First democracy, then centralism.' I must sell to the others first; you can go to the end of the line."

A: "What's that? I have to wait in line? Just what the hell are you driving at? The Party secretary's schedule is very tight. Waiting in line will delay the branch. You'll be held responsible."

B: "I'm not making the branch wait in line. I'm telling *you* to line up."

A: "I'm the leader of the branch. I represent the branch. Just what the hell are you driving at? Let's get one thing straight!" *(raises his hand)*

B: He was going to hit somebody?

A: "Just scratching my head."

B: How can one guy be so screwed up?

A: I saw what was going on and ran over to reason with him. "OK, OK, OK, don't get riled up, Secretary Wu. I'll wrap up whatever you like." *(then, to the meat seller)* "With so many people waiting, why argue with him about such a trifle?"

B: Then let him go ahead and pick.

A *(imitating the tyrant again):* "Now that's the correct attitude toward the Party branch."

B: He's pleased.

A: "OK, here I go, I'm going to choose, I—I don't want this one."

B: How's that?

A: "There are pig's ears in it."

B: How can you have pig's head without pig's ears?

A: "I'm not much of a fan of pig's ears."

B: Here's tongue.

A: "Don't like it."

B: Here's brain.

A: "Don't like it."

B: What do you like?

A: "I like the pig's—uh—the chest!"

B: You mean chops.

A: "Yes. Pork chops."

B: Get out of here! Since when does a pig's head have chops?

A: I was standing nearby and was fed up, too. "Secretary Wu, you're really going too far. What're you being so picky about? Everybody's busy day and night carrying out the Four Modernizations, and you don't even care about the dining hall. If we get off work a little late we can't get a hot meal. We arranged for this meat by ourselves, and now you come and butt in. How come you're suddenly so concerned about us?"

B: Disgraceful.

A: "Just what the hell are you driving at? Let's get one thing straight! Now do you want Party leadership or don't you? Does your democracy have centralism? Did the Party branch investigate this matter of selling pig's head?"

B: You need the Party branch's OK for *this?*

A: "Of course!"

B: They shouldn't sell *any* to you.

A: "What? Not sell any to me? OK. Then I proclaim—it is not permitted to sell pig's head. Tomorrow is Sunday—no one is allowed the day off. Instead we'll have a study discussion session."

B: To discuss what?

A: "A specialized inquiry into pig's head!"

B: A meeting devoted to a plate of pig's head?

A: Everybody blew up when they heard this. "Tyrant Wu is just too absurd. Why wait till tomorrow? Let's go straight to the meeting hall and talk this out right now!"

B: Right. Make him see reason.

A: Tyrant Wu gives the masses no credit at all. He said the masses were hotheaded, giddy. When they went to the meeting room and took seats he said, "Now what the hell are you driving at? All I wanted to discuss was the leadership of the Party and—its relation to pig's head."

B: You've really screwed up Party leadership.

A: "It's just that I don't like to eat pig's ears. Or tongue or brains, that's all. OK, who's got something to say? I'm not afraid. Speak up. And I won't haul out the cudgels or stick you with a 'hat'[2] or make you wear small shoes—or pants—or anything else."

B: Stark naked? Shameless!

A: The masses just couldn't take it any more. One guy leaped to his

2. A "hat" is an undesirable political label.

Stubborn Weeds

272

feet. "Enough! All you can do is babble about 'Party leadership' and lecture about 'political study.' Well, we've heard enough of this singsong. We're fed up with empty talk!"

B: Right. What the masses want is the Four Modernizations.

A: *(continuing to imitate the indignant comrade):* "Who says we don't want Party leadership? All we want is *good* leadership. You know what everyone calls the Party secretary in the unit across the way?"

B: Bosom buddy of the masses.

A: "And you? Exactly what have you done for the Four Modernizations? Do you care one iota about the masses' welfare—day care, dining hall, showers, barbershop? You won't listen to anybody. We wanted to build a bike shed and what did you say? That you needed a new assistant—new bureaucratic deadwood. What for?"

B: To be chief of the bike shed.

A: *(speaking as himself again):* Engineer Wang made *one* suggestion to him and got sent to hard labor for three years. Even now Wu won't admit he was wrong.

B: As stubborn as that?

A: "When Li the technician was doing that scientific experiment, he had a couple of setbacks, remember? Wu closed the lab! Li protested, so naturally Wu accused him of being anti-Party. One night Li sneaked into the lab to work but couldn't work because a lot of big bottles of acid were missing."

B: Where were they?

A: At Wu's house to make brine for a Buddhist holiday!

B: He doesn't worry about getting poisoned?

A: In his own life if he wants to eat pork chops instead of pig's ears, OK—let him. But the way he "leads" us only harms the country and the people.

B: Tell his Party superiors and get him sacked.

A: When he hears that idea, he gets scared. "Just what the hell are you driving at? First democracy, then centralism. You've had your democracy but I haven't centralized yet."

B: Still wants to centralize! If he keeps on like this, it's about time for "the tyrant to bid farewell to his mistress."

A: *(still imitating the tyrant):* "Farewell to what mistress? You can't get me to bid farewell to my mistress."

B: Why not?

A: "The mistress I keep at home loves me."

B: What could that mean?

A: Just then the phone rang.

B: Who was calling?

A: His wife.

B: What a coincidence!

Popular Performing Arts

A: Just look how proud he is—with the receiver in his hand! *(imitating Wu)* "Hear this? It's my mistress!"

B: What?

A *(the tyrant suddenly feels embarrassed):* "No, no, no—not 'mistress'— I said 'biz-niss'!"

B: Holy mackerel.

A *(Wu on the phone again):* "Hello. What's up?"

B: What's up?

A *(imitating Wu's wife):* "Old Wu, do you know what time it is? You haven't even given me instructions on what we eat for lunch."

B: She needs his instructions on lunch?

A *(Wu again):* "Concerning the matter of what our family shall dine on for lunch, the Party branch has studied the matter—yellow croaker with pancakes."

B: So now the branch has become his family? What nonsense.

A: "Did you get that?"

B *(as Wu's wife):* "There's no croaker. How about carp?"

A: "No go. Just what the hell are you driving at? Carp has too many bones."

B: "How about pig's head?"

A: "I don't want pig's head."

B: "How come?"

A: "I nearly came to blows over pig's head!"

B *(as himself again):* Isn't that something? A scuffle with a pig's head.

A: He put the receiver down and looked around. No one was left in the room.

B: Where'd they go?

A: They were so riled up they took off. They put up big character posters all over the place. Here they wrote, "We don't want this kind of Party leader." There they wrote, "We want a *true* democratic spirit." Everybody beseeched the higher levels to sack Tyrant Wu.

B: You can't shrug off the will of the people.

A: Tyrant Wu was so angry his face turned green and his lips blue. He paced back and forth in the empty room, saying, "Boy, will I show *them!*"

B: Still showing off.

A: He didn't go home, so his wife came looking for him. She took one look at all the posters and gasped. "Wow! Hey, Wu, listen, what're you *doing?* The people's posters are all on the mark. You really should change your work style. Think it over! Come on, stop pacing; come home and eat first."

B: Did he go home?

A: He was still angry when he and his wife got there. "Just what the hell are you driving at? Did you buy croaker or not?"

Stubborn Weeds

274

B: Still thinking about that croaker.

A: "Where am I going to get croaker these days? Let's make some nice dumplings. We can get ready-made skins and filling at the market. You can have a couple of nips too."

B: How can she be so nice to him?

A: "What do you mean, eat dumplings? Why did you countermand my instructions? You have disregarded the—the head of household!"

B: A tyrant even at home!

A: His wife exploded. "You've gone too far, old Wu. Not a whit of democratic spirit. More of a tyrant than the Tyrant of Chu. Everyone wants to sack you, and it serves you right! I knew that sooner or later it'd come to this. Tonight our family will hold a plenary session and sack you as head of household too!"

B: Wow. His wife was keyed up.

A: "What? Remove me as head of household? It's not that simple. Don't get ideas just because they've put up posters against me at work. At home, my word is law!"

B: Gee, still so inflexible.

A: His wife was beside herself. "OK, if your word is law, then legislate to yourself. I've had it. I'm taking the kids and leaving. We won't come back unless you change. One of these days, I'm telling you, somebody else will be head of this household."

B: So it really was "bidding farewell to his mistress."

A: "What?" said the tyrant. "Someone else as head of household? Oh, you want to *divorce* me?" He panicked. "Don't leave, come back!"

B: So he came around.

A: "On the head of household question, you must listen to my opinion. As I see it—"

B: What?

A: "First democracy, then centralism!"

B: Still centralizing!

Originally published in Quyi *(Beijing), No. 3, 1979.*

Translated by Thomas B. Gold.

Fast Clappertales and Shandong Fast Tales

Fast clappertales and Shandong fast tales are related but quite distinct forms of popular comic art. They tell stories in rhyme and are performed in a quick, syncopated rhythm to the accompaniment of bamboo or metal clappers. Fast clappertales are in the Beijing dialect, accompanied by bamboo clappers; Shandong fast tales are in the Shandong dialect, accompanied by metal clappers. The contemporary messages in the present examples are only part of their appeal; the forms themselves, which are centuries old, are still well loved by the Chinese masses.

LIANG HOUMIN *Interview in a Moscow Kindergarten*

(Fast Clappertale)

There's a kindergarten in Moscow, where they say
A foreign reporter's coming to visit today,
And, oh, this makes the new leader worry,
So she calls the kids to one side in a hurry!
"Now, kids, you're about to be interviewed, and they might say
What do you have on your dinner plate,
And what kind of clothes do you wear every day
And who's the leader of your state
And what kind of pets do you like for play?
And if they do, what will you say?"

"Auntie, let me, I know what to say!"
"OK, then you certainly may."
"We have potatoes, black bread, and imported rice every day."
"Ooooh, no, no, no! Sit down, sit down, sit down!
If you answer the question that way,
You get *nothing* to eat
And have to stand in the bathroom all day."
That's the scariest thing these kids have ever heard
So no one else dares to say a word.

The leader stands with her hands at her waist
And shouts at the top of her voice:

276

"Now remember what I say,
You must answer this way, you have no other choice.
We have milk and eggs on our dinner plate,
And leather shoes and pretty shirts are what we wear,
Mr. Brezhnev is our head of state,
And our favorite animals are the chimpanzee and the Russian bear.
Is that clear?
"Yes, ma'am, that's clear!"

Now the kids are afraid of forgetting their lines,
So they say them over, time after time:
"Milk and eggs on the plate,
Leather shoes and pretty shirts, what we wear,
Mr. Brezhnev, our head of state,
And the chimpanzee and the Russian bear."
The foreign reporter arrives after a while,
And the leader runs up to greet him with a great big smile:
"Ah, Mr. Reporter, sir,
You may ask *any* question that might occur.
They've all got their lines down pat—
No, no, no, I mean they'll answer freely, just like that.
Oh, for example, you might ask
What do we have on our dinner plate?
And what sort of clothes do we wear every day,
And who's the leader of our state,
And what's our favorite pet for play?
There's no need to ask any more than that, wouldn't you say?"

Now the reporter thinks this is rather strange,
Like something funny's been arranged.
"OK, I'll ask the questions, but I'll make a change
In the order and see what happens!"

"OK, so tell me please,
What are you wearing, anyway?"
"Milk and eggs!"
"Then what do you eat every day?"
"Leather shoes and pretty shirts!"
"And what's your favorite animal, eh?"
"Mr. Brezhnev!"
"Well, then, who are your leaders, please?"
"Russian bears and chimpanzees!"

Performed in Beijing in 1978.

Translated by Jan W. Walls.

Popular Performing Arts

LIANG HOUMIN   *Who's the Lucky One?*

(Fast Clappertale)

The boulevard is smooth and wide,
Poplars grow high on each side.
A bicycle comes whizzing down the road, flying by,
With a young lad pedaling, see him ride!
He's wearing dark glasses and long, long hair,
His clothes are beautiful, cleaned with care,
A rayon shirt of heavenly blue,
And bell-bottom trousers of a darker hue.
That digital watch on his wrist is keen
And that bicycle's a Phoenix Major, Model Eighteen.
He's outfitted with nothing but the best,
But he still feels far behind people in the West!
This is Xiao Jun, a propaganda clerk in the pesticide plant,
It's Liu Tingting he's coming to see, the girl who is his bride-to-be.
He comes flying into the experimental farm, see him ride,
Charging down the narrow path, just so wide,
He sees two people in the cabbage patch spraying pesticide,
And one of them looks like Liu Tingting, his future bride.
"Tingting, Tingting, Tingting!" Listen to him yell,
And people stop and wonder why he doesn't buy a bell.
He's shouting loud and racing, pell-mell,
But he isn't careful, and he loses his wits:
"Whoops! Oh, no!" Splash! "Aw, shit!"
And he lands in the middle of the night soil pit.
Then two people come and pull him out of that dung.
It's Tingting and a young man, Fang Dacheng.
"I've been looking all over for you,
And look at the mess I got into!"
His black shoes turn a browner hue,
His bell-bottoms stick to his legs like glue.
And his body, well—well—it stinks like hell!
Now Fang Dacheng brings him clothes to wear,
And helps him wash his bike with care,
Then says: "Tingting, Xiao Jun has something important to say,
We can check on this experiment later in the day."
Xiao Jun hurries over and says to Tingting:
"Ting, please *give up* this laboratory work
And listen to the advice I bring."
"What? Xiao Jun, I thought you were backing me here,
You even told me to volunteer."

"Oh, that's because *then* I didn't understand,
This work is dangerous, it could get out of hand!
Ting, our relationship has come a long way,
That's why I care for you so much more today.
Darling, I love you because you're young, alive, and in beautiful
    shape,
Your looks even drive the movie directors ape!
They say you're beautiful as a star;
I think you're even more lovely by far!
But you—you have to mess around this dangerous place!"
"Xiao Jun! How can you say that without a blush on your face?"
Look at this vegetable patch, right under your eyes,
There are insects spreading all over the place.
Soon they'll be feeding on this year's crop,
And *none* of our pesticides can make them stop.
Our job is here, with pesticides,
Aren't you a little concerned, deep down inside?
Xiao Jun, I've made up my mind, and I'll confide
I must work in science, side by side
With Dacheng." "Dacheng? Why? Why?
Why take chances showing off with that guy?
What if that poison blew in the wrong place?
You'd ruin the springtime beauty of a fair and tender lovely face."
"Xiao Jun, a ruined face is one person's worry;
We've got to come up with a new pesticide in a hurry!"
"Ting, I'll tell you true, your lovely face means more to me than the
    food I eat and the air I'm breathing,
Without it I simply couldn't go on living.
If you ruined your looks in an experiment,
Oh, I'd kill myself, I'd call it quits, I'd jump back into that night soil
    pit!"
Xiao Jun had even more to tell,
But the factory sounded the back-to-work bell.
Tingting was anxious to get back to work,
Xiao Jun's blood pressure shot up with a jerk.
"Ting—Ting—Ting—"
He cried, but she didn't hear a thing.
Poor Xiao Jun, he's having a fit,
He walks his bike three times around the night soil pit.
Aha! He finally comes up with a plan!
He'll get Tingting's mother to give him a hand.
"Right!" He rides his bike to Tingting's home,
He steps inside and hums and haws and groans and moans.
Mrs. Liu doesn't quite understand:
"What's going on here, young man?"

Popular Performing Arts

Xiao Jun tells her of all the dangers in a laboratory,
And even adds a bit of color to make it seem gory—
"Mrs. Liu, if she ever has an accident in that place,
She'll have nothing but scars all over her face."
"Holy smoke!" Mrs. Liu is really scared.
"My boy, you just wait right there.
I'll get dressed and we'll be on our way."
"Oh, yes, but please hurry, eh?"
Xiao Jun puffs on a cigarette, feeling satisfied,
And munches on some peanuts by his side.
He looks up and sees a smiling photo of Tingting,
Just like a movie star, a beautiful thing,
A perfectly proportioned face,
Not too fat, not too thin,
Two thick eyebrows, curved and fine,
An ideal nose, and big eyes that shine,
Long lashes and lovely lids on those eyes so wide,
Watery, slightly turned up on each side,
Two lovely cheeks, so fair and fine,
Each seems to be brewing its own special wine!
Wow! The more he's hooked, the cuter she gets, the cuter she gets,
      the more he's hooked, his vision fades, he's losing his balance,
He seems to be inside an enchanted palace!
Nine hundred and seventy Tingtings appear in a vision!
Swoon!
Swooning, he lifts up his cigarette,
And grabs another handful of peanuts yet,
But he's so upset he can't tell north from south,
And just pops something into his mouth.
Ah! A hissing sound! He's so upset
He almost ate his cigarette!
But now from the front door, there's a knock,
And Dacheng's sister comes in with a shock!
She's all out of breath and wet with sweat—
"Mrs. Liu, an accident in the plant, I don't know how,
But my brother and Tingting are in the hospital now!"
"Ah?" Mrs. Liu's knees begin to quake.
Xiao Jun's eyes are open wide, his hands are frozen at his side,
From the enchanted palace a moment ago
He's dropped into a hellhole down below.
Dizzily, he turns around and walks outside,
Climbs on his bike and wobbles, slowly, he can hardly ride,
And silently leaves, not a sound is heard,
And to Mrs. Liu, not so much as a word.
Little Fang and Mrs. Liu,
      are off to the hospital as fast as they can go,

To call on Tingting and Dacheng.
When she sees her daughter in bed, where she lies,
Bitter tears come to Mrs. Liu's eyes:
"Tell me, child, how do you fare?
Is the pain more than you can bear?"
But Tingting tries to comfort her mother:
"Mom, the wound's not such a bother
Thanks to little Fang's big brother.
As soon as that old valve blew
Dacheng came running, like an arrow he flew.
Poison blowing everywhere, he didn't care,
He pulled me to where I could breathe fresh air,
Then he ran back through the gas to shut the valve.
Dacheng must have been hurt worse than I."
"Oh, what a fine boy, my, oh, my!
I must go find him and see how he is."
"Oh, yes, you'd better!"
Mrs. Liu has just walked out
When little Fang runs in with a shout:
"Tingting! My brother says to tell you the news,
Your experiment is working,
It's been tested and approved.
They'll start making your formula right away!"
"You don't say!"
Tingting is moved and overjoyed inside,
She can't help feeling full of pride.
Then, the sound of leather shoes outside
Has a familiar ring that's hard to hide:
"Listen, little Fang, that's got to be him!"
Little Fang tilts her ear—
That's queer! These footsteps come and go, sound fast, then slow,
     sound weak, then strong.
Little Fang runs outside to see what's wrong.
It *is* Xiao Jun, what a sight, hands behind his back, circling left and
     right.
He looks up and sees little Fang come out,
And runs right over to ask about—the wound—
"Tell me, little Fang, are Ting's eyelashes still nice and long?"
"What?" Little Fang doesn't know what to say.
She thinks, "He doesn't even care how she feels, anyway,
Or whether her wound is bad or slight,
He only asks if her lashes are all right.
This guy's got something wrong upstairs."
"Go in and see for yourself, if you dare,
Whether she has lashes, I couldn't say."
"Well, OK!"

Popular Performing Arts

Xiao Jun slowly enters the room, and to his surprise,
Tingting is all wrapped in gauze, nothing showing but mouth and
    eyes.
Ah, it's even worse than he had thought at first.
A cold look covers Xiao Jun's face
And sadness spreads all over the place,
As if sending off a corpse.
Tingting asks him this, that, and the other too,
But nothing seems to be getting through.
Finally little Fang can't stand it any more:
"How can you be so reserved at a time like this, anyway?
There must be so many things you want to say!"
"Say? What is there to say? It seems
The past was nothing but empty dreams.
This just hasn't been my day!"
Tingting finally understands what he's trying to say,
And now she sees through him to the core.
With a sigh, he silently walks out the door.
Little Fang takes Tingting by the hand:
"Tingting, you mustn't feel bad, do you understand?
Don't waste your feelings on him any more."
"Little Fang, when he walked out on me today,
He proved he wasn't serious about me anyway.
If it weren't for this accident, maybe he'd stay,
But he would love me only as a pretty thing for play.
I couldn't be happy with him anyway.
True love must be based on something real."
"Oh, Tingting, that's just the way I feel!"
Now the doctors come in and proudly say
Their skills can wipe the wounds away.
Dacheng and Tingting are out in no time,
Hand in hand, shoulder to shoulder, finding new peaks to climb.
Then one day, with sunshine and blossoms, spring comes,
And we hear the sound of fireworks, gongs, and drums.
There's a big celebration at the plant, no less,
For the new pesticide was a great success.
At the head banquet table Dacheng and Tingting sit side by side,
Each with a red flower on the chest.
Looking lovelier than ever before, Tingting's
Face is fresh as the breeze of spring.
Xiao Jun looks up from the crowd, and he's mortified,
He looks around for a corner where he can hide.
Then someone pokes him in the side:
"Say, Dacheng and Tingting are sporting flowers and wearing red,
Doesn't it look like they're being wed?"

Stubborn Weeds

This little joke makes everybody laugh,
Except Xiao Jun, whose face turns red, and then turns green, and
    then turns purple, then turns white—he looks like a
    multicolored neon light.
But see Tingting and Dacheng, each in place,
True love written all over each face.
Who's the lucky one, tell me true!
I'll leave the answer to that one for you!

Performed by the Beijing Ballad and Storytelling
Troupe (autumn 1979).

Translated by Jan W. Walls.

LI HONGJI *The Woolly Sheep*

(Shandong Fast Tale)

Here's the tale of a fellow by the name of Wang
Who let his hair grow very long.
He smeared on grease and oil to make it behave
Then with an electric comb he gave
Himself a great big permanent wave.
From any angle, take a peep, he looks just like a woolly sheep.
Now one day he goes to the bike shop to fill up with air
And the kid behind him sees his hair, and thinks it's a lady there.
"Uh, lady, can I use the pump when you're through?
I've got a basketball to do."
This makes the fellow kind of mad,
And he turns around, looking bad:
"Who're you callin' lady? Damn!
Can't you tell the difference 'tween a woman and a man?
Look here, ace,
I think I'm gonna slap your face!"
"B-b-but your hair's so long, gee,
I couldn't tell if you were a he or a she,
So why hit me?"
Well, I'll be!

Performed for television in Beijing (autumn 1980).

Translated by Jan W. Walls.

Popular Performing Arts

CAO SHUYUN *"Ear to the Wind"*
and "Endless Tongue"

(Shandong Fast Tale)

Once there was a man called "Ear to the wind,"
And there was another called "Endless Tongue."
The two were comrades-in-arms, you might say,
And they met on the street and chatted one day.
"Ear to the Wind, you're great, heaven knows,
You can rise high by shifting as the wind blows."
"Endless Tongue, you too are pretty slick,
You rose to vice bureau chief with one well placed lick."
"Ah, but you can feel a tempest eight thousand leagues away,
And whichever way the winds may blow, higher and higher you go.
Why, you can ride a typhoon through the deep blue,
And stir the sea into a murky brew,
Or you can hide in an anthill when the winds are too cold
Or ride a tornado to heaven, I'm told.
The grass that bends with the wind is nothing compared to you,
You could deal with any wind that ever blew!"
Endless Tongue has hardly said what he has to say
When Ear to the Wind starts jabbering away:
"Dear friend, how would I dare make any claim, before a person of
    your fame?
You're so resourceful, yes indeed, your tongue can grow to meet
    any need.
Whatever the leadership, you can still lick,
And you make it seem such an easy trick.
You want to go to heaven? A stretch of your tongue is a ladder to
    the sky;
You want to cross a river? A flick of your tongue is the best bridge
    you can buy.
A flick of your tongue and Lord Yama[1] would quake
For fear you'd bring his dead awake."
"Oh, such praise, really, I'm inferior to you."
"Ah, such modesty, you're really best, it's true."
"You know, these great abilities of ours
Have all been fostered by our 'superior powers.' "
So saying, the two of them left with a laugh,
While bystanders stayed behind, muttering their wrath:
"Huh! Boast all you will, curry with all your might,

1. Lord Yama is Lord of the Dead in Buddhist mythology.

Stubborn Weeds

7762-1
5-35

But see if you don't end up in a plight!"
And having said this, perhaps we ought
To let everyone give it a bit of thought,
For though this tale occurred under the Gang of Four,
Can we really say that these ways exist no more?

Originally published in Tianjin yanchang, *No. 4, 1979.*

Translated by Jan W. Walls.

CHEN JINBO and *Think It Over*
LIU JUNQUAN
(Shandong Fast Tale)

There's a section chief in our company, Wang is his name,
And playing "bureaucrat" is his favorite game.
"We'll think it over," he always claims,
Or "We'll talk about it," which is just the same.
Now we have a storage shed about to tumble down
So we filled out a form requesting repair
And sent young Huang from Supply to the company
To give it to Section Chief Wang up there.
Wang takes the papers, shuffles them a bit,
Then slowly begins to move his lips:
"No need to panic over this, I'd say,
We'll think it over and make up our minds,
But for now, why don't you get back on your way
And come again in a couple of days."
Two days later young Huang comes back.
The Chief is smoking and reading away.
"He's already thought it over, I declare,
How serenely he sits in the chair."
The Chief half-rises, nods his head,
Then ever so courteously he says:
"And what can I do for you today, let's see,
Is it a wedding? Got some sweets for me?"
"Chief, I've come to ask about our request."
"Request? What request?"
He's let it slip right out of his head!
"The request to repair our storage shed!"
Chief Wang thinks it over and says:

Popular Performing Arts

"Gosh, I've just been so busy these days
I haven't had time to discuss it yet.
For the moment, why don't you just go back
And come again some other day."
Young Huang is miffed, needless to say,
He's already wasted two trips this way.
When four more days have come and gone
He returns again to see Chief Wang.
"Now, about these building repairs—"
"What? Hire yourself a carpenter for home repairs."
He's forgotten about the whole affair!
"Chief, I'd think it over if I were you,
This is our third interview!"
Chief Wang scratches his head in thought,
Then searches through every cabinet and box.
"Gosh! How could it have gotten lost?
Write me another one, what do you say?"
Huang turns around and says: "OK!
I'll get something written up right away!"
Huang spreads his paper, raises his pen, and now
He writes an expose, a long *dazibao*[1]
"We requested three times and got not a word,
A Long March[2] like this is really absurd!
If all of us were like Chief Wang, indeed,
The Four Modernizations would never succeed!"

Originally published in Tianjin yanchang, *no. 3, 1979.*

Translated by Jan W. Walls.

1. A *dazibao* is a critical wall poster.
2. This refers to the "New Long March" i.e., the Four Modernizations.

Glossary and Name List

Attack with Words and Defend with Weapons. This slogan, announced by Jiang Qing in a speech on September 5, 1967, introduced the violent phase of the Cultural Revolution. As the violence increased, each of the combatant Red Guard groups could easily see itself as on the defensive, and the slogan eventually became a mere euphemism for "Charge!" It was not long before it gave way to another slogan: "All-out Civil War!"

Beijing. Peking.

Cadre. In this volume "cadre" is used in the singular to translate the Chinese *ganbu*, which refers to any of a variety of administrators such as factory managers, school principals, government bureaucrats, etc. A cadre is not necessarily a Party member.

Cow Shed. A popular term for any of the confinement areas established for errant cadres and intellectuals ("cow ghosts and snake spirits," in Mao Zedong's phrase) during the Cultural Revolution. Generally, each work unit fashioned its own cow shed in a makeshift manner.

Cultural Revolution. Formally called the Great Proletarian Cultural Revolution and conventionally dated from 1966 to 1972, this massive campaign—the largest in human history—was conceived by Mao Zedong as a final attempt to create unending revolution in China. The results included incalculable dislocation and suffering.

Deng Xiaoping (b. 1904). Vice Premier of the People's Republic and China's most powerful leader in the late 1970s and early 1980s.

Five Black Categories. See "Five Red Categories."

Five Red Categories. In the Cultural Revolution, much of the populace was divided into good ("red") and bad ("black") categories. There was never an authoritative definition of these categories, and popular usage was not uniform. But generally the Five Red Categories were industrial workers, poor peasants, lower middle peasants, revolutionary cadres (those who had joined a Communist organization by 1947), and revolutionary soldiers. Black categories were more confusing. The Four Black Categories usually referred to former landlords, rich peasants, counterrevolutionaries (including spies, former KMT people, "rightists," etc.) and "bad elements," meaning common criminals. The Five Black Categories referred to the same people but counted counterrevolutionaries and rightists as two groups. The Seven Black Categories added two more—capitalists and "capitalist-roaders." Since one's category was inherited, the children of red families were purely red and those of black categories inalterably black.

Four Black Categories. See "Five Red Categories."

Four Modernizations. A plan to achieve the modernization of China's industry, agriculture, national defense, and science and technology by the year 2000. First enunciated by Zhou Enlai at the Fourth People's Congress (January 13–17, 1975), the plan became a dominant policy of the Deng Xiaoping regime in the late 1970s. Also referred to as "the New Long March."

Four Olds. Old ideas, old culture, old customs, old habits—the targets of Cultural Revolution campaigns to "Destroy the Four Olds and Establish the Four News."

Gang of Four. In October 1976, four high-ranking radicals were ousted and made the major scapegoats for the catastrophes of the preceding ten years: Jiang Qing was the widow of Mao Zedong and during the Cultural Revolution was a member of the Central Politburo. Zhang Chunqiao was a vice-premier of the People's Republic and a leading Marxist theoretician. Yao Wenyuan, also a vice-premier, was a political critic of literature. Wang Hongwen, a former Shanghai worker, was a vice-chairman of the Communist Party.

Guangzhou. Canton.

Hua Guofeng (b. 1921). Mao Zedong's chosen successor and the most important transitional figure between the regimes of Mao and Deng Xiaoping. Chairman of the Communist Party from October 24, 1976 until June 29, 1981.

Jiang Qing. Also Chiang Ch'ing. See "Gang of Four."

Lin Biao (1907–71). A vice-chairman of the Communist Party of China before he died and Mao Zedong's "closest comrade-in-arms" from 1966–71. Officially reported to have died in an airplane crash as he was fleeing toward the Soviet Union after failing in a coup d'etat and assassination attempt on Mao in September 1971. (What actually happened is unclear.) Although many people secretly rejoiced at Lin's disappearance, public denunciation was postponed more than two years. He eventually became a *bete noire* to rank with the Gang of Four.

Mao Zedong (1893–1976). Mao Tse-tung. Chairman of the Communist Party of China, 1943–76.

New Long March. See "Four Modernizations."

Qingming. See "Tiananmen Incident."

Red Guards. Youth in the Cultural Revolution who spearheaded the attacks on cadres and intellectuals and eventually on one another. Generally they sought idealistically to uphold Chairman Mao and his ideas, but they were often pawns in local power struggles and ended up doing great damage. Also called "little generals."

Tiananmen Incident. Tiananmen is the Gate of Heavenly Peace in Beijing that stands before the vast Tiananmen Square, symbolic of the political center of China. The Tiananmen Incident refers to April 5, 1976, when hundreds of thousands of people gathered in the square in a spontaneous tribute to Zhou Enlai, who had died on January 8, 1976. April 5 is the date of the Qingming Festival, when the Chinese sweep family gravesites and honor the departed. The crowd had gathered in an anti-totalitarian spirit but was forcibly driven away; the demonstration was declared "counterrevolutionary."

Zhou Enlai (1898–1976). Chou En-lai. Premier of the People's Republic, 1949–76.

Contributing Translators

Thomas B. Gold is Assistant Professor of Sociology at the University of California, Berkeley. His doctoral dissertation concerned dependent development in Taiwan. He studied modern Chinese literature at Fudan University during 1979 and 1980. His previous translations include *Selected Stories of Yang Ch'ing-ch'u* (Kaohsiung: Tun-li Publishing Co., 1978).

Edward M. Gunn has a Ph.D. in Chinese literature from Columbia University and is Assistant Professor of Asian Studies at Cornell University. He is author of *Unwelcome Muse: Chinese Literature in Shanghai and Peking, 1937–45* (Columbia University Press, 1980) and several articles on modern Chinese fiction and drama.

Kenneth Jarrett is a graduate of Cornell University (B.A., 1975) and Yale University (M.A., 1979) and has studied Chinese in Hong Kong and Taiwan. During 1979–81 he was an English teacher at the Shanghai Foreign Languages Institute.

W.J.F. Jenner teaches Chinese literature and cultural history at the University of Leeds in England. He worked in Beijing in the early 1960s. He is author of *Memories of Loyang: Yang Hsuan-chih and the Lost Capital (493–534)* (Oxford University Press, 1981) and editor of *Modern Chinese Stories* (Oxford, 1970).

Dale R. Johnson (Ph.D., University of Michigan) teaches Chinese at Oberlin College. He is the author of *Yuarn Music Dramas* (Ann Arbor: The University of Michigan, Center for Chinese Studies, 1980) and several other articles and translations on Yuan Drama and other aspects of Chinese literature. In 1979–80 he taught English at the Maritime Transport College in Shanghai.

Perry Link is Associate Professor of Oriental Languages at UCLA and specializes in modern Chinese literature. During 1979–80 he was in China doing research on contemporary literature. He is interested in popular thought and is author of *Mandarin Ducks and Butterflies: Popular Fiction in Early Twentieth-Century Chinese Cities* (University of California Press, 1981).

William A. Lyell is Associate Professor of East Asian Languages at Stanford University. His many publications include *Lu Xun's Vision of Reality* (University of California Press, 1976) and a translation of *Cat Country* by Lao She (The Ohio State University Press, 1970). He has just completed new translations of the short stories of Lu Xun.

Denis C. Mair has an M.A. in Chinese from The Ohio State University and has studied and worked three years in Taiwan. He has published translations of several Chinese stories and of *Random Talks About My Mendicant Life* (Armonk, N.Y.: M. E. Sharpe, 1982), the memoirs of a Chinese monk. He is currently working with his brother Victor Mair on a translation of Pu Songling's *Liaozhai zhiyi*.

Bonnie S. McDougall is a translator and editor at the Foreign Languages Press in Beijing. She previously taught Chinese language and literature at Harvard University and the University of Sydney in Australia. Her many publications include *The Introduction of Western Literary Theories into Modern China 1919–1925* (Tokyo, 1971) and *Mao Zedong's "Talks at the Yan'an Conference on Literature and Art"* (Ann Arbor: Center for Chinese Studies, University of Michigan, 1980).

Paul G. Pickowicz is Associate Professor of History at the University of California, San Diego. He is author of *Marxist Literary Thought in China: The Influence of Ch'ü Ch'iu-pai* (University of California Press, 1981) and *Marxist Literary Thought in China: A Conceptual Framework* (Berkeley: Center for Chinese Studies, 1980). He is presently completing a study of Wugong, a rural community in Hebei Province.

Douglas Spelman is a Foreign Service officer stationed in Hong Kong. He has a Ph.D. in modern Chinese history from Harvard University and has taught at Bucknell University. He has also directed the Oberlin program at Tunghai University in Taiwan and the Yale-China Association program at the Chinese University of Hong Kong.

William Tay is Assistant Professor of Modern Languages at the University of California, San Diego, and has taught English at the Chinese University of Hong Kong. He is author of *Orphic Variations: Essays in Comparative Literature (Aofeiersi de bianzou)* (Hong Kong: Su-yeh Press, 1979) and *Literary Theory and Comparative Literature (Wenxue lilun yu bijiao wenxue)* (Taipei: China Times Books, 1982). He has edited three books and written several articles in both English and Chinese on literary theory and comparative literature.

Robert N. Tharp lived for twenty-nine years in Manchuria, until he was repatriated after internment in 1942. He has taught at the Chinese Army Language School, Yale University, and the Defense Language Institute at Monterey, California, where he is currently consultant to the commandant on Chinese language texts and teaching methodology.

Jan W. Walls teaches Chinese at the University of Victoria, B.C., Canada, where he has also served as the director of the Centre for Pacific and Oriental Studies. He formerly taught at the University of British Columbia and served for two years (1981–83) as Cultural Attaché at the Embassy of Canada in Beijing.

Contributing Translators

Ellen Yeung is a language instructor with the San Francisco Community College District and San Francisco State University. She is co-translator of *Field of Life and Death* by Hsiao Hung (Indiana University Press, 1979) and contributed to K. Y. Hsu, ed., *Literature of the People's Republic of China* (Indiana University Press, 1980).